PSYCHOLOGICAL PERSPECTIVES ON RELIGION AND RELIGIOSITY

Is religion to blame for deadly conflicts? Should religious behavior be credited more often for acts of charity and altruism? In what ways are religious and "spiritual" ideas, practices and identities surviving and changing as religion loses its political power in those parts of the world which are experiencing increasing secularization?

Written by one of the world's leading authorities on the psychology of religion and social identity, *Psychological Perspectives on Religion and Religiosity* offers a comprehensive and multidisciplinary review of a century of research into the origins and consequences of religious belief systems and religious behavior. The book employs a unique theoretical framework that combines the "new" cognitive-evolutionary psychology of religion, examining the origins of religious ideas, with the "old" psychology of religiosity, which looks at correlates and consequences. It examines a wide range of psychological variables and their relationship with religiosity. It also provides fresh insights into classical topics in the psychology of religion, such as religious conversion, the relevance of Freud's ideas about religion and religiosity, the meaning of secularization, and the crucial role women play in religion. The book concludes with the author's reflections on the future for the psychology of religion as a field.

Psychological Perspectives on Religion and Religiosity will be invaluable for academic researchers in psychology, sociology, anthropology, political science, economics, and history worldwide. It will also be of great interest to advanced undergraduate students and graduate students across the social sciences.

Benjamin Beit-Hallahmi is Professor of Psychology at the University of Haifa, Israel.

PSYCHOLOGICAL PERSPECTIVES ON RELIGION AND RELIGIOSITY

Benjamin Beit-Hallahmi

LONDON AND NEW YORK

First published 2015
by Routledge
27 Church Road, Hove, East Sussex BN3 2FA

and by Routledge
711 Third Avenue, New York, NY 10017

Routledge is an imprint of the Taylor & Francis Group, an informa business

© 2015 Routledge

The right of Benjamin Beit-Hallahmi to be identified as the author of this work has been asserted by him in accordance with sections 77 and 78 of the Copyright, Designs and Patents Act 1988.

All rights reserved. No part of this book may be reprinted or reproduced or utilised in any form or by any electronic, mechanical, or other means, now known or hereafter invented, including photocopying and recording, or in any information storage or retrieval system, without permission in writing from the publishers.

Trademark notice: Product or corporate names may be trademarks or registered trademarks, and are used only for identification and explanation without intent to infringe.

British Library Cataloguing in Publication Data
A catalogue record for this book is available from the British Library

Library of Congress Cataloging in Publication Data
Library of Congress Cataloging-in-Publication Data
Beit-Hallahmi, Benjamin.
Psychological perspectives on religion and religiosity /
Benjamin Beit-Hallahmi.
pages cm
1. Psychology, Religious. I. Title.
BL53.B373 2014
200.1'9--dc23
2014016888

ISBN: 978-0-415-68286-2 (hbk)
ISBN: 978-0-415-68287-9 (pbk)
ISBN: 978-1-315-74984-6 (ebk)

Typeset in Bembo
by Saxon Graphics Ltd, Derby

CONTENTS

List of tables		*vii*
Preface		*ix*
Acknowledgments		*xi*
1	Defining psychology, defining religion	1
2	Exceptional or natural? The psychological roots of religion	23
3	Social learning and identity	40
4	Explaining variations in religiosity	56
5	Women and religion	89
6	Consequences and correlates of religiosity	109
7	Conversion and convert-dependent groups	151
8	Psychoanalysis and the psychological study of religion	182
9	Secularization and the persistence of religion	201
	Concluding remarks: The new psychology of religion	233
	References	*237*
	Index	*313*

LIST OF TABLES

2.1	Cognitive shortcuts	31
4.1	Nobel laureates 1901–2001 by religious affiliation	79
4.2	The Schwartz list of values	87
5.1	Male and female mean differences, adult sample	97
9.1	Belief in supernatural entities	207
9.2	Strength of religiosity by type of society (percent)	210

PREFACE

Over the past century, academic research has produced many significant, non-intuitive findings about religion and religiosity which deserve to be shared with a wide audience of scholars and students. Over the past twenty years, a new psychology of religion has been formed, or a new social science of religion. The findings and ideas presented in this book have been produced not only by psychologists, but also by sociologists, anthropologists, historians, economists, political science scholars, neuroscientists, psychiatrists, epidemiologists, and even physicists. The reason is not only that religion attracts the attention of scholars in many fields, but that in the psychological study of religion, disciplinary boundaries and labels may be ignored on the road to better ideas. The phenomena we want to investigate do not honor disciplinary boundaries, and academic curiosity no longer follows them. That is why economists and physicists study religion and religiosity, and that is why the intended audience for this book includes students and scholars in all disciplines.

This book, future-oriented and theory-driven, offers a review and an analysis of questions, methods and findings in the psychology of religion and religiosity. It is selective by necessity, as one book cannot do justice to the many significant contributions on every aspect of religious behavior, and must focus on a few topics. Still, it aims at covering the most important issues raised by students of religion. The book will leave the reader with more questions than answers, and that's the way it should be in any serious academic work. It is hoped that these questions will then be pursued to the best of one's talents, tastes, and preferences.

ACKNOWLEDGMENTS

I should first acknowledge my huge debt to Michael Argyle, who was a great mentor and role model for thirty years. Jean-Pierre Deconchy and Laurie Brown served as big brothers and models. I can only wish that I had learned more from the three of them.

I owe a special debt of gratitude to Todd Tremlin, who actually triggered the writing of this book.

Ken Barney, Gabriel Bar-Haim, Jacob Belzen, Yoram Bilu, Catherine Caldwell-Harris, Simon Dein, Jay Feierman, Daniel Gat, Moshe Hazani, Ariela Keysar, Barry Kosmin, Micah Leshem, Raanan Lipshitz, Roger O'Toole, Jerry Piven, Avraham Ronen, Joel Schlosberg, Ruth Sharabany, Mark Pavlick, Wayne Proudfoot, Ilkka Pyysiäinen, Sam Rakover, Henry Rosenfeld, Zvi Sobel, and David Wulff generously shared their knowledge.

Jerry Slater read the manuscript and offered important comments. Stephen Porges read some of the chapters and offered great advice.

My editor at Routledge, Michael Strang, has been most supportive and patient.

The Department of Psychology at the University of Haifa and the University of Haifa Library have offered vital support, and so has the Center for the Study of Secularism in Society and Culture at Trinity College, Hartford, Connecticut. Last but not least, my students may be surprised to hear how much I have learned from them.

1

DEFINING PSYCHOLOGY, DEFINING RELIGION

Religion as a sphere of human activity is regarded as especially challenging for academic research. It is tied to seemingly unique individual behaviors, together with strong collective commitments. The word religion brings to the mind's eye and ear haunting sounds and colors: The music of processions and festivals celebrating ancient (or recent) miracles and triumphs, the wailing of supplicants praying for mercy and asking for intercessions by spirits great and small, and then the silence of contemplation, as well as beautiful objects that were crafted to be worshipped while standing for invisible powers, believers dressing up to follow old traditions on joyful occasions, and barefoot monks begging for their food. It also brings to mind major historical events and upheavals, and many clear reminders of its central role in most human cultures. The resources humans have invested in religion make its importance obvious.

Can the cold (or lukewarm) prose and the dry statistics of academic research portray faithfully this wealth of human experiences? First, it is clear that the study of religion is not a reproduction or promotion of religious activities. There is no need for that. Billions of believers maintain and promote living traditions without any help from academics.

What the academic study of religion aims to do is go behind the actions and search for causes and explanations. With the help of ideas and findings produced by many capable researchers we can arrive at significant generalizations, interpretations, and explanations of religion and religiosity. To achieve that, the first task is the clarification of basic terms, which mark the boundaries of the phenomenon and the attendant explanatory concepts.

Defining psychology

An academic field is defined by (a) a set of questions, and (b) a set of methods for studying these questions. The two sets, (a) and (b), create a unique field, whether

2 Defining psychology, defining religion

chemistry, sociology, or psychology. Psychology is an intellectual endeavor, today mostly based in academic institutions, that aims at understanding and predicting human behavior. In academic psychology the (a) set includes questions about regularities in human behavior, including both observable action and consciousness. Beyond looking for regularities, we seek to explain them through various methods covered under (b). These may consist of experiments, standardized tests (sometimes conceived as mini-experiments), questionnaires, and systematic observations.

Psychology is both a life science and a human science, guided by an evolutionary assumption that connects humans to other animals in terms of both physiology and behavior. It is ahistorical in the sense of looking for the building blocks of human behavior, which are assumed to be stable across time and space. Psychologists share many interests with researchers in the other human sciences, especially anthropology, sociology, political science, and history, but they also stand out in any encounter with other disciplines by aiming to approach the person through the study of individual differences and personality traits.

Observing and defining religion

The whole point of a definition is the classification into two basic categories of human activities – religion and non-religion. There are those who suggest that defining religion is hard or impossible (Guthrie, 1993; Wulff, 1999), and we even encounter well-known researchers who declare that "what constitutes religion is unclear" (Sosis and Bulbulia, 2011, p. 348). This is puzzling, and there is enough reason to disagree. How and why do you study religion if you are not sure how to define it? Those who state that defining religion is impossible actually deal with the same topics and the same concrete phenomena that will be discussed in this book.

What do all religions have in common? What is common to Vietnamese Buddhism, Aztec religion, Roman paganism, the Tallensi tradition, Mormonism, and Hinduism? What is the unity, if there is one, behind this great diversity of behaviors and traditions? The definition must be inclusive and comprehensive. Observable differences among religions, obviously due to history and culture, are relatively marginal to psychology, because it seeks explanations for religion-in-general. That is why in this book, very little will be said about particular traditions, or about differences among denominations. Humans cannot believe in religion-in-general, but in a particular one, just as we don't speak a language-in-general, but in linguistics we can speak of language in general terms and define its essential properties. The concept of religion is an abstraction from countless concrete cases, but we can still talk about religion-in-general because there is a common denominator to all those systems. Concrete examples are considered representative of the psychological unity of all religions.

Religions claim exclusivity, uniqueness, and originality, but the similarities among traditions of supernaturalism are too obvious, and sometimes found in identical or highly similar texts. Thus, the Flood story in the book of Genesis is obviously similar to the story of Deucalion in Greek mythology, and to hundreds

Defining psychology, defining religion **3**

of flood accounts found all over the world. It actually shares some phrases with the Mesopotamian Gilgamesh text of the seventh century BCE. What can be observed is clearly not unity, but uniformity and similarity among religions. We may speak of a multiplicity paradox: Tens of thousands of religions express similar ideas, and, as observers, we may even conceive of one basic religion shared by humanity (Bulbulia, 2005).

Religion is not a realm of psychological functions or structures; it is defined by content, and not by process; by what rather than by how (Beit-Hallahmi, 1989). The essentials appearing in tens of thousands of belief systems lead to the definition: Religion is a belief system which includes the notion of a supernatural, invisible world, inhabited by gods, human souls, angels, demons, and other conscious spirit entities (Beit-Hallahmi, 1989; Beit-Hallahmi and Argyle, 1997). Religious claims and narratives are immediately recognized through their content and special rhetoric. Belief systems will be defined as religions only when those committed to them make specific references to supernatural agents or interventions, and specific assertions about the spirit world. Religious actions are defined solely by their relation to the realm of the spirit world.

A definition of religion delineates what is universal in all the concrete experiences and behaviors that are designated by the actors involved as constituting religion. This designation may not be formal or written. Religious acts are construed in reference to spiritual entities, and being religious is about a particular affirmation of the invisible spirit world and its constituent entities. What we observe every day, in every culture, is individuals discussing souls, spirits, ghosts, gods, ancestors, or demons, who are assumed to inhabit another sphere of existence than ours, but sometimes are reported to be in contact with living humans. This is the irreducible common core, the supernaturalist premise, which unites tens of thousands of religions and billions of believers: "It is the premise of every religion—and this premise is religion's defining characteristic—that souls, supernatural beings, and supernatural forces exist. Furthermore, there are certain minimal categories of behavior, which, *in the context of the supernatural premise*, [italics in the original] are always found in association with one another and which are the substance of religion itself" (Wallace, 1966, p. 52). These minimal (or more than minimal) activities are the derivatives of supernaturalist beliefs. Because the supernaturalist premise is the beginning of all religions, the terms supernaturalism and religion could be used interchangeably.

In the above definition, souls precede other beings, and this is a reflection of their centrality in religious discourse. A supernaturalist belief system does not have to refer to gods, but it does always refer to spirit entities (ancestors, ghosts, angels, etc.) which have some power over humans and can affect their lives.

Rituals are about contacts and negotiations with spirit entities. When we ask participants or officiants at religious rituals to explain the meaning of their actions, they will always refer to beliefs about spirits and contact with them. Prayers and incantations inspire awe, even when they are being pronounced in a language the believers do not understand, as they are believed to reach powerful spirits.

4 Defining psychology, defining religion

The definition presented here follows the tradition of modern research on religion, started in the nineteenth century. According to E. B. Tylor, the "minimum definition of religion" is the belief in spiritual beings. Such beings,

> are held to affect or control the events of the material world, and man's life here and hereafter; and it being considered that they hold intercourse with men, and receive pleasure or displeasure from human actions, the belief in their existence leads naturally, and it might also be said inevitably, sooner or later to active reverence and propitiation.
>
> (Tylor, 1871, I, p. 381)

They include the "souls of individual creatures, capable of continued existence after the death or destruction of the body" and "other spirits, up to the rank of powerful deities" (Tylor, 1871, I, p. 424).

Twenty-five years later, William James stated: "Religion has meant many things in human history: but when from now onward I use the word I mean to use it in the supernaturalist sense, as declaring that the so called order of nature, which constitutes this world's experience, is only one portion of the total universe, and that there stretches beyond this visible world an unseen world of which we now know nothing positive, but in its relation to which the true significance of our present mundane life consists" (James, 1897/1956, p. 51).

James G. Frazer emphasized that,

> [b]y religion, then, I understand a propitiation or conciliation of powers superior to man which are believed to direct and control the course of nature and of human life. Thus defined, religion consists ... a belief in powers higher than man and an attempt to propitiate or please them ... belief clearly comes first, since we must believe in the existence of a divine being before we can attempt to please him.
>
> (Frazer, 1922, pp. 65–66)

Similarly, Meford Spiro stated that "the belief in superhuman beings and in their power to assist or to harm man approaches universal distribution, and this belief—I would insist—is the core variable which ought to be designated by any definition of religion" (Spiro, 1966, p. 96). More recently, a leading sociologist of religion, Rodney Stark, stated that "[t]he core of any system of religious doctrine is a *general account of existence predicated on a description of the supernatural*" (Stark, 2000, p. 305; italics in the original). Saroglou (2011, p. 1323) stated that "[a] set of some or many beliefs relative to what many people consider as being an (external) transcendence—and its 'connection' with humans and the world—is a basic universal component of religion." The emphasis on the supernaturalist premise in defining religion gives us first a clear distinction between religious and secular acts, valid cross-culturally, consistent with believers' experience, whether they are Hindus, Moslems, Sikhs, Baha'is, Buddhists, or members of any other religious group, and including the

Defining psychology, defining religion **5**

phenomena of witchcraft, possession, and the modern "New Age." Observed differences among traditions and historical situations are publicly expressed through different assertions about the spirit world. Different assertions serve as the starting point for different group identities and intergroup conflicts. Adherents to the same religion or to different religions may disagree, and believers may argue about what the spirits want, but they all share a faith in the existence of such entities, which they aim to communicate with and whose presumed wishes they follow.

Religion is not, as sometimes suggested, about "non-empirical" claims. For the believers, gods and angels are as real as any other object. Harris and Koenig (2006) state that "children quiz adults in approximately the same way whether they are grappling with a question about liquids or a question about angels" (p. 518). Not only children, but also some adults may think about liquids and angels in a similar way. William Blake made it clear more than 200 years ago:

Scoffers

Mock on, mock on, Voltaire Rousseau;
Mock on, mock on; 'tis all in vain!
You throw the sand against the wind,
And the wind blows it back again.

And every sand becomes a gem
Reflected in the beams divine;
Blown back they blind the mocking eye,
But still in Israel's path they shine.

The Atoms of Democritus
and Newton's Particles of Light
Are sands upon the Red Sea shore,
Where Israel's tents do shine and bright.

(Blake, 1804/1905, p. 108)

Just like Blake, who affirmed the reality of the mythological Exodus, believers today have no doubts about thousands of miraculous events, such as the Virgin Birth of Buddha, Krishna, Zoroaster, or Jesus, or about the ability of saints and ancestors to grant their wishes for a better life. Subject to culture specifics, the human mind is easily capable of imagining witches casting spells designed to harm unsuspecting victims, heaven and hell, or the trajectories traveled by prayers and offerings as they create their effects. The immediate experience is that of representations, images, and ideas, attached to supernaturalist references. Representations of supernaturalist images are universal. Even "the nonbeliever ... must also have a God representation" as the result of exposure to religious ideation (Rizzuto, 1979, p. 42). In the globalized twenty-first century, it is hard not to have representations of Krishna, Jesus, Moses, Muhammad, or Buddha.

6 Defining psychology, defining religion

Beyond the conscious representations, religions involve the individual in a unique commitment and in a unique network of relationships, concrete as well as imagined. While religion is unique in terms of content, its consequences cannot always be distinguished from that of other ideologies. Other belief systems, tied to commitment, emotion, ecstasy, and transformation, constitute secular ideologies. Some of the more dramatic aspects of religious behavior, including ecstasy or acts of extreme devotion culminating in total self-sacrifice, can be found in secular settings, motivated either by private love or by public nationalism.

While every religion claims to be connected to the unseen world, it operates through visible objects and acts in this world. Some material objects, from temples to prayer beads, holy books, and amulets, are believed to radiate power. It is *mana*, a power that emanates from sacred objects, and humans seek closeness, or physical contact, to such objects, leading to touching them, or to pilgrimage to the locales of relics and tombs. Household shrines, which take the form of sacred objects kept in the home and offering a focus of worship, possess *mana* and are common in many religions.

Pilgrimages were known already in ancient Egypt, where believers went to the tomb of the god Osiris, and the Middle Ages were the heyday of pilgrimage in Europe. Great masses of people take part in pilgrimages, which connect them to *mana*. Voyages to special locations all over the world are initiated in the hope of finding miracle cures, visiting relics (a hair from the beard of the prophet Muhammad or a tooth of Buddha) or tombs, places in which apparitions have been reported, or just mountains considered sacred since time immemorial. Some of them have survived for millennia. The best known is the Kumba Mela, a pilgrimage held every three years in Northern India, which is considered the largest gathering in the world, with tens of millions attending. The pilgrims believe that bathing in the Ganges River will ensure their happiness and salvation, but many of them are likely to contract infectious diseases or get injured in accidents.

Other pilgrimage traditions are much younger, but can be quite powerful in mobilizing the masses. On June 24, 1981, six young individuals reported apparitions of the Virgin Mary, of Christian mythology, in the small village of Medjugorje, not far from the resort city of Dubrovnik, Croatia. They went on to report visions and excursions to heaven and hell. This started a mass pilgrimage which has attracted tens of millions, and is likely to attract millions more in the foreseeable future (Bax, 1995; Berryman, 2001).

Belief in *mana* creates many practices, such as the custom of hanging rags or clothes on the branches of sacred trees, common among Moslems in West Asia and North Africa:

> Holiness is, indeed, to the Palestine peasant a sort of liquid which may be absorbed by physical contact. The man who hangs a rag upon a tree will take from it and wear about his person another rag which has become soaked with the virtue of the place by hanging there.
>
> (Rix, 1907, p. 32; see also Dafni, 2002)

Similar practices, based on the belief in sacred trees which possess *mana*, have been observed all over the world. Charles Darwin reported tree worship, including the hanging of rags, in South America in August 1833 (Darwin, 1839/1965).

The substance of religion: pantheons and souls

The supernaturalist premise unfolds by enumerating the entities in the spirit world. In all religions, there is a hierarchy of spirit entities and the population of the invisible world consists of millions of gods, angels, and demons, as well as saints, humans promoted to a divine or semi-divine status. The spirit world is at the top of a hierarchy which involves humans, with "our" group placed higher than others, and gods placed above humans (Demoulin, Saroglou and Van Pachterbeke, 2008; Meier *et al.*, 2007). The invisible spiritual forces are envisaged anthropomorphically, sharing human qualities, and are usually thought of as male (Carroll, 1979). Various hypotheses have been proposed to account for the denizens of the pantheon in different traditions, and connections have been found between social structure and the spirit world (Underhill, 1975). Swanson (1960) found that high gods, supreme deities in the pantheon, are likely to be worshipped in societies where there are three or more sovereign groups (Peregrine, 1996). When monarchy used to be tied to religion, rulers not only had religious roles, but became gods, sometimes while still alive. In Japan traditional Shinto beliefs include the assertion that the Japanese emperor is descended from the Shinto sun goddess Amaterasu-o-mikami.

Among mortals, the boundaries of human communities extend beyond physical existence. Most spirit entities are human souls before birth or after death, and there is constant contact between spirits and humans, between the living and the dead. In religious mourning, "acknowledgement of the permanent absence of the deceased ... ultimately comes to coexist with belief in the permanent presence of the deceased—but now on another plane of experience, in the afterworld, part of the cosmos and the place to which the bereaved will ultimately repair" (Lutzky, 2008, p. 152–153).

In the religious imagination we find an intimate interaction and movement between life and death, and heaven and earth. Gods and spirits descend to earth, sometimes taking human form, while humans ascend to heaven, sometimes becoming divine. There are stories about sex between gods and humans, and the semi-divine human children of the gods. Here is a story from the book of Genesis (6; 1–4, 6):

> That the sons of God saw the daughters of men that they were fair; and they took them wives of all which they chose. There were giants in the earth in those days; and also after that, when the sons of God came in unto the daughters of men, and they bare children to them, the same became mighty men which were of old, men of renown.

This sounds like a summary of many Greek stories about the sexual intercourse of gods and women and its products, but we find it in the Hebrew Bible.

8 Defining psychology, defining religion

The soul is the means for every human to connect directly with the spirit world. A related idea, prevalent in many religious traditions, is reincarnation, the transmigration of souls. Similar stories about the migration of souls from humans to animals are found in strikingly different settings. According to beliefs among the Wari', an Amazon basin tribe, the spirits of the dead go to an underground world, and return in the form of fish or peccaries, pig-like animals that are a major source of meat for the tribe. Later on, the ancestor-peccaries seek out hunters from their own families and offer themselves to be shot, ensuring that their meat will go to feed the people they love (Conklin, 2001). Among Hassidic Jews, members of a tradition which started in Eastern Europe in the eighteenth century, there has been the belief in the souls of just men transmigrating into kosher beasts, which Jews may eat. These beasts need to be slaughtered only with the sharpest knives, otherwise causing the just men unnecessary suffering. In the fourth century BCE, Pythagoras took a more radical position and advocated the avoidance of meat, because what one eats may come from the body of an animal inhabited by a friend's soul. Such notions express confidence in continuing relationships with the dead, gratitude for their aid, and guilt about animals being killed to feed humans.

In many traditions, belief in an eternal soul, which travels to the world of the spirits, is tied to a belief in spirit possession and to the practice of exorcism. A possession is a special kind of incarnation, and a conflict between the dead and the living, when a hostile soul or a demon takes over a human body because of sins or its own needs. The possessing entity may be the soul of a dead person, a demon, or a unique possessing spirit. Exorcisms are designed to end possession states by driving out the entity that had penetrated a human body, and are practiced today in various traditions, from Maoris in New Zealand, to Hindus, Roman Catholics, and Pentecostals, sometimes resulting in the death of the possessed (Mercer, 2013). A case that attracted much media attention was reported by the American politician Bobby Jindal, the 55th governor of Louisiana, who reported being involved in an exorcism at age twenty-three (Jindal, 1994).

Rituals which consist of negotiating with the souls of animals can be found in cultures which rely on hunted or domesticated animals for survival. This involves apologizing to the hunted species and expressing hope for its preservation and its continuing fertility. Thus, members of the Yurok tribe were described praying to the salmon:

> Tearfully they assured their prey that they meant no harm to his essence, that they were eating only that fleshy part of him that he could well afford to lose, and that they would let his scales return downriver and out into the ocean where they came from, so that from them new salmon could grow—and continue to come into the Yurok's nets.
>
> (Erikson, 1964, p. 104)

There is much evidence of guilt over the killing of animals, expressed in taboos and rituals among hunters (Luckert, 1975). Ideas about the fear of revenge by the souls of slaughtered animals lie at the root of hunting and slaughter rituals, which are best known today in Islam and Judaism (Frazer, 1922).

Belief variations

Brown (1991) collected a list of some 200 "human universals," among them many that are directly relevant to the psychology of religion: Anthropomorphization, taboos, rites of passage, death rituals, beliefs about disease, beliefs about fortune and misfortune, belief in supernatural/religion, myths, and divination. The universality of these ideas demonstrates the psychological unity of humans, who share the same mental mechanisms and face similar challenges.

In the academic study of religion, all beliefs and traditions must be treated equally. The psychology of religion does not need such terms as "primitive," "cult," or "magic" and assumes one unified, psychological realm of experience. Durkheim (1912/1995) already emphasized the unity of "primitive" and "modern" religions. Strenski (1998) describes "a longstanding rejection of invidious distinctions between cult and religion or superstition and religion among students of religion" (p. 360), and Atran (2002) similarly makes no "distinctions between magic and myth, between primitive and modern thought, or among animistic, pantheistic, and monotheistic forms of religion" (p. 8).

There is much psychological and cultural continuity between "official" religious beliefs and para-religious beliefs, which are part of folk tradition and popular practices in every culture. Para-religious beliefs are most often transmitted unofficially and orally, but the unofficial lore is as well known in a given culture as official doctrines. Driskell and Lyon (2011, p. 389) stated that institutional religions and "New Age" share "beliefs regarding the existence of transcendent entities (i.e., the soul or spirit)." Boyer (2001) stated that the realm of religion included both "official" religious ideas, as well as "unofficial" narratives about Santa Claus or witchcraft, produced by the same psychological processes.

"Official" doctrines and "unofficial" popular beliefs and practices are united by a subjectivist worldview (Zusne and Jones, 1982) based on non-materialism. Both religions and para-religious belief systems, such as beliefs in "telepathy," astrology, or communication with the dead, posit a causal system which is both cosmic and personal, challenging the impersonal reality of nature. Events in nature are presumably tied to a coherent, comprehensive system of causality with humans at its center. "New Age" beliefs and practices reflect this kind of supernaturalist thinking (see Chapter 9).

Studies which tried to assess whether believers in orthodox traditions were also likely to hold popular occultism have led to inconsistent results (Bader, Baker and Molle, 2012), but there is a body of research which points to some continuity (Canetti-Nisim and Beit-Hallahmi, 2007; Francis *et al.*, 2013; Francis, Williams and Robbins, 2009; Glendinning, 2006; Mencken, Bader and Kim, 2009; Rice, 2003; Weeks, Weeks and Daniel, 2008; Willard and Norenzayan, 2013; Zusne and Jones, 1982).

10 Defining psychology, defining religion

Witchcraft beliefs involve claims about the manipulation of evil supernatural forces and entities. Pedro Espada, Jr., a politician on trial for corruption in New York City, claimed that "evil spiritual powers" were acting against him, and so he "held up rosary beads and said, 'We Catholics fight that off with this'" (Secret, 2012, p. A28). Mr. Espada went to prison for five years. In the twenty-first century, witchcraft accusations directed at individuals are still heard all over the world, leading to individuals (mostly women) being killed in Africa, India and Papua New Guinea.

The notion of the "primitive" in beliefs and social systems is simply an expression of bias. It is clear that pre-literate cultures possess highly complex social structures and belief systems. We may find in such cultures beliefs which may appear strange, together with others which seem familiar and quite similar to those in the advanced industrial nations of today. The Kurelu people of New Guinea have been described as living in the Stone Age, and that is understandable given their rudimentary technology, but their culture consists of thousands of complex beliefs and customs. The Kurelu believe in friendly and unfriendly ghosts, as well as purification rites to remove the impurity of death. There are exorcisms to drive away ghosts and remind the dead members of the tribe to move on, and during funerals an arrow is shot into the dead body, releasing the soul. Divination is performed by cutting up the innards of small animals (Matthiessen, 1962). Such beliefs and practices have been known in many cultures. Practices of telling fortunes by "reading" animal entrails were well known thousands of years ago among Babylonians, Hittites, Etruscans and Romans.

The Nuer of East Africa believe in a supernatural world controlled by one supreme deity, Akuj, and offer him sacrifices of cattle designed to ensure prosperity and divine blessings. Some members of the tribe are recognized as prophets, who may have contacts with the supernatural world (Evans-Pritchard, 1970). Similar beliefs are found among the Dinka, Himba, Igbo, and other African cultures. To Western observers, they all appear similar to common Biblical ideas.

Ancestors play an important role in many traditions all over the world as denizens of the spirit world. Events in one's life, and especially death and misfortune, are explained as resulting from ancestors' wishes and acts. Fortes observes the virtual identity of African and Chinese ideas about filial piety: "The Tallensi would accept the Confucian ideal of pietas as consisting in 'serving one's parents when alive according to propriety; in burying them when dead according to propriety and in sacrificing to them according to propriety' ... or 'according to ritual'" (Fortes, 1961, p. 179).

In many cultures, paying respects to dead ancestors is believed to ensure a happy life and a good afterlife, and it is better to be on good terms with them (Ahern, 1973; Traphagan, 2004). Here is an example from Taiwan:

> the deceased's spirit needs to be supplied with goods from the world of the living, which is done by burning spirit money and presenting offerings. If the spirit receives these sacrifices, s/he is appeased. If not, the spirit becomes a

hungry ghost, whose ability to wreak vengeance surpasses the good an ancestor can render.

(Gries, Su and Schak, 2012, p. 626)

The Western version of such beliefs is reported among students in the United States, who believe that "rituals carried out after your death affect your afterlife" (Lester *et al.*, 2002, p. 117).

Sometimes, holidays are set aside to honor dead ancestors and relatives, in the expectation that they in turn will protect the living. In the Chinese festival of Qingming ("tomb sweeping day"), the living burn fake money notes and leave cigarettes, oranges and beer at the graves of relatives, which have been cleaned and tidied up. These acts are believed to ensure a good life for the living, and happiness in the afterworld for the dead. The Qingming holiday is similar to Western traditions, such as All Souls Day in its many forms.

The language of miracles

Most religious traditions are transmitted through miracle narratives, which prove supernaturalism in the most literal way by suggesting that religion overcomes the limitations of life and nature. Countless miracle narratives have been circulated in human history, many obviously reused and recycled. They are often defined as events which seem to violate our sense of the "laws of nature" or the "order of nature," but the point of the supernatural premise is to tell us that the true order of nature includes entities and actions which transcend mundane experiences.

For the believers, a myth is a true report of real and important events, proving the power and mercy of the gods, and any interpretation follows from that assumption. Faith is sustained by narratives of past glories and promises of future triumphs. Miracles are always naturalistic claims presented as evidence for the power of spirits and the power of those connected, or obedient, to them (Beit-Hallahmi, 2001a). Their most important characteristic is that they take place in this world, not in the invisible world of the spirits. They are believed to occur through the intercession of benevolent spirit entities, but their effects are totally material, palpable, and provable (at least to the believers) in naturalist terms. When the claim is made that somebody has been cured of cancer, the alleged cure happened right here on earth, and not in the spirit world. In explaining disease and cures, what is unique about miracles is not a deficient knowledge of physiology, which can be found in many purely secular assertions, but the claimed intervention by the great spirits.

Some humans are believed to be miracle workers, having special powers, and claims about individuals with such powers are made in many traditions. Dan Stratton is the pastor of the Faith Exchange Fellowship, a fundamentalist Christian congregation in New York's financial district. His wife Ann has been described as a born-again miracle worker, "whose prayers once supposedly raised a German au pair from the dead on the street in front of the Blue Moon Mexican Cafe in

12 Defining psychology, defining religion

Englewood, N.J. ... Today that woman's alive and well in Germany." Ann Stratton also stated that thanks to her prayers, "[a] woman with brain cancer was healed, another was saved from a hysterectomy and a man came out of a seemingly permanent coma ... a little deaf boy regained his hearing ... her prayers replaced a blind eye in a woman's socket with a healthy, perfectly matched green eyeball" (Chafets, 2006, p. 21).

Many religious narratives contain both supernaturalist and naturalist claims (Beit-Hallahmi, 2001a). Naturalist claims are often found in religious discourse, but do not convey the unique character of religious thinking. While a claim such as "[a] man named Jesus was born in Judea under Herod," is straightforward, naturalistic, and lacking any supporting evidence, it is part of a religious narrative that is anything but naturalistic.

Disasters and miracles are both believed to be part of a divine plan, and a cosmic calculus is evident in both. Humans are believed to be subject to rules of reward and punishment, administered meticulously by the great spirits. Within a religious framework, both disasters and miracles serve to persuade us, not of the reality of the world of the spirits in general, but of one particular belief system and one particular claim to authority, which is better and stronger than those worshiped by other collectivities. "Our" miracles are clearly superior to theirs. Superiority and self-esteem are vital psychological supplies, provided by religions and other ideologies.

Mythologies, written or transmitted orally, present the cosmic order and the centrality of humans in it. This human role, of course, is miraculous, and so is the revelation telling us about it. Humans are naturally attracted to the idea of being at the center of the universe, sharing a cosmic mission. There exists a cosmic plan in which the believer and his group play a central role, and this human role can be understood only within the context of the cosmic script. While many religions report foundational revelations, events which led to their founding, some traditions report confirmatory revelations, which reinforce and sustain long-held beliefs. Through these apparitions specific messages from the spirit world are conveyed, or the presence of spirits and gods directly felt.

The substance of religion: sacrifice

Sacrifice is a way of negotiating with the spirit world which involves a fantasy of reciprocity, with believers asking for intercession and forgiveness. Offerings may take many forms, from mutilating one's body to avoiding speech for long hours, and a great variety of materials are offered to the spirits for their nourishment, from bananas to sheep. Sacrificing one's hair as a part of an initiation rite or a mark of devotion is found in some traditions. Among ultra-Orthodox Jews, all married women keep their hair short and wear a hairpiece (in some groups they shave their heads). In India both men and women sacrifice their hair to the gods. In a rare case of unwitting religious cooperation, hair collected at Hindu temples has been used in recent years for hairpieces purchased by ultra-Orthodox Jewish women.

Defining psychology, defining religion **13**

Sacrificing one's private life is a dramatic religious act. Religious ideals of renunciation, which involve giving up attachments and family ties, are found in many cultures, and individuals are invited to make a major offering by consecrating their lives as clergy, monks, or nuns. In South Asia we find the phenomenon of middle-aged men committing themselves to severing all personal attachments. Laungani (2007) discusses the case of a former High Court Judge in India, who has renounced the material world, abandoned his large and loving family, and has become a sanyasin in search of enlightenment and nirvana. The consecration of virgins is an ancient tradition, re-established by the Roman Catholic Church in 1970. As of 2011, there were 400 consecrated virgins in Italy (Turina, 2011). Consecrated virgins make a public promise of perpetual virginity during a special ceremony, conducted by a bishop, which celebrates marriage to the mythical Jesus Christ. They live alone or with their families, have regular jobs, and are part of the community.

Public infliction of suffering as a form of sacrifice is found in some traditions. Sitting Bull (c. 1831–1890), a Lakota Sioux holy man, pierced his body with skewers when performing the sun dance in honor of the goddess White Buffalo Woman (Uttley, 1993). Piercing with skewers can be observed today among Shiite Moslems in West Asia and Hindus as well as Buddhists in South Asia. Blood shedding in the genital mutilation of children is practiced in various cultures as part of puberty or pre-puberty initiation rites, and is sometimes sanctioned as a religious duty.

Animal sacrifice is a dramatic part of many traditions. The relationship with the sacrificial victim is often complex and ambivalent, as the animal may be worshipped as well as sacrificed. An example is the worship of bull-god, found in Mediterranean cultures as well as in South Asia. Bulls were deified, but sometimes also killed, and worshipped while being consumed. The ritualized killing of a bull survives to this day in a secular form in Latin America, in Spain, and in Southern France as bullfighting.

Animal sacrifice is most common today in Islamic and African cultures, as well as in Afro-Caribbean and Afro-American traditions, such as Voodoo, and its rules are similar to the Old Testament rules, where for each transgression there is a sacrificial atonement. The tradition of the mythological scapegoat, described in Leviticus 16, lives on in Orthodox Judaism, where the custom of sacrificing a chicken on the eve of the Day of Atonement for every member of the family (hens for females and roosters for males) is still prevalent, and hundreds of thousands of fowl are sacrificed every fall in Jewish communities all over the world. The belief is that human sins are transferred to the animal, which will pay for them with its life. In this case, as in others, the projection of sins on a victim is conscious.

The majority of Christians, numbering more than one billion, celebrate the Eucharist, a ritual involving ideas of sacrifice and cannibalism. Participants ingest a piece of bread and drink some wine or grape juice. The believers insist that they are actually engaged in the eating of human flesh and the drinking of human blood. In the words of Pope Paul VI, the ritual involves "the marvelous change of the

14 Defining psychology, defining religion

whole of the bread's substance into Christ's body and the whole of the wine's substance into his blood" (1965, pp. 7–8). Outsiders see only wafers and wine, but the fantasy is powerful and the ritual is at the center of the tradition. This is a case of theophagy, a celebration which involves god-eating, and is found in ancient traditions (Frazer, 1922; Griffiths, 1980). In some preliterate cultures, such as the Ainu of Japan, the bear is considered a god, and rituals of bear sacrifice, in which the celebrants share meat, play a major role in religious traditions (Kitagawa, 1961). Determining the actual emergence of the Eucharist in antiquity is impossible, but similar practices have been observed recently. Zivkovic (2014) described how followers of the Tibetan lama Bokar Rinpoche (1940–2004) ingested red and white pills containing his blood and semen during funeral ceremonies following his death, and stated that in this way they can "merge with his mind" (p. 121).

In the early days of Christianity, this ritual gave rise to rumors and accusations of child sacrifice and cannibalism (McGowan, 1994; Schultz, 1991). In 177 CE, Christians in Lyon were accused of the ritual sacrifice of infants. Their slaves confessed to the truth of the allegations and the entire community was massacred (Cohn, 1975). The accusation that Jews use the blood of Christian children in baking unleavened bread for the Passover holiday, known as the Blood Libel, has been interpreted as growing out of the Eucharist. Simmel (1946) suggested that the anti-Semitic Christian accuses the Jew of the crime which he unconsciously commits when he eats the holy wafer. Dundes (1991) argued that the Blood Libel was a projective inversion of the Christian communion. Those who acted out ritualized cannibalism in the communion selected Jews as their scapegoat, a sacrificial victim. The Jewish Passover celebration, named after the mythical killing of the Egyptian first-born and the survival of the Israelite children, has been interpreted as originating in human sacrifice (Schlesinger, 1976).

A unique worship ritual which involves animals and the loss of human life is that of snake handling. This is a Christian ritual native to the United States, and observed since the early twentieth century among poor Whites in Appalachia. It has led to scores of fatalities. The worshippers defy death and secular authority in proving their devotion (Hood and Williamson, 2008). In 2013, the practice became the subject of a regular television program in the United States, known as "Snake Salvation." On February 15, 2014, one of the show's stars, Jamie Coots, died of a snake bite during a church service. He had refused medical care (The Associated Press, 2014).

Death and religion

Religion's most unique claim, which combines the two worlds, that of nature and that of the spirits, is the denial of death. Avoiding the recognition of death as the end of any individual existence is one of religion's strongest compensators (Beit-Hallahmi and Argyle, 1997). There is evidence of probable afterlife beliefs during the middle Paleolithic period, between 120,000 and 40,000 years ago. The material evidence is of intentional burials, and archaeologists suggest that only ideas about death as a

Defining psychology, defining religion **15**

transition can explain them. The oldest burials are found in the Middle Palaeolithic in West Asia (Ronen, 2012). What we find in them are grave goods, i.e. articles left with the body, mostly food. The investment in grave goods is interpreted as reflecting a wish to help the dead person survive, so to speak, in this new stage of existence. These early humans thought that death was not the end, and the difference between one bowl of food left with a dead child 100,000 years ago and the tombs of Egyptian pharaohs 5,000 years old is just quantitative. The belief animating both is identical: We have to invest in creating the right future for the dead.

"To judge by archaeological evidence … some of the most gigantic constructions, some of the most splendid and extravagant works of art, some of the most complex rituals have all been devoted to the internment, housing and equipping of the dead, in preparation for the journey of the soul beyond the grave" (Stone, 1978, p. 22). What other explanation can account for the massive investment of resources in activities and artifacts which have no direct bearing on survival, at a time when human communities were small and always in danger of extinction? We can speculate about early humans because they had the same brains and the same minds as ourselves. This is the first time we can refer to the denial of death by humans, and this is the beginning of religion.

To say that religion is an expression of death denial is a truism. As Carson McCullers put it, religion is about "the future of the dead" (McCullers, 1940, p. 188). Every day, all over the world, humans are saying farewell to dead relatives, friends, and colleagues. If we ask about the meaning of their acts, whether it is a burial, cremation, or a Zoroastrian ceremony in which the body is devoured by carrion birds, the meaning, we will be told, in most cases, is in the departure on a journey to the spirit world, where the deceased may undergo transformations, but the soul will survive to live on in another container or return to the same body when resurrected.

The illusion of immortality is one reaction to the inevitability of death, the universal threat to every individual human. Within the religious framework, death is not a singular event occurring only once in the history of the individual, but a transition from one form of existence to another. All religions state that dying is only a passage, a transition point in the existence of the soul, as it comes out of a particular human body.

Frazer described religion, with "the almost universal belief in the survival of the human spirit after death" (Frazer, 1933–1936, p. v) at its center, as resulting from the fear of the dead, which is the fear of death itself (Beit-Hallahmi, 2012). Another analysis states:

> Religion, whether it be shamanism or Protestantism, rises from our apprehension of death. To give meaning to meaninglessness is the endless quest of religion … Clearly we possess religion, if we want to, precisely to obscure the truth of our perishing … When death becomes the center, then religion begins.
>
> (Bloom, 1992, p. 29)

16 Defining psychology, defining religion

The terror of death leads to the creation of prominent cultural mechanisms (Becker, 1973; Greenberg *et al.*, 1995; Pyszczynski, Greenberg and Solomon, 2003), with religion being the most important.

And indeed, denying death is part of the daily practice of all religions: "I can testify to the entire world that I know that life is eternal, that it is everlasting, that the grave is not the end, that those who die young or old shall go on living" (Hinckley, 2001, p. 2). This is how a President of the Church of Jesus Christ of Latter Day Saints expressed his faith, which he shares with billions around the globe, of all traditions.

The idea of the soul expresses the denial of death (Roheim, 1932). One can find claims not only about the soul's state of perfection after death, but about the body. Elizabeth Kubler-Ross, a well-known spiritualist, proclaimed that "[p]eople after death become complete again. The blind can see, the deaf can hear, cripples are no longer crippled after all their vital signs have ceased to exist" (quoted in Rosenbaum, 2001, p. 267). Some of the activities attributed to the dead in heaven seem to require working bodies, and not just souls. David Brandt Berg (1919–1994), the founder of Children Of God (known since 2004 as The Family International), reported in 1985 that he had ascended into "the spirit world" and discovered that there was great sex in heaven: "No exhaustion, no tiring, no surfeiting, no impotence, no failures, no dissatisfactions! All was pure joy & love & endless fulfillment, hallelujah! Thank you, Jesus!" (quoted in Kent, 1994, p. 183).

While religions have promised their followers everlasting life through the immortality of the soul, some religious leaders promised their followers literal, physical immortality, and some followers claim to accept that promise. In the 1930s in the United States, a man known as Father Divine was supposed to have given his followers everlasting life: "many of us who are in this place will never lose the bodies we now have. God is here in the flesh, and he is never going away from us, and we will remain here forevermore. This is heaven on earth" (Fauset, 1944, p. 105).

Connecting death and the sacred is found in most religious belief systems. Personal immortality, whether through the rise of one's soul to heaven, or through some form of reincarnation, as well as various promises of resurrection, has been described and promised in religious traditions for many thousands of years, and is indeed the most important function of religion for the majority of believers. It was William James who stated that "[r]eligion, in fact, for the great majority of our own race, means immortality and nothing else" (James, 1902/1961, p. 406). The spirit world is usually the afterworld, or afterlife, which are clearly euphemisms for death and a denial of its reality and finality.

Every encounter with death is a reminder of the spirit world. Atran (2002) reported that people have a pronounced tendency to associate the word "God" with death and sadness. The souls of the dead have always been regarded with fear, to be propitiated or conjured up, but reminders of death are used to shore up religious faith through assurances of immortality. This is what Christianity has promised: "The trumpet shall sound, and the dead shall be raised incorruptible, and

We shall be changed. For this corruptible must put on incorruption and this mortal must put on immortality" (I Corinthians 15: 52–53).

All religions offer us descriptions of the soul's trajectory following physical death and every one of these is an attempt to deny and diminish reality, as it has been witnessed by humans since time immemorial. The most common expressions of the "normal" religious denial of death consist of accounts of the soul's travels through heaven, hell, incarnation and reincarnation, rebirth, and eventually nirvana or resurrection. Redefining death is a way that preserves the self's integrity, as identity is stable through all migrations. The person's real self will experience what happens after death and will preserve his/her unique identity. The connection between each individual soul and the cosmos offers what might be called existential confidence.

It has been pointed out that in some religious traditions, the afterlife is characterized by suffering and darkness. But even in these cases the belief is that death is only a transition to another stage, and another state, of existence. Thus, the finality of death and the finality of life are denied. The dead still have a future, even if it is a bleak one.

Defining the psychology of religion and religiosity

The psychology of religion aims to account for individual religious thinking and its meanings. It applies psychological hypotheses, explanations, and concepts to religious ideation and actions. When an individual refers to Allah, Jesus, hell, or heaven, what are the associated processes, emotions, and motives? What are the associated images? The phenomena to be explained include religions across space and time; not just religions we are familiar with, but all religions, including extinct and ancient practices from the Stone Age to ancient Egypt, Greece, or Rome.

Research on the psychological foundations of religion may rely on experiments, where conditions are controlled and causality is supposed to be determined. Thus, experimenters may create death anxiety in respondents and observe its effects on different beliefs. Many experiments have used priming, which is "the temporary activation of an individual's mental representations ... and the effect of this activation on behavior in an unrelated subsequent task" (Hadnes and Schumacher, 2012, p. 692). Religious priming means the activation of religious ideas by various means, consciously or unconsciously, and its effects are measured.

A second kind of research is concerned not with the foundations of religion, but with religiosity and the effects of religiosity in secular spheres of behavior. When individuals tell us that they espouse a certain belief system, what can we say about the relevant psychological antecedents, and about the relevant behavioral consequences? What does belief in hell or heaven lead to? The question is "Does religiosity make a difference?", and the answer is given in terms of both individual and collective behavior.

What is done first is to measure religiosity, the importance of the supernaturalist premise in an individual's life. For most individuals, this will be expressed in a

18 Defining psychology, defining religion

conscious adherence to any of the many thousands of religions currently in existence, and derivatives such as participation in rituals and meetings or monetary donations. For some individuals, it will be a more eclectic or nebulous commitment to supernaturalism (Chapter 9). Religiosity is a continuous, rather than a discrete, variable. This means that for most humans, investment in beliefs and practices is not an all or nothing question, but a matter of degree. Religiosity measures reflect one's investment of resources in supernaturalism.

Assessing the dimensions of religiosity

Glock (1962) proposed five dimensions for the measurement of religiosity in modern society: ideological, intellectual, ritualistic, experiential, and consequential. This idea has been applied in hundreds of studies.

Dimension 1: Ideological, covering religious beliefs

Support for particular religious beliefs is the main measure of religiosity, which is then related to other beliefs, and to psychological and behavioral indicators (Beit-Hallahmi and Argyle, 1997). Belief is the main measure used in the literature, because that is how every religion measures its successes or failures. It is the content of beliefs that gives meaning to religious acts and everything around them.

A public statement of faith is considered sufficient for membership in many religious groups, and this makes sense from a social-psychological point of view. A public utterance of a creed means a public commitment, and that is what any group, secular or religious, would wish to have. Particular traditions frame beliefs in a credo or a single sentence. Repeating such sentences aloud is a ritual and an act of public commitment. Examples of such are the Kalimat al Shahada ("There is no God but Allah") of Islam, or the Buddham saranam gacchami ("I take refuge in the Buddha") in Buddhism. Data about beliefs are not based on official dogma, but on what believers say and how they respond to religious concepts (Cohen, Shariff and Hill, 2008).

Here are some examples of belief items: In the General Social Survey (GSS), a nationally representative survey of the United States population, six response options are provided for the question:

"Which statement comes closest to expressing what you believe about god?"

1 I know that god exists and I have no doubts about it;
2 While I have doubts, I feel that I do believe in god;
3 I find myself believing in god some of the time, but not at others;
4 I don't believe in a personal god, but I do believe in a higher power of some kind;
5 I don't know whether there is a god, and I don't believe there is any way to find out;
6 I don't believe in god.

Such items are relevant only to religious systems with a concept of a supreme god, but this means a large part of humanity.

> "Which one of these statements comes closest to describing your feelings about the Bible?"

> The Bible is an ancient book of fables, legends, history, and moral teachings recorded by man.
> The Bible is the inspired word of God but not everything should be taken literally, word for word.
> The Bible is the actual word of God and it is to be taken literally, word for word.
>
> (Davis and Robinson, 1999b, p. 1659)

This item is relevant to nominal Christians and Jews.

> "What do you think happens after your body dies?"

> An afterlife of some kind.
> Reincarnation.
> Nothing. Death is the end of personal existence.
> I don't know.
> I don't think about it.
> "Does man have a soul that can exist independently from the body, for example after death?"
>
> (Belyaev, 2011, p. 358)

These two items are relevant to all humans.

Asking individuals whether they believe in an immortal, immaterial soul seems just as useful in assessing religiosity as asking about belief in a god. Afterlife beliefs appear to be associated with the idea of an immaterial essence, potentially dissociable from the biology of life and death. Richert and Harris (2008) found that students who believed in the existence of the soul were also likely to report attitudes reflecting the stance of religious groups in the United States on issues such as stem-cell research.

Dimension 2: Intellectual, covering religious knowledge

Religious knowledge, that is the knowledge of a religion's scriptures and traditions, is not always a good measure of religiosity, simply because many believers seem to be quite ignorant of what are considered basic elements of the religious tradition they claim as their own. There may be a negative correlation between beliefs and knowledge in some traditions. Discussing the United States, two leading researchers stated: "The public on the whole is amazingly ignorant ... For example, 79 per

20 Defining psychology, defining religion

cent of the Protestants and 86 per cent of the Catholics could not name a single Old Testament prophet" (Glock and Stark, 1966, p. 161). Such ignorance is found in many denominations and assuming that nominal members are familiar with their group's doctrine is risky. Limited knowledge by religious Americans extends even to such basic matters as their own religious affiliation, as observed by two sociologists, who claimed that "attempting to classify people by the denomination is problematic given that many people are poorly informed about their actual affiliation" (Driskell and Lyon, 2011, p. 387).

In 2010, a survey in the United States found that atheists and agnostics were the most knowledgeable about religious concepts and traditions, even after controlling for education, compared to those identifying with a religion. Mormons and Jews were in third and fourth places. Afro-American Protestants and Latino Catholics had the lowest scores. Overall, the survey showed that religious knowledge was quite limited. Fifty-three percent of American Protestants did not connect Martin Luther with the Reformation (Pew Forum, 2010).

All these findings demonstrate that the knowledge dimension cannot serve as an effective measure of religiosity, and that data about knowledge should be used with caution.

Dimension 3: Ritualistic, covering participation in religious rituals

Here is an example of a Dimension 3 item:

"How often do you go to a place of worship to pray?"

More than once a day.
Once a day.
Several times a week.
Once a week.
Less than once a week.
Once a month.
Less than once a month.
Never.

Frequency of attendance in religious services is a common index of public religious commitment. Most studies using data on attendance at religious services rely on self-report, which raises the obvious question of reliability. Should we trust what people tell us about their public worship attendance? In the United States more than 40 percent of the population were reporting having attended services ("in the last seven days") until recently. Many have thought such findings physically impossible (i.e. not enough space in places of worship to accommodate 100 million attenders). Using actual time-use diaries, rather than self-reports, researchers found that a more realistic figure would be about 26 percent (Presser and Chaves, 2007).

Does this mean that self-reported attendance should not be used in research? Not at all. The first thing we learn from this over-reporting of religiosity is that it reflects a strong cultural norm, which reflects the reality of culture (but not the reality of behavior). We may still want to use attendance as a variable, because it correlates with other measures and with other attitudes. We should think of responses to questions about worship not necessarily as reflecting reality, but as part of a complex of attitudes and behaviors which should be examined. Hadaway, Marler, and Chaves (1998) suggested that "over reporting is generated by the combination of a respondent's desire to report *truthfully* his or her identity as a religious, church-going person and the perception that the attendance question is really about this identity rather than about *actual attendance*" (1998, p. 127, italics in the original). Brenner (2011) argued that overreporting of religious service attendance in the United States was related to the importance of religious identity for individuals, and so overreporting was a valid measure of high religiosity.

Those who claim regular worship attendance are quite distinct in many ways, as compared to (self-reported) non-attenders, and this is of great interest. The mere fact of claiming to have attended religious services in the past seven days may be tied to other significant variables, such as political attitudes, sexual behavior, or prejudice. Asking people about their private acts of worship, such as praying or reading scriptures, may be an alternative to asking about public worship, but still relies on self-reporting.

Here is such an item:

"About how often do you pray or meditate outside of religious services?"

Never.
Only on certain occasions.
Once a week or less.
A few times a week.
Once a day.
Several times a day.

(Baker, 2008b, p. 173)

Dimension 4: Experiential, covering intense religious experiences

The experiential dimension covers intense religious experiences such as conversion, "speaking in tongues," or mystical experiences (Proudfoot, 1985). Here is an example of a Dimension 4 item:

"Have you ever felt as though you were very close to a powerful spiritual force that seemed to lift you out of yourself?"

(Greeley, 1975)

22 Defining psychology, defining religion

The following items are supposed to reflect daily spiritual experiences:

"I feel God's love for me, through others."
"I feel God's love for me, directly."
"I feel guided by God in the midst of daily activities."
"I feel God's presence."
"I ask for God's help in the midst of daily activities."
"During worship, or at other times when connecting with God, I feel joy which lifts me out of my daily concerns."

(Taken from Unnever, Bartkowski and Cullen, 2010, p. 313)

It may be argued that the above six items reflect belief, rather than experience, but in any case they reflect personal religiosity.

Dimension 5: Consequential

The so-called consequential dimension of religiosity, which sought to measure the effects of religiosity in secular activities was soon dropped by Glock himself, and considered separate from religiosity (Glock and Stark, 1965). It is no longer assessed together with the other ones, but is still of major interest, as it should be. Chapter 6 will survey research on the non-religious consequences of individual religiosity.

Scores based on preferably multidimensional surveys and questionnaires enable us to place the individual on a conceptual religiosity continuum running from 0 to 100 or from 0 to 10, but in most cases not just 0 or 1. From such scores we can proceed to correlations and generalizations. Even when the respondent is allowed only a "yes" or "no" answer, the findings may be significant. The consensus on using religiosity as a continuous variable (0 to 100) and then correlating it with similar continuous variables, such as personality measures, has been challenged by Galen and Kloet (2011), who argued that to learn more about the correlates of religiosity, we need to compare religious individuals, of all levels, to self-declared atheists.

2

EXCEPTIONAL OR NATURAL?

The psychological roots of religion

Popular conceptions of the origins of religion, which ascribe the formation of religious ideas to extraordinary and dramatic events, are encountered often enough. There might be references to mystical experiences or visions, inferred or imagined on the basis of ancient scriptures. Such views tie religion to dramatic, unusual, irregular, or abnormal psychological processes, and mention trances, dissociation, or "altered states of consciousness," induced by hallucinogens or appearing spontaneously (Clark, 1969; Harner, 1973; Lewis-Williams and Pearce, 2005; Vaitl *et al.*, 2005; Wulff, 1997).

These accounts assume that the phenomenon of religion started with individual founders, who, following these exceptional experiences, presented a new belief system to their communities and started leading rituals. The prophet, with his imagined charisma, is able to inculcate this new belief system in a group of followers and create a real commitment. Stories about single founders and mystical experiences in the desert, possibly produced by psychedelic substances, echo mythological accounts, which describe the beginning of a tradition as the result of the miracle of revelation, but bear no relation to the actual history of any religion. Minority experiences, however intense, cannot explain the hold on the majority, and the processes that give rise to religion cannot be abnormal or deviant. Dramatic behaviors get our attention, and deserve it, but don't represent the majority of practices or believers.

It has long been agreed among scholars who use a psychological perspective to study religion that there is no need for specialized psychological concepts which will only apply to religious phenomena, because such phenomena are not *sui generis*.

> There is religious fear, religious love, religious awe, religious joy, and so forth. But religious love is only man's natural emotion of love directed to a

> religious object; religious fear is only the ordinary fear of commerce, so to speak, the common quaking of the human breast, in so far as the notion of divine retribution may arouse it; religious awe is the same organic thrill which we feel in a forest at twilight, or in a mountain gorge; only this time it comes over us at the thought of our supernatural relations; and similarly of all the various sentiments which may be called into play in the lives of religious persons.
>
> (James, 1902/1961, p. 29)

James argued that the affects involved are religious only because of religious ideas.

General psychological theorizing is considered adequate and appropriate to the task of explaining religion, and no unique mental or physiological mechanisms are assumed. Cognitive mechanisms have come to be considered the relevant building blocks: "Whatever explains how language and minds work generally, explains how religious language and religious minds work" (Frankenberry, 2002, p. xv). The universality and robustness of religious ideas shows that they are natural and intuitive, much more so than the ideas of physics, chemistry, or anthropology. Jahoda (1969, p. 146), discussing what he called superstition, stated: "far from being odd and abnormal ... [it] is in fact intimately bound up with our fundamental mode of thinking, feeling and generally responding to our environment." The ubiquity of religious ideas, as well as their persistence, cannot be accounted for by the effect of unusual experiences or altered states of consciousness. The *homo sapiens* brain leads to the creation of religious ideas without any need for help in the form of psychotropic materials or spontaneous hallucinations.

Modern theorizing about supernaturalism as a consequence of universal cognitive mechanisms continues a long tradition, more salient since the eighteenth century, which regards religion as the product of common mental operations. This view locates the sacred not "out there," but in the human psyche (Manuel, 1983). Xenophanes (sixth century BCE) coined the term anthropomorphism when noting the similarity between religious believers and the imaginary representations of their gods, with Greek gods being fair skinned and African gods being dark skinned, and wrote: "if an ox could paint a picture, his god would look like an ox" (Dodds, 1951, p. 181). D'Holbach (1689–1723) used the term anthropomorphism and attributed the origins of religion to infantile helplessness and dependence, just like Sigmund Freud (see Chapter 8). In 1844, Karl Marx proposed that "in religion the spontaneous activity of human fantasy, of the human brain and heart, reacts independently as an alien activity of gods or devils upon the individual" (quoted in Fromm, 1961, p. 82). Thirty-five years later, the eminent American neurologist G. M. Beard observed that "spirits only dwell in the cerebral cells ... not our houses but our brains are haunted" (Beard, 1879, p. 67).

Religion first appears, or is learned and embraced, through the operation of ordinary, automatic, cognitive processing. Several natural mechanisms create the capacity for developing supernaturalist ideas, as well as the readiness to accept these ideas once they have been created. "The naturalness hypothesis as widely understood by cognitive scientists of religion refers to the fact that religious ideas and behaviors thrive on (or are parasitic to) normal human cognitive and psychological processes" (Geertz and Markússon, 2010, p. 155).

Two cognitive modes

One starting point for the analysis of religious thinking is the notion that humans use two modes of information processing and judgment, described as intuitive and reflective (Sperber, 1997), automatic and deliberate (Chaiken and Trope, 1999), System 1 and System 2 (Kahneman, 2003; Stanovich and West, 2000), or "nonreflective beliefs" and "reflective beliefs" (Barrett, 2004). Pacini and Epstein described these two processing styles as,

> an inferential system ... conscious, relatively slow, analytical, primarily verbal, and relatively affect-free; ... has a very brief evolutionary history. The experiential system is ... preconscious, rapid, automatic, holistic, primarily nonverbal, intimately associated with affect, and it has a very long evolutionary history.
>
> (Pacini and Epstein, 1999, p. 972)

The reflective, non-egocentric, mode requires effort, while the intuitive mode is automatic, agreeable, and attractive. Automatic, intuitive thinking is not unique to religion, and predominates in many human actions and affects all decision-making.

The experience of automatic believing, part of System 1, has been described by Daniel Gilbert (Gilbert 1991; Gilbert, Krull and Malone, 1990; Gilbert, Tafarodi and Malone, 1993). The mind's default assumption is to believe what one hears, while disbelieving or doubting requires special effort.

> The asymmetric model of belief and unbelief posits that comprehension automatically implies belief ... to understand something is to implicitly accept it, at least briefly, as a prerequisite to understanding. It then requires a second move to critically evaluate and certify or, alternatively, to 'unbelieve' it. Belief is therefore rapid, automatic, and effortless, whereas the act of unbelief is slow, deliberate, and effortful.
>
> (Pennycook et al., 2012, p. 337)

This means that any information we receive is immediately accepted as valid, and only rarely rejected or analyzed. Even when we read a novel, which is by definition a work of fiction, we imagine the events as real. When we hear ancient mythological stories, we still imagine what is described, including Athena's birth from Zeus' head. Then an additional step is taken when we remind ourselves that these occurrences never actually happened. The picture of Athena's birth (or of Little Red Riding Hood meeting the bad wolf) will stay on in our imagination.

26 Exceptional or natural?

Explaining religion's psychological origins means specifying the processes which make religious thinking possible. The cognitive psychology of religion maps the workings of the imagination which creates souls, gods, angels, and devils. Theories of religion and religiosity assume an infrastructure of unconscious enabling mechanisms which make religion not only possible, but inevitable, automatic, and ubiquitous (Andresen, 2000; Atran, 2002; Barrett, 2004; Boyer, 2001; Pyysiäinen, 2004; Tremlin, 2006). Religious thinking, which means ways of relating to imagined spirit entities, miracles, and mythological stories, is the mind's (and the brain's) default option, characterized by intuitive operations and attractive shortcuts. Every religious belief originates in evolved mechanisms of the human mind, whose last known address is the human brain.

The discovery of certain cognitive biases in children has led to systematic theorizing about the cognitive processes that have created supernaturalism. Historically, this started with the work of Jean Piaget (1896–1980). His observations of young children uncovered a universal tendency toward false inferences about causality, together with egocentricity, anthropomorphism, and animism, in an attempt to make sense of the world (Inagaki and Hatano, 1987; Inhelder and Piaget, 1958; Piaget, 1929, 1962, 1967).

Piaget described three modes of perceiving causality. The earliest is animism, where all objects are believed to share consciousness and volition. Later comes artificialism, where events and objects are believed to be controlled by humans or a human-like consciousness. Children believe that lakes, clouds, rocks, and other natural things were created by humans. The last stage is naturalism, where natural, impersonal forces are used to explain events. There has been an assumption that adults outgrow childish biases and use only naturalism, but this is not the case.

Biases: causality, design, purpose, intention

"Religious ideas, like all kinds of ideas, owe their existence to a raft of specialized tools used in the brain's mental workshop to interpret and organize the world" (Tremlin, 2006, p. 74). Religious ideation is natural and intuitively plausible because of innate mechanisms that lead us to imagine reality in terms of egocentric, anthropocentric, animistic, teleological processes, and to interpret events through intentionality and design.

Human brains look at the environment and it seems like all they see are agency, intention, and consciousness, whether they exist or not. Powerful mechanisms lead to the attribution of consciousness and volition to numerous non-human objects, real and imagined. The apparently universal tendency for over-detecting causality and agency is so powerful because of the cost of not detecting them in ambiguous situations. The ability to recognize threats and opportunities, and to identify intentions, is crucial. The search for causality is vital for human survival, and because of the way it operates humans often cannot tell the difference between intentional actors, imagined intentional actors, and inanimate objects (Tremlin, 2006). They also connect causation to conscious intentions.

Related to the over-detection of causality are several cognitive shortcuts, which pull the mind toward supernaturalist ideation. They undoubtedly overlap, but their analysis as discrete processes provides important insights. Our innate animism, anthropomorphism, Theory of Mind (TOM), dualism, and teleology lead to seeing ourselves as surrounded by minds and by intentions, real (in the case of other people) and imagined (in the case of spirits and objects).

Animism

It is common for humans to attribute beliefs, desires, or intentions to non-human entities, such as animals, or machines, such as cars or computers (Caporael, 1986). The root metaphor of animism, as Pepper (1942) suggested, is the human being. Every event in nature comes about just as we feel our own behavior does, as the result of a wish or conscious intention. This is a direct generalization (or projection) of conscious experience.

Animism is a psychological phenomenon in which humans attempt to understand the world around them by assuming that all creatures and substances share with them the subjective experience of consciousness, including volition. This can be easily observed in young children, who will ascribe volition to clouds moving in the sky, or after hitting a table while running and feeling pain, will hit back at the table, punishing it and inflicting similar pain. Animistic conceptions have always been prominent in culture, and only recently have we begun to develop formal non-animistic ways of looking at the world. Naturalism may be defined simply as looking at the world non-animistically, a method which humanity has developed in the search for an effective control of nature. Naturalistic reasoning is counter-intuitive, unnatural, and hard to develop, as it requires overcoming innate cognitive strategies.

Non-animistic ways of looking at the world have to be taught and require much work. This can most clearly be observed in the historical development of modern science. What we call science, or academic research, is made up of the institutionalization of unnatural and counter-intuitive modes of thinking (Cromer, 1993; McCauley, 2012; Wolpert, 2000). The historical transition from astrology to astronomy and astrophysics, and from alchemy to chemistry, is the transition from animism to non-animistic strategies, but this transition is far from universally accepted.

Anthropomorphism

Human experiences are bound to be expressed through a human vocabulary, and so, naturally and intuitively, we humanize objects by ascribing not only consciousness but a human-like character to everything around us, until we learn better (Guthrie, 1993; Epley, Waytz and Cacioppo, 2007). In the eighteenth century, it was David Hume (1711–1776) who wrote about the "universal tendency among mankind to conceive all beings like themselves, and to transfer to every object those qualities with which they are familiarly acquainted, and of which they are intimately conscious" (Hume, 1757/1875, p. 317). In the twenty-first century, references to inclement weather events or natural disasters give rise to expressions such as "nature's deadly wrath." Positive references to processes and events around us invoke references to "Mother Nature's wisdom." Privately, individuals may interpret a rainstorm that interfered with their weekend plans as a successful attempt by invisible forces to make life hard for them, in retaliation for earlier misdeeds.

The way humans think about spirit entities is unreflective and anthropomorphic. Attempts at "reflective" religious ideation are irrelevant or secondary to the experience of real believers. When we observe religious believers and the way they discuss actions by gods, the gap between intuitive and reflective thinking demonstrates a conflict between official doctrines and intuitive discourse. The expectation that individuals will embrace more "mature," and less anthropomorphic, ideas about deities as they grow older has been shown to be false. Although individuals may report their sincere beliefs about the abilities of the deities to be everywhere at the same time, when asked to discuss a story about the gods, they seemingly forget such beliefs and think anthropomorphically (i.e. a deity cannot be at more than one place at one time). If in such a story God is being addressed by a boy in danger of drowning, believers state that He could help that boy only after taking care of another person in trouble. Ideas about the omnipresence and omnipotence of the gods remain unutilized (Barrett, 1998; Barrett and Keil, 1996).

Theory of Mind

Imagining the mental states of conspecifics carries a clear evolutionary advantage (Dennett, 1989), and so Theory of Mind (TOM) abilities, i.e. ability to understand and predict others' mental states, is crucial for human survival, and makes communication and cooperation possible. As social beings, humans attempt to monitor each other's intentions, beliefs, and wishes. Such attempts are not always successful, because inferring other people's attitudes and beliefs is often done egocentrically, but they mean that humans are busy trying to imagine what happens in the consciousness of others (Nickerson, 1999).

Neuroimaging studies show that when thinking about religious beliefs, individuals rely on brain areas devoted to Theory of Mind activities (Kapogiannis et al., 2009), and believers' framework for viewing their relationship with God is borrowed from their relationships with other humans (Tremlin, 2006). In fact, when "talking to God" through personal prayer, highly religious participants have been shown to use areas of the brain involved in other forms of social cognition (Schjøedt et al., 2009). Religious mentalizing can also be quite egocentric, or at least self-referential. It has been found that positive attitudes toward the self are correlated with positive attitudes towards the image of God (Beit-Hallahmi and Argyle, 1997). McNamara (2009) argued that religious experiences involve the same structures in the brain as those involved in one's self concept. In neuroimaging data, religious individuals were found to be more egocentric when thinking about "God's beliefs." Their social attitudes were correlated more strongly with estimates of "God's beliefs," compared to estimates of other people's beliefs (Epley *et al.*, 2009). Harris *et al.* (2009) suggested that all beliefs, i.e. judgments of "true" or "false" were connected to brain regions involved in self-representation.

This notion of the Theory of Mind is further supported by research demonstrating that a specific region in the human brain (known as the temporoparietal junction) is active in reasoning about the content of other people's minds, as different from their mere physical presence (Saxe and Kanwisher, 2003). Lieberman (2009) argued that the brain processes information about bodies separately from information about minds. This neural differentiation leads to the mistaken assumption that there are two different categories of being.

Dualism

Theory of Mind, mentalizing, or mind perception, is the capacity for people to represent the wishes, intentions, and ideas of other entities, but it is much broader than that (Gray, Gray and Wegner, 2007). Broadening this effort leads to the notion of many other minds around us, and then the notion that some of these minds are not necessarily or permanently housed in human bodies. We imagine the minds of spirit entities in terms of intentions and wishes just like we imagine other persons' minds, but much more power is attributed to some spirits. Theory of Mind leads to the belief in souls surviving death in both humans and animals and to imagined interactions with them.

Mentalizing is related to belief in mind–body dualism, which can be found in virtually all human cultures and this allows for beliefs in souls, reincarnation, and the spirits of deceased family members (Bering, 2006; Bloom, 2004, 2007). These beliefs grow out of the dualistic assumption of a mind that can exist independently of the body it formerly "occupied" (Boyer, 2001). Only if people assume that minds and bodies are two conceptually different entities can they believe that one can exist without the other. Bloom (2007) describes dualism as a "natural by-product of two cognitive systems, one for dealing with material objects, the other for social entities. These systems have incommensurable output" (p. 149).

An important aspect of dualism, which is tied to (or leads to) the belief in a soul, is the experience of subjective consciousness. Private consciousness, which is the source of unique experiences in night dreams, day dreams, and a stream of images and words, is perceived as the true seat of the self. Subjectively, humans experience their consciousness as qualitatively different from their bodies. What makes dualistic beliefs possible is the differentiation between observable bodies and unobservable minds. People know that their thoughts and feelings, emotions, and dreams remain private, whereas their bodies are perceptible to the outside world.

Consciousness also contains the experience, or the illusion, of free will. As Wegner (2005) has suggested, we naturally experience conscious agency, and

30 Exceptional or natural?

believe that our private immaterial self is in control of many physical events, particularly involving our own body:

> The popular solution to the search for free will is that the brain is not the ultimate source of thinking, but there is some nonmaterial self – the soul – that somehow operates to control the body … It is difficult to imagine that such a potent force could just dissolve into nothingness.
>
> (Preston, Gray and Wegner, 2006, p. 483)

It is also difficult to imagine one's private self dissolving, or the imagined selves of others, which supports the idea of an eternal soul. We see the world as populated not just by minds but by souls, which are disembodied minds. Our own private consciousness is the starting point, and we generalize from our own experiences to infer the consciousness of others and the existence of disembodied minds (Bering, 2006, 2011; Bloom, 2004, 2007).

Demertzi *et al.* (2009) carried out two surveys on dualistic beliefs. The one in Edinburgh (with 250 university students) showed a prevalence of support for the separateness of mind and brain. Another one in Belgium (with 1858 healthcare workers and members of the public) found that religiosity was the best predictor of dualistic ideas, namely that the mind and brain are separate, that a "spiritual" part of a person survives death, and that humans possess a soul, separate from the human body.

Teleology

Teleological thinking involves the interpretation of events and objects in terms of purpose, intention, function, and design. Behind it is a belief that every event we observe is willed by a conscious, intentional agent. Children appear naturally predisposed to ascribing intent behind visible acts (Bloom, 2004), and both children and adults demonstrate a bias towards seeing the world as intentionally and purposefully designed (Kelemen, 1999, 2004; Kelemen and DiYanni, 2005; Kelemen and Rosset, 2009). Young children appear to assume that all objects in the world are manufactured for a purpose, and likewise assume that the world also has a creator (Kelemen, 2004), but pervasive, or "promiscuous," teleological thinking is found in all ages. It is difficult for humans to get around the idea that the universe was somehow "created," following some "purpose," "plan," "direction," or "meaning," and to understand that such concepts are human constructions.

Kelemen, Rottman, and Seston (2013) demonstrated that professional chemists, geologists, and physicists from major universities such as Harvard, MIT, and Yale could not escape the automatic preference for the idea that natural phenomena exist for a purpose. The scientists were asked to judge statements such as "Trees produce oxygen so that animals can breathe" or "The Earth has an ozone layer in order to protect it from ultra violet light." This was done under accelerated conditions, so they had little time to reflect. Scientists under time pressure

TABLE 2.1 Cognitive shortcuts

Mechanism	Guiding message
Animism	Consciousness resides in all organisms and objects.
Anthropomorphism	Intention and evaluation reside in all organisms and objects.
Theory of Mind	All minds share desires, feelings, and intentions.
Dualism	Consciousness exists inside and outside bodies and objects.
Teleology	The world around us is the product of designs and intentions.

demonstrated greater acceptance of purpose-based explanations. Chemists, geologists, and physicists showed no less of a teleological bias than English and history professors, though less than a control group of undergraduates.

The importance of cognitive shortcuts in individual believers needs to be demonstrated. If these cognitive mechanisms are indeed the building blocks of religious beliefs, then there should be positive correlations between individual differences in the ways they are used, and individual religiosity. Willard and Norenzayan (2013) measured religiosity, "paranormal" beliefs, and life's-purpose beliefs (e.g. "Things in my life happen for a reason") together with mentalizing, dualism, teleological thinking, and anthropomorphism in two North American samples (n=492 and n=920). They found clear connections, of differing magnitude, among basic cognitive mechanisms and supernaturalist beliefs, thus supporting the general theory. Their main conclusion was that dualism was central to the formation of supernaturalist beliefs, with other mechanisms playing a secondary role: "Dualism is, theoretically, a necessary condition to believe in any disembodied supernatural being ... This includes gods, ghosts, spirits, and the soul. The more people see minds and bodies as separate, the more likely they are to think about and believe in these types of beings" (Willard and Norenzayan, 2013, p. 388).

Inducing the religious mindset

Dualism, animism, anthropomorphism, Theory of Mind, and teleology are intuitive mechanisms which induce the animistic-teleological mindset, and introduce ways of imagining consciousness in other minds. The detection of agency thus might be a precursor of the ability to infer other people's mental states. Human agent detection is "hyperactive" in the sense that even minimal cues can trigger the postulation of agency (Barrett, 2004). Agent-causality is our preferred mode of explanation because it is better to mistake a non-agent for an agent than the other way around (Guthrie, 1993; Barrett, 2004).

It is adaptive to believe that we are surrounded by active, conscious agents, some of which may be malevolent. Detecting intentional agents is valuable for survival, but the brain operates to detect not just biological processes, or activity, but another consciousness or another mind. The survival value of detecting, and negotiating with, other minds is so great that it accounts for this hyper-vigilance. This might be because, for our ancestors, one of the most important threats has

32 Exceptional or natural?

been other humans (Alexander, 1987). Our early experience of our own consciousness and of other conscious beings leads to our belief in the enormous power of the mind, which in religious terms becomes the eternal soul.

Gilbert *et al.* (2000) found that people seek external agents to explain fortunate events. People were found to ascribe agency to an external force when things worked out in their favor, and to attribute benevolence to that agent. Dijksterhuis *et al.* (2008) found that after being subliminally primed with the word "God," believers (but not atheists) were more likely to ascribe an outcome to an external source of agency, rather than their own actions.

Observing the mind (and the brain) we find parallel, collaborative, and (seemingly) opposing processes in co-existence. Most of us use a combination of animistic and non-animistic thinking, depending on our momentary level of egocentrism and anxiety, and on the task at hand. Most humans still hang on to anthropomorphism and notions of design and intentionality as their intuitive way of explaining events around them, and (passively) accept the independence from animism of academic research and its derivative technologies. What is known as superstition represents the dominance of the same cognitive shortcuts (Lindeman and Aarnio, 2007).

Is religion adaptive?

How should the relationship between evolution and religion be characterized: Is religion just a by-product, an accidental output of cognitive processes that evolved for other purposes? Or has it survived and flourished because of its adaptive value?

It has been argued most often that religion results from the basic architecture of the human mind, a by-product and not an adaptation. The mechanisms that create religious ideas (agent detection, Theory of Mind, animism) are in themselves highly adaptive, but religious ideas need not be. While these basic cognitive mechanisms are held to be of survival value, religion itself has been considered a cognitive error, an appendage to more necessary psychological processes (Atran, 2002; Bloom 2004, 2007; Boyer, 2001; Guthrie, 1993; Hinde 1999; Kirkpatrick, 2008; Pyysiäinen, 2009). If this is the case, then religion has survived without being adaptive and without offering believers any real advantage.

Gould and Lewontin (1979) classified religion, together with music, law, and language, as a prime example of a spandrel, an incidental by-product of selected-for adaptation. Spandrel is a structural element which is a by-product of objective needs, and becomes a decorative space. In the medieval cathedral, spandrels became the space for elaborate decorations, and survived without adding to adaptation. Pinker (1997) similarly argued that human art, music, humor, fiction, religion, and philosophy are not real adaptations, but biological side-effects of other evolved abilities.

It is clear that religion contributes to group survival and reproductive success first through higher levels of fertility. World religions have been totally pro-natalist, and some religions have encouraged sexual intercourse between married couples during the wife's most fertile period (Reynolds and Tanner, 1995). This has led to a remarkable growth in the number of Roman Catholics, Hindus, and Moslems, and has been considered a threat to global secularization (see Chapter 9). The question remains whether religion confers other advantages, and it has been argued that religion could not have survived so successfully among humans without making a real contribution to adaptation.

McCullough and Willoughby (2009) suggested that religion may have evolved because of its ability to help people exercise self-control. Another hypothesis is that the evolution of human cooperation could not have proceeded without the support of religious ideas. Supernatural punishment theory suggests that cooperation is encouraged by religion because norm disobedience is dissuaded by the threat of harmful life events or fear of an afterlife punishment (Bering, 2006; Johnson and Bering, 2006; Shariff and Aknin, 2014).

Atkinson and Bourrat (2011) found, in samples from 87 countries, that beliefs about two related sources of supernatural punishment, God and the afterlife, and frequency of ritual attendance, were found to independently predict harsher condemnation of moral transgressions, such as cheating on taxes. The connection between religion and pro-sociality had evolutionary value in the past and has social value at present. This means that religious beliefs and their correlates have played an active role in human evolution (Alcorta and Sosis, 2005; Bering, 2006; Haidt, 2012; Johnson, 2005; Johnson and Bering 2006; Norenzayan and Shariff, 2008; Sanderson, 2008; Wilson, 2002).

Data from different cultures have shown religious communes to be more successful than secular ones (Fishman, 1992; Fishman and Goldschmidt, 1990; Sosis and Bressler, 2003), but Bader, Mencken, and Parker (2006), after examining 454 modern American communes, challenged this generalization and stated that religiosity had no effect on survival.

Priming with supernatural agency concepts predicts increased rates of cooperation with in-group members (Johnson and Bering, 2006; Shariff, Norenzayan and Henrich, 2009). This may contribute to the survival of a particular group, but not to pro-sociality in general (see Chapter 6). It has been suggested that religion promotes trust through ritual participation (Sosis, 2000; Sosis and Bressler 2003) and several experiments found ritual participants to be more cooperative (Ruffle and Sosis, 2006; Sosis and Ruffle, 2003), but Hoffmann (2013) pointed out that the results were of limited significance.

The problem is that biological forces directing organisms towards cooperation had been in existence long before the appearance of *homo sapiens*. Cooperation and altruism at every level are a fundamental aspect of all biological systems, from bacteria to primates (Ohtsuki *et al.*, 2006). There are clear biological imperatives which push organisms to coordinate their activities with those of conspecifics, and even with members of other species (Alexander, 1987; Axelrod and Hamilton, 1981; Field, 2001; Henrich and Henrich, 2007; Sober and Wilson, 1999; Trivers, 1971). Restraints on individual behavior are necessary for social life and have been naturally selected because of their survival value. Impulse control, and a balance

34 Exceptional or natural?

between cooperation and competition, are crucial for individual and species survival.

Both human infants and primates closely related to humans have been observed offering help to vulnerable and incapacitated peers, leading to the idea that caregiving is a primate adaptation (Warneken and Tomasello, 2006, 2007). Humans "cooperate widely and intensely with non-kin … in part through a set of social psychological adaptations that make us extremely sensitive to and influenced by what other people feel and think" (Haidt and Bjorklund, 2008, p. 192), and group life is the key survival strategy for our species. Thus, in the course of evolution, aptitudes requiring interdependence with other individuals of one's species have been added to "selfish" survival skills (Krebs, 2011). Pylogenetically, religions cannot be the real source of any moral codes but, at most, social enforcers of evolved moral responses in some cultures, taking on this role in quite recent times. In this view, a suite of cognitive biases lead to intuitions that support religious beliefs. Some cultural variants of these beliefs are then harnessed by cultural evolution and intergroup cultural competition to enable large-scale cooperation (Atran and Henrich, 2010; Henrich, 2009; Laurin *et al.*, 2012; Norenzayan and Gervais, 2012; Norenzayan and Shariff, 2008; Powell and Clarke, 2012).

If humans are hard-wired to cooperate because of particular phylogenetic forces and then also hard-wired to develop religious beliefs because of a separate set of particular phylogenetic forces, then we see two separate and powerful phenomena, which can be combined in history and culture, but not in the earliest stages of humanity. In historical times and in mass societies, religions might have played a role in channeling the positive behaviors of cooperation, altruism, empathy, and compassion, most often to in-group members, and sometimes beyond a shared identity (see Chapters 3 and 6). Thus, solidarity gets a boost from religion in larger human groups, which appeared fairly recently in terms of evolution. This solidarity was natural in small groups, which characterize most of the evolutionary history of *homo sapiens*. The pro-social benefits of religion, if any, cannot account for its origins and early history.

The adaptive value of practices, beliefs, and narratives

Intuitively and sometimes implicitly, the notion of the adaptive value of any behaviors observed to be universal is attractive. "If it's universal it must have some adaptive value" or "If it has survived for so long, it must contribute to fitness." There are those who reject the idea: "The myth is slow in dying that only adaptive or 'successful' behavior persists in the long run. The history of magic and ritual has contradicted it for thousands of years. Practices which for aeons have failed to influence natural processes are still carried on today" (Cameron, 1963, pp. 265–266).

Nevertheless, acts that fail to affect reality may still offer psychological benefits, thus being adaptive to some extent. Various forms of divination and fortune telling have remained globally popular, despite their uselessness. One example is that of astrology, which in several versions, attracts billions and is a solid part of the mass media (see Chapter 9). One reason is that divination systems, while having no real value, offer humans an illusion of control, power, and knowledge.

A major area of popular cultural activity is folklore, where old and new stories make the rounds and win audiences easily. So-called urban legends are widely circulated and believed, despite their absurd nature, which becomes clear with any genuine reflection (Beit-Hallahmi, 1985). These narratives about human failings are inherently attractive and plausible, clearly gratifying in some ways (Brunvand, 1999). Most urban legends are naturalistic, but a few narrate encounters with ghosts.

Let's look at one story, popular worldwide, "The Kidney Heist." It's about a man in a big city (Paris, London, New Orleans, New York), a tourist or a visiting business executive, who goes out to a bar, drinks a little (or a lot), strikes a conversation with a woman, and then wakes up the next morning in a strange neighborhood, feeling some pain. Visiting the nearest medical facility leads to a shocking discovery. One of the man's kidneys has been removed using the standard surgical procedure for kidney transplants. Of course, when kidneys are removed for transplants, the donor is carefully chosen to match the patients needing them. A kidney removed at random has no value.

What could be the meaning of such a story? It is construed as a crime-and-punishment narrative. What was the man looking for going out at night? Listeners may feel that the man was far from innocent, and deserves his fate, because he was possibly in search of some illicit pleasures. He is probably a married man traveling alone. In some versions of the legend, the woman involved is a prostitute, who acts friendly but leads him to an ambush where he is kidnapped, or maybe puts something in his drink. The story teaches attentive listeners to be wary of big cities, where many temptations and dangers lurk. The swift punishment teaches a clear lesson about resisting temptation. If we look for an adaptive value, it may lie in the support for conventional social norms, which is at play when crime reports are eagerly consumed. Urban legends create a shared emotional experience, and offer a gratifying ending with the sinner severely punished.

Urban legends manage to attract countless millions of believers in many different cultures. An obvious point is that of the similarity between unofficial folklore narratives and religious mythology believed to be true. Urban legends are not far from religion in terms of the psychological mechanisms involved. Narratives, written or oral, which teach believers about negotiating with spirits, are uniquely accessible and attractive, just like urban legends, and offer emotional gratification and relief. With the exception of psychoanalytic writings (see Chapter 8), the psychological study of religion does not offer much in the way of interpreting the themes of religious narratives and the gratifications they offer.

Explaining misfortune

Mentalizing is not abstract. It is done in the context of explaining miracles and misfortunes. Flood myths, common around the world, explain imaginary disasters, and, by inference, other misfortunes, as the gods' response to human iniquity.

36 Exceptional or natural?

Before the coming of biomedicine, any illness was a serious threat, often lethal, which was accorded much significance as part of a meaningful and morally ordered universe. Disease explanations, like ideas about mortality and immortality, reflect evolved ways of coping by finding meaning and moral order where none exist. Both death and disease are turned from human tragedies into evidence of cosmic justice.

Folk theories of disease causation refer to (a) divine retribution for human transgressions, (b) the acts of evil spirits, or (c) evil intentions and evil deeds coming from living humans in the form of sorcery (Foster, 1976; Murdock, 1980; Simpson, 2011). Souls of the dead, who now inhabit the world of the spirits, play a significant role in theories of disease causation. Most evil spirits are human ghosts, and they are responsible, according to traditional theories, for much misfortune, disease, and death. As Frazer (1933–1936) noted, the spirits of the dead are most often held responsible for specific cases of sickness and death. In ancient Hindu doctrines a husband's death was believed to be a consequence of his wife's sinfulness, and so calls for sati, where the wife's 'fire-bath' on the husband's funeral pyre is the ultimate means of expiation (Weinberger-Thomas, 1999). The recent AIDS epidemic in Africa has been interpreted within the framework of historically prevalent theories, which explain it as resulting from witchcraft and divine wrath in response to the breaking of taboos (Ashforth, 2001; Forster, 1998; Kalichman and Simbayi, 2004; Manglos and Trinitapoli, 2011). The millions of AIDS deaths have been seen by those who follow these theories as validating them beyond any doubt.

In children and adults, culturally transmitted supernaturalist teachings co-exist with culturally transmitted naturalism, and individuals are able to use both. This can be observed in the way children learn about the biological and the supernaturalist conceptions of death (Harris and Koenig, 2006; Talwar, Harris and Schleifer, 2011). They may acquire the correct biological concepts first, and then learn supernaturalist ideas about souls and immortality. These seemingly contradictory kinds of knowledge may co-exist for most individuals in many cultures (Astuti and Harris, 2008; Harris, 2011a, b; Harris and Giménez, 2005; Richert and Harris, 2006). Clearly, religious and biological notions are not utilized in the same context. In the context of physical death, biology dominates, but in the religious context, the soul is talked about as active and conscious (Harris, 2011b).

Legare and Gelman (2008) and Legare et al. (2012) found that individuals use both natural and supernatural explanations to interpret the very same events and that there are multiple ways in which both kinds of cognitions coexist in individual minds. Contrary to traditional accounts of cognitive development, the findings demonstrated that reasoning about supernatural phenomena is an integral and enduring aspect of human cognition. Individuals seem to conceive of two kinds of causal explanations, proximal and ultimate. Even if an individual follows the biomedical model and believes that micro-organisms constitute the proximate causes of illness, she may still think that at the same time "somebody up there" makes the ultimate decision on who is going to be hit by those micro-organisms.

This dual causation model, where religion overrides biology, is not tied to traditional culture, and may be encountered in modern, seemingly secularized individuals (see Chapter 9).

Religious emotionality and art

Explaining religious ideas seems insufficient, because what might be called religious emotionality comes to mind. William James, quoted above, stated that "religious love is only man's natural emotion of love directed to a religious object" (James, 1902/1961, p. 29), but this seems to discount the power of love and the power of religious commitment. Religion is often analyzed with the help of analogies from human behavior which involve commitment and emotionality (Beit-Hallahmi, 1989). In thinking about religious love, art and politics seem like useful reference points.

Works of art are capable of creating powerful emotions, and that is why we value them so highly. What happens when we listen to *Under Milk Wood*, the great radio play authored by the poet Dylan Thomas (Thomas, 1954), or to Beethoven's Ninth Symphony, or when we view Rembrandt's *Militia Company* (1642), or Edward Hopper's *Nighthawks* (1942)? The many millions who have been exposed to these works have been transformed and drawn by the hypnotic power of art, which some would compare to the power of religious rituals.

Religion may indeed be viewed as a form of art, a symbolic product of anxiety, desire, and imagination expressed in a social milieu.

> Like any art, religion is a product of tension ... between the urge to satisfaction and life, and recognition of the inevitability of suffering and death ... Its most effective expressions are generated, as in all arts, by individual creative effort, but they depend more than other arts upon tradition and membership in a community.
>
> (Firth, 1981, p. 584)

Art offers not only tension, but also relief, which is the other part of the esthetic response cycle.

The psychoanalyst Donald Winnicott coupled religion and art time and again, as two phenomena belonging to the "intermediate area" where illusions are created (Winnicott, 1971; see Chapter 8). Religious thinking can be compared to artistic thinking, reflecting a "regression in the service of the ego," which is the readiness to regress from reality in favor of imaginary respites (Kris, 1952).

The process of artistic creation is a model for understanding the process of developing religious ideas and rituals. Religious fantasies appear to serve the needs of both the creative artist and the audience. The mechanism of identification, which is so essential to art, lets every member of the audience participate in the unfolding drama on stage. In the case of religion, it is a drama set on a cosmic stage (Beit-Hallahmi, 1989).

Limitations and questions

The cognitive approach to religion pays only limited attention to variance in religiosity, because it focuses on what we all share, namely cognitive mechanisms. Despite these common mechanisms, which create the naturalness of religious ideas, humanity in general as well as particular human populations have displayed a great deal of variation when the actual investment of resources in religion is measured. General explanations of religion are faced with the problem of explaining individual and group differences in religiosity, as well as major historical changes.

There seems to be a gap between the description of universal cognitive mechanisms, the result of evolutionary developments in the human brain, and living religious systems of belief and practice. Here is how one scholar described our topic of study:

> Religion provides human beings with an opportunity to cope with their problems in the realm of fantasy. Relatively free from the checks and limits of reality they can express both their hopes and their fears in more intense form than when confronting real dangers ... Relatively powerless themselves, they conceive of the universe as an ordered system functioning under a definite set of rules known to them alone.
>
> (Moore, 1983, p. 29)

What could be noted is that the meaning offered by religion, as Moore himself observed, is totally anthropocentric, and this is the kind of meaning system humans naturally prefer.

If we go back to the "Stone Age" Kurelu of New Guinea (Chapter 1) we encounter elaborate structures of beliefs and practices, which have evolved over millennia, but it is the basic processes that make the elaborate narratives and rituals possible. For religious thinking to function, the psychological infrastructure must be there, and it is there in the form of tenacious dualism, mentalizing, and teleology. This infrastructure started the rudimentary forms of religion more than 100,000 years ago. Different traditions were created throughout history, because of local variations in environment, culture and identity. Regardless of historical changes, the default mode is there, and it is of animistic-intuitive thinking.

The explanations for the creation of religious ideation through basic cognitive mechanisms, presented in this chapter, leave us with further questions:

1. How to explain individual differences in religiosity? These may be explained by differences in cognitive mechanisms, individual traits, or situations (see Chapter 4).
2. How to explain the most important predictor of religiosity, namely being female? (see Chapter 5).
3. How to explain the specific contents of beliefs, rituals, and myths? Such questions seem to be ignored in the case of most traditions (see Chapter 8).

Secularization challenges theories which assume that the forces pushing humans to create and support religious ideas are constant and eternally present. Western Europe and East Asia show the highest levels of secularization, but no one will suggest that historical changes occurred because of modified brain architecture. The reality of secularization, together with the persistence of religion, hints at a multiplicity of factors which determine the centrality (or marginality) of religious thinking (see Chapter 9).

3

SOCIAL LEARNING AND IDENTITY

In the discussion of individual and collective supernaturalism, one simple fact is often overlooked: that all aspects of religion and religiosity are socially learned. The most common way individuals become committed to a particular religion is by being born into it, and that is how most believers have acquired the identity they so often proudly proclaim. Individual religious identity is, in the vast majority of cases, totally predictable in terms of culture and intergenerational continuity. A believer's specific persuasion is actually determined at the moment of birth, and formed as a specific identity, not related to conviction or choice. Of about one billion Hindus, the vast majority are the products of a Hindu family, and the vast majority of self-identified adult Roman Catholics similarly grew up in a Catholic family. Ninety-nine percent of the world's religious believers have followed parental and communal teachings in acquiring the belief system they hold.

A related socio-biological fact is that the number of followers of any religious tradition is determined by fertility rates. The number of Catholics (1.2 billion) and Moslems (1.6 billion) in the world has been rising dramatically, not because more individuals have recognized that the messages of the Roman Catholic Church or of Islam are so persuasive and have converted, but because more and more babies are born to Catholic and Moslem mothers, and are more likely to survive today than they were a century ago, thanks to modern biomedicine.

Within any specific religious family and community, children are a captive audience. They are "cradle" Roman Catholics or "cradle" Moslems, or "cradle" Hindus (recently, the terms "DNA Catholic" or "DNA Hindu" have appeared). A similar idea, which moves from the biological to the social is the "sociological believer," who is automatically ascribed an identity by his own community and by outsiders, because of his birth (Roy, 2010). Some atheists have been raised by atheist parents, of course, and people with religiously unaffiliated parents are more likely to claim no religion (Baker and Smith, 2009).

Gary Becker put the matter within the framework of culture:

> Individuals ... cannot alter their ethnicity, race or family history, and only with difficulty can they change their country or religion. Because of the difficulty of changing culture and its low depreciation rate, culture is largely a 'given' to individuals throughout their lifetimes.
>
> (Becker, 1996, p. 16)

Another social scientist observes:

> the content of individuals' religious beliefs correlates very strongly with the beliefs of their communities ... the fact of belief does not correlate with the content of belief but does correlate with ... the believers' social context. Moreover, these correlations are radically stronger that the bulk of correlations taken seriously in the social sciences.
>
> (Hardin, 1997, p. 260)

All this may seem self-evident, but it is not so to everybody. One still encounters analyses which focus on individual choice, and describe a conscious decision to embrace a belief system as leading to affiliation. Religious identity as a choice is simply irrelevant for most of humanity, but psychologists (and others) are still denying the basic facts of life when they offer a totally fictional framing for religious involvement:

> Religious affiliations require a variety of costly behaviors to join and remain in good standing within the group: elaborate rituals and rites of passage, public commitments of faith and devotion, contributions of time and money, wearing special clothing, and/or reading and learning various scriptures are just a few examples to illustrate this point.
>
> (Preston, Ritter and Hernandez, 2010, p. 582)

This description applies to very few believers. It chooses to overlook the way in which religious affiliation, for most of humanity, is ascribed at birth, with the individual involved having no say in the matter and simply being born and socialized into a particular identity. Maintaining a religious identity, for most adults in this world, does not require much of an investment. Hindus or Catholics who do not observe any of the prescriptions and proscriptions of their traditions are not likely to receive a termination notice in the mail. Excommunication or shunning are still practiced, and as painful as they may be, are found only in relatively small groups, such as the Amish, Mennonites, Plymouth Brethren, Jehovah's Witnesses, and the Baha'is.

42 Social learning and identity

Here is another puzzling description:

> Participation in a religion has certain costs for the participant, which include the time and effort involved in learning a religion and practicing it, the loss of opportunity to engage in other beneficial activities (opportunity costs), and risks such as the avoidance of modern medical care or extended fasting … To learn the emotionality and associated language of a religion requires a long developmental (ontogenetic) exposure to the belief system. Opportunity costs include the inability to associate with other groups because one's specific beliefs may be considered irrational or contra-evidentiary.
>
> (Fincher and Thornhill, 2012, p. 67)

Fincher and Thornhill portray the acquisition of religious beliefs and practices as individual "participation," that is, taking an active part voluntarily, a matter of personal choice and conscious effort. The possibility of choice and preference in individual religious identities is a modern phenomenon, a symptom of secularization (Chapter 9). The idea that learning a religion requires effort is totally unrelated to reality, and another part of reality is the illusion of individual choice. Religious believers may use a rhetoric of choice about their faith, naturally wishing to present deliberation, rather than compliance, as the way which led them to their religious stance. When presenting, or defending, a religious (or political) position, introducing the story of a personal voyage by a seeker is more persuasive than describing oneself as a passive receptacle.

Davidson (2008, p. 102) criticized those who assume "that religion is purely a matter of personal choice (if your religion is holding you back, you can easily switch to one that does not)." There is even a description of choosing a tradition in a process in which statistical evidence for the secular consequences of religion is evaluated and weighed:

> By observation alone one might notice the benefits of religious participation. If the happiest, most prosperous people in one's community are deeply religious, that fact alone may confer a kind of face validity on claims of divine concern and intervention in mortal lives. Equally if not more powerful are signs that failure to adhere to religious obligations is associated with misfortune.
>
> (Livingston, 2005, p. 101)

This description completely ignores the cultural trasnsmission of beliefs and behavior. It is like suggesting that people learn to fear the number 13 because they have noticed that it is consistently tied to mishaps.

Social teaching and learning

For the vast majority of individuals, acquiring a religious identity (and the associated belief system) is like learning their native language, and children do not have more choice in learning religion than they have in acquiring a mother tongue. Children go through cultural immersion, with countless orally transmitted references, some written sources, and many ritual acts. Religious behaviors, beliefs, and experiences, are simply a component of culture and cultural experience, and so are regularly transmitted from generation to generation, in the same way as any other cultural component such as cooking, health practices, and political ideologies. There are numerous kinds of knowledge that parents don't teach children, because they are clearly unprepared for them. We don't expect a three-year-old to be taught chemistry, but they will be exposed to supernaturalism.

That is how Michael Argyle first introduced the social learning theory of religion:

> This theory states that religious behaviour, beliefs and experiences are simply part of the culture, and are regularly transmitted from generation to generation, in the same way as all other customs. This view has of course been held, and there is much evidence for it, for example the fact that children reared in different parts of the world tend to acquire the local religious beliefs. To some extent we assume this theory when we talk of the different religions of different countries, for it is assumed that these are relatively unchanging and will persist in time.
>
> (Argyle, 1958, p. 143)

We take it for granted that children will follow in their parents' footsteps, and they do. Social learning, despite its seeming simplicity (and maybe because of it), remains the best explanation for most religious actions. It is the best explanation for the overall prevalence of religion, for individual religiosity, and for the most varied and the most dramatic of religious acts and movements. To the question, "Why do people believe in God?" the best answer remains: "Because they have been taught to believe in God." The social learning of religion means that individuals believe in Krishna, Jesus, Jehovah, or Osiris, only because their parents taught them these specific beliefs. The variety of religious traditions and the correspondence between the dominant tradition in the social environment and the religious beliefs of the individual are the most obvious proofs to the validity of the social learning approach, which is also able to explain what are considered intense religious experiences.

Supernaturalism is inherently accessible, and children learn just one local version of it and in most cases become inexorably attached to it. Here is how Oliver Wendell Holmes put it:

> We are all tattooed in our cradles with the beliefs of our tribe; the record may seem superficial, but it is indelible. You cannot educate a man wholly out of the superstitious fears which were early implanted in his imagination; no matter how utterly his reason may reject them.
>
> (Holmes, 1872, p. 226)

44 Social learning and identity

As we look closer at more unusual and "esoteric" religious actions it becomes clear that they are socially learned, just like the less esoteric ones (Spanos and Hewitt, 1979). Conversion, although enjoying much scholarly attention, is a rarity among the world's billions of believers. Even in the most dramatic cases of religious conversion, there is no acceptance of new belief systems without prior exposure and learning (Chapter 7). The freedom to choose and decide is indeed a modern experience (or illusion) shared by Westerners living in mostly secularized cultures (Chapter 9), and in some countries, conversion still means risking one's life.

Mystical experiences, considered unique and individual, are totally culture-dependent. We know that the specific content of visions, the most intense and personal of religious acts, is wholly predictable from exposure to certain ideas, which are always learned. Visions of the Holy Virgin occur exclusively among Catholics or those exposed to Catholic ideas. They have never occurred among Orthodox Jews, and we easily understand why.

Through kinship children acquire, or inherit, not only religious identity, but also ethnicity, sports fanships, and other group attachments. One area which is similar in more than one way to the learning of religion is the inheritance of political identity, where parental influence has been demonstrated quite decisively (Jennings and Niemi, 1974; Renshon, 1977; Sears and Funk, 1999). In the case of political identity, as in the case of religion, no choice is involved: "party identification originates at a stage of childhood before the ability to understand political issues and to evaluate party performance is fully developed" (Kroh and Selb, 2009, p. 561). Many individuals stick to their political identities despite challenges and disconfirmations, just like well-known cases of faith persistence in the face of disconfirmation (Chapter 7).

Socialization

The credibility of religious ideas is only relative, and tied to time, place, and identity. We find evidence for spontaneous biases, as described above, such as design, purpose, Theory of Mind, animism, anthropomorphism, but these do not create spontaneous religious beliefs, without cultural input. The innate readiness to accept religious ideas will not lead to belief or commitment without exposure. Cognitive shortcuts or biases create "receptivity, not generativity" (Banerjee and Bloom, 2012, p. 8). Only with the culturally given transmission of ideas about gods and spirits will children acquire particular content (Gervais and Henrich, 2010; Gervais *et al.*, 2011).

Socialization is the process which makes an individual child a member of a unique group and makes possible the absorption of the group culture. It means, within any given culture, conveying to children reliable, credible information about the human, social, and natural worlds around them. Fichter (1973) described objective socialization as "the process by which the society transmits its culture from one generation to the next and adapts the individual to the accepted and approved ways of organized social life" (p. 29), and subjective socialization as "a process of learning which goes on in the individual while he is adapting to the people around him" (p. 30).

Cavalli-Sforza (1993) noted that the way religious ideas and tradition are transmitted hardly differs from biological heredity. What is inherited from parents is first, a nominal affiliation, which is most obvious, and second, according to Myers (1996) even the level of religiosity. Family, friends, and formal religious education, have been consistently linked with greater religiosity in youth and young adults (Erickson, 1992).

The central roles of parents and the family in the acquisition (or the inheritance) of religious identity has been noted and demonstrated often (Baker-Sperry, 2001; Clark, Worthington and Danser, 1988; Ecklund and Scheitle, 2007; Flor and Knapp, 2001; Glass, Bengtson and Dunham, 1986; Iannaccone, 1990; Myers, 1996; Wilson and Sherkat, 1994). Parents' religiosity easily constitutes the strongest and most reliable influence across studies of adolescents (Myers, 1996), and mothers are thought to be more influential than fathers (Bao *et al.*, 1999; Benson, Masters and Larson, 1997; Gunnoe and Moore, 2002). Vermeer, Janssen, and De Hart (2011) found that parental religiosity and especially parental church attendance are important predictors of juvenile church attendance.

Belief systems are not acceptable to most people unless they are shared with members of a social group. Csibra and Gergely (2009) suggested that because individuals, especially children, are vigilant regarding cultural information, this may lead them towards judging communicated information as culturally relevant, and then towards embracing it (Harris *et al.*, 2006). Individuals always regard as natural and obvious whatever beliefs they grew up with, and believers in every one of the tens of thousands of religions in the world make similar claims with much conviction, but in the vast majority of cases fail to persuade those born into other cultures. In many traditional cultures, the historical reality has been of one religious worldview dominating the culture, creating a totalistic situation. Encountering other worldviews creates a problem for believers, but the apparent challenge is easily met in most cases.

If socialization is to be defined as the mechanism creating plausibility for a meaning system, then it is clear that connecting that plausibility to primary relationships is likely to make socialization more effective. Adults provide religious models for children, and the readiness to believe is based on the acceptance of authority. Socialization of the young is done by significant others, those with whom they have emotional ties, and to whom they feel a natural dependence. Intensive parenting and dependency, characteristic of the human family, lay the groundwork for the social learning of identity.

For most of human history, individual religious identity was, together with language and cultural heritage, part of the attachment to a "tribe" (real or metaphorical). In traditional cultures, it is the parents' duty, and in modern cultures their right, to socialize their children into religious faith, as part of the parental role. As Quinn (2005) describes it, parents produce culturally valid adults and have the power to do it. Parents speak about instilling pride in the group's legacy, and pride

46 Social learning and identity

buttresses loyalty. The process in which the majority of believers have acquired their identities is almost seamless, smooth, and conflict-free. It also takes place at a very early age, and most believers have learned all they will ever know about their inherited tradition by age ten.

We are acutely aware of socialization when we observe the process that leads to joining new religious movements. We are less aware of the way the acquisition of religious beliefs and identity is carried out by those who raise children and teach them beliefs and identity. Children learn specific religious beliefs through exposure to many moving stories, especially triumphal narratives about contacts between the world of the spirits and human heroes who are close to the gods. Believers, young and old, are constantly socialized and re-socialized through rituals, sermons, prayers, and festivals: "the rituals of religion tend to be so frequent, elaborate, evocative and mandatory that they provide very strong guidelines for faith" (Firth, 1981, p. 584). Repeated rituals in the form of holidays and festivals celebrate miracles and triumphs and strengthen the faith, and so religion "persists on the basis of a constant rehearsal of its complicated dramas, woven as they are into the whole rhythm of social and cultural life" (Geertz, 1966, p. 177).

Findings on religious beliefs in children simply reflect the learning of local culture. A child may believe in the special powers of gods, ancestors, witches, or angels only because adults have taught it such beliefs (Harris and Koenig, 2006). In cultures where the concept of God is central to the religious belief system, research has shown that by age four, children have learned that it represents an immortal and omniscient entity (Barrett, Newman and Richert, 2003; Barrett, Richert and Driesenga, 2001; Gimenez-Dasi, Guerrero and Harris, 2005; Knight *et al.*, 2004; Richert and Barrett, 2005; Woolley, 2000).

In addition to the descriptions of supernatural entities and their qualities, what are the more subtle messages conveyed by parents around religion and religious traditions? Most often the child senses the special importance and uniqueness attached to this realm, as a special kind of anxiety surrounds what is considered the sacred in every culture. An ambivalent parental message will result in a reduced commitment. The process which children undergo is not designed to encourage reflection, consideration, or deliberation. It is designed to create loyalty, and it does, especially in situations where religious pluralism exists, and defection is a possibility. At some point a child may be explicitly reminded of the loyalty he owes to family traditions. This may create an association for life in the child's memory between the family members asking for it and group loyalty. Children learn that they are members of a community and owe it their allegiance. Not only parents, but the whole community forms children's beliefs (Kelley and De Graaf, 1997).

It is universally assumed that parents have the absolute right to indoctrinate their children, and the issue of children's rights is rarely mentioned. This may be challenged as children's rights are being considered in the context of various cultural practices. "Have the parents sought valid consent from their children before baptizing them soon after birth?" (Ng, E.M.L., 2002, p. 492). Certain initiation rites, such as genital mutilation, are considered abusive, and it is clear why (Denniston *et al.*, 2006). Sometimes the imposition of religious beliefs and practices by parents can be lethal. Where medical care is withheld in favor of "faith healing," the cost is often borne by children who never had a choice, but die or suffer without proper health care. These extreme cases illustrate the total powerlessness of children in relation to inherited and imposed religious identity (see Chapter 6).

"The persistence of religion largely depends on how successfully one generation indoctrinates its offspring" (Myers, 1996, p. 858). We have clear quantitative evidence showing that a greater investment in socialization inside the family is related to higher levels of parent–child continuity (Beit-Hallahmi and Argyle, 1997; Bengtson *et al.*, 2009; Gunnoe and Moore, 2002; Hunsberger and Brown, 1984; Lenski, 1963). We should expect differences in socialization policies and strategies, based on the particular history of any religious tradition. Minority groups would tend to enforce selective contacts or minimal contacts with the wider society around them. For the individual, self-categorization means locating oneself within the prevailing social categorization system. Research has shown that children in heterogeneous schools mastered religious categorizations by age nine, but those in homogeneous schools only at age eleven (Takriti, Barrett and Buchanan-Barrow, 2006; Waillet and Roskam, 2012).

To assess continuity and the impact of childhood socialization, we may ask "What religion were you raised in?" or "What was your religion at age sixteen?" and then compare it to religious commitment at present. Discontinuity will be affected by secularization (Chapter 9) and by the motivation of the rare convert (Chapter 7). Differences in strategy should be related to differences in resulting loyalties. There are differences among denominations in the effectiveness of religious training, which can be measured by looking at the endurance of beliefs, or the percentage of those who are still loyal to their religion when they come of age.

Children's experiences

What do children learn? Religion is most often transmitted and learned not as a belief system, but as a collection of narratives (myths, stories). Religious belief is first and foremost the acceptance of certain narratives, which are taken to be true and important. In addition to specific beliefs, children acquire a basic commitment to doctrine and authority. Any individual believer is not expected to know all details of doctrine and mythology, but he is supposed to accept the authority of those who are defined as experts on doctrine.

For any individual, the reality of religion is learned as part of the acquisition of family attachments and group culture. Religious identity creates a special kind of group loyalty and identity, which may be the prototype of tribal and national loyalty. Religious loyalty is psychologically tied to kinship, and conversion or religious exogamy (intermarriage) are experienced as a betrayal. The term "defection" has been used to denote leaving the religion you have been raised in or a religion you have joined later on (Wright, 1987).

48 Social learning and identity

It is quite natural then to speak of loyalty, or defection, in a religious context. In return for loyalty, the individual can enjoy security, a sense of belonging, support for self-esteem and many concrete material rewards. A powerful attachment is formed, and any slight to the collective identity is an insult to the self. "Faith and family, blood and belief, are what people identify with and what they will fight and die for" (Huntington, 1993, p. 190). Children learn from their parents in a special way, which binds ideas to emotions. Parental beliefs are deliberately and consciously transmitted. Within-family transmission is more important than other factors, such as formal teaching, recruitment campaigns, or peers. The parents have a monopoly on forming children's habits and beliefs, if not personality. Public ceremonies and holidays in the family circle reinforce and mobilize commitment periodically. Children are not full participants, but the effects on them are robust.

"'[B]ecoming religious' is, in the main, such a subtle part of the person's total socialization process that except for formalized ceremonies, one is seldom conscious that anything is happening" (Chalfant, Beckley and Palmer, 1981, p. 74). The process of teaching and learning is personal for most participants, except in the formal settings of religious education, where children (and adults) acquire familiarity with official doctrines. Sometimes, identification with the parents is conscious: "Two little boys, Sammy and Marty, both seven, are having a discussion, over milk and cookies, about God. Sammy says he believes in God and Marty replies he isn't quite sure there is a God. Sammy says that everybody believes differently about God—some people believe there is a God and some don't. "But," Sammy adds, "it doesn't matter what you believe as long as it's the same thing your Daddy believes. So I'll go on believing there is a God." "Yes," Marty nods in agreement, "you're supposed to believe what your Daddy believes. So I'll go on believing that maybe there is and maybe there isn't a God" (Rokeach, 1981, p. 192).

Social learning takes place through identification and modeling, conscious as well as unconscious. To most believers, religion appears as a total ideology with a sense of the "natural" and the "real" which they have inherited, and without which it is impossible to conceive the world they inhabit. Religious socialization is not just about learning a particular belief system, but a general introduction to the supernaturalist premise, the notion of the invisible world shared by all religions. But the message the child hears is one of uniqueness and superiority, rather than of similarity. "We" share a system which is true and ultimate; "they" believe in nonsense. The teaching of identity means teaching group solidarity. This is done by "activities [that] serve to validate group members, by advancing narratives of moral and spiritual truth or even superiority … narratives are embodied in rituals, stories, songs, and dances that are explicitly taught to children by parents and other adults in the community" (Dunham *et al.*, 2013, p. 7). These experiences create strong ingroup preferences in children (Dunham *et al.*, 2013).

The local belief system is introduced to the child through numerous references to invisible entities, together with visible and tangible objects and acts, from home shrines to festivals. The social learning of religion presents religious ideas as part of social reality. The received social consensus may have little to do with individual preferences.

> It is not necessary to set up a special teaching situation in order to inculcate in the young the most consistent and constantly manifested traits of the family culture-complex. Very special educative situations indeed are needed if one is to eradicate the effects of this most facile sort of acculturation. It is safe to assume that the nucleus of one's personal religion has been acquired in this automatic way.
>
> (Sullivan, 1964, p. 81)

If social learning is indeed the more important variable in creating religiosity, then social variables, rather than personality traits, should play a primary role in predicting it. The question to be answered in the study of individual religiosity becomes the individual's reaction to cultural traditions and socialization. The impact of personality is most significant when individual reactions to socialization deviate from the majority norm.

Groups and identities

The overwhelming effects of tradition on the individual and the reality of one's limited choices in defining a separate identity are reflected in the terminology of identity. Often, biological metaphors are used to denote religious identity, in such terms as roots, and sometimes the language is more ambiguous, such as heritage or legacy. In most human cultures, religious identity is determined by kinship, and considered immutable, like "race." A related aspect of social reality is the idea of allowing an adoption only by parents who match the supposedly inherited religious identity of the adoptee. This idea has been a legal requirement in some countries, and reflects a belief in the biological inheritance of religion (Schwartz, 1991).

In the case of mixed religious ancestry, identity (or "biological" heritage?) is sometimes expressed by fractions. Hanif Kureishi, the well-known British writer, said, "My children are only a quarter Moslem" (noted on December 31, 2010 on France 24/7 at 13 hours GMT). "Quarter-Moslem" may be surprising, but "half-Jewish" is less so. Such expressions reflect first of all a biological conception of inheritance, similar to conceptions of race in many cultures. In terms of social reality, "quarter-Moslem" means the psychological forces acting on a given individual or family. The use of fraction may reflect a fractured or divided identity, or the probability of beliefs and claims transmitted to a descendant, given the forces acting on those involved.

Religious individuals identify with and participate in a cohesive community, sharing norms, beliefs, and actions. Most humans are hostages to identity, and they have never known any other identity or culture than their own. Identity, in the most general sense means belonging to a collectivity and sharing a reality (or a fantasy) of common destiny, interests, and values as well as a "collective memory"

50 Social learning and identity

of the past (Halbwachs, 1992). Identity also means the creation of an "imagined community" (Anderson, 1991), or a "community of destiny," which forms the basis for identification and the feeling of power. But the community is not just an imagined one; it is quite real, and every religion creates communal actions of ritual. Believers belong to the imagined community of believers, which may have more than a billion members, but they also belong to an immediate congregation.

Religion has "identity functions" in being a foundation for group identity and for individual self-esteem. Individuals enjoy the experience of belonging and acceptance, and many would enjoy the feeling of superiority often provided by religious groups. Believing means taking part in a social system, belonging to a community, and achieving intimacy with real and imaginary others.

"The function of the group ethic, of course, is simply to maintain the group" (La Barre, 1970, p. 14). The first goal and the basic necessity for every group is survival. This necessitates group integration and the creation of a common worldview, at least in matters relevant to the group's existence and activities. There must be solidarity, expressed through mutuality and cooperation in relationships, and participation, in the sense of individuals having a sense of involvement in reaching common goals. Group cohesion, created by common loyalties to imaginary beings, has great survival value. Members of the most successful groups have a strong sense of group identity and know the rights and obligations of membership. The collective identity of religious communities is deliberately and consciously fostered, in addition to its unconscious, spontaneous components. What keeps religions alive is their differences, which must be emphasized and elaborated at all costs, as they are crucial for identity maintenance. As Zerubavel (1982) states:

> There are many ways in which groups can and do stress their in-group unity as well as their distinctiveness vis-a-vis other groups. Language, emblems, dress, and dietary laws are just a few of the various characteristics almost universally employed by groups in order to distinguish group members from 'outsiders'.
>
> (Zerubavel, 1982, p. 284)

Purity rules are also about identity. Thus, food taboos serve as identity markers, which are always tied to self-esteem and superiority (Tajfel and Turner, 1986). Individuals feel superior to members of their caste who choose not to observe the taboos, or sometimes to non-members who naturally do not observe them. The arbitrary and sometimes symbolic meaning of food taboos can be illustrated with the case of the Nation of Islam in the United States, which expects its followers to avoid cornbread and okra, because they have been identified for so long with Afro-American culture and the history of slavery. The group seeks to renew Afro-American identity, and the rejection of such foods clearly symbolizes that (Evans, 2008). In this case we know the circumstances that led to the definition of an object as tabooed. In most other cases the historical roots of a custom are unknown, but its function as an identity marker is clear. In most cases identity markers are explained in terms of revelations from the spirit world, but are secondary to the essential core of a tradition.

Wunn (2003) described religious groups as follows:

> 1) Religions … are not defined by the similarity of their traits, but by a clear distinction from other religions. 2) Religions consist of groups of followers … and not of independent individuals. 3) Religions as units are defined by their relation to groups of believers of other religions and not by their relation to members of the same religion … religions are not accidental sets of individuals with similar religious ideas and practices, but units of devotees who recognise each other as members of the same belief-system. Therefore, religion … is … the natural result of a consensus concerning religious thought and acts which is distinct from that of other religions.
>
> (Wunn, 2003, p. 397)

Work by Tajfel (1978, 1981) showed that social categorization based on minimal (arbitrary) similarity is a sufficient condition for in-group solidarity and discriminatory social behavior. The simplest dichotomization into "we" and "they" (or "greens" vs. "blues" in sports practice) creates a division of our social world into one in-group and at least one out-group. We know that children understand arbitrary social categorization around age five (Aboud, 2003; Diesendruck and haLevi, 2006; Dunham, Baron and Carey, 2011; Dunham and Emory, 2014; Heiphetz, Spelke and Banaji, 2014).

Minimal social categorization is amazingly powerful (Brewer, 1979; Tajfel, 1981). Social demarcations are introduced when the need to emphasize the "we," as different from or opposed to "they," is felt. Collective identity is then expected to manifest itself in the individual's consciousness and behavior, in his "social self." The experience of community is the most important function of tradition for most people. Being in a group in which they feel valued and accepted, even special, just because they belong, is deeply rewarding. I am not alone, I am part of a "we," an "us," which affects my individual power. In the case of religion the impact of social categorization is multiplied by parental messages to children, expressing the traditional uniqueness and awe tied to religion. For many religious adults slighting their faith means doubting their intrinsic worth.

High in-group identification and positive attitudes toward one's in-group are often connected to negative attitudes toward other groups (Gramzow and Gaertner, 2005). Vilification, ridicule, and dehumanization are sometimes directed at those who belong to other faiths or tribes, to draw the line between "us" and "them." Our evolutionary heritage will push us in that direction: "Our forebears had a tendency to treat members of out-groups … with contempt and sometimes murderous aggression" (Oatley, 2004, p. 29). Because religion is tied to both group cohesion and individual self-esteem, it contributes to positive social and individual integration, but also to many inter-group conflicts all over

52 Social learning and identity

the world. The reality of social categorization, whether in the case of religion or in other identities, leads to various cognitive distortions in deductions about the self and others such as out-group homogeneity bias, in-group favoritism, and stereotyping (Fiske and Taylor, 2013). Social categorization is accompanied by evaluation, and intimately tied to the management of self-esteem. Individuals express an overvaluation of the in-group, thereby enhancing their self-esteem, and a parallel systematic underevaluation of the out-group. The result may even be described as in-group narcissism. "It is always possible to bind together a considerable number of people in love, so long as there are other people left over to receive the manifestation of their aggression" (Freud, 1930, p. 114). Tajfel (1981, p. 255) defined social identity as "that part of the individual's self-concept which derives from his knowledge of his membership of a social group together with the value and emotional significance attached to that membership." Zavalloni (1975) listed the following elements in a "social identity cluster": sex, nation, religious origin, political ideology, social class, family situation, age group, and profession. A social persona, or identity, is composed of numerous collective categories, or sub-identities, which make up our social position.

The concept of religious identity seems to be intuitively simple. We assume that the act of self-identification stems from an internal selection process, leading to a more or less stable commitment, and often demonstrated in some other behaviors. "Religious identity" is then a hypothetical structure, found somewhere "inside" a person, which will lead her to respond with a brief identity label when asked about affiliation and belonging. Identity is experienced by the individual as creating obligations: "I am a Catholic, and this means that I should hold certain beliefs and follow certain practices." Reminding an individual of a religious identity label makes that sub-identity salient.

We need to determine the behavioral consequences, if any, that may be tied to an identity label. As Zavalloni (1975) suggests, just because a person states and knows an identity label group, what does that reveal about commitment level, or about effects on individual behavior? What is the meaning, for the individual, of "belonging"? It may be positive, negative, or indifferent. The majority of believers share an "identity religion," which, while reflecting low ego-involvement, constitutes a significant and social psychological reality. How much time and effort do individuals invest in considering their religious identity options? Most humans spend very little time thinking about their religious identity. For the majority of nominal believers, religious identity is indeed simple and marginal, without much commitment or investment (Beit-Hallahmi, 1989).

Here is a description of identity religion in its Moslem version:

> [I]dentity religion is experienced as something akin to family, ethnicity, race, or nationality. Identity religion thus is something into which people believe they are born rather than something to which they convert after a process of study, prayer, or reflection. Identity religion, in this basic form, understands co-religionists to be a part of the same group (perhaps even regardless of their

personal beliefs). *Identity* religion is less likely to emphasize shared theological beliefs and more likely to emphasize shared histories, cultures, ethnicity, and traditions. People may consider themselves Muslims on the basis of ethnicity, even though they have not been inside a mosque for twenty years and even though they know little about the *Qur'an*.

(Gunn, 2003, p. 201, italics in the original)

Identity, so easily formed, is given up only with difficulty. Dawkins (2006) notes that some atheists he knows quite well still display loyalty to "tribe," family, or community, by regularly attending religious services, without any real faith. And indeed large-scale research shows that under conditions of continuing secularization, individuals identify as belonging to dominant historical traditions, despite the absence of any behavioral commitment to that tradition. This can be observed today in Europe, where rates of religious observance have declined sharply, but individuals still identify with the traditional labels of Roman Catholic, Anglican, or Lutheran (see Chapter 9). This indicates that early and seemingly minimal socialization leads to robust learning of a loyalty to identity without attendant behavior. Catholics, Jews, and others keep their identity badges not because of a history they did not experience, but thanks to the traditions they experienced directly through community and family (Inglis, 2007).

The power of group identity

Insecurity and self-enhancement, individual and social, may lead to conflicts which are identity inspired and automatic. The idea of being elected and belonging to a superior group is a powerful compensation for subjectively felt deficiencies. Religious identity may be more forceful than other kinds, because of the notion of election and superiority. The idea of being chosen is found in every case of religious ideology. Members of many religious groups believe that their group has been chosen to share in revealed absolute truth, and that their group is the vanguard in a cosmic project. The belief that one is playing a role in this cosmic script must have some effect on self-esteem.

Within a social reality of religious pluralism and competition, measurable social distances among different groups are maintained, and they will affect intimate social contacts across group boundaries. Ysseldyk, Matheson, and Hymie (2010) consider a desire for a positive social identity as an explanation for religiosity. Hogg, Adelman, and Blagg (2010) argue that identification with groups reduces uncertainty, and religions especially reduce feelings of self-uncertainty through the belief systems they offer. Uncertainty reduction influences obedience to religious leaders, which may culminate in immoral behavior.

It has been suggested that by their very nature, religious communities will enter states of tension and conflict with out-groups, and that such conflicts will galvanize group identities. "The symbolic and social boundaries of religion (no matter how fluid or porous) mobilize individual and group identity in conflict, and sometimes violence, within and between groups" (Wellman and Tokuno, 2004, p. 291). When civil wars are defined in religious terms, they are less likely to be settled (Svensson, 2007). Neuberg *et al.* (2014) looked at 194 ethnic, religious, and national groups around the world and found that what they called *religious infusion*, the extent to which religious activities and discourse permeated everyday life, led to more serious conflict through heightened prejudice and discrimination.

Atran and Ginges (2012) argued that religious identities and loyalties will lead to interminable conflicts, because the believers become immune to the impact of actual outcomes and incentives. Issues are likely to be defined as sacred when a threat to the group or the group's identity is perceived (Sheikh *et al.*, 2012). When individuals experience an event as threatening their identity, they may react emotionally and may be easily mobilized by leaders to react violently.

Thus, religious group identities lead to significant social consequences. Beit-Hallahmi and Argyle (1997) stated that religious group identities and solidarities will lead to in-group cooperation but also to conflicts among groups. Atran and Henrich (2010) argued that religion is connected with both within-group pro-sociality and between-group enmity and point to the similarity between secular nationalism and religion in this respect. McCrae (1999, p. 1211) stated that religion was "a cause for which to live, or die, or kill," but this is often true of nationalism.

When considering analogies for the strong commitments, attachments, and conflicts created by religion, nationalism seems highly relevant. A leading anthropologist agrees:

> Rather like religion, nationalism has a bad name in the modern world, and, rather like religion, it more or less deserves it. Between them (and sometimes in combination) religious bigotry and nationalist hatred have probably brought more havoc upon humanity than any two forces in history, and doubtless will bring a great deal more.
>
> (Geertz, 1973, p. 253)

Religion inspires cooperation among genetically unrelated individuals by invoking a new identity which is above that of family or clan, and nationalism has been doing the same thing, with considerable success. Individuals have been ready to sacrifice their lives for the nation, or express their loyalty in less lethal ways, often with a great deal of sentimentality. A national anthem brings tears to some eyes, and the national flag symbolizes a common fate and greatness. What we find in nationalism is a strong commitment and sometimes high emotionality, inspired by a secular set of beliefs.

There are national mythologies, relating great victories and glories, together with ideas of superiority and election, but there are no references to the spirit world, only to the fatherland (or motherland). Those who died fighting for the nation are not promised a glorious afterlife, but only to be remembered forever by their compatriots. Nationalism, like religion, uses and extends kinship metaphors, expanding the natural solidarity of family and clan to create an imagined brotherhood of compatriots. Comparing religion and nationalism points to a clear difference, which is the reliance on supernaturalism in the case of religion, and on common fate and identity in the case of nationalism. The latter promises its adherents only historical triumphs, while the former promises immortality and cosmic victories.

More connections between nationalism, politics, and religion in the dynamics of identity and loyalty are discussed in Chapters 4 and 6.

4

EXPLAINING VARIATIONS IN RELIGIOSITY

Given the presumed universality and uniform action of the psychological mechanisms involved in the making of religion, the question of individual differences in religiosity is especially intriguing. If we all possess the same brain architecture, how is it that individual humans differ so much in the way it is expressed? Basic cognitive mechanisms must interact with individual differences and social conditions to determine individual religiosity.

Observing differing levels of involvement in religion raises the question of whether the differences are not only quantitative but actually qualitative, and there may be in reality different kinds of individual involvement in religion. The concepts of social learning and social identity can account for most religious involvements (see Chapter 3), but research on religious movements, religious experiences, and converts has shown that the religiosity of a significant minority among believers may be qualitatively and quantitatively different (see Chapter 7). William James proposed a distinction between the once-born "healthy minded" and the twice-born "sick souls" (James, 1902/1961). The former were optimistic and well-adjusted; the latter depressed, ridden by guilt, and in a permanent crisis. These individuals may change dramatically and experience elation and zest as the result of conversion. Then they sometimes become leaders and models for others.

Beit-Hallahmi (1989) described two distinctive styles of religiosity, denoted by the terms of art (high involvement) vs. identity:

> One is the low-involvement religion, the religion of identity, learned within the family of origin and having little emotional significance; and the other is the high-involvement religion, often the religion of converts, who learned it outside their family of origin and invest much emotional energy in it.
>
> (Beit-Hallahmi, 1989, p. 100)

The research shows that nominal believers simply don't know much about the religious tradition they nominally embrace, nor do they report much in the way of emotional experiences. Holding religious beliefs while keeping them marginal in one's life-space, as opposed to keeping faith closer to the center of one's existence, should have measurable consequences and reflect a qualitative difference between the two kinds of involvement.

The separation of believers into a low-involvement majority and a high-involvement minority is not a modern phenomenon, and is not the result of secularization; we can find different levels of commitment in all historical periods and in all types of groups. What we have observed is that high involvement may be tied to discontinuities in the learning of identity, as James suggested. The road to an all-consuming religious identity, always a minority option, may be paved with anxiety and conflict (see Chapter 7).

Religious rebels, who may sometimes turn out to be founders of new movements, and those who choose to commit their lives to religion, develop these careers out of conflict and crisis. The majority of believers just follow, rather than lead or create new beliefs, but it is the variations in the behavior of this majority that need explaining, just like those among the intense minority. These variations are not in the form of a clear dichotomy, and lend themselves to being measured as continuous variables.

Situational determinants of religiosity

The most common explanations for stronger religious involvement offered by historians, sociologists, anthropologists, or psychologists use the terms deprivation, frustration, suffering, crisis, vulnerability, and insecurity. They may refer to objective, material conditions, or subjective, psychological factors. The literature also uses terms like estrangement, isolation, marginality, alienation, or anomie to describe the context of religious yearnings. Glock stated that religious activities "are likely to compensate for feelings of deprivation rather than to eliminate its causes" (1964, p. 29), while Stark and Bainbridge (1987) described religion as providing "supernatural general compensators," imaginary rewards wished for when real rewards are unavailable. Duschinsky (2012) described worldwide fundamentalist movements as a reaction to the upheavals of modernization and economic insecurity. Deprivation and distress explanations predict that with less frustration and anxiety, religiosity would decrease for both individuals and groups (see Chapter 9).

It is important to emphasize that the deprivation-compensation hypothesis, which starts with the terminology of strain, crisis, and dislocation, is used in the literature of history and the social sciences not just to explain religious phenomena, but to explain ideological commitment in general, secular ideologies, and secular political movements (Smelser, 1962). In research on nationalism, revolts, revolutions, political attitudes, or even on historical changes in psychological theories, deprivation explanations are most common (Beit-Hallahmi, 1992). This

58 Explaining variations in religiosity

may be regarded as reflecting a negative view of existence, but it has remained dominant for a reason. One does not have to be uniquely pessimistic to recognize the prevalence of insecurity, anxiety, and victimization in so many human lives.

Writing in 1844, Karl Marx formulated the best known description, poetic and psychological, of religion as a response to deprivation:

> Religious suffering is at the same time an expression of real suffering and a protest against real suffering. Religion is the sigh of the oppressed creature, the heart of a heartless world, and the soul of soulless conditions. It is the opium of the people.
>
> (Marx, 1964, pp. 43–44)

In 1852, Marx described how despair leads to salvation dreams, which will never be fulfilled:

> In the sphere of consciousness, men ... made an eschatology of their unrealized yearning for fulfillment, and the idea of God expressed at once their desperate hope in the beneficence of a world become strange and their awful submission to it.
>
> (quoted in Birnbaum, 1973, pp. 170–171)

A century later, a similar view was most clearly expressed by Davis (1948):

> The greater his [man's] disappointment in this life, the greater his faith in the next. Thus the existence of goals beyond this world serves to compensate people for frustrations they inevitably experience in striving to reach socially acquired and socially valuable ends.
>
> (Davis, 1948, p. 532)

Often, the references to crises and upheaval in the literature are general and describe factors affecting masses of people. Because not every individual responds to stress by joining religious groups (or secular ones) and making serious social and psychological commitments, it is clear that individual vulnerabilities or personality factors must play a role and should be considered when examining specific cases (Beit-Hallahmi, 1992). Glock, Ringer, and Babbie (1967) stated that being female, unmarried, old, with little income, and little education are all forms of deprivation that would lead to greater religious involvement.

Deprivation: case studies and regularities

The scholarly literature offers thousands of case studies which demonstrate the connection between deprivation of all kinds and increasing religiosity and the appearance of new religious movements and the readiness to join such movements (Beit-Hallahmi, 1992; Beit-Hallahmi and Argyle, 1997). Among individuals and social groups, religious awakening as well as the appearance of new religious ideas, are tied to problems and anxieties (see Chapter 7). Harris (1981) suggested that in the United States, any religious awakenings in the twentieth century were the result of frustration with the lack of worldly progress in society, and that the failure of the American Dream to become reality has pushed Americans in the direction of supernaturalist solutions, but the relationship between material deprivation and religious commitments may be attenuated by other factors (Schieman, 2010).

Joining a new religious movement (NRM) has been interpreted as a response to crisis situations and individual alienation, alleviated by a promise of salvation. Wilson (1967, p. 31) proposed that new religious movements (NRMs) emerge because of "stresses and tensions differentially experienced within the total society ... disturbance of normal social relations, for instance in the circumstances of industrialization and urbanization ... Insecurity, differential status anxiety, cultural neglect." These terms are not unique to Western nations. Describing the situation in Japan after 1945, which led to the success of many new religions, McFarland used the term "disintegration" (McFarland, 1967).

Among the indicators of maladjustment leading to religious commitment we find lower socioeconomic status which leads to joining NRMs in Japan (Miller, 1992), and being widowed which made individuals more likely to join a spiritualist organization (Nelson, 1972). Carroll (1975) showed that the recent extermination of the buffalo led particular native American tribes to join the Ghost Dance of 1890, and population decline was another factor (Thornton, 1981). Looking at the development of new religious movements in Africa, Assimeng (1986, 1989), Nukunya (1992), and Pfeiffer (2002) concluded that the success of such groups had to do with their use of "healing" and "salvation," meeting the needs of an impoverished population, and especially women. Witch killing, which seems incomprehensible, is a scapegoating ritual in reaction to economic insecurity. Miguel (2005) demonstrated that the frequency of witch killing, but not of other murders, rises with the incidence of extreme rainfall, which threatens agriculture. Similarly, possession phenomena in many cultures have been interpreted as expressions of discontent by deprived groups (Lewis, 1966).

Sociologists have proposed a distinction between sect and church, and between sect-religiosity and church-religiosity. The former is marked by commitment and emotionality, the latter by routine and structure. Sect-type groups are also characterized by a converted membership and by separatism towards the larger society (Beit-Hallahmi and Argyle, 1997; Wilson, 1967). Those with lower incomes and education are more likely to be committed to a "sect-like" religiosity, meaning more emotionality and more traditional beliefs. Conservative Protestants in the United States have been disproportionately female, rural, poor, elderly, and less educated (Gay and Ellison, 1993). In terms of wealth accumulation, conservative Protestants in the United States have remained at the bottom of the ladder, behind other religious groups, and their situation is unlikely to change, to some extent because of their religious beliefs which devalue material rewards (Keister, 2008).

60 Explaining variations in religiosity

The connection between poverty and sect membership has been noted often. Gillin (1910) described sects as protest groups of the poor in the USA. Clark (1965) examined 200 American sects and noted that none of them was interested in earthly social reform. Schwartz (1970) stated: "People join sects because they seek to redress the lack of deference and esteem they feel is rightfully theirs" (pp. 40–41). Gans (1972, p. 284) stated that "Pentecostal religion would probably not survive without the poor." Sales (1972) found that in bad economic times, conversion rates to authoritarian churches went up. Similarly, during periods of heightened economic insecurity, Americans have been found to be more likely to attend churches that strictly adhered to doctrine (McCann, 1999).

Findings show that,

> classes of people experiencing relatively limited secular opportunities (such as minorities, women, and the young) are more likely than others to choose sect membership over mainline church membership ... a general decline in secular opportunities, such as that which occurs during recessions, will make sectarian groups more attractive.
>
> (Iannaccone, 1994, p. 1201)

Kaplan (1965) described sect-type religiosity among the lower class as "religious escapism."

Smith and Faris (2005) showed that in the United States such groups as Jehovah's Witnesses, black Baptists, Southern Baptists, and Pentecostalists were lower in socioeconomic status (measured through income, education, and occupational prestige). In terms of beliefs, these are groups that proclaim an imminent salvation and "tend toward more openly expressive, informal, emotional, and 'Spirit-filled' styles of worshipp" (p. 102). Driskell and Lyon (2011), summarizing a 2005 survey of 1721 Americans, stated: "We find Evangelical Protestants less likely to be engaged in political and civic activities for reasons ... that may be tied to beliefs about personal salvation."

The prediction that suffering and poverty would lead to higher levels of religiosity has been put to the test by looking at cross-national data. Norris and Inglehart (2004) suggested that economic insecurity is tied to the persistence of religion, and that is why religiosity has declined in wealthy nations, and not in poor ones. They described "the absence of human security as critical for religiosity" (p. 14). Cross-national differences in religiosity are then explained by economic modernization, which reduces any need for religious reassurance (Inglehart and Baker, 2000; Norris and Inglehart, 2004). Barro and McCleary (2003) found that economic development leads to lower levels of individual religiosity. Mourao (2011) studied the factors affecting the number of Catholic priests in 38 European countries, covering the period 1950–2006. The findings showed that economic development was the most important determinant of the ratio of Catholic priests to Catholic population, explaining the significant decline between 1950 and 2006. Urbanization, migration, and changing fertility rates were contributing factors. This was interpreted as supporting theories of historical secularization.

Ritual attendance rates are higher in nations suffering economic inequalities without offering a safety net (Gill and Lundsgaarde, 2004; Norris and Inglehart, 2004). In an analysis of 60 nations, Ruiter and van Tubergen (2009) found that religious attendance is primarily affected by personal and societal insecurities, as well as by parental and national religious socialization and the general level of urbanization. Lower income and being unemployed was also tied to attendance, and there was a high negative correlation between national welfare expenditure and ritual attendance. Brandt and Henry (2012) used data on 216,249 participants in 90 cultures and found that individuals low in income and education were more religious. In wealthy countries this relationship was mediated by a measure of psychological defensiveness. Hanson and Xiang (2013) found that Christian denominations with stricter religious doctrines attracted more converts in countries where risks of natural disaster or disease outbreak were greater and where government provision of health services was more limited.

Existential insecurity, which means worrying about economic survival, is tied to the continued importance of religion in developing nations. Moreover, Norris and Inglehart (2004) suggest that growing up with insecurity creates a stronger religious commitment for life. Aarts *et al.* (2010) showed that improvements in the quality of life in 26 nations, as measured by the United Nations Human Development Index, had a significant, negative effect on attendance. Cragun and Lawson (2010) suggested that economic development of countries ultimately leads to a secular transition, curtailing the growth of these religious groups. A similar survey using data from 114 countries showed that lower rates of employment in agriculture, together with growing income security and equality, led to a decline in religiosity (Barber, 2013).

Solt, Habel, and Grant (2011) looked at data from countries around the world over two decades and at a time-series analysis of the United States over five decades. They found that economic inequality had a strong positive effect on the religiosity of all members of a society regardless of income. Their conclusion is that greater inequality yields higher religiosity by increasing the extent to which wealthy people support religion and have the power to shape the attitudes and beliefs of those with fewer means. An additional prediction is that greater economic inequality increases the vulnerability of the poorer members of a society, and should raise their religiosity level (Norris and Inglehart, 2004). A survey in 40 nations found that inequality increases religious service attendance, as well as support for the involvement of religious organizations and leaders in politics, and weakens support for secularization, especially among the poor (Karakoç and Baskan, 2012).

If we find a high level of religiosity in a developed nation, and the best-known case is the United States, it may be related to a high level of economic inequality, which leads to insecurity being experienced by a majority in the population. The absence of a welfare state (as developed in Europe) may be a

62 Explaining variations in religiosity

primary source for its pervasive religiosity (Höllinger, Haller and Valle-Höllinger, 2007; Verweij, Ester and Nauta, 1997). Ruiter and van Tubergen (2009) concluded that the United States is an exceptional case, and is likely to remain so because of its religious history, urbanization, and socioeconomic inequalities. Delamontagne (2010) found that social inequality (measured by inequalities in education and income) was highly predictive of religiosity in the United States. Another reason for insecurity in the United States is the high level of violence, compared to other developed countries.

The correlation between deprivation and religiosity has been found in comparisons of individual states within the United States, with religiosity higher in poorer states. Gray and Wegner (2010) looked at differences in religiosity in individual states, and related them to a "suffering index." The suffering index was based on rates of infant mortality, cancer deaths, infectious disease, violent crime, and environmental pathogens. They found a positive correlation between a state's level of suffering and its religiosity, as measured by belief in God, r (48)=.69, p <.001. The connection between suffering and religiosity is demonstrated also by the finding that in the United States, individuals who report praying often and claim that it brings results are likely to be women, fundamentalists, African-Americans, those with less education and income, the widowed, and the elderly (Pargament, 1997). Similar findings by Baker (2008b) showed that those with fewer resources and social status pray more often.

The economic insecurity hypothesis, proposed by Norris and Inglehart (2004), has been put to another global test by Diener, Tay, and Myers (2011). They started with what they see as a paradox: if religious individuals report a higher subjective well-being (SWB), why is the number of the unaffiliated growing? They found that nations which suffer from poverty, hunger, and low life expectancy were likely to be highly religious. In these nations, religiosity was associated with subjective well-being (SWB), so that religious people had a higher SWB in poor, religious nations but not in wealthy, secularized nations.

This finding has been replicated in New Zealand by Hoverd and Sibley (2013). The relationship between economic deprivation (measured by census data on the respondent's neighborhood), religiosity, and SWB was measured in a representative national sample in New Zealand (n=5984). The religiosity measure was self-reported affiliation ("Do you identify with a religion and/or spiritual group?") A total of 2657 (44.4 percent) respondents identified as affiliated and 3327 (55.6 percent) as unaffiliated. Individuals living in prosperous areas reported higher levels of SWB regardless of affiliation, while people living in poor neighborhoods reported higher SWB only if they were religiously affiliated.

A related issue is that of social trust, which reflects one's sense of security in society. Low trust clearly reflects deprivation and insecurity, and should be tied to religiosity. Data from the Gallup World Poll for 109 countries and 43 US states indicated a robust, negative relationship between self-rated importance of religion in daily life and social trust, defined as the share of a population that thinks people in general can be trusted (Berggrena and Bjornskov, 2011).

Crisis and revitalization movements

Some religious movements start as deliberate attempts to reconstruct a culture in response to crisis (Wallace, 1956). Hundreds of historical movements have been analyzed as religions of crisis or religions of protest and resistance, including Voodoo (Pierre, 1977), modern Pentecostalism (Flora, 1973), the Rastafarians (Kitzinger, 1969), the Bwiti in West Africa (Fernandez, 1982), and the Great Awakening in northern New York in the 1840s (Barkun, 1986). In preindustrial societies, NRMs have been known as "crisis cults," including so-called Cargo Cults (Burridge, 1975; Worsley, 1957) and Ghost Dances (La Barre, 1970; Mooney, 1965; Thornton, 1986). Among historical periods that gave rise to crisis religions, we should mention the United States in the nineteenth century, with a wealth of salvation movements, the rise of Spiritualism, and the founding of many new religions (e.g. Christian Science, Mormonism, Seventh Day Adventists, Theosophy), and the United States in the 1960s where many religious movements were started, such as ISKCON ("Hare Krishna").

Sometimes attempts at revitalization lead to catastrophes. The Chinese Taiping movement in the mid-nineteenth century led to a major civil war, where possibly 20 million were killed. Its leader claimed to be the son of the Christian God and the brother of the mythological Jesus. He also attacked the feudal regime and laid out a plan for a modernized China. The movement mobilized the poor masses into a force that became a real threat to the ruling Manchu dynasty. The rulers would have been defeated without the intervention of Britain and the United States on their side (Platt, 2012).

The Ghost Dance, a rebellion by native Americans against White settlers, started as a totally non-violent apocalyptic dream, which led to a disaster. It represented a traditional response to externally imposed oppression and deprivation. Its doctrine was based on the theme of the coming triumph of the natives over the Europeans, material prosperity of the natives at the expense of Europeans, the resurrection of the dead, and the return to pre-colonial bliss, including the reappearance of buffalo herds. The eventual outcome would be a renewal of native existence, forever free of death, disease, and misery. To bring this about, natives had to perform the sacred dance. Believers were also exhorted to discard all warlike behaviors (La Barre, 1970; Lanternari, 1963; Mooney, 1973).

The largest wave of the Ghost Dance movement rose in 1890 in the western United States, when 45 North American tribes, inspired by the prophet Wovoka, were involved. Wovoka presented himself as the messenger of a messianic kingdom, soon to be established under Jesus Christ. In Wovoka's visions, the native dead would appear around God's throne, the natives would recover their lands and their lost way of life, while the Whites would disappear. The Ghost Dance itself was designed to secure communication with the dead and hasten the coming of the messianic age. Men and women, dressed in white, danced in circles, singing "revealed" songs and reaching ecstasy. Wovoka's followers also believed that they were immune to bullets. The Ghost Dance of 1890 ended with the massacre at

64 Explaining variations in religiosity

Wounded Knee, South Dakota, on December 29, 1890, in which chief Sitting Bull and between 150 and 300 Sioux were killed. Wovoka survived the Ghost Dance, died in 1932, and is buried, under the name Jack Wilson, in western Nevada.

The Ghost Dance has been compared to Cargo Cults, a collective term for a variety of nativist movements which have appeared most often in Oceania, and promoted the belief in obtaining "cargo," i.e. manufactured goods and wealth, through spiritual means. Sometimes the expectation is that ancestors would return, delivering the "cargo" (Lanternari, 1963; Maher, 1961; Worsley, 1957). In all of these cases, as we judge them today, we regard the natives as victims of European colonization, and we recognize their deprivation and oppression. We should recall that earlier generations saw them as savages committing acts of terrorism.

One successful revitalization movement is described by Wallace (1970), who shows how the Seneca tribe in North America, suffering every possible disaster since 1650, and a total disintegration at the end of the eighteenth century, was reborn in the nineteenth century thanks to a religious vision. After a long period of decline and demoralization, the Seneca were revitalized by the Seneca chief Ganiodayo (Handsome Lake, 1735–1815) in 1799. His visions called for the adoption of a puritan-like ethic. Handsome Lake was changed by the visions from an alcoholic to a prophet who saved his people. His new religion introduced the confession of sins as its main ritual and banned whiskey and witchcraft. Later on the movement spread among the Iroquois, and still exists among the Iroquois in northern New York and Canada.

Situational uncertainty

The idea that religious beliefs serve to block threats to one's sense of certainty, stability, and security has been proposed and tested in several experiments (Burling, 1993; Hogg, Adelman and Blagg, 2010; Li *et al.*, 2010; McCann, 1999). Religion helps satisfy the need for order, explanation, and prediction by providing a sense of illusory control (Kay *et al.*, 2008; Kay *et al.*, 2009; Kay, Moscovitch and Laurin, 2010b). Van den Bos, Van Ameijde, and Van Gorp (2006) showed that uncertainty led participants to be more protective of their beliefs and religious identity. Laurin, Kay, and Moscovitch (2008) found that a threat to beliefs in personal control led to a stronger belief in a controlling God. Kay *et al.* (2010a, c) proposed that religion helps to maintain the belief in an orderly world and found that feeling a loss of control is tied to belief in God or "spiritual forces." They also review evidence showing that when the stability of external control structures (e.g. government) is threatened, religious belief increases.

Kay, Moscovitch, and Laurin (2010b) found that exposing individuals to random or uncertain occurrences will increase religious conviction. Rutjens, van der Pligt, and van Harreveld (2010) showed how a desire for certainty pushes individuals towards holding religious beliefs. McGregor, Nash, and Prentice (2010) placed participants in anxiety-provoking or neutral situations, which included asking whether they would give their lives for their faith. The anxiety-inducing condition caused participants to become more committed in their convictions.

Greenaway, Louis, and Hornsey (2013) manipulated participants' sense of control and found effects on beliefs in "precognition." Some participants read a paragraph offering support for the notion of precognition, while others read a statement refuting the notion. Individuals exposed to the confirmation were more likely to endorse statements such as "I am in control of my own life," "My life is determined by my own actions," and "I am able to live my life how I wish." In another experiment, participants who experienced a loss of control and then read the same paragraphs reported an increased sense of control after reading the good news about precognition, unlike those who read the disconfirmation.

Believers imagine deities as attachment or love objects. Dutch members of Christian student organizations suffered a decrease in well-being and donated less money to charity when reminded that God could exclude them from his sight (Van Beest and Williams, 2011). Experimental manipulations of loneliness, such as receiving a prediction that the participant is destined to be alone later in life, or watching a loneliness-inducing brief video, resulted in greater belief in supernatural agents, such as ghosts, God, or the devil (Epley *et al.*, 2008). There is related evidence that the need to belong does push individuals in the direction of greater religiosity (Gebauer and Maio, 2012). Manipulations of social exclusion have been found to foster greater religious belief in both Western and non-Western societies (Aydin, Fischer and Frey, 2010). These results suggest that religious beliefs may help people shore up threats to their sense of social connectedness and may serve this buffering role for low-status individuals. There is also neural evidence for an association between religiousness and reduced uncertainty. Inzlicht *et al.* (2009) found reduced reactivity in the anterior cingulate cortex (a system involved in anxiety and self-regulation) among participants with stronger religious beliefs. They concluded that religious beliefs defend against anxiety and minimize the subjective experience of failure.

Terror Management Theory (TMT)

TMT proposes that the awareness of death is humanity's main cultural problem, and suggests that death awareness is managed through cultural beliefs that offer transcendence via non-religious (scientific or artistic contributions, raising children) and/or religious (promises of afterlife bliss) ways.

> Cultural worldviews consist of humanly constructed beliefs about the nature of reality that are shared by individuals in a group that function to mitigate the horror and blunt dread caused by the knowledge of the reality of the human condition, that we all die ... Successful cultural worldviews allow people to control death anxiety by convincing them that they are beings of enduring significance living in a meaningful reality.
>
> (Pyszczynski, Greenberg and Solomon, 2003, p. 16)

66 Explaining variations in religiosity

Religion naturally plays a major role as a cultural worldview: "TMT posits that religion improves subjective well-being and mitigates existential distress, which are beneficial for staying alive and reproducing in a self-conscious animal explicitly aware of the inevitability of death" (Solomon, Pyszczynski and Greenberg, 2010, p. 91). Illusory beliefs, rituals, and art seem to have no clear survival value, but on reflection we must realize that they play an important role in relieving anxiety and allowing culture to survive (Becker, 1973; Greenberg *et al.*, 1995).

TMT has inspired experiments in which participants experience mortality salience and its effects are measured. When confronted with death reminders, individuals will defend cultural traditions (Greenberg, Solomon and Arndt, 2008; Dechesne *et al.*, 2003), including their religious beliefs, religious identity, or nationalism (Greenberg *et al.*, 1995). Religion appears to protect adherents from the anxiety of eventual death (Vail *et al.*, 2010). Vail, Arndt, and Abdollahi (2012) found that death reminders had no effect among atheists, but among Christians it raised religiosity and enhanced denial of the competitor deities Allah and Buddha. Among Moslems, death reminders raised religiosity and enhanced denial of Jesus and Buddha. Norenzayan and Hansen (2006) similarly found no effect on non-religious participants, but interestingly found that mortality salience increased Christians' belief in non-Christian supernatural entities like Buddha and "Shamanic spirits."

A few experimental studies have attempted to identify the causal direction in the relation between death anxiety and religious belief, and while many of these studies find that religious individuals bolster their belief in the face of death, the critical data for non-religious individuals are far more equivocal. Osarchuk and Tatz (1973) found that mortality salience strengthened afterlife beliefs among believers, but had no effect on non-believers. It has also been found that the connection works in the other direction. Raising doubts among firm believers led to increased death anxiety (Friedman and Rholes, 2007). Jong, Halberstadt, and Bluemke (2012) found that mortality salience did produce some residual beliefs even in atheists.

Vess *et al.* (2009) examined whether reminders of death motivate individuals strongly invested in a religious worldview (i.e., fundamentalists) to rely on religious beliefs when making medical decisions. Raising awareness about mortality led those high in fundamentalism to endorse prayer as an effective cure. Following reminders of death, fundamentalists were more likely to support religiously motivated medical refusals and reported an increased willingness to rely on faith alone for medical treatment.

Variance in individual predispositions: biology

Behind individual differences in religiosity, as well as the total absence of religiosity in atheists, there must lie a biological substratum (Saler and Ziegler, 2006). Research has looked at two biological aspects of individual differences: genetics and brain mechanisms. Numerous studies have reported genetic influences on religiosity

(Koenig *et al.*, 2005, 2007; Truett *et al.*, 1992). Waller *et al.* (1990) reported significant heritability coefficients for general views about the value of religion. Olson, Vernon, and Harris (2001) together with Bradshaw and Ellison (2008), reported similar findings. Political attitudes have been found to show similar levels of heritability (Funk *et al.*, 2013).

Self-transcendence (ST) is a measure of religiosity and support for occultism. Urgesi *et al.* (2010) found that damage to the left and right posterior parietal regions induced an increase in ST. Borg *et al.* (2003) found that the number of serotonin receptors correlated negatively with scores for self-transcendence—higher scores on self-transcendence tied to lower numbers of receptors. Nilsson *et al.* (2007) reported that genes connected to serotonin are associated with religiosity. Parkinson's disease, related to lower dopamine production, is tied to lower religiosity (Butler, McNamara and Durso, 2010).

Asp, Ramchandran, and Tranel (2012) hypothesized that patients with prefrontal cortex damage would have a "doubt deficit," which would be expressed through higher authoritarianism and fundamentalism. Ten patients with bilateral damage to the ventromedial prefrontal cortex (vmPFC), ten patients with damage to other brain areas, and sixteen medical control patients were compared on authoritarianism, fundamentalism, and specific religious beliefs. vmPFC patients scored significantly higher on authoritarianism and religious fundamentalism.

High intensity religiosity: religious experiences

The literature on religious experiences or mysticism refers on the one hand to reportedly spontaneous, personal experiences leading to written or oral testimony and related religious commitment ("mystical experiences"), and then to the findings from mass surveys which ask respondents about private experiences. Religious experiences or mystical states are by definition private events, like dreams, that we know about only by first-person reports. Laubach (2004, p. 242) offered the following description: "perceptions of psychic intrusions into the stream of consciousness that are interpreted by the actor as not originating within the self's normal information channels."

Religious visions reported by individuals (Berryman, 2001; Zimdars–Swartz 1991), possession experiences, glossolalia (speaking in what sounds like an unknown language), snake handling (Hood and Williamson, 2008), and conversion (see Chapter 7) engage the observer's curiosity and challenge researchers. Often such rare experiences are reported by those living a totally religious life. Well-known mystics in history felt compelled to report them publicly, even though they were said to be indescribable and unutterable (Belzen and Geels, 2003). Individual experiences reported by religious devotees or leaders become part of religious histories and traditions, and sometimes lead to the formation of new movements. While such experiences are reported as spontaneous, a psychological interpretation will regard them as being the product of combined brain processes and social learning (Proudfoot, 1985).

68 Explaining variations in religiosity

Over the past fifty years, one can find mass surveys of believers who report having had intense experiences in response to direct questions in the survey. These are examples of the questions used in such surveys:

> Have you ever been aware of or influenced by a presence or power, whether you call it God or not, which is different from your everyday self?
>
> (Hay, 1982)

> Would you say that you had ever had a "religious or mystical experience," that is a moment of sudden religious insight or awakening?

Large surveys are important in assessing mass beliefs (Beit-Hallahmi and Argyle, 1997). With representative samples of the United States population, a survey in 2004 showed that 37 percent responded to the item "I feel God's presence" by "many times a day or most days" and 22.4 percent of the population never or almost never had the experience (Underwood, 2006).

What unites most reported private experiences is an alleged contact with a sensed presence, or "another consciousness" (Persinger, 2001). This can be viewed as a personalization or concretization of essential supernaturalist beliefs, which revolve around the existence of spirit entities. An illusory sensed presence or the conviction that another person or another consciousness are close by have been produced by the stimulation of particular brain areas (Arzy *et al.*, 2006; Booth and Persinger, 2009; Persinger and Healey, 2002). Another common description is of an experience of mystical union with a deity or with nature (Hood and Chen, 2013).

The particular content of private religious experience is totally determined by cultural learning and tradition: "to have religious experiences, man must acquire a religious tradition" (Sunden, 1959, quoted in Belzen, 1996, p. 187; Proudfoot, 1985). Some traditions and some social settings will increase the frequency of reported experiences. Data from a 2005 American national survey show the poor are more likely to be affiliated with conservative religious movements, more often report visions, hearing the "Voice of God," or miraculous healing (Baker, 2009). In a group of meditators, fourteen meditators were told about "the function that always has been attributed to meditation in religious-mystical traditions" (experimental group) and twenty-one meditators were told about "the therapeutic function meditation may have" (control group). After four weeks of daily practice, seven members of the experimental group and no members of the control group reported having religious experiences (Van Der Lans, 1987, p. 406).

Halloy (2012) and Halloy and Naumescu (2012) described how spirit possession is learned as individuals master the required cultural expertise. Novices start by observing audience reactions towards the possessed persons and then learn to regulate their own emotional states. Then they develop the specific somatic pattern typical to the group. Spanos *et al.* (1986) demonstrated how glossolalia could be easily taught. Seventy percent of trained subjects spoke fluent glossolalia following two training sessions (see also Kildahl, 1972). Together with social learning, there is an individual, causative part (Luhrmann, Nusbaum and Thisted, 2010). With the same exposure, not every individual will have such an experience, and it is assumed that personality factors and neural states play a role in creating this behavior (Beit-Hallahmi and Argyle, 1997).

The personality dimension of schizotypy consists of a tendency to hallucinate and have other anomalous perceptual or cognitive experiences, but also enables those who have it to be creative in art or literature, and to be religious (Claridge, 1985). Jackson (1997) found a positive correlation between schizotypy and reported religious experiences. The schizotypy items with the strongest correlations were "Do things sometimes feel as though they were not real?" (.43), "Do you believe in telepathy?" (.40), and "Do you believe that dreams can come true?" (.30). Confirming earlier findings, Hood and Chen (2013) reported that the Hood (1975) Mysticism Scale (M Scale) correlated with schizotypy scores and with beliefs in "extrasensory perception."

It is assumed that as brain processes mirror all behaviors, unusual subjective experiences will be tied to unusual brain states. Some reported religious experiences are definitely connected to brain syndromes. Azari *et al.* (2001) found that during religious recitation, religious participants activated a particular frontal–parietal circuit. They concluded that religious experiences were a cognitive process mediated by a pre-established neural circuit. Previc (2006) suggested that hyperreligiosity is a major feature of mania, obsessive-compulsive disorder (OCD), schizophrenia, and temporal-lobe epilepsy (TLE), caused by highly activated dopaminergic systems. Hallucinations during epilepsy and paranoid schizophrenia are involved in so-called mystical experiences. Sacks (1985) suggested that mystical visions may be the result of "migraine aura," which may lead to hallucinations.

Clinical observations and systematic studies over the past 150 years support an association between religious experiences and epileptic seizures, especially in individuals with temporal lobe epilepsy (Devinsky, 2003). The evidence is quite clear that temporal lobe epilepsy is tied to hyper-religiosity (Trimble and Freeman, 2006), religious conversions (Dewhurst and Beard, 1970), and claimed spirit possession in Voodoo (Carrazana *et al.*, 1999). Slater and Beard (1963) reported religious ideation and multiple conversions in individuals with a psychosis-like epilepsy. Waxman and Geschwind (1975) described what has been named the Waxman-Geschwind syndrome in some patients with chronic temporal lobe epilepsy, which includes hyper-religiosity and conversion.

Is it possible that famous mystics in history suffered from specific brain syndromes? Saver and Rabin (1997), after a thorough survey of the medical literature, offer diagnoses for several well-known mystics and religious leaders. St. Catherine of Genoa (1447–1510) had her first vision at age twenty-six, which led to a conversion, and was the author of two celebrated books of visions. She is diagnosed as a possible epileptic. Teresa of Avila (1515–1582), widely popular in her native Spain, was a Catholic saint, whose visions have been recorded for posterity. Her ecstatic writings have inspired numerous artists and writers, including

70 Explaining variations in religiosity

George Eliot, Thomas Hardy, and Simone de Beauvoir. She is diagnosed as a probable epileptic.

Emanuel Swedenborg (1688–1772) was trained as a mining engineer and made significant contributions to the technology of mining and metallurgy. At age fifty-five, he started having visions of angels, heaven, and hell. He declared that for thirty years he was in daily contact with the "spiritual world." According to his visions, the world is divided into three regions: the heavens, the hells, and the world of spirits. These visions were contained in his many books, and the movement he inspired is known as the New Church signified by the New Jerusalem in the Revelation. Saver and Rabin (1997) described him as a probable epileptic, in addition to suffering from mania and schizophrenia. Ann Lee (1736–1784), the founder of the Shakers, and Joseph Smith, Jr. (1805–1844), the founder of Mormonism, were also described as possible epileptics.

Ramachandran and Blakeslee (1998) suggested that some individuals with temporal lobe epilepsy suffer from an overstimulation of "saliency pathways," described as follows:

> These pathways recognize the emotional significance of events ... Patients who suffer from such conditions experience things that resonate with many religious traditions around the world: *Every* object and event – not just salient ones – would become imbued with deep significance, so that the patient would see "the universe in a grain of sand" and "hold infinity in the palm of his hand." He would float on an ocean of religious ecstasy, carried by a universal tide to the shores of Nirvana.
>
> (Ramachandran and Blakeslee, 1988, p. 183)

Devinsky and Lai (2008) proposed that the two levels of religiosity, normative beliefs and ecstatic religious experience, may be localized in the frontal and temporal regions of the right brain hemisphere. While events in the temporal lobe may evoke subjective religious experiences, changes in frontal lobe functions may contribute to increased religious interests in the individual as a permanent trait.

In addition to the reported "sensed presence" of cultural spirit entities, which characterizes so-called mystical experiences, individuals report feeling the presence of loved ones who have died. This has been known as "grief hallucinations" (Baethge, 2002), bereavement hallucinations (Persinger, 1988), "hallucinations of widowhood" (Rees, 1971), or "hallucinations associated with pathologic grief reaction" (Wells, 1983). MacDonald (1992, 1994) investigated which factors increased the likelihood of reporting contacts with the dead, and found that such reports appeared together with other claims about unusual experiences and "arise out of the uncertainty of life and the human condition and appear most frequently among those subject to the most change and stress. Women, blacks ... report higher instances of deja vu, telepathy, clairvoyance, and communication with the dead" (p. 35). Recency of widowhood affects the likelihood of having such experiences.

Out-of-body and near-death experiences

Since the 1970s, reports of near-death experiences (NDE) have attracted much attention in the popular media and have produced a number of best-selling books. For the believers, NDE reports may represent evidence of miracles. Most published descriptions of NDE use such terms as "bliss," "strong lights," and "serenity." Contrary to popular notions, most NDE reports are not about "bliss" and "peace," and some are totally negative (van Lommel *et al.*, 2001), while many "near-death" experiences come from individuals who were by no means close to dying (Owens, Cook and Stevenson, 1990). Temporal lobe irregularities are correlated with so-called near-death experiences (NDE), which sometimes lead to conversions (Britton and Bootzin, 2004; Groth-Marnat and Summers, 1998).

Because the circumstances preceding NDE (illness, accident, suicide, or anesthetics) have only a minimal effect on reported experiences, there must be an invariant, specific, neurophysiological mechanism behind them (Vaitl *et al.*, 2005). One explanation is that lower levels of oxygen cause the brain to react, in an attempt to restore normal oxygen supply (Mobbs and Watt, 2011). Another explanation is that near-death experiences are a subset of more common out-of-body (OBE) experiences. The latter, known as autoscopic phenomena, are illusory own-body perceptions, involving the duplication of one's body in external space. Autoscopic hallucinations are related to damage in brain regions tied to body sensation, perception, and motion.

OBE and autoscopic experiences represent paroxysmal disorders of body perception and cognition (or body schema) (Blanke *et al.*, 2003). Such paroxysms may appear in the oxygen-deprived brain and create NDE. Individuals reporting out-of-body experiences also reported more perceptual anomalies associated with specific measures of temporal lobe instability and body-distortion experiences. These results are consistent with a disruption in temporal lobe and body-based processing which causes OBE experiences (Braithwaite *et al.*, 2011). McCreery (1993) studied the personalities of people who report out-of-body experiences (OBEs). The schizotypy scale discriminated between the OBE subjects and controls.

Cognitive abilities and styles: analytical thinking, intelligence, and intellectualism

Mentalizing

If mentalizing is crucial to religious thinking, then individuals with problems in Theory of Mind, such as those with autistic spectrum disorders, will be expected to demonstrate lower religiosity. This indeed has been found in samples of autistic individuals in Canada and the United States (Norenzayan, Gervais and Trzesniewski, 2012). Individuals with Asperger's syndrome, an autism spectrum disorder, are less likely to see purpose behind the events in their lives, and this may undermine

72 Explaining variations in religiosity

intuitive support for supernatural agent concepts and reduce belief in God (Baron-Cohen and Wheelwright, 2004).

Intuitive vs. analytic style

Religiosity may be tied to the general tendency to rely on intuition versus reflection (see Chapter 2). "An analytic cognitive style denotes a propensity to set aside highly salient intuitions when engaging in problem solving" (Pennycook *et al.*, 2012, p. 335). An analytic style predicted lower religious and occultist beliefs when controlling for cognitive ability as well as sex, age, political ideology, and education (Pennycook *et al.*, 2012). Gervais and Norenzayan (2012b) also found that thinking analytically increases disbelief among believers and skeptics. Shenhav, Rand, and Greene (2012) suggested a causal link between intuitive thinking and a belief in God.

Colzato *et al.* (2010) compared a laboratory measure of local processing bias, the Navon hierarchical figures task (Navon, 1977), in groups of secular individuals, Orthodox Jews, and Roman Catholics in Israel and Italy. The secular persons had greater local processing bias than did the religious participants, even though all participants had been matched for educational background, IQ, and age. Aarnio and Lindeman (2005) examined connections between occult beliefs (e.g. "psychic power") and education, gender, and analytical and intuitive thinking in 3141 Finnish students. University students had fewer occult beliefs than vocational school students, partially due to their preference for analytical thinking. Intuitive thinking was positively connected with occult beliefs. Women's less analytical thinking partially explained their readiness to embrace occult beliefs, compared to men. Burris and Petrican (2011) presented evidence showing that atheists, compared to religious individuals, process emotions differently. Atheists' experiences appeared to be less vivid and less emotionally evocative relative to those of religious individuals, which may be related to a hyper-analytical style.

Intelligence

Overall, the correlation between IQ and religiosity has been found to be negative, but small. Sherkat (2010) examined the impact of religious affiliation, religious participation, and beliefs in the inerrancy of the Bible on verbal ability, and found that both inerrantist beliefs and affiliations with sectarian-style groups have substantial negative effects on verbal ability. Zuckerman, Silberman, and Hall (2013) performed the most comprehensive meta-analysis of 63 studies, which showed a significant negative association between intelligence and religiosity with mean r of $-.24$. Three possible explanations were proposed: higher intelligence may be negatively correlated with conformity; higher intelligence may be tied to an analytic thinking style (see above); higher intelligence helps in coping and may make religious compensators unnecessary.

Highly gifted groups

Several studies followed up children with outstanding (top 1 percent) IQ scores or with exceptional mathematical abilities. These longitudinal studies help uncover the precursors to later worldviews, because many of the gifted children did become part of the science-technology elite (Ferriman, Lubinski and Benbow, 2009). Starting in 1922, Terman and his colleagues studied 1528 gifted youth with IQs greater than 135, and a mean IQ of 151, who had been followed as long as they lived. Not too surprisingly, members of the gifted group excelled in academic work. Almost one-tenth of the 856 males became academic researchers (77), more than one-tenth (85) earned law degrees, and 48 earned medical degrees. Their religiosity was investigated repeatedly and the findings were consistent. At mid-life, in 1941, 45 percent of the group were unaffiliated with any religion (as compared to 6 percent in the general population at the time). Sixty-two percent of the men and 57 percent of the women claimed "little religious inclination" (Terman and Oden, 1959). This notable level of secularity was consistent throughout life (Holahan and Sears, 1995). Politically, the group was judged to be more liberal than the general population, and those with an IQ over 170 were the most liberal (Holahan and Sears, 1995).

Intellectualism

Beyond intelligence, some individuals are marked by intellectualism, a total commitment to scholarship, and high levels of analytical, non-intuitive thinking. They are likely to end up with academic careers and spend their lives at research universities. What about university students, some of whom are marked by intellectualism? Findings about religiosity in this group have been collected for a long time. In 1950–1951, Goldsen *et al.* (1960) carried out a survey (n=2975) of male students at eleven campuses across the United States. Religiosity was negatively correlated with the quality of the institution. The percentage of students who believed in God was at Harvard, considered the best, 30 percent; at UCLA 32 percent; at Texas, considered weak, 62 percent; and at North Carolina 68 percent. Zelan (1968) analysed 1958 data on graduate students in the United States, and found 25 percent were religious "nones," 80 percent of whom had been raised in some religion. This pattern was accentuated in elite universities. Caplovitz and Sherrow (1977) found that apostasy rates rose continuously from 5 percent in low ranked universities to 17 percent in high ranked universities. Niemi, Ross, and Alexander (1978) reported that at elite colleges, organized religion was judged important by only 26 percent of students, compared with 44 percent of all students.

When religiosity among academics is examined, the basic question is simple: How different are they from the general population? Stark, Iannaccone, and Finke (1996, p. 435) claimed that "scientists, professors, and graduate students are less religious than the overall population, the estimated differences are small, on the order of a few percentage points." In reality, surveys of religiosity among academics

74 Explaining variations in religiosity

in the United States have consistently showed a huge gap separating them from the general population (Ecklund and Park, 2009; Gross and Simmons, 2009). This was clear already in surveys carried out in the United States early in the twentieth century, which found a majority of nonbelievers among academics (Ament, 1927; Lehman and Witty, 1931; Leuba, 1916). Vaughan, Smith, and Sjoberg (1963) polled 850 physicists, zoologists, chemical engineers, and geologists listed in *American Men of Science* (1955) on church membership, attendance, and belief in the afterlife. Of the 642 replies, 54 percent had religious affiliations different from those of their parents. Larson and Witham (1997) reported 60 percent non-theists in a random sample taken from *American Men and Women of Science* in 1996.

Ecklund and Scheitle (2007) surveyed 1646 academics in physics, chemistry, biology, sociology, economics, political science, and psychology at twenty-one elite research universities in the United States. They were significantly less religious than the general population, leading to the thought that they came from another culture, or constituted one. Almost 52 percent identified themselves as having no current religious affiliation, compared with only 14 percent of the general population. Among them 33.5 percent were atheists, and 30.2 percent agnostics (for a total of 63.7 percent non-theists), while in the general population of the United States, atheists made up less than 1 percent, as did agnostics (Kosmin and Keysar, 2009). While 14 percent of the general population called themselves "evangelical" or "fundamentalist," less than 2 percent of the academics did. Fifteen percent identified as Jewish, compared to 2 percent in the general population. Both sectarian Protestants and Catholics are underrepresented among academics (Ecklund and Scheitle, 2007; Gross and Simmons, 2009).

One set of attitudes that correlates with low religiosity is the commitment to research. Those who are research oriented score lower on every measure of religiosity or "spirituality." Stark (1963) reported that a commitment to an academic career excluded a commitment to religion. That a commitment to an academic career, and not high intelligence, is the causal factor which affects religiosity among academics was shown by Ecklund and Park (2009). They compared 1386 academics to a group of 375 Americans with advanced degrees, who should have a similar capacity. The percentage of Catholics in the graduate degree group was 27.9, while among academics it was 9.0. The percentage of atheists in this group was only 3.8 percent, compared to 33.5 percent among academics. Chapter 6 includes a brief discussion of religiosity among physicians, who (like engineers) are much more religious than those committed to basic research. This illustrates the practical and psychological gap between science and technology. At the same time, those applying technology, like engineers and physicians, are charged with finding concrete solutions, rather than theoretical innovations, in their daily work, and live with more stress and insecurity.

Differences by academic disciplines have been noted. Among academic psychologists, 50 percent were atheists and another 11 percent were agnostic, while professors of accounting, finance, and nursing tended to be the most religious (Gross and Simmons, 2009). Surveys of applied psychologists have shown that 50 percent of them state that they have no religious preference, compared to 7 percent of the American public (Beit-Hallahmi, 1977b; Ragan, Malony and Beit-Hallahmi, 1980; Shafranskee, 1996). American psychiatrists, like other physicians, are more conventional in their beliefs than academics but they are still less religious than the general population, i.e. their patients. Sixty-five percent of psychiatrists reported a belief in God, compared to 77 percent among all physicians (Curlin *et al.*, 2007a). In Canada, 54 percent of psychiatrists were believers (Baetz *et al.*, 2004), and a survey of 231 psychiatrists in London found that only 23 percent reported a belief in God, reflecting cultural differences (Neeleman and King, 1993).

While most studies have looked at academics in Western nations, only one survey looked at academics in the developing world. A sample of 1100 Indian scientists from 130 universities and research institutes were asked about their religiosity in 2007–2008 (Keysar and Kosmin, 2008). To the question "What do you believe about God?," 12 percent were atheists and 13 percent agnostic, 26 percent believed in a personal God without doubts, 15 percent believed with doubts, and 30 percent did not believe in a personal God, but did believe in a higher power. The results showed a higher level of religiosity compared to academics in the United States, but a degree of secularity significantly higher than that of the Indian general population. According to Norris and Inglehart (2004) there may be no more than 5 percent atheists in the Indian population. These results must reflect India's unique cultural history, together with the negative correlation between intellectualism and religiosity, which may be global. Bourget and Chalmers (2013) carried out a global survey of 1972 philosophers at 99 of the world's "leading departments of philosophy." Almost 73 percent of the respondents defined themselves as atheists.

Jewish ancestry as a factor

Jewish over-representation has been noted in the literature on the social origins of scientists and academics. "In fact, among the most creative and elite groups of scientists most estimates suggest that 20 to 30% come from Jewish families" (Feist and Gorman, 1998, p. 13). This is while Jewish ancestry can be claimed by only tiny minorities in most nations. Jewish over-representation among eminent academics parallels the notable Jewish presence in modern elites of all kinds: political, financial, and creative (Slezkine, 2004). What does it mean in terms of religiosity or religion?

Secularization among Jews has been vigorous and thorough ever since it started in the eighteenth century. It meant that Jewish identity has been maintained by individuals who were no longer observing most Judaic commandments, and that Jewishness became only minimally related to Judaism (Beit-Hallahmi, 1993). Most modern Jews are highly secularized, scoring low on every measure of religious belief and religious participation in every known study.

In the twentieth century, Jewish self-identification has been consistently reported as having similar or identical consequences to secularity or irreligiosity. In many cases the reader of research articles can conclude that "Jewish" and "No

76 Explaining variations in religiosity

religion" are almost interchangeable. Here is how one sociologist in the 1960s interpreted the "no affiliation" and "Jewish" labels in research:

> "No religious affiliation" was assumed to indicate a low value on conformity and an individualistic approach. "Jewish" was considered a liberal designation because of the high level of education of this group, its low degree of organized religion, and its political liberality.
>
> (Reiss, 1967, p. 122)

Jewish over-representation among academics is related to secularity and modernity, rather than to Judaic traditions, but Jewish history may have contributed to the radical secularization Jewry has undergone. If modernization means urbanization, literacy, and mobility, Jews were clearly ahead of other groups, which must have prepared them well for modernity and its challenges (Slezkine, 2004).

The eminence effect

Quite early on, an "eminence effect" was noted, with the more eminent scientists being less religious than others. In the best known early surveys, starting in 1914, James L. Leuba mailed a questionnaire to leading scientists asking about their belief in "a God in intellectual and affective communication with humankind" and in "personal immortality." "I do not see any way to avoid the conclusion that disbelief in a personal God and in personal immortality is directly proportional to abilities making for success in the sciences in question" (Leuba, 1916, p. 279). Later on Leuba (1934) found that only 32 percent of "greater" scientists believed in God, compared with 48 percent of "lesser" ones; the figures for belief in immortality were 37 percent and 59 percent.

Roe (1952) interviewed sixty-four eminent scientists, nearly all members of the prestigious National Academy of Sciences or the American Philosophical Society. She reported that, while nearly all of them had religious parents, only three were seriously active in church. All the others had long since dismissed religion, and it played no part in their lives. A few were militantly atheistic, but most were just not interested. Bello (1954) studied research scientists, under age forty, judged by senior colleagues to be outstanding. Of the eighty-seven respondents, forty claimed to be "agnostic or atheistic" and an additional nineteen claimed no religious affiliation. There was a massive over-representation of unaffiliated and secularized Jews, and an under-representation of Roman Catholics.

Larson and Witham (1997, 1998) performed an exact replication of the 1914 and 1933 surveys by Leuba. They used the same wording, and sent their questionnaire to 517 members of the United States National Academy of Sciences from the biological and physical sciences, many of them Nobel Laureates. The return rate was slightly over 50 percent. The results showed that the percentage of believers in a personal God among eminent scientists in the United States was 27.7 percent in 1914, 15 percent in 1933, and 7 percent in 1998. Belief in personal immortality was slightly higher (35.2 percent in 1914, 18 percent in 1933, and 7.9 percent in 1998). The highest percentages of belief were found among eminent mathematicians (14.3 percent in God, 15.0 percent in immortality). Biological scientists had the lowest rate of belief (5.5 percent in God, 7.1 percent in immortality), with physicists and astronomers slightly higher (7.5 percent in God, 7.5 percent in immortality).

The findings demonstrate, first, that the process of turning away from religion among the most eminent scientists had been continuing over the twentieth century (as reported also by Ecklund, Park and Veliz, 2008 for academics in elite institutions), and, second, that in the United States, eminent scientists, with only 7 percent believing in a personal God, present a mirror image of the general population, where the corresponding percentage hovers around 95 percent in various studies. Lipset (1982) argued that the correlation between low religiosity and academic eminence paralleled the correlation between left-wing political positions and academic eminence.

What do we know about the minority of academics who pursue a research career while being traditionally religious? MacPherson and Kelly (2011) hypothesized that these individuals may have higher levels of creativity and positive schizotypy, expressed through having hallucinations, delusions, and magical ideation (Claridge, 1997). A comparison of 222 scientists (most from the natural sciences) and 193 controls showed that positive schizotypy and creativity was related to variance in religiosity among scientists, but not among controls.

The most eminent scientists

The Nobel Memorial Prize is awarded each year in physics, chemistry, physiology or medicine, peace, and literature. Since 1968, the Bank of Sweden Award in Economic Science has provided an entrée for the social sciences. The Nobel Prize is universally regarded as recognizing the highest achievements in science, literature, and humanitarian efforts. Its recipients are a unique population of remarkable individuals, who represent a modern cultural ideal of personal creativity.

Beit-Hallahmi (2003) used the biographical directory by Sherby and Odelberg (2001) to determine the religious affiliation and religiosity of 696 Nobel laureates between 1901 and 2000, who in terms of nationality represent mainly the USA (282: 41 percent), Britain (77: 11 percent), Germany (68: 9.7 percent), and France (51: 7.3 percent). Behind them were Sweden (26), Switzerland (14), Austria (13), Denmark (13), the Netherlands (13), and Italy (12). Other nations have smaller representations.

Sherby and Odelberg (2001) note in the introduction to their directory that obtaining information about religion was particularly difficult with this population. As they report, it was most difficult to locate information regarding affiliation in most cases, and this is for individuals who are public celebrities. Only 49 percent of laureates could be clearly classified (as Roman Catholic, Protestant, Jewish, Unitarian, or Other). Of the remaining 51 percent, 20.26 percent were classified

78 Explaining variations in religiosity

as None, apostates (e.g. "from Christian background") or No Record (!!). It should be noted that five of the economics laureates, who received the award fairly recently and are world famous, are listed as No Record. For almost 35 percent of laureates, the classification was speculative, ambiguous, and generic, such as "Protestant" (no denomination), "Christian," or "Most probably Christian." This was an indication of how reluctant many laureates were to align themselves with any denominations.

Table 4.1 shows a severe under-representation of Catholics in the science fields (they are well-represented in literature). Those 18 percent of the Nobel laureates that were listed as Jewish do not represent a religious group, but an ethnic label. We know that the vast majority of them are thoroughly secular. As to those openly identifying themselves as Nones, two things should be noted. First, they are the largest group among the literature laureates (31 out of 97). Second, they were found among the laureates as early as the first decade of the twentieth century.

Among Nobel laureates, the "eminence effect" (Leuba, 1916) has been demonstrated again. Eminence accentuates differences in both religious affiliation and religiosity between scientists and the general population, so that eminence in natural and social sciences (and even in literature) is clearly tied to a personal distance from religion.

What the findings regarding the Nobel laureates and the US National Academy of Sciences show is that since the nineteenth century, an international intellectual elite, committed to the life of the mind, and made up of creative and highly secular individuals, has been very much in existence. Those studied by Leuba in 1914 and those awarded the Nobel Prize in the early years, between 1901 and 1950, had had their formative years in the nineteenth century (among those awarded the Nobel Prize before 1920, most were born before 1850).

Intellectualism and religiosity: explanations

The basic findings have been summarized by Feist and Gorman (1998, p. 13): "Scientists in general, and eminent scientists in particular, are conspicuous in … an almost complete absence of current religious faith." This has been noted whenever the subject has been studied (Eiduson and Beckman, 1973; Feist, 2006). The case of the United States, where most of the research has been done, presents us with a puzzle: a highly religious population, by all measures, produces a group of individuals who display a high degree of secularity. It is clear that academics should not be a representative sample of the population they came from, but this is a unique phenomenon historically and psychologically. What could be the proximate psychological processes involved?

It has been suggested that low religiosity does not appear in individual academics during the years of academic training, but results from the tendency of those already lower in religiosity to select an academic career (Beit-Hallahmi and Argyle, 1997; Ecklund and Scheitle, 2007; Wuthnow, 1985). There is a long process of selection and self-selection that produces an academic (Finkelstein, 1984). Much

TABLE 4.1 Nobel laureates 1901–2001 by religious affiliation

All fields									
Jewish	Protestant (denomination specified)	Catholic	Unitarian	Other	None	"Protestant" (no denomination)	"Christian" or "Most probably Christian"	"From X background"	No record
124	104	72	9	33	84	53	78 + 82	33	24
Total = 697									
Science									
Jewish	Protestant (Denomination specified)	Catholic	Unitarian	Other	None	"Protestant" (No denomination)	"Christian" or "Most probably Christian"	"From X background"	No record
94	69	33	6	15	47	39	58 + 59	24	12
Total = 467									

80 Explaining variations in religiosity

has to do with family background, as the values and ideals dominant in the family are crucial. Gross and Simmons (2006), looking at public opinion data in the United States, found that conservative political views, Republican Party affiliation, and evangelical identity are tied to lower confidence in higher education and ascribing less occupational prestige to professors. Sherkat (2011) found that sectarian Protestants, Catholics, and people with fundamentalist beliefs had significantly lower levels of scientific literacy when compared with secular Americans. This is likely to affect their aspirations and career choices.

Hardy (1974) noted that Catholics and conservative Protestants were underrepresented in academia, and related this to values and ideals. Intellectualism means independence, which is not promoted in highly religious families. Granger and Price (2007) found that individuals holding fundamentalist beliefs and having been raised in a fundamentalist family are much less likely to pursue academic science training. Both religious commitment and an academic career can be predicted quite early on, in adolescence. Academics and scientists are expected to excel in critical thinking, originality, and independence. The early experiences of a gifted child in an environment that values academic achievement and independence would lead to the choice of an academic or professional career. Curiosity, intellectualism, critical or skeptical thought, and/or personal dedication to a branch of knowledge could be recognized by age eighteen in many adolescents (Hardy, 1974; Hoge and Keeter, 1976; Roe, 1952), and some of these qualities emerge much earlier. Ecklund, Park, and Veliz (2008) noted that age sixteen was a turning point, with future academics switching to a nonaffiliated status at that age.

A psychodynamic interpretation would suggest that, in addition to their creativity and high intelligence, some of these individuals had a strong wish to create distance between themselves and their parents. Eiduson (1962) described the individuals in her group of highly eminent scientists as intellectually gifted children, whose fathers were often absent, had limited intimacy with their families, and found nurturance in intellectual life, turning to reading, puzzles, and fantasies. They valued logic and emotional control, built a set of "intellectual fences" to defend themselves against problems or disturbances at home, came to value innovation and difference, while tolerating the ambiguity and uncertainty which this might create, and developed into intellectual rebels, channeling their aggressions into their academic work.

Personality traits and religiosity

How are individual differences in religiosity related to personality? Dittes (1969) offered an individual deficiency framework combining personality traits and situational pressures when he stated that religion "is associated with awareness of personal inadequacies, either generally or in response to particular crisis or threat situations … with a strong responsiveness to the suggestions of other persons or other external influences; and with an array of what may be called desperate and generally unadaptive defensive maneuvers" (p. 616). This is reminiscent of Freud's notion of religion as wish fulfillment in response to the human condition (Freud, 1927; see Chapter 8).

Regarding the search for the "religious personality," here is one summary:

> What we are able to conclude about the modal believer or religious person in Western society today is that person is probably more conventional, more likely to be a female, older rather than younger, unmarried, of lower education, more likely to be authoritarian, dogmatic and suggestible than is the non-religious person.
>
> (Beit-Hallahmi and Argyle, 1997, p. 251)

One possible research strategy in the search for the "religious personality" could be to look at the lowest end of the religiosity continuum. Once we paint a picture of atheists, who proclaim an absence of supernaturalist beliefs, we can then ask whether the highly religious present a mirror-image. What we are able to conclude about the typical atheist in Western society today is that that person is more likely to be a male and with higher levels of education and income. We may also speculate about their mentalizing ability, analytical style, intelligence, and intellectualism, as reported above. Atheists are more liberal, less prejudiced, less authoritarian and suggestible, less dogmatic, more tolerant of others, law-abiding and compassionate. Such findings have been reported in the United States, Australia, and Canada (Beit-Hallahmi, 2007). Atheists may be alienated non-conformists in some countries, but they may be conformists in the Czech Republic or in Eastern Germany, where they constitute a majority. About their subjective well-being there is no consensus. It is interesting to note that Maslow (1970), in a study of the fifty-seven individuals in history he judged to be self-actualized, having achieved the highest level of personality development, included very few religious individuals.

Are the highly religious just the opposite of atheists? The picture is more complex, first because of the many assessment instruments and the theoretical concepts involved. In this chapter and in Chapters 5, 6, and 7, a more detailed picture will be presented.

Individual differences in attachment

Attachment theory, which grew out of psychoanalysis (see Chapter 8), describes the process of developing security (or insecurity) feelings in the child and their consequences in adulthood. Attachment theory assumes that interpersonal styles in adults, namely the ways of dealing with attachment, separation, and loss in close personal relationships, stem directly from the mental models of oneself and others that were developed during infancy and childhood.

With an emphasis on panhuman experiences and innate tendencies, Bowlby's attachment theory proposed that the infant's early experiences with caregivers determined the internal working models (IWMs) that were central to individual

82 Explaining variations in religiosity

personality formation. In his own words, his main departure from everything his colleagues stood for is as follows:

> No variables have more far-reaching effects on personality development than a child's experiences within the family. Starting during his first months in his relation to both parents, he builds up working models of how attachment figures are likely to behave towards him in any of a variety of situations, and on all those models are based all his expectations, and therefore all his plans, for the rest of his life.
>
> (Bowlby, 1973, p. 369)

The theory assumes that the human baby is hard-wired to seek a caretaker and find security as soon as it comes out of the womb (Bowlby, 1969, 1973). This search is either met with success, leading to a sense of security (in most cases), or fails with lifelong insecurity as a result (Bowlby, 1973). For evolutionary adaptive reasons the child is motivated to develop an IWM of attachment to significant others, based on actual experiences with the primary caregiver in infancy. Bowlby (1969) posited that the internal working models of self and parent prefigure adult expectations regarding the worthiness of the self and the availability and responsiveness of others in general.

Bowlby's IWM includes beliefs about self-worth, about trusting others, and about closeness in intimate relationships. The mother's sensitivity to the infant's needs is a condition for the formation of a secure attachment. Security in attachment leads to competence, autonomy, and sociability later on. The notion of the family as the secure base from which the developing child is able to explore the world with confidence is central. Beyond universal experiences, individual differences are accounted for by individual histories. Attachment styles can be characterized as secure, avoidant, or anxious/ambivalent. Secure adults find it relatively easy to get close to others. Avoidant adults are somewhat uncomfortable being close to others. Anxious/ambivalent adults find that others are reluctant to get as close as they would like.

Kirkpatrick (2005) argued that attachment theory includes all the universal components and individual difference components that are crucial in order to answer the normative question (Why are people religious?) and the question of interpersonal differences (Why are different people religious in different ways?). How does attachment theory account for religion? Religion stems from the basic search for an object, which may be construed as the attempt to recapitulate the original (real or imagined) closeness with the mother, and leads us throughout life towards intimate relations with other human beings, or towards devotion to imaginary religious objects.

Individual differences in childhood attachment experiences should result in interpersonal differences in religious faith later on in life: "perceptions of having a personal relationship with a parent-like deity, can well be understood as manifestations of an evolved psychological system called the *attachment system*"

(Kirkpatrick, 2005, p. 16). Fantasies of a personal relationship with a parent-like deity or supernatural agent can be found in all traditions. Such patterns of submissive identification seem to be panhuman and must have grown out of our evolutionary history. This interpretation clearly follows Sigmund Freud's ideas about childhood experiences and god as a father image (see Chapter 8).

Attachment theory looks at variations in early experiences and IWM formation, and tries to predict the resulting patterns of religious beliefs: "To the extent that religion really does involve the activation and operation of the attachment system, individual differences in attachment experience should be related to individual difference in religious belief" (Kirkpatrick, 2005, p. 125). At the group level, different parenting styles are related to cultural differences in religious beliefs: "behavioral patterns of IWMs ... lead ... to certain ways of thinking about God and the perception of some kind of God-beliefs as plausible ... another kind of parenting reliably produces a different pattern. Which kind of belief about God has the most staying power in a given culture depends largely on whatever particular attachment schemata are prevalent or normative in that culture, which in turn depends on the kinds of early attachment experience people typically experience in those cultures" (Kirkpatrick, 2005, p. 125). Granqvist, Mikulincer, and Shaver (2010) suggested that religious beliefs satisfy relational concerns and in particular attachment needs. The imagined relationship with God in religious believers is an attachment relationship and is especially beneficial to individuals who are insecurely attached (Kirkpatrick and Shaver, 1992). A more secure attachment to God serves as a stress buffer and helps individuals who had suffered a personal loss in coping with grief (Ellison *et al.*, 2012; Kelley and Chan, 2012). In a study of 400 adults in the United States, those having an avoidant attachment style were most likely to identify themselves as either atheist or agnostic (Kirkpatrick, 2005).

Only a few studies tested the theory on children. De Roos, Idedema, and Miedma (2001) tested an attachment model of differences in God concepts among kindergarteners. Subjects were seventy-two kindergarteners (mean age sixty-three months) from two elementary schools. Children's concepts of self, other, and God were measured using structured questionnaires. Harmony and closeness in the teacher–child relationship predicted a loving God concept, but a punishing concept of God was not related to any of the independent variables. This was explained by the children's internal working models of self. Cassibba, Granqvist and Costantini (2013) tested whether mothers' security of attachment predicted their children's sense of God's closeness. A total of seventy-one mother–child dyads participated (children's mean age=7.5). Children were told stories about attachment-activating or attachment-neutral situations, and then were asked to indicate God's closeness to the children in the stories. Children of secure mothers indicated greater closeness than children of insecure mothers. The mothers' religiosity and attachment to God were unrelated to the outcomes.

Research on adults has shown that individual differences in attachment styles are related to individual differences in religiosity. Attachment to parents has proven to predict adolescent and adult religiosity (Granqvist, 2002). Securely attached adults

84 Explaining variations in religiosity

exhibit more stable religiosity, close to the one they were raised with (Granqvist 2002; Granqvist and Hagekull 1999; Granqvist and Hagekull 2000). A study of college students found that with an increase in adult attachment anxiety, the frequency of petitionary prayer went up (Byrd and Boe, 2001). Individuals with insecure attachment displayed an emotion-based religiosity marked by relatively sudden changes (Granqvist and Hagekull 1999; Kirkpatrick, 1997, 1998).

Individuals without a love relationship were found to be more religiously active (Granqvist and Hagekull, 2000; Kirkpatrick, Shillito and Kellas, 1999; Granqvist and Hagekull, 2003). Granqvist and Kirkpatrick (2004) found that individuals who described their mothers as cold and distant were more likely to have had religious conversions, and that such conversions should be viewed as a fantasy compensation for an attachment deficit. Granqvist and Hagekull (2001) found that a childhood insecure attachment to the mother were strongly related to holding positive beliefs about astrology, the occult, "parapsychology," and UFOs in a Swedish sample (see Chapter 9 for additional findings on "New Age").

Authoritarianism

Authoritarianism is a belief complex that combines conformity, submission to authority, respect for tradition, and hostility towards out-groups. The original F-Scale (Adorno *et al.*, 1950) contained the following items, which are still being used today, among others:

> Young people sometimes get rebellious ideas, but as they grow older they ought to get over it and accommodate.
> Our social problems would be largely solved, if we could somehow get rid of immoral, dishonest and simple-minded people.
> What we need are fewer laws and institutions, and more courageous, indefatigable, and devoted leaders, in whom the people can put their faith.

Studies since the 1950s have found that authoritarianism is on average greater for individuals with the most orthodox beliefs, and is highest for Catholics and fundamentalists. This trait has been found to correlate with religiosity in studies all over the world. It was also found to hold for Moslem fundamentalists, in a study of students at Kuwait University, and for Moslem, Hindu, and Jewish fundamentalists in Canada (Beit-Hallahmi and Argyle, 1997). Rubinstein (1996) found the religiosity–authoritarianism correlation among Moslem Palestinians and among Jewish Israelis. Hunsberger, Owusu, and Duck (1999) found that right-wing authoritarianism and religious fundamentalism were correlated in samples of Moslem and Christian university students in Ghana, but a study of 267 Moslem students in Indonesia found that only intrinsic religiosity, but not doctrinal orthodoxy was tied to authoritarianism (Ji and Ibrahim, 2007). Van Pachterbeke, Freyer, and Saroglou (2011) found that a combination of religiosity and authoritarianism reduces pro-social reactions.

Cognitive processing

It has long been suggested that religiosity is tied to rigid, stereotypical thinking, expressed in an intolerance of ambiguity and uncertainty (Furnham and Ribchester, 1995; Watson *et al.*, 1999). Sagioglou and Forstmann (2013) found that, in a field study in Western Europe, a religious setting increased ambiguity intolerance, and exposure to Christian religious concepts among European respondents increased self-reported ambiguity intolerance and judgment certainty about social judgments. Rokeach (1960) defined a dimension of personality which he called "dogmatism," or the "closed mind." Individuals who scored high on his dogmatism scale were found in experiments to be rigid in their thinking, intolerant of ambiguity, and unable to deal with new information. Rokeach found among American students that Roman Catholics had the highest dogmatism scores, followed by Protestants, with nonbelievers having the lowest scores. This was confirmed in later studies, except that Protestants in the American South had higher scores than Catholics (Beit-Hallahmi and Argyle, 1997). In a study of 532 US Roman Catholic adolescents and their parents, it was found that those described as "indisriminately antireligious" were the lowest on dogmatism, compared to all others (Thompson, 1974). Not surprisingly, political conservatism has also been associated with dogmatism.

The concept of need for closure has been proposed as a trait broader than dogmatism (Webster and Kruglanski, 1994). It has been described as "the desire for a definite answer on some topic, any answer as opposed to confusion and ambiguity" (Kruglanski, 1989, p. 14). Saroglou (2002b) administered the Need for Closure Scale (NFCS), the Religious Fundamentalism Scale, and a religiosity scale to 239 respondents. Fundamentalism and religiosity predicted a high need for closure.

The Big Five dimensions

The Big Five dimensions of personality, widely accepted and applied, are Openness, Conscientiousness, Extraversion, Agreeableness, and Neuroticism. Hills *et al.* (2004) and Robbins *et al.* (2010) suggested that there was possibly no relationship between religiosity and the Big Five dimensions, and Paunonen and Jackson (2000) suggested that Big Five dimensions accounted for only 7 percent of the variance in religiosity.

Saroglou (2002a, 2010) and Lodi-Smith and Roberts (2007) conducted independent meta-analytic reviews of studies on the Big Five correlates of religiosity, with most studies done on students from North America. Both reviews concluded that the traits of Agreeableness (warm and kind) and Conscientiousness (responsible and goal driven) were correlated with religiosity, though the correlations were low. Other studies (McCullough, Tsang and Brion, 2003; McCullough *et al.*, 2005; Taylor and MacDonald, 1999) reported similar findings. In a meta-analysis of Big Five personality traits, non-believers were shown to be more open to new experience, less extroverted, less conscientious, and less neurotic than believers (Roccas *et al.*, 2002).

86 Explaining variations in religiosity

Galen and Kloet (2011) challenged these findings and their interpretation. Although church members were higher in Agreeableness and Conscientiousness, they suggested that these findings were largely eliminated when controlling for demographic variables. They argued that the one personality dimension which distinguished religious church members from secular individuals was Openness (i.e. intellectual, unconventional). This was suggested already by McCrae (1999), one of the fathers of the Big Five model. High scorers on Openness tend to be nonconforming and liberally minded (Roccas et al., 2002; Schwartz and Huismans, 1995). Duriez, Soenens, and Beyers (2004) reported that Openness was negatively related to orthodoxy, and according to Streib et al. (2010), apostates have higher scores on Openness. Krauss et al. (2006) reported negative correlations between Openness, authoritarianism, and fundamentalism. So there is much agreement on low Openness being tied to religiosity, and the disagreement is about other Big Five traits. It is interesting to note that similar findings have been reported in research on the correlations between Big Five and political commitments. Openness has been found to be negatively correlated with conservative political attitudes (Gerber et al., 2010; McCrae, 1996; Mondak et al., 2010).

Self-enhancement and religiosity

When individuals are asked to describe themselves in terms of stable traits or actual behavior, accuracy cannot be expected. It is not just a matter of cognitive limitations, but of the motivation to describe oneself favorably, following cultural norms. According to Batson (2011), self-reports should not be used to establish motives, because people might not know why they have done something or if they do know they might not be willing to tell. This is true regardless of religiosity, but it has been repeatedly shown that religiosity is correlated with positively exaggerated self-presentation, or self-enhancement. It has been assumed that individuals differ in the dispositions towards a socially desirable self-presentation, and that variation in self-presentation is related to religiosity (Sedikides and Gebauer, 2010). Religious individuals will present themselves, when asked, in a more positive light than their non-religious peers, demonstrating the effects of "social desirability" or "impression management" (Batson, Naifeh and Pate, 1978; Gillings and Joseph 1996; Pearson and Francis, 1989; Trimble, 1997).

In another form of self-enhancement, most people tend to describe themselves as above average on desirable characteristics, and the phenomenon has been called the better-than-average effect (BAE). Eriksson and Funcke (2014) analyzed self-judgments of desirable characteristics in fifteen nations and found that the BAE was stronger in more religious countries. In two online surveys of 1,000 Americans, the BAE was stronger among more religious individuals. In an experimental setting, reminders of religious beliefs increase impression management concerns among believers (Gervais and Norenzayan, 2012a).

Some researchers have proposed that the connection between self-enhancement and religiosity isn't just correlational, but causal. Batson and Stocks (2004, p. 147) stated that "[f]eeling good about oneself and seeing oneself as a person of worth and value play a major role in much contemporary religion." Sedikides and Gebauer (2010) found that socially desirable responding (SDR) and religiosity were in a positive relation in samples that placed higher value on religiosity (United States > Canada > United Kingdom; Christian universities > secular universities). This was interpreted as showing that religiosity is partly driven by self-enhancement.

Values, personality, and attitudes

Values are defined by Schwartz (1992) as desirable, trans-situational goals, varying in importance, that serve as guiding principles in people's lives. Schwartz (1992) has proposed that motivational values can be classified into a number of distinct categories including universalism, benevolence, and power. The Schwartz list of values includes Achievement, Benevolence, Conformity, Hedonism, Power, Security, Self-direction, Stimulation, Tradition, and Universalism.

Schwartz and Huismans (1995) found that religiosity is positively related to values such as Tradition and Conformity that emphasize the preservation of the status quo and negatively related to values like Universalism, Stimulation, or Self-direction, which expresses openness to new experiences and change and to independent thinking. Further meta-analyses have led to the conclusion that religious people tend to favor values representing social and individual order (Tradition, Conformity, and to a lesser extent, Security) and to dislike values that promote openness to change and autonomy (Stimulation, Self-direction), while nonbelievers were more likely to endorse Universalism, Hedonism, Stimulation, Self-direction, Achievement, and Power (Saroglou, 2010; Saroglou, Delpierre

TABLE 4.2 The Schwartz list of values

Power	Social status and prestige, control or dominance over people and resources.
Achievement	Personal success through demonstrating competence according to social standards.
Hedonism	Pleasure and sensuous gratification for oneself.
Stimulation	Excitement, novelty, and challenge in life.
Self-direction	Independent thought and action-choosing, creating, exploring.
Universalism	Understanding, appreciation, tolerance, and protection for the welfare of all people and for nature.
Benevolence	Preservation and enhancement of the welfare of people with whom one is in frequent personal contact.
Tradition	Respect, commitment, and acceptance of the customs and ideas that traditional culture or religion provide the self.
Conformity	Restraint of actions, inclinations, and impulses likely to upset or harm others and violate social expectations or norms.
Security	Safety, harmony, and stability of society, of relationships, and of self.

Source: Schwartz, 1992

88 Explaining variations in religiosity

and Dernelle, 2004). These differences parallel those in political tendencies. Caprara *et al.* (2006) questioned 3044 voters for the major coalitions in the Italian national election of 2001. In their preference for values, center-left voters were higher in Universalism, Benevolence, and Self-direction and lower in Security, Power, Achievement, Conformity, and Tradition. Reiss (2000) noted that self-reported religious salience was associated with high desire scores for honor and family, and with low desire scores for independence. In the United States, more religious parents have been found to favor obedience rather than autonomy in children, which is often perceived as tied to upholding traditional moral values. This finding has been consistently reported over many decades (Ellison and Sherkat, 1993; Starks and Robinson, 2007). Bouchard (2009) demonstrated that "traditionalism" (comprising authoritarianism, religiousness, and political conservatism, which correlate with each other to a high degree) may be a specific trait with high heritability.

Cultural specificity and individual traits

Recognizing the importance of cultural context and the interaction between individual dispositions and the cultural environment has been a major theoretical advance. Cultural religiosity interacts with commitments and personality traits in adult members of society. Galen and Kloet (2011) showed how individual traits interact with group membership within the same culture. Roccas and Schwartz (1997) proposed that relations between church and state in a given nation would affect the associations between values and religiosity. Data from Roman Catholic nations (n=2274) showed that in the nations with adversary relations between church and state in the preceding years (Poland, Czech Republic, Hungary), religiosity correlated more positively with Universalism, less positively with Conformity and Security, and more negatively with Power and Achievement, compared to nations with good relations between church and state (Italy, Spain, Portugal).

Gebauer, Paulhus, and Neberich (2013) looked at the traits of agency (reflecting competence, uniqueness, and ambition) and communion (reflecting warmth, relatedness, and morality) in relation to religiosity. Communion is the tendency to be concerned about closeness to others, while agency is the tendency to be self-interested and assertive. Communion may contribute to religiosity, while agency would be independent of religiosity. The authors assumed that because communal individuals conform to dominant culture, they would be more religious in religious cultures and least religious in nonreligious cultures, and because agentic individuals define themselves at a distance from the dominant culture, they would be most religious in nonreligious cultures and least religious in religious cultures. Data from 187,957 individuals in eleven cultures confirmed this hypothesis. The relations are not universal, but the assumption that communal individuals are conformists and agentic individuals are non-conformists is universally valid.

These findings, which connect variations in religiosity, individual differences, and culture, lead to the notion of the varying congruence between the individual and the surrounding religious environment.

5

WOMEN AND RELIGION

The greater religiosity of women, demonstrated in consistent research findings over the past 100 years, is one of the most important facts about religion. Most research on religion is in reality research about women, who are actively supporting, maintaining, and sometimes keeping alive religious establishments, institutions, and organizations worldwide (Beit-Hallahmi, 1989; Beit-Hallahmi and Argyle, 1997; Francis, 1997; Miller and Stark, 2002; Stark, 2002b). When we describe and interpret behavior tied to religiosity, it is likely that we are really describing typical female behaviors (Myers, 2012a). It has been claimed that women are attracted to more marginal religious groups: "The predominance of women in ecstatic, possession, mystical, and healing cults is a worldwide fact" (Ellwood, 1979, p. 68). However, more extensive research shows that women play a major role in sustaining mainstream denominations.

The difference between men and women had never been predicted by any general theories about religion. It often seems counter-intuitive, because religious organizations, institutions, and traditions are developed and controlled by men, often described as supporting the subordination of women. When we observe what religious doctrines everywhere say about women, the content and nature of male fantasies is clear and uniform. Women are the target of taboo and derision in most traditions, described as evil and impure (Piven, 2003). If the world of religious figures and ideas was created by men, reflecting their wishes, why are women so willing to adopt this masculine universe and commit themselves to it? Attempts to create an alternative female pantheon ("Goddess religions") have clearly failed (see Chapter 8).

We can describe the belief universe of the committed religious believer anywhere as a pyramid, made of three tiers. The top of the pyramid is the religious pantheon, populated by imaginary, invisible creatures. Then we have actual humans who constitute the religious hierarchy. The broad base of the pyramid is

90 Women and religion

made up of the followers, who are the largest group, made up mostly of women. A study of 1376 religious congregations in a large American city found that the ratio of women to men among members was almost two to one (65.25 percent and 34.75 percent respectively), but only 11 percent of congregations (significantly smaller ones) were headed by women (Cnaan and Helzer, 2004). A similar gap in terms of membership and leadership, regardless of egalitarian ideology, was observed in two Theravada Buddhism groups in the United States (Cadge, 2004). As we get closer to the top of this pyramid, we find fewer and fewer females. The pantheon, which includes gods, angels, demons, founders, and prophets, has only a minority of women (Carroll, 1979).

Women's religiosity has been interpreted as a hidden rebellion:

> For thousands of years women had rebelled. They had made a fortress of religion—had buried themselves in the cloister, in self-sacrifice, in good works—or even in bad ... always busy in the illusions of heaven or of hell ... the Church had been made by the woman chiefly as her protest against man ... the man had overthrown the Church chiefly because it was feminine.
>
> (Adams, 1931, p. 446)

If there was a rebellion, it remained invisible.

The findings

Overall religiosity measures

Data on levels of religiosity for men and women in forty-nine Western and eight non-Western cultures (Japan, Taiwan, China, South Korea, India, Albania, Azerbaijan, and Turkey) show that in every single case women are more likely to describe themselves as religious, as compared with men, with ratios ranging from 1.05 in Brazil to 1.69 in Estonia (Stark, 2002b). In the largest data pool anywhere in the world, women in the United States have been found to score significantly higher than men on all measures of religiosity used in public opinion polls (Gallup and Lindsay, 1999). Sullins (2006) reported that being female was significantly correlated with self-reported religiosity among Catholics, Protestants, Hindus, and Buddhists. Inglehart and Norris (2003) reported on religiosity in seventy-four nations (including eight Moslem majority nations, India, China, and Brazil), divided into three levels of economic development, i.e. agrarian (21), industrial (32), and post-industrial (21). Women were more religious than men in all of them. The differences were largest in post-industrial nations and smallest in the agrarian ones.

Anderson (1993) reported that in the Soviet Union a higher level of religiosity among women was observed in both the European republics, with their Christian heritage, and in the republics of Central Asia, historically part of the Islamic world. González (2011) found that in Kuwait, the overall level of religiosity was uniformly high, but women still outscored men in self-ratings of religiosity. The significantly higher religiosity of Jewish women in the United States (where about 40 percent of world Jews live) has been noted in numerous surveys (Hartman and Hartman, 2011).

Describing religiosity in Russia, Belarus, and the Ukraine in the post-communist era, (Titarenko, 2008) reports that in all three nations women make up the majority of believers. Older women are always the most committed group: "religion is more important for women rather than for men, and more important for the older generation" (2008, p. 249). Czechs are highly secular and Slovaks highly devout, and the two nations share much of their history, but women score higher than men on religiosity in both (Froese, 2005). In the Ukraine in the 1990s, 50.9 percent of women, but only 36.3 percent of men described themselves as religious (Gee, 1995). In Russia in 1996, among those who defined themselves as believers, 31 percent were men and 69 percent women, while among those defining themselves as atheists, 29 percent were women, and 71 percent men (Kääriäinen, 1999). In surveys since 2000, where Russian religiosity levels have been growing, females still lead the trend (Evans and Northmore-Ball, 2012). A 2005 survey in Korea showed that 50 percent of the men and 40 percent of women defined themselves as non-religious (Kim et al., 2009). In another large-scale survey of 6172 Koreans, women made up 64 percent of 1320 Buddhists, 64 percent of 1465 Protestants, 67 percent of 472 Catholics, and only 47 percent of 2915 atheists (Park et al., 2012). Liu (2010) reported women in Taiwan to be more religious.

Sex differences appear already among children. Girls demonstrate higher levels of religious observance, belief, and experience than boys (Donahue and Benson, 1995; Flor and Knapp, 2001; Kay and Francis, 1996; Levitt, 2003; Smith et al., 2003; Regnerus, Smith and Smith, 2004). The same is true for adolescents (Benson, Donahue and Erickson, 1989) and for college students (Bryant, 2007). Religiosity rises with age, but older women are significantly more religious than older men (Levin, Taylor and Chatters, 1994).

In a study of highly gifted individuals, who showed outstanding mathematical (and verbal) abilities at age thirteen, and went on to academic and creative careers, the Allport-Vernon-Lindzey Study of Values, which measures interest in six themes: Theoretical, Economic, Political, Aesthetic, Social, and Religious, was given at age thirteen and at age thirty-three. The highest scores for males both times were Theoretical, Economic, and Political. For females it was Social, Aesthetic, and Religious (Lubinski, Schmidt and Benbow, 1996). In the Terman longitudinal study of highly gifted children (who were generally low on religiosity; see Chapter 4), women were more likely to be religious (McCullough et al., 2005). A survey of Canadian psychiatrists (718 men and 457 women) found that the women were significantly higher on all measures of religiosity (Baetz et al., 2004).

Women's commitment to religion means that the extent and meaning of secularization actually depends on them (Aune, Sharma and Vincett, 2009). Among those with little or no religious beliefs, agnostics and atheists, the probability of finding women is low. In atheist organizations in the US, women make up around 7 percent of the membership (Beit-Hallahmi, 2007). In surveys, men make up 70 percent of those who describe themselves as atheists, and 75 percent of those choose the term "agnostic" (Keysar, 2007). In representative surveys of the US and Canadian populations, the unaffiliated were found to be mostly male (Feigelman, Gorman and Varacalli, 1992; Hadaway, 1989; Veevers and Cousineau, 1980).

Beliefs and attitudes

The differences between men and women in belief are not always large, but they are most consistent. Demertzi *et al.* (2009) found that women were more likely to believe mind and brain are separate and that some spiritual part of humans survives death. Women in the United States were 1.34 times more likely than men to believe in an afterlife and a World Value Survey of 132,746 adults in 71 nations in 1990–1997 showed that women are 1.36 times more likely to believe in an afterlife (Roth and Kroll, 2007). In Sweden in 1956, 52 percent of men and 72 percent of women believed "in a God who oversees the world" (Tomasson, 1968).

Islamic doctrine includes the belief in Jinn, spirits who may become malevolent and possess humans, and in the "evil eye." Khalifa *et al.* (2011) and Mullick *et al.* (2013) surveyed Moslems in Britain and in Bangladesh, and found that females were significantly more likely to hold beliefs about Jinn and the "evil eye" and about their causative role in physical and mental illnesses. In the United States, women have been more likely to believe in the existence of Satan, hell, and demons (Baker, 2008a).

Men are more likely than women to change their affiliation (Hayes, 1996), and women are more conservative or orthodox, holding firmly to central and traditional beliefs in any religion (Gay and Ellison, 1993; Roald, 2001). The differences are especially striking in cultures with an overall low level of religiosity. Such is the case with post-communist Russia, where the rate of belief in God was found to be 32 percent for men, and 57 percent for women (White, McAllister and Krishtanovskaya, 1994).

Jelen and Wilcox (1995) found that women in the United States, more than men, wanted government to support all religious groups, contrary to the majority understanding of the constitution, and women were significantly more likely to support prayers in public schools, ruled to be unconstitutional in 1962 (Schwadel, 2013). In a survey of forty nations (which included the Moslem majority nations of Bangladesh and Turkey, European and American nations, as well as India and Japan) Karakoç and Baskan (2012) found that women were less likely to support secularization of national politics.

We can speak of a dimorphic religious imagination, with women holding different images of deities and saints. For them God is seen more as a healer, supportive, loving, comforting, and forgiving, rather than instrumental (Nelsen, Cheek and Hau, 1985; Sered, 1987), while males see him as a supreme power, a driving force, a planner and controller (Wright and Cox, 1967).

Religious experiences

The ratios of women to men among those reporting religious experiences in response to surveys are 1.32 in Britain (Hay, 1982), and 1.20 in the USA (Back and Bourque, 1970). This difference is found in childhood and at age nine to ten more girls say they have experienced "God's closeness" (Tamminen, 1994). Women are also more likely to report apparitions and contacts with deceased relatives (Greeley, 1987; Kalish and Reynolds, 1973; MacDonald, 1992; Zimdars-Swartz, 1991). Almost 90 percent of stigmatization cases, in which Christian believers display skin lesions which represent wounds attributed to Jesus in Christian mythology, have involved single young women, who were often members of religious orders (Whitlock and Hynes, 1978). Women make up the majority of participants in possession cults (Lewis, 1966).

Ritual attendance

This is the most visible indicator of sex differences. If we visit places of worship around the world, we will immediately realize that (older) women make up the majority of those in attendance. This has been noted often: "In the 1950s, the sociologist Gabriel Le Bras said that when religious practice declines the last block of faithful at Sunday Mass consists of old women" (Dogan, 2002, p. 141). Data from 2004–2005 on self-reported worship attendance in twenty-two European countries showed women to be higher in every single case. In France, 4.9 percent of men and 8.7 percent of women reported attending regularly, while 57.9 percent of men and 45.0 percent of women never attended. In Denmark, 2.5 percent of men and 3.6 percent of women reported attending regularly, while 40.3 percent of men and 25.8 percent of women reported never attending. In Portugal, 19.7 percent of men and 35.9 percent of women reported attending regularly, while 31.6 percent of men and only 16.7 percent of women reported never attending (Nicholson, Rose and Bobak, 2009). Anthropological observations in India indicate that women make up the majority of those attending Hindu temples.

In traditions where ritual attendance by women is ignored or discouraged, such as Islam and Judaism, this is naturally reversed (Anderson, 1993; González, 2011; Loewenthal, MacLeod and Cinnirella, 2002; Roth and Kroll, 2007; Sullins, 2006). In the Islamic world, while women are discouraged from attending mosque services, they dominate some popular practices, such as pilgrimages to saints' tombs. In these sanctuaries, a popular "women's religion" is practiced (Mernissi, 1977). Television rituals are the perfect opposite of pilgrimage, but we know that among viewers of televangelists in the United States, women are over-represented (Buddenbaum, 1981; Stacey and Shupe, 1982).

If we look at reported private prayer, outside of religious services, the sex ratio is higher here than for any other religious activity. Gorer (1955) found a ratio of 1.87 for English adults. In a survey of adults in the United States, 18.8 percent of men and 8.8 percent of women reported never praying, while 20.3 percent of men

94 Women and religion

and 36.2 percent of women reported praying several times a day, for a ratio of 1.78 (Baker, 2008b), and similar differences are reported for private Bible reading (Roth and Kroll, 2007). Pargament (1997) found that in the United States, individuals who claim that praying helps are predominantly women, and when prayers are unanswered, women will produce "God-serving justifications" (Sharp, 2013).

Popular and para-religious beliefs

Here the differences between men and women are even more robust than those relating to institutional religion. Women are eager customers for practices which promise direct contacts with the world of the spirits or claim to operate with help from invisible powers and energies. They are much more likely to believe in astrology, ghosts, "psychic healing," reincarnation, "telepathy," and fortune-telling, and this has been confirmed in numerous cultures (Adams, Easthope and Sibbritt, 2003; Belyaev, 2011; Emmons and Sobal, 1981; Lindeman and Aarnio, 2007; MacDonald, 1994; Markle, Petersen, and Wagenfeld, 1978; Mencken, Bader and Kim, 2009; Rice, 2003; Vyse, 1997; Wuthnow, 1976; Zeidner and Beit-Hallahmi, 1988). The typical occult believer has been characterized as a female with little education (Zusne and Jones, 1982), but sex differences persist even among the better educated. In 1999, a survey of 3569 university students in Argentina, Brazil, Colombia, Uruguay, the United States, Austria, Germany, Great Britain, Italy, and Portugal found that females were both more religious and more involved in esoteric beliefs and practices (Höllinger and Smith, 2002).

Glendinning and Bruce (2006) found that women are more likely to be involved with divination (horoscopes, astrology, fortune-telling and tarot), as well as with "alternative medicine." Most of the customers for "alternative medicine" have been female (Kellner and Wellman, 1997; Millar, 1997; Shapiro, 2008; Singh and Edzard, 2008). Bader (2003) noted that among those claiming to have been abducted by UFOs or being ritual abuse survivors they are respectively 63 percent and 100 percent female.

The typical "New Age" customer is a middle-aged woman (Driskell and Lyon, 2011; Farias, Claridge and Lalljee, 2005; Heelas and Woodhead, 2005; Streiker, 1991). Streiker (1991, p. 50) stated that the "New Age ... is largely of, by, and for women." Research on spirituality, just like research on "New Age," shows that women make up the majority of followers, and Mencken, Bader, and Kim (2009, p. 77) suggested that "[s]pirituality may be perceived as a form of femininity" (cf. Furseth, 2005; Glendinning and Bruce, 2006). Heelas and Woodhead (2005) stated that 80 percent of those involved as either practitioners or clients in what they call self-spiritualities, are female (more on "New Age" and spirituality in Chapter 9).

Summarizing the research on religiosity in women, we see that the most pronounced differences are found in measures of belief, which constitute the core of religiosity. The generalization is statistical, which means that not all women are more religious than all men, but any woman chosen randomly anywhere in the world will be more religious than a man similarly chosen. The findings are clearly not tied to Christianity or Western culture, and are just as pronounced in such cultures as India, Japan, China, Israel, Ethiopia, and Turkey (Inglehart and Norris, 2003; Stark, 2000; Wondimu, Beit-Hallahmi and Abbink, 2001).

Deprivation and women's religiosity

Deprivation and frustration are likely to increase religiosity (Chapter 4). In many cultures today, being a woman still means being powerless, illiterate, and poor. Reporting on the greater religiosity of women in the Soviet Union and then in post-communist Russia, Anderson quotes an unnamed tourist guide "who explained that there were greater numbers of women in church 'because women suffer more'" (Anderson, 1993, p. 209). It is clear that while both men and women share the human condition, their locations, real and imagined, in human power structures are far apart (Woodhead, 2008).

Men control all human institutions and organizations, and the status of women in religion, both in the imagined pantheon and in real organizations, reproduces the lot of women in most human collectivities. "There is not a single society known where women-as-a-group have decision-making power *over* men or where they define the rules of sexual conduct or control marriage exchanges" (Lerner, 1986, p. 30). When being female is coupled with lack of attachments, religious involvement is more likely (Beit-Hallahmi and Argyle, 1997). Anderson (1993) reported on "surveys which demonstrated that up to 50 per cent of many congregations were single women" (p. 209).

Sexuality is one area where women are deprived and victimized. Women have rarely had the freedom to express their sexual impulses. Moreover, women in all cultures suffer from predatory male sexuality. Beit-Hallahmi (1997) suggested that religions sometimes offer women a shelter from the male mode of defining and controlling sexuality, which views women as sex objects and regards unattached women as easy prey. Religion sacralizes maternity, which is another shelter from male advances. We know that in some religious movements founded or dominated by women (Shakers in the United States or Brahma Kumaris in India), chastity becomes the rule, and sexuality is avoided. Such groups will have only a few male members. Some reports of mystical experiences in women have been interpreted as reflecting diverted sexual energy (Beit-Hallahmi, 1996).

Coercive sexual experiences create lifelong suffering, and childhood sexual abuse is a shattering experience. Women who report childhood abuse are two and a half times more likely to be depressed in adulthood, and over three times more likely to be depressed if they experienced both physical and sexual abuse (Wise *et al.*, 2001). Victimization naturally leads to increased fear and insecurity. Deprivation creates openness to supernaturalist consoling messages and often leads members of oppressed groups to imaginary compensations and magical acts (Beit-Hallahmi, 1989, 1992).

The finding that women are the majority of participants in possession cults has been explained as arising from two forms of deprivation. First, women's diet in many cultures is inferior to men's, and vitamin and calcium deficiencies affect the nervous system and create what is judged culturally to be a possession state (Kehoe and Giletti, 1981; Wallace, 1961). It has also been proposed that while nutrient deficiency may play a role, it is the stresses and strains in the lives of women that create the setting for possession states (Raybeck, Shoobe and Grauberger, 1989). In both instances, women react to oppression by men, who deprive them of an adequate diet and then hold the power and deny them the support that would relieve their stressful experiences.

It has been noted that revivalist or fundamentalist movements around the world, active since the 1970s, have enjoyed support from women (Brink and Mencher, 1997; Hardacre, 1993). Women's support for Islamist movements has received much attention (Mahmood, 2005; Natchwey and Tessler, 1999). Blaydes and Linzer (2008) analyzed survey data from 11,462 Moslem men and 10,914 Moslem women in eighteen countries and concluded that support for fundamentalism among women (and men) was tied to having lower socioeconomic status and being poorly educated, and poorer countries were likely to have more women with fundamentalist beliefs. A traditional marriage and family life, prescribed by fundamentalists, were women's best chance for some economic and personal security under precarious conditions. In the relatively secular West, women are expected to develop an independent career and still be the homemakers. Because of the stress over multiple responsibilities, women are the majority of those involved in "spirituality" (Woodhead, 2009).

The evidence about the many deprivations women suffer seems sufficient to explain women's high investment in religion, but there is one clear problem. In many cases of hardship and suffering a whole population of both sexes shares the same conditions, but women still emerge as much more religious. When compared to other deprived and oppressed groups, women display a higher openness to supernaturalist beliefs. Rice (2003) found that in the case of para-religious ideas (astrology, ESP, ghosts, "psychic healing," and reincarnation) American women are more likely to be believers than African-Americans, thus suggesting a significant difference between oppressed groups. Women may constitute an oppressed group with a unique investment in religiosity, which may be conceived as not just quantitatively, but qualitatively, different. What is involved is an evolved pattern of feminine coping, which is most often, but not always, tied to biological sex.

Sex differences and religiosity

To explain sex differences in religiosity means suggesting how reported psychological and physiological sex differences are directly related to religious activities. Cataloging the findings that show significant differences between men and women is not enough. The task is that of locating the predisposing factors or predisposing conditions that would lead to a greater investment in super-naturalism.

Basic openness to beliefs

The first and most general question is about the encounter with the supernaturalist message. If religious beliefs are the product of universal cognitive mechanisms, then differences in their salience in any individual should be related to religiosity (Chapter 2). Willard and Norenzayan (2013) measured mentalizing, dualism, teleological thinking, and anthropomorphism, together with religious and para-religious beliefs, in 1412 individuals in North America.

Table 5.1 reports their findings on the differences between men and women.

As expected, women scored higher on religiosity, but also on each measure of the four cognitive mechanisms that are supposed to produce it. Female superiority on these scores is related to a greater openness to certain beliefs, and in this case "official" religiosity, para-religious beliefs, and life's-purpose beliefs, which are all related.

Mentalizing, or Theory of Mind, one of the mechanisms measured with women being superior (Table 5.1), is basic to supernaturalist thinking. It has been demonstrated that mentalizing deficits are indeed correlated with lower religiosity (Norenzayan, Gervais and Trzesniewski, 2012), and these deficits, which in their extreme form are connected to the autistic spectrum, are much more common in men.

Intuitive thinking style (Chapter 2) is positively related to religiosity (Pennycook et al., 2012; Shenhav, Rand and Greene, 2012). It has often been suggested "that women's behavior is more often directed by sensitivity and intuition" (Höllinger and Smith, 2002, p. 242), and, in terms of the dichotomy between intuitive and analytic style, it is clear that men think more analytically and less intuitively than women (Lieberman, 2000; Pacini and Epstein, 1999). King, Wood, and Mines (1990) found males scoring higher on critical thinking tests, and a survey of superstitious and pseudo-scientific beliefs of British secondary school students (n=2159) found that at all ages females were less skeptical than males (Preece and Baxter, 2000). The greater empathy of women (see below) acts to reduce critical thinking, and female neuro-hormones lead to the suppression of negative judgments, as shown by Bartels and Zeki (2004). Belenky et al. (1986), expressing a feminist viewpoint, described a feminine "learning style," which is open to new ideas, because doubts and disbelief are set aside and empathy is in charge. They recommend a "connected knowing" mode, which "precludes evaluation, because

TABLE 5.1 Male and female mean differences, adult sample

	Anthro	Teleology	Dualism	Mentalizing	Paranorm	Purpose	Religiosity
Male	3.14	4.70	3.68	19.09	2.63	4.58	4.61
Female	3.48	5.00	3.90	23.67	3.18	5.27	5.31

All differences are significant at the .001 level.

Source: Willard and Norenzayan, 2013, p. 386

98 Women and religion

evaluation puts the object at a distance, places itself above it, and quantifies a response to the object that should remain qualitative" (p. 101).

Studies of influenceability, suggestibility, and persuability have shown a consistent sex difference in favor of women (McGuire, 1969; Roberts, 1991). Eagly (1978) suggested that the greater influenceability of women may be explained as due to the propensity to yield, inherent in the female sex role, and to the tendency for women to be oriented to interpersonal goals in group settings more than men.

Psychological dimorphism

Over human evolutionary history, men and women have faced different problems and challenges in life (and largely, but not exclusively, each other) and therefore have differently evolved decision-making mechanisms and processes (Barash and Lipton, 2001; Campbell, 2002; Geary, 1998). Evolutionary psychologists have observed that women feel threatened by isolation and diminished intimacy, while men feel threatened by anything that smacks of diminished prestige and authority (Barash and Lipton, 2001).

The notion of a psychological dimorphism has been repeatedly proposed. In small-group interactions, women were the expressive leaders, while men were instrumental and goal-oriented (Parsons and Bales, 1955). Spence and Helmreich (1978) described the dichotomy of orientations in females and males as communion versus agency (see Chapter 4). Beck (1983) proposed two personality dimensions, sociotropy and autonomy, which may create a vulnerability to depression. Sociotropic individuals, mostly women, concerned about maintaining close relationships, may become depressed after experiencing an interpersonal failure or loss. Autonomous individuals, mostly men, are excessively concerned with their sense of self-worth, based on achievement and control. Blatt (1990) proposed two developmental courses: (1) "interpersonal relatedness," involving the development of the capacity to establish mature, satisfying, and reciprocal relationships with others; (2) "self-definition" focused on the development of a stable, positive self-definition. Not surprisingly, the first characterizes women, and the second, men.

Personality differences

There is much evidence for significant personality differences between men and women, including emotion processing and expression (Everhart et al., 2001). On standard personality inventories, women score higher on Affiliation and Nurturance, and men higher on Dominance and Aggression. Del Giudice, Booth, and Irwing (2012) used a United States sample of 10,261 individuals and the 16PF questionnaire, and found only 26 percent overlap in male and female distributions on personality dimensions. Individualism, low sociality, nonconformity (tied to dominance and testosterone), and a preference for logic in reasoning are more heavily male than female traits (Kenrick et al., 2010; Weisberg, DeYoung and Hirsh, 2011). There are sex differences in cognitive style, with women in many societies being more field dependent than men, except among the Inuit where conditions foster the independence and equality of both sexes (Berry, 1976; Witkin, Goodenough and Oltman, 1979).

Empathy, defined as the vicarious affective response to another person's feelings, is more pronounced in females (Feingold, 1994), and they tend to be more accurate judges of personality traits than men (Vogt and Colvin, 2003; Chan et al., 2011). Women are clearly readier to express feelings, admit dependence, and demonstrate interpersonal caring, sensitivity, and warmth. Fumagalli et al. (2009) found that men were more utilitarian in what was described as emotional and personal decision making and Fumagalli et al. (2010) concluded that the brain areas active in utilitarian decisions are organized differently in men and women.

In all cultures males are less nurturant and less emotionally expressive, while women are more submissive and passive, anxious, and dependent (Campbell, 2002). "[W]omen tend to manifest behaviors that can be described as socially sensitive, friendly, and concerned with others' welfare, whereas men tend to manifest behaviors that can be described as dominant, controlling, and independent" (Eagly, 1995, p. 154).

Adolescent self-esteem in females is based on appearance and close relationships, but on achievements in athletics and academics, and moral behavior in males (Harter, 1999). Men's self-esteem is susceptible to comparison with same-sex others only (Major, Sciacchitano and Crocker, 1993), but women's self-esteem is susceptible to comparisons with both women and men (Martinot et al., 2002; Guimond et al., 2006). Males score higher on standard measures of global self-esteem with the largest effect emerging in late adolescence (Kling et al., 1999). Block and Robins (1993) found that between the ages of fourteen and twenty-three, self-esteem in males rose, while in females it declined. At age twenty-three, women with high self-esteem valued relationships with others. At age twenty-three, men with high self-esteem were more emotionally distant and controlled in interpersonal relations.

Wrangham and Peterson (1996) proposed the Demonic Male Hypothesis, accounting for the innate and extreme violence of human males. Males are much more likely to die violently and to commit homicide and suicide at any age. They are responsible for 90 percent of violent acts worldwide, while women make up only 6.51 percent of murderers, and only 7.26 percent of robbers (Kanazawa and Still, 2000), but men have marched off to their deaths in war throughout history, and quite often they were not being violent, but extremely obedient in their willingness to be sacrificed.

Males exceed females on physically risky forms of sensation seeking and a variety of physically dangerous activities such as involvement in crime, dangerous sports, injury proneness, and volunteering for drug experiments or hazardous army combat (Zuckerman, 1994; Kerr and Vlaminkx, 1997; Poppen, 1995). As a result, there are large sex differences in mortality from accidents. Men risk their lives not only because of choice. What should be remembered is that every year about 2.3 million people die of work-related accidents and illnesses, and the vast majority are men, whose physical abilities are utilized in mines, fields, and construction sites to keep the world going.

Differences such as greater verbal and physical male aggressiveness and risk-taking seem to be innate (Geary, 1998), and all anti-social behavior is much rarer among women (Moffitt et al., 2001). Byrnes, Miller, and Schafer (1999) found women lower in risk taking in every area examined, but certain traits (intellectual risk taking and physical skills) produced larger differences. Females,

> express more fear, are more susceptible to anxiety, are more lacking in task confidence, seek more help and reassurance, maintain greater proximity to friends, score higher on social desirability, and at the younger ages at which compliance has been studied, are more compliant with adults.
>
> (Block, 1976, p. 307)

Sex differences in dominance emerge early in the preschool years and at about the same time in all cultures (Maccoby, 1988). As children, boys are observed to be competitive and aggressive. Girls are sociable and helpful, and enjoy social contact for its own sake. When boys are confronted with a conflict involving fairness they tend to argue it out or take their ball and go home, but girls will try to resolve the issue through compromise. If compromise fails, girls will generally change the activity rather than disband the group (Cyrus, 1993).

Females, starting in childhood, are less competitive than males, show less evidence of hierarchical organization in groups, are less interested in leadership, and are more concerned with maintaining relationships of mutuality and reciprocity (Campbell, 2002; Gabriel and Gardner, 1999). Women assume more responsibility for relationship maintenance and social support (Turner, 1994; Belle, 1982). Eibl-Eibesfeldt (1989) suggested that throughout human evolution, the social style of females provided the basis for maintaining the long-term stability of social groups. Vocational interest measures show males to be more object-oriented, and females more people-oriented (Lippa, 2005), and when looking at their paid work and careers women express more interpersonal and altruistic concerns than men (Marini et al., 1996). Douvan and Adelson (1966) stated that,

> For the girl the development of interpersonal ties ... forms the core of identity, and it gives expression to much of developing feminine eroticism ... What the girl achieves through intimate connection with others, the boy must manage by disconnecting, by separating himself and asserting his right to be distinct.
>
> (Douvan and Adelson, 1966, pp. 347–348)

The importance of close relationships for women, and especially friendship with other women, marks women's encounter with the human communities that convey the religious message. Women are more likely to become converts through a social network, while men act as more independent seekers. The effect of intimate attachments is clear also for de-conversions or defections (Wright, 1986). Sered (1994) studied religions dominated by women and found them to be characterized by intense in-group relationships. Brasher (1998) and Ozorak (1996) looked at women's activities in American congregations and concluded that relationships, especially with other women, were a major source of support and gratification.

Psychopathology

Neuroticism scores are lower in males, compared to females, and high levels of in-utero testosterone are associated with low neuroticism scores within-sex (Fink, Manning and Neave, 2004). There is much evidence showing that women have stronger guilt feelings, and are more intro-punitive than men (Wright, 1971). Women are more often diagnosed with disorders of internalized conflict, such as eating disorders, depression, cyclothymic disorder, panic disorder, and phobia, while men suffer more often from acting-out disorders, such as substance abuse and antisocial personality (Simon, 2002). In a 1996 survey of 1050 Americans, 447 females and 603 males, there were significant differences in ways of handling anger, with women choosing "Talked to someone else" and "Prayed for help from God" more often, and men choosing "Had a drink or took a pill" (Simon and Lively, 2010, p. 1566). Men score higher on measures of the Dark Triad, i.e. psychopathy, marked by callousness and limited empathy, Machiavellianism, marked by social charm and manipulativeness, and narcissism, marked by feelings of entitlement, superiority, vanity, and exploitive behavior (Jonason, Li and Czarna, 2013).

There is a consistent body of research indicating that women are more affected by stressful situations. Women are more than twice as likely as men to suffer from stress-related disorders, including major depressive disorder, post-traumatic stress disorder, and several anxiety disorders. Data from large-scale epidemiological surveys indicate that panic disorder is two and a half times more common in women than in men (Lewis-Hall *et al.*, 2002).

Apparently, estrogen makes the brain more vulnerable to stress, and high levels of estrogen may enhance responses to stress, making women more vulnerable to depression and post-traumatic stress disorder (PTSD) (Shansky *et al.*, 2004). The lifetime prevalence of PTSD for women, about 10.4 percent, is more than twice that for men. In the United States, it has been estimated that between 2.3 percent and 3.2 percent of men and between 4.5 percent and 9.3 percent of women meet the diagnostic criteria for major depressive disorder at any given moment (Depression Guideline Panel, 1993). Data from a representative survey of twenty-nine countries, including Britain, the United States, Japan, Mexico, Brazil, Nigeria, India, China and Turkey, showed that in every case women were more likely to be depressed (Hopcroft and Bradley, 2007). A survey of the American population in 1996 found that the prevalence of depressive symptoms in women was related to the higher level of intense and persistent anger (Simon and Lively, 2010).

Schizoaffective disorders are more common in women, while schizophrenia is more common in men. Borderline personality disorder (BPD), defined as "a pervasive pattern of instability of self-image, interpersonal relationships, and mood, beginning in early adulthood and present in a variety of contexts" (Majid, 2010, p. 116), is diagnosed in three-quarters of all cases in women. This finding has been confirmed cross-culturally (Huang *et al.*, 2014).

While bipolar disorder affects males and females in equal numbers, the disparity is clear in rates of major depression and subclinical depressive syndromes. The higher levels of depression found in women, starting in adolescence, has been explained as the result of "ruminative coping" or "overthinking," a tendency to focus inwardly and passively on one's emotions, and on negative experiences. The difference in rumination behavior, which may have an underlying biological cause (Parker and Brotchie, 2004), is thought to be directly related to depression, and it has been found as early as age nine (Nolen-Hoeksema, 2003).

On measures of the schizotypal personality, females score higher on Ideas of Reference and Odd Beliefs/Magical Thinking and Cognitive/Perceptual Dysfunction, while males score higher on No Close Friends and Constricted Affect (Raine, 1992). The "feminine" side of schizotypy is tied to reporting religious experiences (Beit-Hallahmi and Argyle, 1997).

Language and fantasy

Men and women use language differently. Tannen (1990) defined male to female communication as "cross-cultural communication," because "[w]omen speak and hear a language of connection and intimacy, while men speak and hear a language of status and independence" (Tannen, 1990, p. 42). Men tend to tell stories that make them look good, while women tell stories that make them look foolish. Women excel in listening, while men act as storytellers to raise their self-worth (Tannen, 1990, 1994).

Koppel, Argamon, and Shimoni (2003) found that female writing is "involved" while male writing is "informational." Male writing was typical of nonfiction while female writing was typical of fiction. Newman *et al.* (2008) analyzed a database of over 14,000 text files from 70 separate studies and found that women used more words related to feelings and social interaction, while men referred more to object properties and impersonal topics. Mulac *et al.* (2013) described what they call the gender-linked language effect (GLLE), where the language of females is perceived as reflecting higher socio-intellectual status and aesthetic quality and of males higher on dynamism, because women use more intensive adverbs, longer sentences, hedges, directives, dependent clauses, and sentence initial adverbials than men.

There are clear differences in the use of humor, with women initiating few humorous exchanges in groups, compared to men. Men create and circulate aggressive jokes, with women as targets, while women prefer less aggressive humor. Women stand-up comics use more self-directed humor (Brodzinsky and Rubien, 1976).

Women's dreams involve relationships and loss, while men are likely to dream about fighting, protecting, and competing, almost always with other men (Moffitt, Kramer and Hoffmann, 1993). A survey of 2,000 Germans about their nightmares found that for men nightmares about losing a job or violence were more common, while for women common themes were sexual harassment or losing a loved one (Schredl, 2010). When ready-made fantasies are consumed, women make up the audience for soap operas and romance novels (which account for nearly half of all fiction titles purchased in the developed world), while men watch aggressive sports, or follow "hard" political and economic news.

Conversion narratives by men focus on gaining status and/or interpersonal distance, while narratives from women might have more emphasis on relationships. Men tend to focus solely on themselves as the central character, whereas women tend to focus on someone other than themselves, and men describe themselves as clever whereas women describe themselves as foolish (Knight, Woods and Jindra, 2005).

The biological substratum

Some sex differences in basic anatomy and physiology are clear: men are larger than women, while women live longer and men suffer from higher mortality rates starting in infancy. Women reach maturity earlier than men, and men are more physically aggressive. The feminine complex of physiological and psychological traits, often thought of as reflecting weakness, confers a clear advantage in longevity. Despite their longer life expectancy, women complain more often about physical and psychological symptoms, suffer more often from chronic illnesses, and consume most primary health care.

On many traits, men show greater variance than women, and are disproportionately found at both the low and high ends of the distribution. Boys suffer from a higher prevalence of neurodevelopmental disorders. It has been known since the late nineteenth century that more boys than girls were mentally disabled or learning disabled. Dyslexia is four times more common in males than in females, 70 percent of students in special education are boys, and boys are four times as likely as girls to be diagnosed with attention deficit hyperactivity disorder (ADHD). Boys predominate in autism, Asperger, stuttering, or bedwetting, but boys are also more likely to reach the top percentiles in mathematical ability or IQ.

Human sex differences start with basic physiology, including such things as the immune system and the digestive system. Differences have also been observed in brain architecture, with sexual dimorphism and asymmetries in the human cerebrum, and in brain functioning (Hines, 2004). Males and females differ even in basic cognitive strategies. Processing in females entails more elaboration of content. Processing in males is more likely driven by schemas or overall themes (Guillem and Mograss, 2005). Weisenbach *et al.* (2014) suggested that all emotion processing in females and males takes place through different neural pathways. There are apparently substantial sex differences in the neural mechanisms underlying the

104 Women and religion

processing of emotionally influenced memory (Cahill *et al.*, 2004), affective imagery (Bradley *et al.*, 2001), and sadness (Schneider *et al.*, 2000). George *et al.* (1996) looked at brains of men and women during self-induced mood changes, and found that women activated a wider portion of their limbic system (tied to emotion and memory) during transient sadness, despite similar self-reported changes in mood.

Baron-Cohen (2003) argues that there are three kinds of normal human brain: "empathizing" (type E), "systemizing" (type S), and "balanced" (type B, which combines types E and S). On average, men have a type S brain, while the female brain is predominantly type E. Empathizing means identifying another person's emotions and thoughts, and responding to them with an appropriate emotion. Systemizing is the drive to analyze, explore, and construct a system. The systemizer figures out how things work, but systemizing gets you nowhere in most day-to-day social interaction. At its extreme, the systemizing brain is autistic (the "extreme male brain"). This dimorphism is tied to hormone levels.

In a study of 112 males and 100 females (mean age 8.59 years), Auyeung *et al.* (2009) found that fetal testosterone related positively to male-typical play in both boys and girls. Baron-Cohen, Lutchmaya, and Knickmeyer (2004) found that fetal testosterone levels were related to the development of typically "masculine" and "feminine" behaviors. At age four, language development, quality of social relationships, and interests were all tied to fetal testosterone.

The total involvement of the female body in procreation, through pregnancy, birth, and nursing, leads to a huge impact on consciousness, transmitted through hormones and physiological changes, together with direct experience, fantasies, and memories. For most women in the world, the cord connecting sexuality and procreation has not been severed, and where it has been, it serves to remind us that it is a recent development, changing something that has been central over evolutionary history. Cárdenas, Harris, and Becker (2013) found that women's attentional bias towards infants was significantly stronger and stable than men's. This was viewed as reflecting women's central role in infant care which led to an evolved greater sensitivity to infants. Motherhood and the metaphor of motherliness are central in women-dominated religions (Sered, 1994), and leave their mark in the traditions dominated by men. The monthly ovulation cycle in women has been shown to affect behaviors related to mating, as well as beliefs and attitudes. In the United States, being in the ovulatory phase of the cycle led women to support the candidacy of Barack Obama in the 2008 presidential election (Navarrete *et al.*, 2010). Looking at the effects of ovulation on religiosity, Durante, Rae, and Griskevicius (2013) found that in two samples (275 and 502 women), there was an interaction between hormonal effects and relationship status. Ovulation induced lower religiosity (as well as political liberalism and in support for Obama) in the 2012 presidential election among single women. Among attached women, the ovulatory phase was tied to higher religiosity, political conservatism, and support for the Republican candidate Romney. This was interpreted as related to mating strategies.

Differences in the processing of social and emotional stimuli, tied to physiological differences in neuro-hormones, are at the root of differences in bonding and social interaction. Bartels and Zeki (2004), in a study of young mothers, found that both romantic and maternal love activate many of the same specific regions of the brain, and lead to a suppression of neural activity associated with critical social assessment of other people and negative emotions or judgments. The brain regions activated are the same ones as respond to brain-produced oxytocin and vasopressin. These neuro-hormones have been shown in animals to be both sufficient and necessary to induce both mother–infant bonding and male–female bonding. Human attachment mechanisms apparently overcome social distance by deactivating networks used for critical social assessment and negative emotions. This is more pronounced in females, shown in their greater empathy and readiness for attachment (Porges, 1998). The male brain secretes less oxytocin and less of the calming neurotransmitter serotonin than the female brain. Hormones such as testosterone and vasopressin set the male brain up to seek competitive, hierarchical groups in its constant quest to prove self-worth and identity. Personality differences between men and women are less pronounced with aging, as women become more independent, and men more family and community oriented. This must be related to changes in hormonal levels, which become more homogenized with age (Helson and Wink, 1992).

Biological explanations of sex differences are sometimes criticized, and the suggestion is made that social learning is what makes men and women different, and that individuals are socialized according to sex-role expectations prevalent in their culture (Bradshaw and Ellison, 2009). But why are these expectations so similar in so many cultures, and why do both men and women find it so easy to comply with them? The challenge is to account for what must be an amazing uniformity in socializing across cultures. If it's "cultural conditioning" or construction, why is it so similar in all cultures (Barash and Lipton, 2001)? Let us look at male violence. Those who propose socialization accounts would have us believe that men, whether in China, India, or Brazil, are expected to be aggressive, and just meet social expectations. Why are those expectations identical in every culture without exception? And how do we account for the universality of personality dimorphism, with women everywhere being so people-oriented and men being so competitive?

Accepting the notion of the biological factors underlying behavioral differences does not confer any advantage on males. They are, after all, just as much the victims of biological determinism, which sentences them to a life with higher chances for autism, learning disabilities, drug addiction, prison, and an earlier, sometimes violent, death (Kanazawa and Still, 2000). So, is biology destiny for both men and women? This powerful determinism, just like any of our generalizations, is probabilistic. Most men in this world will never commit either homicide or suicide, and personality differences between men and women are more likely to have an impact than extreme violence or pathology.

Coping styles

Lazarus and Folkman (1984) differentiated between problem-focused coping, which involves cognitive and behavioral efforts to decrease stress, and emotion-

106 Women and religion

focused coping, which involves efforts aimed toward changing and modifying the affective reactions accompanying stressful events. Long (1990) showed that women are more prone to use emotionally oriented coping and seek more social support in stressful situations when compared to men. Pearlin and Schooler (1978) reported that men use more effective coping strategies than women and Folkman and Lazarus (1980) found that, on the job, men show a tendency to use more problem-oriented strategies than women. Women are more likely to seek help, which means admitting weakness and accepting another person to take control (Cohen, 1999; Sen, 2004). Ilfeld (1980) suggested that in coping, women use more resignation and rationalization than men and are less prone to use direct action.

Tamres, Janicki, and Helgeson (2002) found that women were more likely than men to use strategies that involved verbal expressions to others or the self, seek emotional support, ruminate about problems, and use positive self-talk. These differences, which fit traditional stereotypes about women's and men's roles in society, were consistent across studies, supporting a dispositional-level explanation of emotion-focused coping (Ptacek, Smith and Zanas, 1992). The feminine coping strategy is characterized by risk avoidance and a search for real or imagined security. A 1989 study of coping styles in adolescents, which surveyed 4367 adolescents in thirteen nations (Australia, Brazil, China, Greece, India, Israel, Kuwait, the Netherlands, the Philippines, Russia, Turkey, the United States, and Venezuela), led to the following conclusion: "We find it a fascinating comment on gender that females responded ... more like lower ... SES groups and more like minority than majority groups! This occurred within all socioeconomic groupings and most countries" (Gibson-Cline, 1996, p. 267).

Bjork and Cohen (1993) reported that women reacted more often to stress by turning to religion. Seeking religious consolation, defined as meaning, comfort, and/or inspiration when faced with personal problems, is more common among women, and is understood as a search for emotional support, compared to more practical concerns for men (Ferraro and Kelley-Moore, 2000).

Psychological femininity

The idea of femininity as a personality trait sums up the basic psychological differences between men and women and introduces the theoretical possibility that higher religiosity is a matter of psychological femininity. One of the clearest formulations of psychological femininity states that "the feminine (not simply female) voice adheres to a calculus of development through attachments and connectedness, rather than growth through separation and substitution" (Thompson, 1991, p. 391). It is evident that some men may adhere to this voice as well. Thompson (1991) found that both men and women who had a feminine self-image on the Bem Sex Role Inventory were more religious, especially as measured by prayer and other devotional activities. In a study of 411 undergraduates, Mercer and Durham (1999) found that those with a feminine or androgynous orientation, of both sexes, were higher on a mysticism scale. Francis and Wilcox (1996, 1998) affirmed that femininity was predictive of greater religious involvement in their studies of UK adolescents, adults, and clergy. Herman (1996) found that adult men and women with a masculine orientation were significantly less "spiritual" than androgynous or feminine individuals.

Mahalik and Lagan (2001) examined the importance of gender ideology, not gender orientation. They sampled seminarians and undergraduate men and found that the men who adhered to traditional masculinity norms were less religious. Their findings are consistent with the thesis that masculinity norms thwart being religious. Thompson and Remmes (2002) found that a feminine orientation predicted older men's self-assessed religiosity. When traditional masculinity norms were rejected, older men participated in church services and private devotion.

Sherkat (2002) examined the self-reported religious involvement of those with varying sexual orientations. Because homosexual males are found to score higher on psychological femininity, while lesbians are found to score lower, then we should expect a corresponding difference in religiosity. The findings show that heterosexual females are the most religious on all measures, being most similar to homosexual men. There is a connection between sexual orientation and religiosity, with heterosexual women being most religious, followed by homosexual men, homosexual women, and heterosexual men.

The priesthood in many cultures presents indications of androgyny, or of an ambiguous and conflicted sexual identity. Francis (1991) tested British candidates for the clergy, men and women, and concluded that male clergy are more feminine, and female clergy more masculine, than the averages for their sexes, and male ministers have been found to be more feminine than average (Francis et al., 2001; Robbins et al., 2001). Clergy seem to be quite different from the general population in terms of sexuality and sexual orientation. Wolf (1989) concluded that about 40 percent of American Roman Catholic priests were homosexual. Sipe (1990) interviewed 1000 Catholic priests, half of them in therapy, and 500 of their sexual partners, and concluded that 20 percent were in a homosexual relationship, and 20 percent in a stable relationship with a woman. Thus, religion as an institution may be maintained by a mass of heterosexual women followers and a group of male religious professionals who are far from following heterosexual masculine norms.

As suggested above, the feminine coping strategy is characterized by anxiety, risk avoidance, and a search for real or imagined security, using others as a source of comfort. The "feminine" in human coping is not limited to women. Ingram et al. (1988) reported that "feminine"-typed adults of both sexes showed increased ruminative and depressive tendencies. Looking at the involvement of adult women in the world of spirits, invisible powers, and miracles, we find that many of their activities have to do with securing good fortune for one's family. Anxiety and helplessness lead to coping through ritual and fantasy, rather than instrumental action. Men do engage in such acts sometimes, but the challenge is to explain why women do it more often. Cramer (1991) found that individuals who score higher on psychological femininity, whether males or females, were more likely to use

108 Women and religion

typically female defense mechanisms of turning against the self, while those higher on masculinity, whether males or females, were more likely to use male defenses of turning against others.

The human condition, as suggested above, is not identical for men and women. Moreover, the two sexes approach it with differing strategies. The male psyche, on average, will be dominated by developmental vulnerability, risk taking, aggression, independence, and relative skepticism, showing the effects of masculine neuro-hormones. Reacting to distress, men will resort to externalizing, sometimes harming those around them. In the female psyche, fear, which leads to aggression in males, will lead to attachment, internalization, and help seeking. Low aggression, empathy, suggestibility, guilt, and sympathy will lead to love, but taking care of children and men, and tending to their needs, rather than one's own, is a heavy burden, growing with the victimization of women by violent men.

Taylor *et al.* (2000) proposed an innate difference in reaction to stress, named "tend and befriend." Tending consists of nurturing acts to protect oneself or one's children. Befriending is the creation and maintenance of social networks that promote safety. Both behaviors reduce stress. Animal and human studies demonstrate that, like fight or flight, tend and befriend is a physiological response. It is induced by oxytocin, as well as female reproductive hormones. Bekker (2001) suggested that women's reactions to stress are affected by the presence (or absence) of care-needing children.

Turning to the world of supernatural agents and miracles fits many "feminine" traits and conditions. Women's people-orientation leads to dependence on real and imaginary objects, from fortune-tellers to angels. Those who nurse and nurture humanity seek their compensation in imaginary objects, in the absence of real support and the presence of much deprivation. We should think of Dalit ("Untouchable") females in India, who may hope for a better life in a future incarnation, but will settle for much less than that, in the form of protection from evil spirits for their own children. Any illusion of control will serve to relieve their constant desperation, as the world of spirits and miracles expresses indeed the sigh of the oppressed creature.

Research on the effects and correlates of religiosity sometimes shows differential effects for men and women which are likely to be related to differing levels of involvement in religious activities (Maselko and Buka, 2008). This should be kept in mind and noted (see Chapter 6). Future research should tell us more about the psychological femininity complex, whether in religious or non-religious contexts, and about sex differences in the learning of religious ideas as they relate to personality. Let us not forget that there are still hundreds of millions of devout men, active in all traditions. We should find out more about their (relative) femininity, and, because femininity is tied to longevity, we should explore the hormonal pathways which possibly give a longevity advantage to religious men (see Chapter 6).

6

CONSEQUENCES AND CORRELATES OF RELIGIOSITY

The impact of religiosity often extends to behaviors and events which have no necessary connection with religious doctrines or practices, and sometimes may be tied to religious prescriptions and proscriptions. This chapter will review the consequences and correlates of religiosity for individuals, which often become significant for collectivities. There will also be gaps between the two levels. Both positive and negative effects have been observed, and the issues are whether the effects observed are significant, and whether they could be attributed to factors unique to religion and religiosity.

Religiosity and impulse control

In everyday life, "morality" most often refers to impulse control, especially regarding sexuality, and then to altruism or selflessness. All cultures share an ideal of self-control, which may be considered a primary virtue, leading to other laudable behaviors. The ideal conveyed to children is that of rising above bodily needs, conquering the weaknesses of hunger, elimination, disease, sex, and death. This universal ideal regards maturity as the ability to set limits on the gratification of physical needs. The newborn baby is pure body, and as such is the opposite of culture and society. Its body has to be conquered externally and internally. Surrendering to the body in pleasure, or in pain and disease, is experienced as a failure, as nature wins over culture and our conscious will. Victory over the body is achieved in asceticism, fasting, celibacy, or athletic feats, and it expresses the triumph of spirit and culture over nature in the most direct and decisive way. Impulse control is described as the ability and the will to resist a temptation which would otherwise lead to actions harmful to the self or others. Both secular and religious individuals share a universal shame complex around surrender to the body and its weaknesses. Self-control is the master virtue, because it overcomes selfish

110 Consequences and correlates of religiosity

and antisocial impulses for the sake of what is best for the group (Baumeister and Exline, 1999). Universal socialization towards self-control precedes the use of religious ideation.

It has been suggested that religion's manifest influence on well-being operates through promoting self-monitoring and building a sense of mastery (Blaine, Trivedi and Eshleman, 1998; Koole *et al.*, 2010; McCullough and Willoughby, 2009). Benson (1992) stated that religion discourages self-destructive behavior by "promoting environmental and psychological assets that constrain risk-taking" (p. 218) as well as "a system of norms and values that favor personal restraint" (p. 216). This has been tested among prisoners, where religiosity has been correlated with a reduction in argumentative behavior and the likelihood of fighting (Kerley, Matthews and Blanchard, 2005; Kerley, Allison and Graham, 2006).

How does religiosity promote self-control? Baldwin, Carrell, and Lopez (1990) subliminally primed women with a scowling picture of the Pope, or another disapproving person, after they read a sexually permissive passage. Catholic women exposed to the disapproving Pope rated themselves lower on morality and competence, but non-Catholic women did not. For Catholic women, exposure to the Pope activated feelings of disapproval and shame for what was perceived as their previous immoral act and motivated self-control to restore a sense of approval.

Rounding *et al.* (2012) found that experimentally inducing religious thoughts increased college students' ability to endure an unpleasant physical experience, delay gratification, and persist at an unpleasant task. In another experiment on self-control, exposure to religious primes (heaven, bless, holy, prayer, cross) was more likely to lead to resistance to temptation (Randolph-Seng and Nielsen, 2007). When religious themes were made implicitly salient, people exercised greater self-control, but Inzlicht and Tullett (2010) reported mixed evidence for a relationship between religious beliefs and executive control.

In a meta-analysis of sixty studies, Baier and Wright (2001) found evidence for the deterrent effects of religiosity on hedonistic behaviors such as gambling, premarital sexual intercourse, and illicit drug use. Religiosity predicts less abuse, and less dependence on psychoactive substances, which are tied to pleasure and loss of control.

Adolescence

During adolescence, humans, especially males, reach a peak in sensation-seeking, leading to risky and self-destructive behaviors. This has been traced to unique features of the human brain, especially its heightened responses to rewards (Bjork *et al.*, 2011; Steinberg, 2008). Religiosity has been found to be a protective factor against the many dangers of adolescence, from delinquency to drug abuse and a variety of high-risk behaviors (Donahue and Benson, 1995; Furrow, King and White, 2004; Johnson *et al.*, 2001; King and Furrow, 2004; Pearce *et al.*, 2003; Rohrbaugh and Jessor, 1975; Salas-Wright *et al.*, 2012; Sinha, Cnaan and Gelles,

2007; Wills, Yaeger and Sandy, 2003). Sabatier *et al.* (2011) found in a sample of 1077 adolescents from France, Germany, Poland, and the United States that in all four cultures religiosity had a positive relationship with family orientation and life satisfaction.

In the United States, church attendance has been found to be related to adolescent health-enhancing practices, including exercise, sufficient sleep, dental hygiene, and seatbelt use. For adolescents who are at risk because of poverty and family history, ritual attendance is a protective factor, reducing the probability of delinquency, drug use, and later maladjustment (Regnerus and Smith, 2005; Smith, 2003). Religiosity in American adolescents is associated with lower levels of depression and hopelessness, and is inversely related to thoughts of suicide, attempted suicide, and actual suicide (Smith, 2003; Yonker, Schnabelrauch and DeHaan, 2012). Religious involvement reduces delinquency only where church membership is the norm (Barrett *et al.*, 2007; Jessor, Turbin and Costa, 1998; Regnerus, 2003; Stark, 1996).

Smith and Snell (2009) looked at a representative sample of individuals aged eighteen to twenty-three in the United States, and found that religiosity correlated positively with self-esteem, physical health, and academic achievement, and negatively with drug abuse, delinquency, and risky sexual activities. On the other hand, Hunsberger, Pratt, and Pancer (2001) compared college and high school students who reported being raised in "no religion" families with peers who reported being raised in Christian homes. They found few differences in adjustment, and individuals' current religiosity was very weakly (positively) related to adjustment. French *et al.* (2008) and Sallquist *et al.* (2010) reported positive effects of religiosity on adolescents in West Java, Indonesia, and interpreted the results as tied to the collectivist context of religion there.

Sexuality and marriage

Religiosity is negatively correlated with sexual activity, as measured by total sexual outlet (Beit-Hallahmi and Argyle, 1997). Religious involvement has been tied to less frequent premarital sexual activity and to higher rates of premarital abstinence, fewer lifetime partners, and less frequent intercourse (Koenig, McCullough and Larson, 2001; Barkan, 2006).

Religious adolescents initiate sexual activity later and report fewer sexual partners than their less religious peers (Bearman and Brückner, 2001; Hardy and Raffaelli, 2003; Fielder *et al.*, 2013; Miller and Gur, 2002; Regnerus, 2007). Paul *et al.* (2000) followed 935 individuals in New Zealand from ages three to twenty-one and found that religious activity at age eleven predicted sexual abstinence at age twenty-one.

A survey of almost 98,649 individuals in forty-six nations found that individual religiosity affected attitudes towards divorce, abortion, prostitution, and homosexuality, but this interacted with the national religious context of their larger environment (Scott, 1998; Finke and Adamczyk, 2008). Scheepers, Te

112 Consequences and correlates of religiosity

Grotenhuis, and Van Der Slik (2002), in a survey of 16,604 inhabitants of fifteen countries, found that individual religiosity affected attitudes towards moral transgressions, but the effect was stronger in more religious countries and negligible in more secularized countries.

Religious individuals are more likely to get married and stay married (Strawbridge *et al.*, 2001). Both church attendance and the personal relevance of religion are positively correlated with marital satisfaction (Mahoney *et al.*, 2001). Religious couples communicate more effectively and use better conflict resolution strategies (Mahoney *et al.*, 1999). Domestic violence and marital infidelity are less common among religious couples, while their divorce rates run anywhere from 13 to 16 percentage points lower (Ellison and Anderson, 2001; Ellison, Bartkowski and Anderson, 1999; Fergusson *et al.*, 1986; Mahoney *et al.*, 2001; Mahoney and Tarakeshwar, 2005).

Crime

Findings on criminal behavior and religion have been mixed. Some measures of religiosity are negatively correlated with deviance of all kinds. Large-scale surveys of adults find that a wide range of offences and deviance is affected, including rape and other crimes of violence (Albrecht, Chadwick and Alcorn, 1977; Baier and Wright, 2001; Bainbridge, 1989; Cochran and Akers, 1989). However, religiosity appeared to serve as a weaker deterrent on serious crimes such as murder and theft. A meta-analysis of sixty studies shows a moderate correlation between religious behavior and belief and the deterrence of crimes (Baier and Wright, 2001). Other researchers have concluded that religious affiliation does not have a significant deterrent effect on unlawful behavior (Evans *et al.*, 1995; Benda and Corwyn, 1997). Jensen (2006) found that homicide rates were higher in nations where beliefs in God and the devil were prevalent, such as the United States, and lower in more secular countries, but in an analysis of twenty-six years of data involving 143,197 people in sixty-seven countries, Shariff and Rhemtulla (2012) found that belief in hell is associated with reduced crime.

Surveys in the United States have consistently shown that atheists have been the least trusted group, because they are perceived as having rejected the basis of moral solidarity and cultural membership in American society (Edgell, Gerteis and Hartmann, 2006; Gervais, Shariff and Norenzayan, 2011). Are atheists more likely to be involved in criminality or deviance? Ever since the field of criminology got started, and with it research on the religious affiliation of criminal offenders, the fact that the unaffiliated and the non-religious had the lowest crime rates has been noted (Bonger, 1943). According to von Hentig (1948), having no religious affiliation is the best predictor of law-abiding behavior. There is no reason to doubt the validity of this generalization today. The prisons are not filled with atheists, and they are rare among those punished for serious crimes.

Well-being, mental health, and physical health

Subjective well-being (SWB)

Religious people, on average, report higher levels of subjective well-being (SWB), happiness, and life satisfaction (Diener and Clifton, 2002; Ellison, 1991; Ellison and Fan, 2008; Ferriss, 2002; Myers and Diener, 1995). In the United States, fundamentalism has been linked to physical and mental well-being (George, Ellison and Larson, 2002; Pargament, 2002; Sethi and Seligman, 1993, 1994). In most studies, frequency of worship attendance is the most consistent correlate of SWB (Ferriss, 2002), although several studies found that private religious involvement was also related to well-being (Ellison 1991; Krause, 2003). Most of the research has been conducted using North American samples, and most study respondents have been of Christian background, but are further findings from research in other cultures (e.g. Abdel-Khalek, 2006, 2010; Abdel-Khalek and Eid, 2011; Roemer, 2010a; Tiliouine and Belgoumidi, 2009).

There is some evidence that an atheist identity can almost match religiosity in contributing to well-being. Mochon, Norton, and Ariely (2011, pp. 9–10) compared average well-being of the non-religious with the well-being of the affiliated in the United States and "estimated that some 47.3% of adherents are less happy than Atheists, 21.9% are less happy than Agnostics, and 14.4% are less happy than those who report no affiliation." Witter *et al.* (1985) concluded that the effect of religious involvement accounted for 2 to 6 percent of the variance in subjective well-being. Religion is less potent than health and loneliness, but it is just as or more potent than education, marital status, social activity, age, sex, or race (Chamberlain and Zika, 1988).

Mental health

What happens in the encounter between severe mental illness and religion? In a European survey, outpatients with schizophrenia or schizoaffective disorders were more religious than the general population (Huguelet *et al.*, 2006). Doering *et al.* (1998) found that higher religiosity predicted worse outcomes in cases of schizophrenia and schizoaffective disorder, possibly because it would lead to religious delusions. Borras *et al.* (2007) found that a religious understanding of their illness in schizophrenia seriously interfered with treatment, and a survey of bipolar patients also reported that religious beliefs interfered with treatment (Logan and Romans, 2002), but Gearing *et al.* (2011) stated that the implications of religious delusions for treatment adherence was not detrimental in all cases. A survey of 406 individuals with persistent mental illness in Los Angeles found that more than 80 percent used religious beliefs or activities during half of their total "coping time." Religious activities, such as prayer or reading the Bible, were tied to more severe symptoms and greater impairment (Tepper *et al.*, 2001). A supportive religious environment may not always lead to positive outcomes. A British study of patients

114 Consequences and correlates of religiosity

with schizophrenia found that those having religious delusions had a longer psychiatric history and suffered from more extensive symptoms, compared to patients without religious delusions. The authors hypothesized that this may result from such individuals coming from more religious families, where their delusional ideas were tolerated and did not lead to seeking treatment (Siddle *et al.*, 2002). How should these findings be interpreted? Religious ideas could in no way be regarded as playing a causal role in psychotic behavior, and what we observe here are desperate coping manoeuvres by an impaired brain. What should be of interest are the ways the majority of brains use religious ideas in facing adversity.

In general, religiosity is tied to higher self-esteem (Beit-Hallahmi and Argyle, 1997), greater emotional stability (Saroglou, 2002a), and decreased levels of anxiety (Koenig *et al.*, 1993) and depression (Le, Tov and Taylor, 2007; Smith, McCullough and Poll, 2003). Belief in an afterlife is associated with lower levels of depression, anxiety, anger, and paranoid ideation (Flannelly *et al.*, 2006). An online survey of adult Americans (n=1629) found a positive correlation between frequency of prayer and the perception of God as either remote or not loving and several different forms of psychopathology, but a perceived intimate relationship with a loving God was negatively related to pathology (Bradshaw, Ellison and Flannelly, 2008).

Although research findings are not unequivocal, the weight of the evidence suggests that religiosity is positively related to mental health (Hackney and Sanders, 2003; Koenig and Larson, 2001; Loewenthal, 2007; Smith, McCullough and Poll, 2003), and the correlation has been found across religions (Abdel-Khalek and Eid, 2011; Abdel-Khalek and Naceur, 2007; Koenig, Zaben and Al Khalifa, 2012). In an exception to most studies, Roemer (2010b) reported that in a Japanese sample depression was positively related to religious beliefs and religious activities. Loewenthal *et al.* (2000) reported that religiosity level, rather than specific religious ideas, positively affected mood in Protestants and Jews under stress.

Maselko and Buka (2008) found that among women, having stopped or started attending services since childhood was correlated with increased rates of anxiety, and marginally increased alcohol dependence, but men who changed their frequency of service attendance were less likely to suffer from major depression. Individuals who reported never attending services did not suffer from mental illness any more than those attending regularly or those who changed their attendance patterns.

Believing that some negative life event is the result of divine punishment has obvious detrimental effects on mood (Pargament *et al.*, 1998). Those who believe in demonic influences or a punishing God tend to have poorer mental health outcomes than those who believe in a benign, supportive God (Ano and Vasconcelles, 2005). McConnell *et al.* (2006) reported that negative religious coping (e.g. endorsing the item: "wondered whether God had abandoned me") was related to serious psychological problems, such as anxiety, depression, and paranoid ideation.

While mourning for a loved one, recurrent thoughts of God's punishment and abandonment were moderately associated with stronger grief reactions (Lee, Roberts and Gibbons, 2013). Krause and Wulff (2004) found that individuals who had more doubts about their faith were less satisfied with their health, and experienced more symptoms of depression (Krause, 2006a). The deleterious effects of religious doubt was naturally greater in members of the clergy. The negative effects of religious strain for individual believers have been noted in other studies (Exline, Yali and Sanderson, 2000).

Lazarus and Folkman (1984) stated that "a belief in a punitive God can lead a person to accept a distressing situation as punishment and to do nothing about mastering or managing the situational demands" (p. 160). Jacobson (1999) found that religiosity was associated with more fatalistic views, and those without a religious affiliation were the least fatalistic. Sharf, Stelljes, and Gordon (2005) reported that cancer patients used fatalistic or religious attitudes as a mode of coping with uncertainty about impending illness, but another study argued that religious fatalism may be a response to chronic illness rather than a contributor to unhealthy behaviors (Franklin *et al.*, 2007).

The relationship of religiosity to suicidal ideas and acts have been studied since the nineteenth century. Findings in the United States point to a clear negative relationship between religiosity and suicidality (Alcantara and Gone, 2007; Chen *et al.*, 2007; Dervic *et al.*, 2004; Lizardi and Gearing, 2009; Rasic *et al.*, 2011). The level of religious consensus or homogeneity in a community reduces suicide rates (Ellison, Burr and McCall, 1997).

Globally, there are large differences among traditions, with low rates of suicide in most Islamic countries (but not all of them). Hinduism and Christianity are tied to higher rates, with Buddhist and secular countries having the highest. The ten countries with the highest suicide rates in 2011 were Lithuania (Roman Catholic majority), Russia (nominal Christian majority with 43.5 percent non-religious), Belarus (42 percent non-religious), Latvia (Christian majority with 21 percent non-believers), Estonia (71 percent non-believers), Hungary (historically Catholic, with 45.4 percent non-religious), Slovenia (Catholic majority, with 30 percent non-religious), Ukraine (62.5 percent non-religious), Kazakhstan (70 percent Moslems, 2.8 percent atheist), and Finland (Lutheran majority, with 21 percent non-religious). All of these countries, except Finland, are post-communist. Since 1991, these countries experienced a "suicide epidemic," and it has been tied to the transition to capitalism and the ensuing economic crisis (Brainerd, 2001). Religious factors have only a limited impact under such cataclysmic conditions.

Effects on physical health

The protective effect of religiosity in terms of morbidity and mortality has been investigated mostly by looking at the connection between worship attendance and physical and psychological health (Benjamins *et al.*, 2003; Krause, 2010; Maselko, Gilman and Buka, 2009; Nicholson, Rose and Bobak, 2010).

The main problem with most studies is that they have relied on self-report for both religiosity and health. While the findings from such studies may be faulted,

116 Consequences and correlates of religiosity

there are other findings which rely on mortality data or objective health measures, such as blood pressure (Sørensen *et al.*, 2011). Hummer *et al.* (1999), in a study of US adults, found that persons who never attended church were nearly twice as likely to die in a follow-up period as persons who attended church weekly. This has been reported quite consistently, and the magnitude of difference has been an additional six years of life (McCullough *et al.*, 2000; Sullivan, 2010). This has been found also in Denmark (la Cour, Avlund and Schultz-Larsen, 2006), Finland (Teinonen *et al.*, 2005), and Taiwan (Yeager *et al.*, 2006). The effects of religiosity on mortality has been found to be stronger for women than for men (see Chapter 5). It should be noted that no effects of religiosity have been found for cases of cancer or heart disease, which lead to a majority of deaths in many countries (Blumenthal *et al.*, 2007).

Explaining the positive effects of religion

The stress reduction hypothesis, which is behind much of the research, assumes that anything that reduces stress is good for the individual psychologically and physically. These stress–reducing effects may appear at the brain level. Inzlicht *et al.* (2009) found that religious conviction is associated with reduced distress in response to errors. Inzlicht and Tullett (2010) tested a neural signal associated with defensive responses to errors and found that religion acted as a buffer against anxious reactions to errors.

Claims about the benefits of religion in terms of prosperity, health, and longevity have been made for thousands of years. There is one big difference, however, between the historical claims about the power of religion to bring about happiness and delay natural or unnatural death, and the suggestions made in recent studies. All traditions have explicitly claimed that only a particular kind of belief, prayer, or sacrifice will keep you healthy and safe. The research in recent decades ignores this essential claim, and all religions are assumed to be equal in their power of ensuring health. The references are always to generic "attendance," "prayer," "belief," or "salience." The implication is that all religious systems are equally helpful. Assuming the equivalence of all religions is totally alien to the lived experience of religious believers, and quite consistent with secularization (see Chapter 9).

To explain the positive effects of religion, health practices, meaning and coherence, and social support have been suggested as the main factors.

Health behaviors

The most common explanations for the correlation between religiosity and health or longevity assume that religiosity is connected to avoiding risk factors (smoking, alcohol, sexual activity, psychosocial stress, and in some cases, consumption of meat). Those with any religious involvement display better health behaviors than those with no involvement (George, Ellison, and Larson 2002; Gillum and Holt, 2010; Hummer *et al.* 1999; Oman *et al.*, 2002; Strawbridge *et al.*, 1997, 2001). In

Consequences and correlates of religiosity **117**

the Israeli Jewish population, Shmueli and Tamir (2007) found among religious people a lower prevalence of reported stress, less smoking, and a healthier diet, with less meat, dairy products and coffee, and much more fish.

Health-conscious Seventh Day Adventists have a longer than average life expectancy (Berkel and de Waard, 1983; Fonnebo, 1992) and members of the Church of Jesus Christ of Latter-Day Saints (Mormons), who avoid alcohol, tobacco, and caffeine also enjoy a considerable longevity advantage (Enstrom and Breslow, 2008; Merrill, 2004). Mormons even look healthier than others and are easily spotted thanks to their "glowing" faces, according to one study (Rule, Garrett and Ambady, 2010). In Africa, religious involvement leads to avoiding risky sex, reducing the spread of HIV infection (Garner, 2000; Gruenais, 1999; Takyi, 2003).

Meaning and coherence

One explanation for the correlation between religiosity and psychological well-being is that religious belief systems may provide meaning and reassurance (Inzlicht, Tullett and Good, 2011), but they may provide even more than that in some cases. Mahoney *et al.* (2005) showed that an attitude of regarding one's body as sacred was directly related to positive health outcomes.

Religious beliefs are considered to be a stress buffer (Steger and Frazier, 2005), because meaning systems (whether religious or secular) provide a "sense of coherence" (Antonovsky, 1979). A demonstration of the religious way of providing meaning and coherence was given by Leo Tolstoy in 1869. He described one of the characters in *War and Peace*, as he coped with despondency:

> If there is a God and future life, there is truth and good, and man's highest happiness consists in striving to attain them. We must live, we must love, and we must believe that we live not only today on this scrap of earth, but have lived and shall live forever.
>
> (Tolstoy, 1966, p. 340)

The hope engendered by religious faith may be an important factor mediating the generally positive association between religion and well-being (Snyder, Sigmon and Feldman, 2002; Vilchinsky and Kravetz, 2005), and helps individuals with depression (Murphy *et al.*, 2000). Religion may also offer help through denial and positive illusions, which may be useful in some situations.

The belief that the world is just, part of most supernaturalist systems, enables individuals to confront the physical and social environment as though they were stable and orderly (Lerner, 1980). Belief in an afterlife, which reduces the terror of death may also influence emotional well-being (Dechesne *et al.*, 2003), and is associated with better recovery in bereavement (McIntosh, Silver and Wortman, 1993; Smith, Range and Ulmer, 1992). But Becker *et al.* (2007) state that the data do not allow for a definite answer on whether all religious beliefs effectively

118 Consequences and correlates of religiosity

influence bereavement. However, it has also been suggested that religiosity is far from being an automatic stress buffer (Pargament, 1997) and that real catastrophes, such as the Holocaust, undermine religion's capacity to offer meaning and solace (Brenner, 1980).

Social support as an explanation

This explanation assumes that all religious traditions offer the same kind of social support. The solidarity felt by members of a religious congregation together with the sense of belonging to the imagined community of believers should have positive effects on well-being. Beyond this general feeling, there are real personal friendships formed in the congregation. It has been argued that "religious (and other group) participation is itself linked to psychological well-being and social integration, simply because it offers social involvement rather than isolation" (Brown, 1988, p. 57; Hayward and Elliott, 2009; Krause, 2008; Krause and Wulff, 2005).

Some researchers have claimed that religious social support is unique in form and quality (Ellison and George, 1994). Krause, Ellison, and Wulff (1998) have stated that there may be "qualitative, as well as quantitative, differences in the effects of support offered in secular and religious settings" (1998, p. 727). Theoretically, it may be assumed that religious support combines normal fellowship with a sense of cosmic mission fostered by religious beliefs, thus creating a unique form of support. This has been repeatedly challenged, and it has been suggested that the support offered in a religious context is no different than social support in secular settings (Joiner, Perez and Walker, 2002; Willoughby *et al.*, 2008).

Beit-Hallahmi and Argyle (1997) considered within-congregation friendships a crucial factor in creating social support, and reported relevant findings. More than one-third (37 percent) of church members in a British sample rated their church friendships as closer than other ones. Krause (2008) found a positive relationship between involvement with a church friend and life satisfaction. In a study of 310,000 church attenders in Australia, 24 percent said that their closest friends were in their church, and another 46 percent had some close friends in it (Kaldor, 1994). Identical effects were found in the case of unemployed Moslem men in Britain. Mosque membership and the social support of the community enabled individuals under stress to cope much better with their situation (Shams and Jackson, 1993).

Lim and Putnam (2010) suggested that it is the group-based social contact and support in the congregation, rather than an inherently religious message that leads to life satisfaction. Confirming the explanation proposed by Beit-Hallahmi and Argyle (1997), they found that friendships developed in the congregation are crucial to well-being. It is church-based friendships that create the relationship between religiosity and life satisfaction (Lim and Putnam, 2010). Okulicz-Kozaryn (2010) found that only the kind of religiosity which promotes social capital (i.e. beneficial relationships) predicts high life satisfaction. On the other hand, forms of religiosity that do not promote social capital do not predict high life satisfaction. It is not religiosity per se that makes people happy, but rather the social setting it offers.

Galen and Kloet (2011) challenged the research on social support, arguing that the weakly religious should not be regarded as representing the completely nonreligious. Thus, Krause (2006b) compared the effects of church-based social support and secular social support on health in late life by comparing older Christians who go to church more than twice a year and older people who do not go to church as frequently. His conclusion was that religious support was superior. Galen and Kloet argued that a comparison such as Krause's did not offer a true contrast between religious and secular support, because only religious individuals were involved. To correct that, they compared 326 church members with 342 members of the local branch of the Center for Inquiry (CFI), a secular humanist group. No differences in social support were found. This means that there is nothing unique in religious groups in terms of the attachment of members and the gratifications they receive. The same attachment and the same gratifications could be found in secular groups.

Summarizing the explanations presented so far, one researcher stated:

> The psychological processes by which religion affects subjective well-being and psychological and physical health are interesting and important, and research on them is easily justified; however, they have very little to do with religion per se, and there is nothing that necessarily leads from an interest in these processes to a focus on religion.
>
> (Funder, 2003, p. 214)

Genetic factors

One problem with correlations between psychological traits and physiological measures is that they may all be determined by innate factors. The possibility that both religiosity and good health (physical and mental) may be in part the result of hard-wired personality differences should be considered. Optimism, which may correlate with religiosity and longevity, may be a reflection of innate factors. One is born with a physiological complex which leads to the genotype of optimism and good health, which under certain conditions may be tied to religiosity. Innate qualities of better physiology, optimism, conformism, and sociability may lead people to religious congregations. Risk-aversive people are more likely to both display greater religiosity and to exhibit positive health practices and pro-social behavior (Ellison and Levin, 1998; Regnerus and Smith, 2005).

Individuals who are healthy and sociable are more likely to attend religious services, and this is how many of the correlations reported in the literature are produced. Stroope (2012), using a large national sample in the United States, found that embeddedness in congregation-based friendship networks was tied to both public religious activity and heightened religiosity. Sullivan (2010) suggested that regular attendance at religious services is tied to having closer relationships with friends and family, which means that individual sociability may be a relevant trait (Idler and Kasl, 1997; Oman et al., 2002; Strawbridge et al., 2001).

120 Consequences and correlates of religiosity

The longevity advantage of religious men may be related to their psychological and possibly physiological femininity. Because women live longer, and are significantly more religious than men (see Chapter 5), it is possible that men who live longer may differ in their hormonal functioning (Viña *et al.*, 2005)

Doubts and criticisms

It has long been recognized that religiosity is tied to self-esteem and better functioning in individuals (Beit-Hallahmi and Argyle, 1997), but many of the interpretations offered for findings about the positive consequences of religiosity have been challenged. Wilkinson and Coleman (2010) and then Baker and Cruickshank (2010) found that strong beliefs, whether atheistic or religious, make a positive contribution to happiness and to facing the challenges of old age. Galen and Kloet (2011) made a similar suggestion.

If religious beliefs are beneficial, we should expect religious doubt to be harmful. Galek *et al.* (2007) examined the connections between religious doubt and mental health in an American sample of 1629 adults. Religious doubt, described as "emerging from the recognition of suffering and evil in the world" had a negative effect on mental health. These effects were found across various measures, including depression, general anxiety, interpersonal sensitivity, paranoia, hostility, and obsessive-compulsive symptoms. This kind of correlational finding ignores the possibility that certain personality traits push individuals in the direction of doubt, oppositionality, and non-conformity. Recognizing "suffering and evil in the world" is not objective or automatic. It is totally dependent on individual dynamics (see Chapter 8; Freud, 1928; Beit-Hallahmi, 2006–2007).

Explanations for the effects of religiosity on physical health have been challenged most often, because the claims have been dramatic, and studies on the benefits of religion for health have been criticized for methodological flaws, and, more seriously, for the religious commitments of the researchers involved (Sloan, 2006; Sloan and Bagiella, 2002; Sloan, Bagiella and Powell, 1999). Sloan (2007) stated that the evidence was too weak and inconsistent to justify the claims made, which have often been extravagant. Two biologists have described the religion-biology connection as follows: "A large literature indicates that the relationships between religiosity and mental health and freedom from coronary disease and certain cancers typically are positive" (Fincher and Thornhill, 2012, p. 72). Any claims about "freedom from coronary disease and certain cancers" must reflect extreme gullibility, and are puzzling when made by academic researchers.

One basic methodological problem in numerous studies has been that of reliance on self-report and reverse causality. If individuals report on religious attendance and then on their health, "we cannot exclude the possibility that those in poor health were prevented from attending services and that this accounts for the observed associations" (Nicholson, Rose and Bobak, 2009, p. 526). As noted above, this limitation is overcome with the use of objective medical data. Mochon, Norton, and Ariely (2008) found that attending religious services regularly had a positive impact

Consequences and correlates of religiosity **121**

on well-being, but so did regular exercise and yoga sessions. They interpreted the results as showing that any regular participation will make a difference.

Most research on religiosity and health has been done in the United States, and Chaves (2010) suggested that the findings may be only valid on one side of the Atlantic. When research is done in places where biomedicine is highly advanced, it is obviously the main factor in determining health. It would be interesting to look at the effects of religiosity in places like India, Ethiopia, or Afghanistan.

The ideology that seems to drive much of the research is first religiosity, and then positive thinking and the popular idea of "mind over matter" (Sloan *et al.*, 2000). The great progress achieved in biomedicine has been possible because of the decline of teleological and animistic thinking and the growing reliance on basis sciences. This is clearly a problem for some believers. The mind-over-matter fantasy has some secular versions, such as the repeated suggestion that cancer may be caused by psychological factors, or treated with the help of psychotherapy (Coyne, Stefanek and Palmer, 2007; Coyne *et al.*, 2009; Gorin, 2010; Stefanek, McDonald and Hess, 2005).

The promotion of religious practices and beliefs as solutions for medical problems results from the strong religious commitments of some medical professionals. This has been demonstrated by Curlin *et al.* (2006) and Curlin *et al.* (2007a), who analyzed data from a 2003 survey of 1144 American physicians, which showed that religious physicians were more likely to believe in the positive effects of religion on health and in the desirability of introducing religion into the physician–patient interaction. For 181 Jewish and for 117 non-affiliated physicians, their low religiosity was tied to a lack of faith in the positive effects of religion on health and the absence of enthusiasm about mixing religion and medicine (Curlin *et al.*, 2007b; Stern, Rasinski and Curlin, 2011). It is also possible that both Jews and the unaffiliated are conscious of their minority status when it comes to discussing religion in a medical setting.

The religionist agenda of the religion and health movement becomes clear when data interpretation turns to action prescriptions. Matthews *et al.* (1998) proposed that,

> [f]amily physicians can encourage patients to make use of potentially health-promoting religious resources from patients' own religious traditions. Where appropriate, religious patients might be encouraged to pray more—whether individually or with others. If already attending a church, synagogue, or mosque, they might be encouraged to continue. They might be encouraged to meditate. They might be encouraged to attend worship, engage in religiously based mourning rituals, seek and ask forgiveness from significant others, or read holy writ.
>
> (Matthews *et al.*, 1998, p. 123)

Koenig (2002, p. 26) suggested that if there was a positive connection between religiosity and health, "interventions could be administered to already religious

122 Consequences and correlates of religiosity

persons to help increase their religiousness." In this case, the emphasis is on existing traditions. There have been more activist views. An earlier survey showed that among American psychiatrists holding evangelical Christian beliefs, one-third were committed to discouraging non-religious patients from actions that ran counter to their own Christian beliefs (Galanter, Larson and Rubenstone, 1991).

In addition to positive advice,

> many of the new spirituality advocates have no hesitancy about rejecting certain spiritual beliefs that they consider ill-advised or harmful, as for example, the belief that illness is punishment from God. They recommend steering patients away from such beliefs. We have, therefore, a revolutionary new claim abroad in the land, that physicians have the task of screening out unhealthy from healthy religious beliefs and practices.
>
> (Lawrence, 2002, p. 75)

In this vein, Koenig (2008a, p. 202) stated that "it may be necessary to gently challenge beliefs that are being used defensively to avoid making important life changes or attitudinal shifts." He also stated that "[p]rayer with a religious patient can have a powerful positive effect and strengthen the therapeutic alliance. This, however, can be a dangerous intervention and should never occur until the psychiatrist has a complete understanding of the patient's religious beliefs and prior experiences with religion. Prayer should only be done if the patient initiates a request for it, the psychiatrist feels comfortable doing so, and the religious backgrounds of patient and psychiatrist are similar" (Koenig, 2008a, p. 203). Koenig (2008a) was addressing an audience of British psychiatrists, and his prescriptions met with some objections (Hansen, 2010; Poole and Cook, 2011).

The most puzzling part of the research on the effects of religion on health has been the work on the efficacy of prayer. Believing that prayer can cure the sick may be viewed as a religious reaction to the success of secular biomedicine. In a 2003 poll, "84% of Americans said prayers for others can have a positive effect on their recovery, and 74% said that would be true even if they didn't know the patient" (Kalb, 2003, p. 54). Moreover, 72 percent thought "that praying to God can cure someone even if science says the person doesn't stand a chance" (Kalb, 2003, p. 48). Matching this expression of popular confidence, research has been carried out since the 1980s on the efficacy of prayer in helping with various medical problems, with millions of dollars being spent. There have even been claims about the positive effects of intercessory prayer on wound healing in nonhuman primates (Lesniak, 2006). There is evidence that prayer may affect the physiology of those who pray (Bernardi et al., 2001; Masters and Spielmans, 2007). Stødkilde-Jørgensen, Geertz, and Roepstorff (2009) looked at the brains of Christians during silent prayers, and suggested that prayer stimulates the dopaminergic reward system. Wiech et al. (2008) found that with Catholics, looking at a religious image decreased pain. This effect was not found among non-believers or with secular images.

For thousands of years, believers have claimed that only specific prayers, addressed to specific spirit entities, could help, but not a generic prayer. One significant aspect of prayer efficacy research is its ecumenicity. The prayers have been directed at a "nonsectarian, higher power" (Cadge, 2009, p. 301), and prayers coming from all religions and all believers are considered equally effective. At least one of the recent "miracle" studies has been exposed as a fraud (Cha, Wirth and Lobo, 2001), and the results of the whole enterprise are expectedly pathetic (Andrade and Radhakrishnan, 2009; Cadge, 2009; Dossey and Hufford, 2005; Hodge, 2007; Masters and Spielmans, 2007; Carey, 2006; Roberts *et al.*, 2009; Sloan, 2006; Sloan and Ramakrishnan, 2006). What the researchers obviously did not know is that the last word on the subject (i.e. prayer has no effect) was said already in 1872 (Galton, 1872). The religious commitment of those involved is clear. Here are representative statements: "We need not wait until all the answers are in before employing prayer adjunctively" (Dossey, 2000). Likewise, Harris *et al.* (1999) recommended distant prayer as an "effective adjunct to standard medical care."

What those carrying out the research have never spelled out were the channels of influence through which prayer affects physiology. The true crucial test would be assigning patients with medical problems to a prayer-only experimental group. This is actually being done in "faith healing," with tragic results. We know that in the real world people also issue spells and curses, and we should expect the next stage of this research program to address them.

The challenge of aggregate measures

The findings on the largely beneficial effects of religiosity on individuals have been challenged by the different picture that emerges from research that looks at individuals in the aggregate. While the literature reports that more religious individuals are healthier, better-behaved, and happier, when we look at large groups of individuals living in a particular territory, the picture is completely reversed.

That is how the "religious engagement paradox" is described:

> Curiously, irreligious places (nations, states) and highly religious individuals tend to exhibit high levels of health, wellbeing, and prosociality. Religious engagement correlates negatively with prosociality and well-being across aggregate levels (countries and American states), and positively across individuals (especially, as noted earlier, in more religious countries).
>
> (Myers, 2012a, p. 916)

This paradox persists whenever we look at large groups or nations. Religiosity is clearly good for individuals, at least in some ways, but religion as a social force is less beneficial.

As Myers (2012a) noted, irreligious nations exhibit high levels of health, well-being, and pro-sociality. Koenig and Larson (2001) noted that the vast majority of

124 Consequences and correlates of religiosity

Scandinavians are atheists or nonreligious. At the same time, Scandinavian nations tend to experience the highest levels of subjective well-being (SWB) in the world (Diener, Kahneman and Helliwell, 2010; Zuckerman, 2008, 2009). The Columbia University Earth Institute published in 2013 its World Happiness Report. This report identifies the countries with the highest levels of happiness in the 2010–2012 surveys as Denmark, Norway, Switzerland, the Netherlands, Sweden, and Canada. The United Nations Human Development Index, published since 1990, which combines measures of life expectancy, literacy, education, living standards, and GDP per capita, and other global indices of the quality of life, published annually, always list less religious nations (Norway, Iceland, Australia, Luxembourg, Canada) at the top.

Similar lists of "the best country to live in" or "the best country for children," which use data on public health, longevity, education, health care, and income disparity include the familiar names of less religious nations: Norway, Sweden, Australia, Canada, the Netherlands, Iceland, and Belgium. At the bottom of such lists are African countries, Moslem countries (Bangladesh, Pakistan, Egypt, Morocco, and Yemen) and India. Inside the United States, if the fifty states are ranked in terms of average health, Vermont, Hawaii, New Hampshire, Massachusetts, and Minnesota are the top five. Mississippi, Louisiana, Arkansas, West Virginia, and South Carolina make up the bottom five. It turns out that the bottom five states are among the most religious, while the top five are among the more secular (Gray and Wegner, 2010).

Life expectancy is one clear measure of the quality of life in any nation. Looking at the global ranking, it becomes clear that religiosity is negatively correlated with longevity. If religiosity affects longevity positively, do we expect more religious nations to have longer life expectancies? Do the more religious people of Ethiopia live longer than the less religious people of Japan? The answer is obvious. The United States Central Intelligence Agency publishes an annual life expectancy ranking of 223 world nations and territories. Among the top thirty, are, as expected, Japan, Australia, France, Canada, Sweden, Iceland, the Netherlands, and Norway (the United States was number fifty in 2013). The bottom thirty is made up of African countries and Afghanistan, the last well known for religiosity.

The United States is often looked at as a laboratory for testing crucial hypotheses about the effects of religiosity. If religiosity guarantees well-being, the United States should be a happy place, but the reality is somewhat different. In 1997, Ralph Reed, executive director of the Christian Coalition, a right-wing religious lobby, stated that the United States was,

> the most devoutly religious nation in the entire world… a nation undergirded by faith, built by faith, and enlivened by faith. It is not a faith in word alone, but an active, transforming faith. Look around today and what you will see are the fruits of our national faith.

> (Reed, 1997, p. 27)

Nevertheless, Reed described "[s]ocial pathologies once imagined only in our darkest nightmares are a daily reality" (Reed, 1997, p. 28). Compared to other wealthy nations (per capita GNP over $20,000), or other English-speaking nations, the United States has (in addition to economic insecurity) the highest rates of violence and imprisonment, as well as other social pathologies such as the highest teen pregnancy rate.

The findings by Diener, Tay, and Myers (2011), reported above, seem relevant to the aggregate paradox. They showed that in nations which suffer from poverty, hunger, and low life expectancy, religiosity was correlated with SWB, and religious individuals had a higher SWB in poor nations but not in wealthy and secularized nations.

Religiosity as detrimental to well-being

By definition, any situation where stress is increased because of religion is detrimental, as well as situations where proper medical care is rejected, or when religious rituals involve mutilation. The genital mutilation of children, which is customary in some religious traditions, has been regarded more and more frequently as a form of child abuse. Female genital mutilation has been targeted for elimination by the United Nations, and the genital mutilation of males is coming under increasing criticism (Terhune, 1997). Various practices attract much attention, because of their shocking nature, despite their rarity. Cases of child death caused by exorcism are still reported (Bottoms et al., 1995). In India, cases of Sati or widow-burning continue to be reported (Bhugra, 2005; Vijayakumar, 2004; Weinberger-Thomas, 1999), as well as Sallekhana, suicide by starvation among the Jains (Braun, 2008). In West Africa "spirit children," identified as dangerous, are killed immediately after birth (Allotey and Reidpath, 2001).

Less horrifying phenomena are more common. In the United States, it has been found that Protestant fundamentalists support, and practice, the corporal punishment of children (Ellison, 1996; Ellison, Bartkowski and Segal, 1996; Gershoff, Miller and Holden, 1999; Grasmick, Bursik and Kimpel, 1991; Grasmick, Morgan and Kennedy, 1992; Straus, 1994). While some of those discussing this used terms such as "discipline," academics have called it "violence against children" or "child abuse" (Bottoms et al., 1995, 2004; Capps, 1992; Greven, 1991). There is evidence that fundamentalist beliefs among both Jews and Christians are associated with a greater likelihood of child abuse (Bottoms et al., 2004; Shor, 1998).

Religious leaders sometimes abuse their power over the helpless and the gullible (Bottoms et al., 1995; Rodarmor, 1983; Nielsen, 2003), and sexual misconduct by clergy has attracted much attention. Saradjian and Nobus (2003) found that religious beliefs held by the clerical offenders removed inhibitions and were instrumental in facilitating offending behavior against children. Stout-Miller, Miller, and Langenbrunner (1997) found, in a survey of 397 students at a southern United States university, that 50 percent of those who reported having been sexually victimized as children came from evangelical/fundamentalist backgrounds,

126 Consequences and correlates of religiosity

but actual involvement with church activities was inversely related to the risk of abuse. Individuals reporting having been abused by non-relatives were either from liberal Protestant backgrounds or from non-believing families.

Religious beliefs are directly harmful when real medical problems are not treated with proven medical means. This may happen in two situations: where populations do not have access to biomedicine, or where biomedicine is available but rejected (Forster, 1998; Kirby, 1997). Worldwide, we find congregations and individuals practicing "faith healing," the origin of many reported miracles (Rose, 1971; Harrell, 1985; Randi, 1989). Rose (1971) demonstrated the absurdity of claims about "faith healing," which involve denial and delusion. Glik (1986) interviewed 176 individuals who had attended "healing" groups, and compared them with 137 who had received regular primary care. Those who had attended healing groups reported better health and subjective well-being, while their physical state was no better than that of controls. Pattison, Lapins, and Doerr (1973) analyzed 71 cases of "healings" and found no change in physical condition, despite subjective claims and beliefs that individuals had been healed by the casting out of sins. MMPI (Minnesota Multiphasic Personality Inventory) profiles for these 71 cases showed higher denial scores. Miettinen (in Holm, 1991) studied 611 cases of "healings" in Finland. There was no evidence of physical improvement, but the clients (450 women and 161 men), of limited education and social status, experienced subjective change, attributed to suggestibility and personal instability.

The fantasy of a world without evil in the form of illness has cost the lives of many children and adults (Bottoms et al., 1995; Hughes, 2004; Terhune, 1997; Woolley, 2005). The best known group that rejects biomedicine has been Christian Science, whose members have lived shorter lives because of this rejection (Simpson, 1989; Wilson, 1956). The group has been in decline for decades, and some have tied it to members' disappointment with its message (Singelenberg, 1999; Stark, 1998; Richardson and Dewitt, 1992). Asser and Swan (1998) reported on 172 child fatalities caused by medical neglect in twenty-three US religious groups. Most of these cases, which occurred between 1975 and 1995, involved Christian Science, the Church of the First Born, and the Faith Assembly.

Hobart Freeman (1920–1984), the founder of the Faith Assembly advocated the complete avoidance of modern medicine, relying instead on prayers.

> Sickness and disease have been repeatedly defeated by maintaining a positive confession of faith in the face of all apparent evidence to the contrary ... When genuine faith is present it alone will be sufficient, for it will take the place of medicines and other aids.
>
> (quoted in Beit-Hallahmi, 1998, p. 130)

This statement represents the view of countless traditions and groups. In the Faith Assembly, 100 members and their children were reported to have died between 1970 and 1990 because of their refusal to seek medical care (Beit-Hallahmi, 1998;

Hughes, 1990). Some group members have been sent to prison for depriving their children of medical care.

Opposition to vaccinations because of religion can be found all over the world, with tragic consequences (Rodgers *et al.*, 1993). Polio, once known as infantile paralysis, remains endemic in only three countries, Pakistan, Afghanistan, and Nigeria, because of opposition to vaccination on the part of Islamic religious leaders, who have described it as a plot by Western governments (Antai, 2009; Jegede, 2007; Obadare, 2005). Religion plays a role in the opposition to organ donations, which have become a crucial part of biomedicine, and thus millions of lives are affected (Boulware *et al.*, 2002).

Religion and pro-social behavior

Morality is defined here as "prescriptive judgments of justice, rights, and welfare pertaining to how people ought to relate to each other" (Turiel, 1983, p. 3). This definition is designed to steer us away from cultural conventions: "Moral judgments are primarily about welfare, justice, and rights, distinguishable from judgments about conventional uniformities" (Turiel and Neff, 2000, p. 279). Concerns about harm and fairness are universally salient and accompanied by anger. In all cultures, children learn early on to distinguish between rules in the moral domain and social conventions. They identify moral issues as those having to do with welfare and physical harm, psychological harm, fairness and rights, or positive behaviors (Nucci, 2001).

Brown's (1991) work on universals in human behavior supports the notion of pan-human moral ideals. Among the cultural components found everywhere are moral sentiments; right and wrong; murder proscribed; rape proscribed; sexual regulation, including incest prevention; and redress of wrongs. It is clear that controlling aggression is foremost, and then controlling sex.

In Jainism, Hinduism, and Buddhism, we find a strong historical emphasis on purity and on the relationship of status to purity, together with the primacy of *Ahimsa*, the prohibition on violence. If we look at the Five Precepts, the basis of Buddhist moral ideals, we find a clear hierarchy. The first precept is to avoid killing or harming living beings. The second is to avoid stealing, the third is to avoid sexual misconduct, the fourth is to avoid lying, and the fifth is to avoid intoxication. The descending order of severity is clear.

Are religion and morality universally connected? Swanson (1960) stated:

> The people of modern Western nations are so steeped in these beliefs which bind religion and morality, that they find it hard to conceive of societies which separate the two. Yet most anthropologists see such a separation as prevailing in primitive societies.
>
> (Swanson, 1960, p. 153)

Stark (2002a) found that religion sustains the moral order only when it is based on belief in powerful and morally concerned gods, and that only 23.9 percent of the

128 Consequences and correlates of religiosity

427 cultures in the cross-cultural database acknowledge gods who are active in human affairs and supportive of human morality.

Moralizing religion and moralizing gods appear when large, differentiated groups first develop (Roes and Raymond, 2003). It has often been claimed that only the expectation of supernatural reward and punishment, meted out by omniscient, but invisible entities, can cause humans to give up their natural selfishness and recognize the needs of others. In the fifth century BCE, Athenian historians asserted that only fear of the gods kept humans close to the word of the law, while the absence of such fear led to lawlessness (Powell, 2001). The Roman Cicero, in *De Natura Deorum* (45 BCE) wondered whether, without fear of the gods, trust and cooperation among humans will be lost and, with them, justice.

Cicero's concern has been reiterated in the form of two questions:

1   Could the institutions of society survive without an authority believed to originate from the spirit world?
2   Could individuals who reject supernaturalism be moral?

With growing secularization and the reality of atheism and atheists, these questions took on some immediacy or, in some circles, even urgency.

> It is one of the oldest of sociological generalizations that ... common moral understandings must ... rest upon a common set of religious understandings that provide a picture of the universe in terms of which the moral understandings make sense.
>
> (Bellah, 1975, p. ix)

If it is indeed religion that provides moral coherence, how can society survive without it, and how could atheists be moral in any way?

John Locke stated that non-believers should not be trusted, because "promises, covenants, and oaths, which are the bonds of human society, can have no hold upon an atheist" (Locke, 1689/1983, p. 51). George Washington, echoing John Locke, warned in his Farewell Address (1796):

> Where is the security for property, for reputation, for life, if the sense of religious obligation desert the oaths which are the instruments of investigation in courts of justice? And let us with caution indulge the supposition that morality can be maintained without religion ... reason and experience both forbid us to expect that national morality can prevail in exclusion of religious principle.
>
> (quoted in Horwitz, 1986, p. 213)

The best known and most quoted modern warning about amoral atheists is found in Dostoyevsky's *The Brothers Karamazov* (1880). Mitya reports a conversation with an atheist: "'But what will become of men then?' I asked him, 'without God and immortal life? All things are lawful then, they can do what they like?' 'Didn't you know?' he said laughing, 'a clever man can do what he likes'" (Dostoyevsky, 1880/1999, p. 557).

Conservative authors have been warning the world about the dire consequences of the decline in the authority of religion. Hegel observed that,

> Reverence for God, or for the gods, establishes and preserves individuals, families, states; while contempt of God, or of the gods, loosens the basis of laws and duties, breaks up the ties of the family and of the State, and leads to their destruction.
>
> (Hegel, 1832/1962, p. 103)

Herbert Spencer asserted that "the control exercised over men's conduct by theological beliefs and priestly agency has been indispensable" (Offer, 1994, p. 93), and Charles Darwin wrote that,

> A man who has no assured and ever present belief in the existence of a personal God or of future existence with retribution and reward, can have for his rule of life, as far as I can see, only to follow those impulses and instincts which are the strongest or which seem to him the best ones.
>
> (Darwin, 1887/2004, p. 94)

William James, writing in 1891, described the difference between a religious and a secular morality in terms of energy, music, and objective power:

> [I]n a merely human world without a God, the appeal to our moral energy falls short of its maximal stimulating power. Life, to be sure, is even in such a world a genuinely ethical symphony; but it is played in the compass of a couple of poor octaves, and the infinite scale of values fails to open up ... When, however, we believe that a God is there, and that he is one of the claimants, the infinite perspective opens out.
>
> (James, 1897/1956, p. 211)

James, an ambivalent but consistent defender of religion (Joshi, 2003), was implying that atheism may be a true risk factor on the road to an immoral symphonic performance.

The idea that the elite can give up religious illusions, but that the spread of unbelief among the masses would lead to anomie has had some currency. Jean-Jaques Rousseau (1712–1778) openly suggested that the basis for public order is the belief in a powerful divinity, to be enforced by the state (Dacey, 2008). Voltaire (1694–1778), to whom Christianity was an "infamy," found faith useful, and once silenced a discussion about atheism until he had dismissed the servants, lest in losing their faith they might lose their morality (Law, 2006). Voltaire's rhetorical question was "What restraint, after all, could be imposed on covetousness, on the secret

130 Consequences and correlates of religiosity

transgressions committed with impunity, other than the idea of an eternal master whose eye is upon us and will judge even our most private thoughts?" (quoted in Manuel, 1983, p. 66). On another occasion, Voltaire said: "I want my attorney, my tailor, my servants, even my wife to believe in God; and I think that I shall then be robbed and cuckolded less often" (Borg, 1988, p. 6).

Irving Kristol, an American conservative author (1920–2009) followed Voltaire and the ancient idea of the Noble Lie:

> If God does not exist, and if religion is an illusion that the majority of men cannot live without ... let men believe in the lies of religion since they cannot do without them, and let then a handful of sages, who know the truth and can live with it, keep it among themselves ... atheism becomes a guarded, esoteric doctrine—for if the illusions of religion were to be discredited, there is no telling with what madness men would be seized, with what uncontrollable anguish. It would become the duty of the wise to publicly defend and support religion, even to call the police power to its aid, while reserving the truth for themselves and their chosen disciples.
>
> (Kristol, 1949, p. 443)

Exemplary moral behavior and moral rehabilitation

Those extolling the moral benefits of religion can justifiably point to numerous cases of exemplary moral commitment. "The highest flights of charity, devotion, trust, patience, bravery to which the wings of human nature have spread themselves have been flown for religious ideals" (James, 1902/1961, p. 210). All over the world, it is Roman Catholic nuns, and members of other religions, who, because of religious ideals, have been taking care of terminal patients in hospices or the severely retarded, just as once they took care of lepers, those who will never get better, in a form of altruism which cannot be easily matched. It is a heroic way of life, day by day, which expresses an ideal of total self-sacrifice. There are medical workers who work in hospices or with incurable cases, but they have not taken vows to avoid pleasures and shun any other commitments. Religious individuals have been ready to adopt children with disabilities and give them a home, an exemplary, selfless act.

Religious organizations are recognized for their role in humanitarian relief (Berkley Center, 2008; Clarke, 2007; Clarke, Jennings and Shaw, 2008). There are many religious individuals helping the unfortunate all over the world and showing great humanity, and religious pacifists who have been imprisoned, or executed, for their moral objection to war (Colby and Damon, 1992; Matsuba and Walker, 2004).

Another phenomenon is that of a dramatic moral transformation in individuals and communities, produced by a religious conversion or revival (see Chapters 4 and 7). We can point to inspiring cases of converts saved from a life of crime and drug dependence, but the overall efficacy of religious conversions with criminals and addicts remains to be proven.

Consequences and correlates of religiosity **131**

The lessons of history argument

If we are going to present anecdotes of selfless acts and exemplary behavior, we will be challenged with many more contrary cases. It is easy to compile long lists of horrifying events inspired by religion over the course of human history, in recent times, or even the present moment (Munson, 2005). Apocalyptic and messianic prophecies have sown death, destruction, and suffering all over the world. Between 1095 and 1291, untold millions died in the Crusades, and a leading historian wrote that "the Holy War was nothing more than a long act of intolerance in the name of God" (Runciman, 1951, p. 480). Jonathan Z. Smith (1982, p. 110) emphasized that Christianity should not be singled out, as "religion has rarely been a positive, liberal force. Religion is not nice; it has been responsible for more death and suffering than any other human activity." Pinker (1997, p. 555) stated: "Religions have given us stonings, witch-burnings, crusades, inquisitions, jihads, fatwas, suicide bombers." A contrary view is expressed by Myers: "We also have religion to thank for much of the antislavery, civil rights, and antiapartheid movements, and for the faith-based founding of hospitals, hospices, and universities" (Myers, 2012b, p. 93). Founding hospitals and universities is praiseworthy, but giving credit to religion for "the antislavery, civil rights, and antiapartheid movements" is unwarranted (see below). In the case of the abolition of slavery, for example, historians give more credit to the Enlightenment (Martinez, 2012).

The Nazi Third Reich was far from being a secular enterprise, and most Nazi leaders made frequent references to the Christian God in their speeches and writings (Bartov and Mack, 2001; Lewy, 1964; Probst, 2012; Steigmann-Gall, 2003). Most Nazis came from Christian homes (in 1933, 95 percent of Germans were Christians), and in Nazi-occupied Europe, the political forces that supported the occupier were often religious. Long before modern genocides, there were religious texts commanding the total annihilation of some human groups. The Hebrew Bible offers us narratives of the extermination of the Midianites and the Canaanites by the Israelites, as ordered by divine authority (see Numbers 31; 1 Samuel 15). These blood-curdling narratives are totally fictitious, but they reflect very real ideals. Apparently, they were invented to justify exclusionary attitudes towards non-Israelites. Those who composed them more than two millennia ago were not worried about anybody being outraged by them. Moore (2000) claimed that the readiness to persecute and kill people of different religious and political persuasions in the defense of "moral purity" had its origins in the monotheism of the Hebrew Bible, but it is clear that followers of other traditions were just as committed to lethal intolerance.

The reality of European colonialism, starting in 1492, was one of genocidal cruelty, often sanctioned by religious authorities. Christian missionaries were often part of the colonial enterprise which enslaved whole continents, and a few of them protested eloquently, but the majority did not (Hanke, 1974). In recent times, it was secular intellectuals who were prominent in the global anti-colonialist struggle, most visibly in the cases of Algeria, Vietnam, and Palestine. Anti-colonialist

132 Consequences and correlates of religiosity

movements were likely to be made up of the least religious. During the years of United States military intervention in Vietnam (1954–1975), those with no religious affiliation were most opposed to the war. In the 1960s civil rights movement in the United States, most of the white activists involved were unaffiliated or Jewish, and an inverse relationship was found between religiosity and support for the movement (Beit-Hallahmi and Argyle, 1997).

The apartheid regime in South Africa (1948–1994) was being led and supported by devout Christians and opposed by atheists. Under apartheid, South Africa did not admit atheists or agnostics as immigrants, despite its desperate efforts to increase the white population. This was justified, as atheists were indeed likely to oppose government policies. Looking at the Jewish community in apartheid South Africa is instructive, as religiosity again correlated with support for the regime. Jews, constituting only 2 percent of the white South African population, made up 50 percent of all activists arrested for opposition to apartheid. But who were they? Just like other whites, religious Jews supported the regime. The activists, who made up most white members of the African National Congress (now the ruling party in post-apartheid South Africa), were atheists of Jewish descent (Shimoni, 2003).

Moslems are a minority in India, and so the target of majority (Hindu) violence. When Moslems are a majority, as in Egypt or in Pakistan, they treat the religious minorities there as badly as they are treated in other countries. Shinto religion did play a major role in the rise and fall of the Japanese empire, Nazism's global ally (Hardacre, 1991). Japanese Zen Buddhism, widely considered meditative and pacifist, was actually an enthusiastic supporter of the imperial regime and Japan's war policies (Victoria, 2006). In the twenty-first century, massacres have been carried out by Buddhists, and directed at Moslems, a minority community, in Myanmar and Sri Lanka (Fuller, 2013). Buddhists should not be singled out, because followers of all religions have been guilty of such crimes, with the exception of religious pacifists, who are found in many groups.

In response to the challenge to the status of any religion as a source of moral inspiration, apologists will hasten to bring up the horrors committed by the atheist dictators Stalin, Mao Zedong, and Pol Pot (Adolf Hitler is usually added to the list, but he remained a Roman Catholic to his last day) and the evil brought about by secular nationalisms and revolutions. Examples of historical atrocities committed by secular and religious movements could be easily multiplied, but the psychological question is the effect of religiosity on individual behavior. Will any religious individual picked at random be more or less pro-social compared to an atheist?

Developing a moral compass

The panhuman experience is that parents are the carriers of morality, as they convey to their children a fantasy of a world ordered by right and wrong, reward and punishment. Socialization in all cultures focuses first on impulse control and then on competition–cooperation skills. Ethical reasoning everywhere involves the capacity to transcend self-interest (Singer, 1981), because going beyond the

Consequences and correlates of religiosity **133**

egocentric perspective is the starting point for sympathy and concern, leading to responses in terms of justice and fairness.

The academic study of moral development has largely ignored religion. Jean Piaget, who pioneered moral development theory, believed that the ethic of cooperation and justice is learned in interaction with peers (Piaget 1932/1965). Lawrence Kohlberg argued that religiosity and moral reasoning are inherently unrelated, and justice-based moral reasoning develops out of perspective-taking abilities developed in social interaction: "When members of religious groups attempt to support the content of moral beliefs, they fall back on the general forms of moral judgment or moral principles ... that develop regardless of religious affiliation" (Kohlberg, 1981, p. 303).

In individual development, the earliest moral intuitions appear before any learning about supernatural agents, and innate empathic arousal together with internalized empathy are the motivating force behind moral orientation (Hoffman, 2000; Decety and Batson, 2009; Zaki and Mitchell, 2013). References to divine authority are sometimes used by parents to bolster their authority in disciplining children, and examples can be found in all cultures (Geertz, 1960). Nunn (1964) found that this "coalition" with divinity was prevalent among parents who were ineffectual and powerless.

Kohlberg (1981) described six stages of moral development, and only the three top stages are of concern here. Stage 4 reflects a social-order perspective and accepts outside rules without internalizing. Stage 5 reflects a social contract perspective, with individuals holding different views, but cooperating in a democratic society. Stage 6 is an ideal position of following universal justice principles, without any other considerations. Conservative religious individuals exhibit increased preference for Kohlberg's conventional stage 4 and decreased preference for the principled reasoning that is exhibited in stages 5 and 6 (Deka and Broota, 1988; Richards, 1991).

Religion and individual generosity

Religious individuals are perceived as being more moral (Hout and Fischer, 2002) and likable than are nonreligious individuals (Bailey and Young, 1986). Regular churchgoers are perceived more positively than those who do not regularly attend church (Isaac, Bailey and Isaac, 1995). Along the same lines, professionals who actively express religious beliefs are rated as more intelligent, likable, trustworthy, and moral, relative to those who do not espouse religious beliefs (Bailey and Doriot, 1985). Widman, Corcoran, and Nagy (2009) showed that individuals with strong Christian beliefs were more likely to rate others displaying a cross as more moral than others not displaying such a symbol.

Altruistic behavior has been defined by Ben-Ner and Kramer (2011) as a sacrifice of one's resources for the benefit of others, representing a trade-off between one's self-interest and a regard for others. Pro-sociality is similarly defined as the tendency to behave so as to benefit another individual or other individuals,

134 Consequences and correlates of religiosity

and cooperation is the ability to work with others, while achieving mutually beneficial outcomes. Psychological experiments have tried to assess the religiosity–generosity connection usually by measuring the behavior in response to introducing religious ideas into the respondent's consciousness.

Galen (2012) critiqued the research on religious pro-sociality, because the experimental and quasi-experimental literature regarding pro-social interactions (e.g. sharing and generosity) was unrelated to results from naturalistic studies. Conceptual problems in the interpretation of this literature include separating the effects of stereotypes and in-group biases from impression formation, as well as controlling for self-report biases in the measurement of religious pro-sociality. Galen also criticized the practice of comparing high levels of religiosity with "low religiosity," rather than with the completely nonreligious.

Research on altruism relies on three levels of behavior: self-report, actions in an experiment, and behavior in the real world. These levels are rarely connected. Batson, Schoenrade, and Ventis (1993) described a gap between self-reported readiness to help and actual behavior in religious individuals. The motivation for positive self-presentation is clear (see Chapter 4). Batson (2011) argued against considering the behavior of saints and martyrs as evidence for altruism. The possibility that their motivation has been fundamentally selfish, and they were consciously thinking about future fame cannot be excluded (Batson and Gray, 1981; Batson *et al.*, 1989). Worrying about reputation may be considered extrinsic to "pure" altruism, but may lead to good deeds nevertheless. Those who want to be considered saintly, and do saintly things, are better than those who earn a reputation by exploiting others. The nameless nuns who are taking care of the dying or the retarded gain no worldly recognition or fame. They may expect afterlife rewards only, just like many believers, but their selflessness remains the purest we can find or imagine.

When college students in the United States were given a chance to cheat and to perform an act of helping, there was no correlation between their eventual behavior and their religiosity level (Beit-Hallahmi and Argyle, 1997). Saroglou *et al.* (2005) summarized a series of studies by stating that the impact of religiosity on pro-sociality was limited, but real, because religious individuals not only reported altruistic actions and empathy, but were also judged as being altruistic by their peers, who presumably knew them well. Pichon, Boccato, and Saroglou (2007) primed subjects with positive religious terms (heaven, miracle, salvation), neutral religious terms (altar, steeple, incense), or control words. Those primed with positive religious concepts were able to recognize pro-social words (e.g. help, support) faster, suggesting an activation of pro-social ideation. Participants were also given an opportunity to pass out pamphlets promoting charity, and those primed with positive religious words took more pamphlets to distribute. Malhotra (2010) showed that pro-social actions among church attenders in the United States could definitely be expected on Sunday, the day of worship, when religion, and religious norms, were salient. Moslem students in India who were in training to join the clergy were significantly more cooperative and more generous than other students (Ahmed, 2009).

Pichon and Saroglou (2009) manipulated the religious context of a hypothetical person in financial need, by providing a picture of the person either in front of a church or a gymnasium. Religious context increased self-reported intentions to help the person if he was presented as homeless, but not if presented as an illegal immigrant. Priming with religious ideation has been found to increase vengeance taken against another person, but this was affected by personal submissiveness (Saroglou, Corneille and Van Cappellen, 2009). Furthermore, without the experimenter's suggestion to seek revenge, religious primes actually increased pro-social behavior (Saroglou, Corneille and Van Cappellen, 2009). Blogowska, Lambert, and Saroglou (2013) showed that religiosity may lead to both helping and harming members of out-groups, depending on situational variables.

Helping in-group members is probably more likely, as some studies have shown. Orbell *et al.* (1992) tested whether religiosity would make a difference in the Prisoner's Dilemma game, which gives players opportunities to cooperate with partners. Effects were found only among Mormons in Utah, interpreted in terms of support for other Mormons. Shariff and Norenzayan (2007) demonstrated that religious concept activation resulted in allocation of more money to in-group members than to out-group members. Bulbulia and Mahoney (2008) demonstrated that New Zealand Christians were more altruistic toward Canadian Christians than were New Zealand citizens to other New Zealand citizens. Sosis and Ruffle (2004) found that members of religious kibbutzim in Israel were more willing to cooperate when anonymously paired with a member of the kibbutzim than with a city resident.

Tan and Vogel (2008) found that individuals (especially strongly religious people) were more likely to transfer money in an anonymous trust game to more religious partners. Similar findings have been reported by Fershtman, Gneezy and Verboven (2005) and Ben-Ner *et al.* (2009). Data from a survey of one mainline Protestant denomination in the United States showed that conservative members donated more money, donated more to the local church, and to other religious organizations, while liberal members donated more to secular charities (Lunn, Klay and Douglass, 2001). A study of tipping at restaurants in the United States concluded that the religious feel that they can tip less because they may be donating money to charity or doing other good deeds (Sachdeva, Iliev and Medin, 2009). Eckel and Grossman (2004) found that religious individuals donated mainly to religious organizations, where some benefits were expected. Similarly, Iannaccone (1998) stated that many of those donating to religious organizations were rewarded directly.

Johansson-Stenman, Mahmud, and Martinsson (2009) found that both Hindus and Moslems in Bangladesh trusted co-religionists more than they trusted followers of other religions, but this had no effect on behavior in a trust experiment. When the targets of one's good deeds are not labeled, do religious people feel more empathy towards their fellow humans and are more likely to provide help to a person in need? Ahmed and Salas (2009) conducted cooperation experiments in India, Mexico, and Sweden, and no effects of religion were found. Tan (2006)

136 Consequences and correlates of religiosity

tested whether religiosity would affect individual generosity in games where one player decides on the sum to be given to another, but found no effects. Anderson and Mellor (2009) and Anderson, Mellor, and Milyo (2010) argued that the effects of religion on cooperation and trust in laboratory experiments have been minimal, if any. Similar findings in studies done with different cultures have been reported by Fehr *et al.* (2002), Karlan (2005), and Bellemare and Kröger (2007).

Laboratory experiments on generosity and trust have been criticized, and researchers have attempted to carry out more field studies (Danielson and Holm, 2007). Wuthnow (2000) reported that individual members in church prayer groups in the United States were more forgiving in interpersonal relations. Ahmed and Salas (2013) showed that religiosity had no effect on cooperation in economic games, but a religious setting did. Participants who were tested in a chapel were more cooperative and attributed positive attitudes to others. Hadnes and Schumacher (2012) experimented with 359 entrepreneurs in Burkina Faso, who were primed through an interview that asked them about moral codes, amulets, and ancestral rites. Those primed showed significantly greater generosity in an economic game. The authors argued that this resulted from a combination of egalitarian norms, the idea of being watched by "powers" (Shariff and Norenzayan, 2007), and expectation of supernatural punishment if norms were transgressed.

Parochial altruism: the problem of love thy neighbor

What emerges from the research is that most religiously inspired altruism is parochial, limited to in-group members (Bernhard, Fischbacher and Fehr, 2006; Hoffmann, 2013). Hall, Matz, and Wood (2010) concluded that "religious humanitarianism" is largely directed at in-group members, and Norenzayan and Shariff (2008) stated that religious pro-sociality is primarily in-group altruism. Duriez (2004) and Saroglou (2006) suggested that not only does religiosity fail to reliably predict universal helping behavior but also that it is a mistake to even hold such an expectation. It should be kept in mind that the preference for religious in-group members is found in the case of most sub-identities, such as sex, age, race, and nationality (Fiske and Taylor, 2013). The issue is that religion is sometimes considered an exception.

Looking at the historical evidence, it is clear that traditional religious morality is most often ethnocentric, a call for in-group solidarity, which means that moral compassion ends at the boundary of the religious community. It is interesting to note that this has been expressed in ancient writings, which were quite explicit about it. "Love they neighbor" is one of the best known imperatives in the world, and is widely regarded as a call for unconditional, universal love for humanity. However, if we go back to the original source, we discover something totally different. The "Love thy neighbor" commandment quite explicitly covered only members of the tribe. The original verse states: "Thou shalt not avenge, nor bear any grudge against the children of thy people, but thou shalt love thy neighbor as thyself: I am the Lord" (Leviticus 19: 18). Many other Biblical injunctions commanded Jews to treat in-group members differently than non-Jews. The Hebrew Bible also contains notable verses that call for compassion for those outside the tribe, such as "Thou shalt not oppress a stranger: for ye know the heart of a stranger, seeing ye were strangers in the land of Egypt" (Exodus 23: 9). Such verses, remarkable as they are in expressing universalist ideals, are far fewer than those emphasizing in-group loyalty.

Biblical writings illustrate the meaning of morality as group loyalty and the psychological effects of real and imagined kinship in moral judgments and ideals.

> The evidence that lies before us in great abundance points to organized religion as an expression of tribalism ... charity and other acts of altruism are concentrated on their coreligionists; when extended to outsiders, it is usually to proselytize and thereby strengthen the size of the tribe and its allies ... The conflict among religions is often instead an accelerant, if not a direct cause, of war ... The goal of religions is submission to the will and common good of the tribe.
>
> (Wilson, 2012, pp. 258–259)

Even parochial altruism reduces selfishness and helps others in the community (Myers, 2012a), but the indifference (or hostility) towards out-groups is a problem.

According to Max Weber, some religious traditions were able to move from parochial to universal altruism: "The great achievement of ethical religions, above all of the ethical and asceticist sects of Protestantism, was to shatter the fetters of the sib" (Weber, 1951, p. 237). Historically, kinship has been the foundation of social solidarity. The Enlightenment morality transcends kin, tribe, and nation. "Moral progress has consisted in the main of protest against cruel customs, and of attempts to enlarge human sympathy" (Russell, 2008, p. 30). Moral progress since the Enlightenment is characterized by an expanding circle of moral concern encompassing not just members of one's ethnic, political, or religious group, but also wider humanity and even some nonhuman animals (Singer, 1981). Pinker (2011) described the "expanding circle" of empathy caused by modern transportation and communications, and the "escalator of reason" caused by fast-expanding education and literacy, leading to a more peaceful world. The process has been described as inevitable:

> In the course of human cultural development there has been a gradual though faltering progression toward enlarging the area brought within a single ethical system. The logical (and undoubtedly necessary) end of such an evolutionary process is the establishment of a world community and the permanent elimination of borders that limit the application of basic ethical codes.
>
> (Goldschmidt, 1954, p. 107)

Today, most of those who pronounce the Love Thy Neighbor imperative have in mind true universalism, but the reality of in-group solidarity is often stronger.

138 Consequences and correlates of religiosity

Preston and Ritter (2013) found that, for Americans, the term religion, perceived as more limited, activated in-group pro-sociality, while the term God led to pro-sociality beyond group boundaries. McFarland, Brown, and Webb (2013) reported that scores on an Identification With All Humanity scale, administered to several samples cross-culturally, were unrelated to religiosity or religious upbringing.

Being watched

Being watched may have several meanings: First, the religious one, which means imagining a god or a spirit (e.g. an ancestor) watching over an individual or a group; second, being watched by a superior; and third, being watched by peers. In all cases, a transgression may lead to actual punishment, or an event perceived as a punishment (disease or death believed to be caused by the ancestor), or to a loss of reputation.

The idea of being watched and punished by supernatural agents should lead to pro-social behavior (Bering, 2006; Johnson and Bering, 2006; Norenzayan and Shariff, 2008). The supernatural monitoring hypothesis suggests that thinking about God might make believers feel as if their behavior is being monitored. Gervais and Norenzayan (2012a) found that in believers, an explicit God prime created self-awareness similar to thinking about being watched by other people. A God prime increased socially desirable responding among believers. Bering, McLeod, and Shackelford (2005) showed that respondents who were led to believe they were in the presence of a ghost were less likely to cheat. Children told that they were in the presence of an invisible, but watchful person ("Princess Alice") were less likely to cheat (Piazza, Bering and Ingram, 2011).

Shariff and Norenzayan (2007) tested whether people must imagine being watched to behave generously. Respondents gave more money to an anonymous stranger in a game if they had been previously exposed to religious words, regardless of personal religiosity. Benjamin, Choi, and Fisher (2010), who replicated this priming, failed to find any effect. However, the impact of religious concepts was identical to that of secular law-enforcement concepts ("jury," "contract," or "police"). These findings clearly show that religious stimuli do affect behavior even in a secularized culture, but also that secular impulse control stimuli had the same effect as "God." The authors themselves stated: "we showed that implicit activation of concepts related to secular moral institutions restrained selfishness as much as did religious suggestion" (Shariff and Norenzayan, 2007, p. 807). Apparently, "police," "jury," and "God" induce a general tendency to be good (or appear good), and not just to avoid transgressions (Randolph-Seng and Nielsen, 2008). Harrell (2012) found that reward-related primes, whether religious (heaven) or secular (appreciation) elicited generosity. Ma-Kellams and Blascovich (2013) found that using "science" terms, such as "laboratory," "hypothesis," or "theory" also led to more positive behaviors. Apparently, science is imagined by many people as a positive authority, enjoying a pro-social halo. We may conclude that the transition from religious to secular social control seems smooth and well-established, despite the powerful legacy of historical traditions.

Honesty and corruption

Although religion is a good predictor of positive attitudes about honesty, the evidence on actual integrity in religious people is inconsistent (Donahue and Nielsen, 2005). Weaver and Agle (2002) reviewed research regarding religion and ethical behavior and found no differences between religious and nonreligious persons in dishonest behavior or cheating. One study, in fact, suggested that students in a religious school were more likely to cheat than those in a secular one (Guttman, 1984), but Perrin (2000) found that religious students were less likely to be dishonest. Much research on ethical judgments has been done on business administration students, with most studies showing a positive correlation between religiosity and proper ethical responses (Conroy and Emerson, 2004; Kurpis, Beqiri and Helgeson, 2008). Bloodgood, Turnley, and Mudrack (2008) tested the effects of ethics instruction, religiosity, and intelligence on cheating in a sample of 230 business students. Religiosity turned out to be more influential than the other two factors in reducing the likelihood of cheating. Randolph-Seng and Nielsen (2007) found that participants who were primed with religious words cheated significantly less than participants who were primed with neutral words.

Humans spend most of their waking hours as economic actors, workers, and consumers, and are likely to encounter ethical problems. Parboteeah and Cullen (2002) surveyed 3450 managers from twenty-eight countries, and found that managers in more religious countries showed more acceptance of unethical behavior. Asking individuals about their willingness to justify acts which are ethically suspect is a measure of loyalty to normative behavior. Using data on 63,087 individuals from forty-four countries, Parboteeah, Hoegl, and Cullen (2008) found that religiosity was negatively related to such willingness. Parboteeah, Hoegl, and Cullen (2009) hypothesized that a higher religiosity in a nation will lead to stronger work obligation norms in individuals. Data on 62,218 individual respondents from forty-five countries supported the hypothesis. Vitell (2009) surveyed the literature and argued that religiosity was tied to stronger ethical norms in both business people and consumers, but the evidence does not seem very strong.

Corruption means that public resources are used illegally, for the benefit of a few officials and those connected to them. Since 1995, an organization known as Transparency International has been rating the nations of the world on corruption, as measured by the enforcement of conflict of interest and corruption laws. The least corrupt countries are New Zealand, Finland, Sweden, Singapore, Norway, the Netherlands, Australia, Switzerland, and Canada. The most corrupt include Burundi, Equatorial Guinea, Venezuela, Chad, Libya, Angola, Democratic Republic of Congo, Cambodia, Guinea, Kyrgyzstan, and Yemen. What is easily noted is that the least corrupt nations are those that are the most secularized. The same nations lead the ratings on measures of quality of life and human development (see Chapter 9). The most corrupt are more religious. Paldam (2001) found that Catholics, Orthodox, and Moslems were more corrupt than Protestants, and differences were tied to prosperity levels.

140 Consequences and correlates of religiosity

Political and social attitudes

For most of human history, supernaturalism was used to legitimize political authority in many cultures. Aristotle (384 BCE–322 BCE), in his *Politics*, suggested that autocratic rulers should put on a show of religiosity to exploit popular beliefs about divine reward and punishment. In Plato's (427 BCE–347 BCE) plan for an ideal state, the lower classes must believe that the social order had supernatural sanction, being unable to consider it a purely human creation and still regard it as binding. This idea became known as the Noble Lie. Defenders of Plato mention that he also hoped that the upper class would believe that lie for the good of the state. More recently, religious organizations have been involved in preserving the old order all over the world. Progress towards democracy and equality has been resisted. On December 8, 1864, Pope Pius IX issued the Encyclical known as Quanta Cura (Condemning Current Errors) in which he condemned freedom of speech and conscience, as well as the idea of "the people's will," expressed in general elections. Behind it was the idea that truth had been revealed (through the Church), and individual humans cannot be trusted to express their views. How does religiosity affect political views where humans are allowed to speak and debate more openly?

A well-known critic has described the historical role of Christianity as follows:

> It has been, at all times and everywhere, the steady defender of bad governments, bad laws, bad social theories, bad institutions. It was, for centuries, an apologist for slavery, as it was an apologist for the divine right of kings.
>
> (Mencken, 1930, pp. 305–306)

Another assessment states: "Religion not only bids the deprived to accept their lot, but maintains that it is the just outcome of rules that are the best possible, indeed, in some instances divinely inspired" (Stark, 1964, p. 702).

Does religion always side with the rich and powerful, as McLeod (1981) claims? Many other historical examples could be cited. During the Industrial Revolution, the Church of England cooperated with the owners of industry, and in the early nineteenth century the British Parliament acted to construct Church of England parishes in south-east England in response to the French Revolution (Homan, 1986). We find an echo of that in the words of the Reverend Henry Ward Beecher, a leading abolitionist, who stated in 1875 that "no man in this land suffers from poverty unless it be more than his fault, unless it be his sin" (McLoughlin, 1970, p. 150). In 1877, Beecher preached against the railroad strikers: "the necessities of the great railroad companies demanded that there be a reduction of wages ... It was true that $1 a day was not enough to support a man and five children, if a man would insist on smoking and drinking beer. Was not a dollar a day enough to buy bread? Water costs nothing." Beecher's well-fed congregation reportedly laughed in accord (McLoughlin, 1970, pp. 98–99).

Writing about life under the apartheid regime in South Africa, Paton (1948), describes that effect of religion as an anesthetic for the oppressed:

> And indeed this Msimangu is known as a preacher. It is good for the government, they say in Johannesburg, that Msimangu preaches of a world not made by hands, for he touches people at the hearts, and sends them marching to heaven instead of to Pretoria ...Yet he is despised by some, for this golden voice that could raise a nation, speaks always thus ... They say he preaches of a world not made by hands, while in the streets about him men suffer and struggle and die. They ask what folly it is that can so seize upon a man, what folly is it that seizes upon so many of their people, making the hungry patient, the suffering content, the dying at peace? And how fools listen to him, silent, enrapt, sighing when he is done, feeding their empty bellies on his empty words.
>
> (Paton, 1948, pp. 90–91)

Leuba (1937, p. 197) wrote about those in the United States who wanted "to preserve at all cost, for the masses, a religion preaching humility, obedience to established authority, and renouncement of earthly possessions in exchange for the imperishable treasures of heaven." Pope (1942) described a mill town in the southern United States where the mill workers joined small sects which substituted religious status for social status, and the clergy always sided with employers during strikes (Earle, Knudsen and Shriver, 1976). Billings (1990) presented a case where, not far from the town that Pope (1942) studied, religious leaders were on the side of labor unions, but this was obviously an exception to the rule. In the late twentieth century, it was the conservative Protestant leader Jerry Falwell who stated that "[l]abor unions should study and read the Bible instead of asking for more money. When people get right with God, they are better workers" (quoted in Potts, 2008, p. 54).

Is there a general relationship between religiosity and basic political stances? The correlation between a rejection of supernaturalism and radical political views has been demonstrated repeatedly (Beit-Hallahmi, 2007). Rutchick (2010) found that exposure to religious images pushed Christians, but not others, towards more conservative political views. An earlier survey concluded that "no empirical study has ever found a relation between doctrinal orthodoxy and political liberalism or radicalism" (Argyle and Beit-Hallahmi, 1975, p. 107; see also Froese and Bader, 2008). Burris, Branscombe, and Jackson (2000) found a connection between religiosity and patriotic symbols, while Saroglou, Corneille, and Van Cappellen (2009) and Van Cappellen et al. (2011) found that religious primes activated submissive thoughts, which the authors described "in its broad sense, including obedience, compliance, conformity, dependence, restriction of free will" (p. 144). In a representative sample of Americans, religiosity was positively correlated with greater trust in authority (Wisneski, Lytle and Skitka, 2009).

Social psychologists have studied Just World beliefs, which assert that people generally get what they deserve, and the social order produces the right outcomes.

142 Consequences and correlates of religiosity

Religions offer ideas that "can encompass an incident of seeming injustice within the larger framework of ultimate justice, (so that) in effect, there are no innocent victims, no injustices, in the ultimate sense of things" (Lerner, 1980, p. 164). This may help in coping, as indicated above, but Just World ideas have their darker side. Such beliefs (or illusions) lead to the derogation of victims, as the oppressed and deprived are held responsible for their lot in life. The political implications are clear: Just World believers hold conservative views. There is a marked tendency for religious people to have stronger beliefs in a just world (Begue, 2002; Dalbert *et al.*, 2001; Furnham, 2003; Rubin and Peplau, 1975; Sorrentino and Hardy, 1974), and this means that religiosity may be tied to victim derogation and an absence of compassion (Galen and Miller, 2011; Pichon and Saroglou, 2009). A value survey with a representative sample of 1400 Americans found that respondents who rated salvation high were significantly less likely to show compassion for the poor and minorities (Rokeach, 1969).

Jacobson (1999) reported that, in the United States, greater religiosity was correlated with fatalistic views and passive acceptance of the social order, but Curry, Koch, and Chalfant (2004) found no relationship between religious affiliation, religious involvement, and support for greater economic equality. Data on 24,000 Moslem respondents from twenty-five countries showed similar results, with no relationship between religiosity and redistributive preferences (Pepinsky and Welborne, 2011). Scheve and Stasavage (2006a, b) showed that attending religious services more often will reduce support for government spending on unemployment benefits, health care, and social welfare. They suggested that religious individuals prefer lower levels of wealth redistribution as long as they derive psychological benefits from religion, which buffer individuals against adverse life events and serve as a substitute for the welfare state. Guiso, Sapienza, and Zingales (2006) found that religiosity was correlated with opposition to redistribution policies. Williamson and Carnes (2013) found that in the United States, states with large populations of evangelical Christians had less generous parental leave policies. Gill and Lundsgaarde (2004) and Scheve and Stasavage (2006a, b) reported a negative relationship between religiosity level (measured through belief in God and attendance) in a nation, or in individual states in the case of the United States, and the scope of welfare state arrangements.

These findings, and their interpretations, have been challenged. Davis and Robinson (2006) proposed that,

> in many countries where Catholicism, Eastern Orthodoxy, Judaism, or Protestantism predominate, the religiously orthodox are to the right of modernists on cultural issues of abortion, sexuality, family, and gender, but to the left of modernists on issues of economic justice.
>
> (Davis and Robison, 2006, p. 168)

This proposition has been tested and supported, using data from large-scale surveys, in the United States, Europe, and the Islamic world (Davis and Robinson, 1996,

1999a, 1999b, 2001). Using national surveys in seven Moslem-majority nations (Algeria, Bangladesh, Egypt, Indonesia, Jordan, Pakistan, and Saudi Arabia) with 9847 respondents, showed that Islamic orthodoxy (measured by support for making the state subservient to Islamic law) was positively related to support for distributive justice (Davis and Robinson, 2006). Junisbai (2010) confirmed these findings in Kazakhstan and Kyrgyzstan, two additional Moslem majority countries.

How does the connection between religious orthodoxy and the desire for distributive justice translate into support for political parties and voting patterns? It does not. Davis and Robinson (1999a) reported that their findings had no effect on voting behavior in the case of Italy. Cross-cultural research on attitudes and voting patterns has shown that religion is the best predictor of major political views. Religiosity and church attendance are far better predictors of vote choice in advanced industrial democracies than income or class (Dalton, 2006; Norris and Inglehart, 2004). Norris and Inglehart (2004, p. 201) stated that "almost three-quarters (70 percent) of the most devout ... voted for parties on the right." Roemer (1998) found that when voters had to choose between a secular party favoring the redistribution of wealth and a religious, anti-redistribution, right-wing party, the religious poor will vote for the latter. De La O and Rodden (2008) showed that in advanced democracies, religion breaks the ties between the poor and left-wing parties. So, how do we reconcile the two sets of research findings? If orthodox religiosity is tied with support for distributive justice, why do religious people vote for parties which oppose it? The answer may have to do with the kind of issues that divide conservatives and liberals, and are sometimes known as "cultural issues." They cover the status of women, reproductive rights (birth control, abortion), homosexuality, nonmarital sexuality, suicide, and euthanasia. Attitudes towards these issues are usually packaged together with economic justice questions in the political platforms of right-wing and left-wing parties. In reaction to "cultural issues," more religious voters, who are ready to support the distributive justice principles of the left, support conservative parties in elections (De La O and Rodden, 2008). These "cultural issues" may be perceived as tied to the core identity of those who identify as religious above all else.

Inglehart and Norris (2003) analyzed data from the World Values and European Values Surveys in seventy-four countries, collected between 1995 and 2001, and showed that the prevalence of support for gender equality was negatively correlated with religiosity, and positively with female literacy rate, use of contraception, and political representation. A five-item scale was used, such as "On the whole, men make better political leaders than women do" (Inglehart and Norris, 2003, p. 31). The five countries with the highest scores on equality were Finland, Sweden, West Germany, Canada, and Norway. The five lowest were Nigeria, Morocco, Egypt, Bangladesh, and Jordan.

There is a relationship between religiosity and attitudes towards the rights of minorities. In the United States, being a conservative Protestant means a reluctance to grant civil liberties to unpopular groups (Reimer and Park, 2001). Gay and Ellison (1993) found that members of African-American Protestant churches were

144 Consequences and correlates of religiosity

the least tolerant of those with unpopular views, while the unaffiliated were the most tolerant. Katnik (2002) looked at the willingness to extend civil liberties to those who want to overthrow the government by revolution, which is certainly a very liberal criterion, and used data from thirteen industrialized countries. The religious had lower levels of tolerance than the unaffiliated, and, regardless of denomination, frequent church attendance predicted lower tolerance.

Radical students on American campuses in the 1960s were more likely to come from families that were identified as Jewish, agnostic, or atheist, and self-identified atheists are more radical than self-identified agnostics (Beit-Hallahmi and Argyle, 1997). Nelson (1988) found that in surveys with representative samples of the US population between 1973 and 1985, disaffiliation from churches was tied to political liberalism. Using a representative sample of the US population between 1973 and 1977, Hadaway and Roof (1979) found that individuals raised as "nones" who remained unaffiliated were more liberal in politics and morals than those who later became religiously affiliated. Religiosity has continued to play a role in United States politics, and has been tied to support for the Iraq invasion in 2003 and to militarism in general (Barker, Hurwitz and Nelson, 2008; Froese and Mencken, 2009; Smidt, 2005). In the 2012 presidential elections religious identity was an important factor. Most of Romney's (Republican) support came from Protestant voters, and 70 percent of the unaffiliated voted for Obama.

Roccas (2005) showed that the pattern of correlations between individual values and religiosity resembles closely the pattern of correlations between values and nationalism. Both are correlated with conservative values and negatively correlated with openness to change. Roccas, Schwartz, and Amit (2010) confirmed the hypothesis that identification with one's nation correlates positively with conservation values and negatively with openness to change values. These findings would lead to a prediction that ties religiosity and nationalism to political conservatism.

Deity images and social ideals

Deity images are related to social and political attitudes among believers because they are a projection of one's personality traits. Greeley (1975, p. 79) argued that "[t]hose whose religious imagination has a propensity to a warmer, affectionate … more loving representation … will also be … more gracious and more benign in their response to political and social issues." This strictly Freudian projection hypothesis has been tested. Piazza and Glock (1979) reported that belief in a God who ordains social life as compared to one that affects personal life is correlated with conservative political views. Similarly, Greeley (1988, 1989, 1991, 1993) found that among Americans, imagining God as a mother, lover, or friend is tied to more liberal political positions. Devout Christians who imagined God in anthropomorphic terms (more like themselves) were much harsher when considering punishments for those violating the Biblical Ten Commandments (Morewedge and Clear, 2008). For Americans in a 2005 national survey, angry and

Consequences and correlates of religiosity **145**

judgmental images of God were correlated with more punitive attitudes about criminal punishments and more support for the death penalty (Bader *et al.*, 2010).

In the United States, positions regarding abortion and the death penalty (which is still common there, though long abolished in other Western nations) are hotly debated. Individuals who support the death penalty and oppose abortion, or vice versa, are accused of being inconsistent. A consistent life ethic (which is the official stand of the Roman Catholic Church), opposes both. Unnever, Bartkowski, and Cullen (2010) investigated what God image was tied to a consistent ethic position. Using data from the 2004 General Social Survey in the United States, the findings showed that individuals who believed they had a close relationship with a loving God image were likely to hold a consistent life ethic.

Froese and Bader (2008) correlated the image of God (in terms of engagement and authority) with political attitudes in eight Western nations (Australia, France, Hungary, Ireland, Latvia, New Zealand, the Slovak Republic, and the United States). God images were strongly related to attitudes about abortion and sexuality, but inconsistently related to ideals of economic justice. The United States was the exception, with Americans showing the effects of God images in all areas.

Using data from a 2005 survey on a representative sample of the United States population, Mencken, Bader, and Embry (2009) examined the relationship between measures of social trust and two God images. Among highly religious individuals, a loving God image ("forgiving," "friendly," "kind," and "loving") was tied to more social trust, while an angry God image ("critical," "punishing," "severe," "wrathful," "angered by human sins," and "angered by my sins") was tied to less trust. Froese, Bader, and Smith (2008) found that holding an image of a wrathful God, who actively punishes sinners, was significantly related to the denial of civil liberties to unpopular groups.

Prejudice and ethnocentrism

The term prejudice has been widely used in the social psychology literature to refer to unfavorable intergroup perceptions, judgments, or attitudes. Allport (1958, p. 10) provided the following definition: "Ethnic prejudice is an antipathy based upon a faulty and inflexible generalization. It may be felt or expressed. It may be directed toward a group as a whole, or toward an individual because he is a member of that group." Research on prejudice and intolerance, extending over a century, has consistently shown that religiosity is correlated with more prejudice, authoritarianism, intolerance, and punitive attitudes (supporting harsh penalties, including death). The correlation has been consistently reported in all traditions and cultures.

An early study of ethnocentrism and anti-Semitism led the authors to conclude that "those who reject religion have less ethnocentrism that those who seem to accept it" (Adorno *et al.*, 1950, p. 213). Looking at a representative sample of the United States population, Rokeach (1969) reported "religious devoutness to be positively rather than negatively related to bigotry, authoritarianism, dogmatism

146 Consequences and correlates of religiosity

and antihumanitarianism" (Rokeach, 1969, p. 4). Similar correlations have been reported since (Hunsberger and Jackson, 2005; Rowatt, Franklin and Cotton, 2005; Rowatt et al., 2009; Shen et al., 2013). Paloutzian and Kirkpatrick (1995) listed prejudice and right-wing authoritarianism as a major negative influence of religion in American society. The religiosity-prejudice connection in Europe was investigated in 1999 by using eleven nationally representative samples (n=11,904). The findings showed that the religiously affiliated, and those who attended church more often, were more prejudiced than the non-affiliated. A measure of religious particularism was used, from "there are no important truths in any religion" to "there is only one true religion," and it was highly correlated with prejudice. The authors concluded that this particularism was especially influential (Scheepers, Gijsberts and Hello, 2002). In a survey of almost 150,000 respondents in twenty-seven countries, the non-religious were the most tolerant, and the correlation between religion and intolerance was present in all religious denominations, with the exception of Buddhism. Protestants and Catholics were very similar, while Moslems were higher in intolerance, and Hindus even higher (Guiso, Sapienza and Zingales, 2003). There has been at least one attempt to reduce religious prejudice experimentally (Rothschild, Abdollahi and Pyszczynski, 2009), but such experimental manipulations can rarely be attempted in the real world.

Experimenters have used priming to assess the relationship between religiosity and prejudice. Johnson, Rowatt, and LaBouff (2010) found that subliminal exposure to religious words increased racial prejudice toward African-Americans using both overt and covert measures. Participants were exposed subliminally to Christian words (Bible, Jesus, heaven) or neutral words (shirt, butter, hammer). Regardless of pre-existing religiosity, activation of religious concepts significantly increased covert prejudice toward African-Americans. LaBouff et al. (2011) recruited participants as they passed by a religious or non-religious structure in Western Europe. With a religious stimulus, participants reported more negative attitudes toward non-Christian groups, more conservative political attitudes, and more personal religiosity, regardless of their belief in God. Johnson, Rowatt, and LaBouff (2012) found that religiosity and spirituality correlated positively with more negative attitudes toward out-groups. They also found that individuals subliminally primed with religious terms showed increases in negative attitudes toward value-violating out-groups, regardless of self-reported religiosity, indicating the causal role of the religion.

Ginges, Hansen, and Norenzayan (2009) found that attending religious rituals strongly predicted support for suicide attacks and parochial altruism among both Israelis and Palestinians. Bushman et al. (2007) demonstrated that reading stories which depict violence "in the name of God" increases aggression toward strangers. The experimental manipulation was reading narratives which advocated violent retaliation, credited either to the Bible or to "ancient scrolls" without specifying the source. Later, participants played a competitive game. Participants were more vindictive if they had previously read the story credited to the Bible, and if the violence was said to be "sanctioned by God." This effect was much larger for believers than for non-believers.

Oliner and Oliner (1988) studied the truly heroic behavior of individuals who saved the lives of Jews in Europe during the Holocaust, but reported that religiosity had no effect in these cases. Varese and Yaish (2000) found that "religiosity and altruism are negatively related; the less religious one is, the more likely she is to rescue. A plausible explanation for this negative effect is that a very religious person might be more receptive to anti-Semitism" (p. 320). It seems that the net contribution of majority religion in the Holocaust in terms of altruism was negative. What we should keep in mind is that altruism in this case meant risking (or losing) your life, so those who did not join the miniscule group of rescuers should not be judged harshly.

Explaining the religion–prejudice connection

Religious hostility and competition, inspired by myth and doctrine, play a role in creating specific prejudices, especially when groups compete over the idea of being the elect, and claim the same historical tradition. Glock and Stark (1966) suggested that American anti-Semitism was partly due to Christian teachings, and found that 86 percent of Southern Baptists agreed that "[t]he Jews can never be forgiven for crucifying Christ," compared with 60 percent of other Protestants and 46 percent of Catholics. These findings were replicated for Protestant clergy (Stark *et al.*, 1971), Lutherans (Kersten, 1971), and Mormons (Mauss, 1968) in the USA, and for Christians in the Netherlands (Eisinga, Konig and Scheepers, 1995). Pargament *et al.* (2007) showed that the perception of Jews as a threat to Christianity predicted anti-Semitism among students in the United States. These findings cannot account for other prejudices which are still prevalent. Using a representative sample of 783 Dutch respondents in 1990–1991, Konig, Eisinga, and Scheepers (2000) differentiated between religious anti-Semitism, measured by such items as "Jews remain responsible for the death of Jesus" and secular anti-Semitism, measured by such items as "Jews have too much power in the financial world." They concluded that "Christian beliefs do not only induce religious anti-Semitism, but indirectly secular anti-Semitism as well. Anti-Semitism still is the inevitable right hand of Christology ... even in the very secularized Dutch context" (p. 384).

Higher religiosity has long meant having less progressive views on racial equality in the United States across religious subcultures (Edgell and Tranby, 2007). A meta-analysis of fifty-five studies demonstrated that greater religiosity significantly predicted negative attitudes toward racial out-groups, and found that only agnostics were tolerant (Hall, Matz and Wood, 2010). The authors concluded that religious individuals are racist because, as belief systems, both religiosity and racism are tied to conformity and traditionalism. They stated that "[o]ther races might be treated as out-groups because religion is practiced largely within race, because training in a religious in-group identity promotes general ethnocentrism, and because different others appear to be in competition for resources" (Hall, Matz and Wood, 2010, p. 126).

Prejudice may be triggered by felt threats. According to terror-management theory (Greenberg *et al.*, 1986), outsiders are easily perceived as threats to the

148 Consequences and correlates of religiosity

established worldview, on which death-transcendence illusions are based. Greenberg *et al.* (1990) found that reminding Christians of their mortality leads to increased hostility towards Jews. Okulicz-Kozaryn (2011), in a comparative study of seventy-seven countries, found that religious diversity in a population is experienced as a threat and lowers well-being.

Prejudice is obviously related to intergroup bias (Hewstone, Rubin and Willis, 2002), and the prevalence of religious bigotry has been interpreted as showing that the moral obligations owed co-religionists do not extend to outsiders (Beit-Hallahmi and Argyle, 1997; Bernhard, Fischbacher and Fehr, 2006). This "groupness" component focuses on religion as a social identity and the goals of protecting and cooperating with the in-group (Preston, Ritter and Hernandez, 2010). Religions foster in-group expressions of preference and superiority, centered upon the beliefs than one's group is more important than other groups, and intragroup expressions of group cohesion and devotion centered upon the beliefs that the group is more important than any individual members (see Chapter 3). Religious intergroup bias exists among numerous religious groups, including non-Western ones (Islam and Hewstone, 1993). Experiments using priming of religious concepts provide further evidence that when one's religious identity is made salient, there is greater intolerance toward the out-group members, in terms of both religion and ethnicity (Johnson *et al.*, 2010). The religion–prejudice correlation is clearly connected to the correlation between religion and conservative political attitudes. The Enlightenment ideals of universalism and equality are often not fully embraced by religious individuals. This is reflected by research on values (see Chapter 4), which shows religiosity tied to the values of traditionalism (Inglehart and Baker, 2000) and political conservatism (Roccas, 2005).

What is socially and politically significant is that a strong religious commitment may interfere with support for religious freedom and tolerance, as the concern of group members for their own rights does not extend to the rights of others and of other groups. As has often been observed, the irreligious are likely to defend the rights of believers. As one observer put it: "Atheism is a European legacy worth fighting for, not least because it creates a safe public space for believers" (Zizek, 2006, p. A 23).

There has been a gradual decline in prejudice in many Western countries, which is directly tied to secularization (see Chapter 9). This change has led to greater tolerance of minorities and more social contacts (including marriage) across religious boundaries.

Consequences, congruence, and cultural specificity

Chapter 4 introduced the notion of congruence between the individuals and the surrounding religious environment, which has been shown to have significant consequences. Most studies that have found positive correlations between religiosity and happiness, which is typically seen as a universal effect of religion, have been done in the United States. The effect may be different in countries where believers

Consequences and correlates of religiosity **149**

are in the minority. This hypothesis was tested in an analysis of the World Values Survey data in the United States, the Netherlands, and Denmark in 2000 (Snoep, 2008). Seven indicators of religiosity and a single question on life satisfaction were correlated. The correlations between religiosity and happiness were low and positive. The correlations are higher in the USA (average + 0.13, most significant) than in the Netherlands (average + 0.05, none significant) and Denmark (average + 0.05, none significant). Lavric and Flere (2008) used several measures of religiosity and two measures of psychological well-being in a cross-cultural survey of university students in five countries: Slovenia, Bosnia and Herzegovina, Serbia, the United States, and Japan. In the two countries with higher levels of religiosity, Bosnia and Herzegovina and the United States, positive correlations between religiosity and psychological well-being were found.

Eichhorn (2011) looked at life satisfaction data, obtained from the World Values Survey, from forty-three European and English-speaking nations. Individual religiosity was positively correlated with life satisfaction in nations where average religiosity was higher, indicating a role for societal conformity. Using the World Values Survey, Lun and Bond (2013) found that reports of life satisfaction and happiness were positively correlated with measures of religiosity. In cultures where religious socialization was more dominant, reports of religious practices were positively related to subjective well-being, but the relationship was negative in cultures where religious socialization was less common.

Gebauer, Sedikides, and Neberich (2012) examined data on 187,957 individuals in eleven countries, and found that where religion is less salient, being religious confers fewer or no benefits. In countries where religiosity was not a majority position, religious individuals did not report higher self-esteem. Okulicz-Kozaryn (2010) used data on 100,000 respondents from seventy-nine nations, from Albania to Zimbabwe, and found that the contribution of religion to life satisfaction depends on cultural context, and religious people were happier only in religious nations. Stavrova, Fetchenhauer, and Schlösser (2013) hypothesized that religiosity contributes to subjective well-being where it is considered normative in a given nation. Their data showed the effect to be stronger in religious countries with dominant negative attitudes towards non-believers. Preference for secular values, emphasizing autonomy and rejecting tradition, was related to life satisfaction in individuals, but the direction of the relationship was determined by the individual's nation score on the Human Development Index. In nations scoring low, the relationship between secular values and life satisfaction was negative. In nations scoring high on the HDI countries there was a negative relationship in Waves 1 and 2 of the World Values Survey, which turned positive in Waves 3 and 4. The findings show the congruence between societal and individual values, with a gradual change process in high HDI nations (Li and Bond, 2010).

An interaction between genetically determined personality disposition and culture led to positive or negative effects of religiosity on well-being in research comparing European Americans with Koreans. Individuals who were genetically higher on social sensitivity enjoyed well-being if they were Koreans and more religious. For European Americans this effect was not found. The cultural context, which in the case of Korea emphasizes religious affiliation, made the difference (Sasaki, Kim and Xu, 2011).

Using a sample of 187,957 respondents from eleven religiously diverse cultures Gebauer *et al.* (2013) found that both individual and collective religiosity weakened the relationship between personal income and psychological adjustment because of religious anti-materialist norms. Religious individuals in religious cultures reported better psychological adjustment when their income was low rather than high. As reported above, Diener, Tay, and Myers (2011) found that religiosity was associated with subjective well-being (SWB) in nations that were more religious, but also poor, and not in wealthy nations, which are also more secularized. Cultures may be dominated by religiosity, or not, which affects families and the religious socialization of children (Kelley and De Graaf, 1997). Sabatier *et al.* (2011) found that the positive connections between religiosity, family orientation, and life satisfaction among adolescents were stronger in high religiosity cultures (Poland and the United States) as compared to the low religiosity culture of Germany.

7

CONVERSION AND CONVERT-DEPENDENT GROUPS

Most religious behavior is rather undramatic, but the natural tendency of observers and researchers is to look at individuals demonstrating costly involvements. We are enthralled by enthusiasm and readiness to sacrifice, and look with amazement at the total commitments and unshaken loyalty of those who prove it by committing their lives to a group or dying for it. Where there is a price to be paid, and serious sacrifices are made, and when a person joins a despised minority, we are rightly impressed and intrigued. Most researchers can only look at intense religious commitments and experiences from the outside, and this was already true of William James (1902/1961). This is clear when commitment leading to self-sacrifice is observed. Secular loyalty to nations and movements, leading to death on the battlefield, raises fewer questions than the loss of life for religious ideals. Conversion seems like a mysterious, sudden, and powerful transfer of loyalty and attachment, which runs counter to the way most humans acquire a religious identity. It is a rare phenomenon, occurring in the small minority of believers who have strayed away from family and community and embraced a new identity.

Converts and convert-dependent groups are inherently attractive to students of religion because they demonstrate the reality of heightened religious motivation and commitment. Students of religion have looked closely at the phenomenon of conversion. First, because it is dramatic in the phenomenological sense, sometimes accompanied by reports of "mystical states," visions, and hallucinations. It may be said that such fascinating cases are unrepresentative, but they may represent more common processes, significantly and conveniently magnified. Conversion has been believed to be religion in its purest form (Clark, 1958), as "[t]he experience of conversion ... affectively stirs up and assuages the same existential anxieties that incite religious belief in the first place" (Atran, 2002, p. 173). Research on conversion may indeed illuminate the dynamics of high involvement in religion,

152 Conversion and convert-dependent groups

covering the founders of new movements, religious leaders, clergy, and committed members. Every founder of a new religion is by definition a convert. Founders may experience a conversion through a "creative illness," with "the spontaneous and rapid recovery accompanied by a feeling of elation ... the conviction of having discovered a grandiose truth that must be proclaimed to mankind" (Ellenberger, 1970, pp. 449–450).

Conversion is not universally praised. Virginia Woolf, in *Mrs. Dalloway*, has a contemptuous view of conversion, and in the late 1930s, Cole (1942, p. 377) observed about the United States that "[t]he number of conversions is steadily becoming smaller. Except among a certain class of Negroes, it is no longer the fashion in America to 'get religion.'"

Within religious discourse, conversion is a miracle. Every religion tells us stories of miracles and transformations, which for most people remain stories about events that happened long ago and far away. For a few others, they are part of their personal history, which they are ready to share. These cases of rebirth should command serious attention first because sometimes what they represent are indeed positive transformations. The lame do not start walking, and the blind do not enjoy the sweet light of day, but those who find themselves psychologically tortured, self-destructive and desperate, sometimes (not often) emerge from darkness and belie everything that happened earlier in their lives.

William James described conversion in behavioral terms as a crisis, caused by depression and anxiety, which creates an openness or hunger for change:

> To be converted, to be regenerated, to receive grace, to experience religion, to gain an assurance, are so many phrases which denote the process, gradual or sudden, by which a self hitherto divided, consciously wrong, inferior and unhappy, becomes unified and consciously right, superior and happy, in consequence of its firmer hold upon religious realities.
>
> (James, 1902/1961, p. 160)

The self can radically change, as happened to newly converted Black Moslems in the United States:

> The true believer who becomes a Muslim casts off at last his old self ... He changes his name, his religion, his homeland, his "natural" language, his moral and cultural values, his very purpose in living. He is no longer a Negro ... he is a Black Man: divine, ruler of the universe, different only in degree from Allah himself. He is no longer discontent and baffled, harried by social obloquy and a gnawing sense of personal inadequacy. Now he is a Muslim, bearing in himself the power of the Black Nation and its glorious destiny.
>
> (Lincoln, 1961, pp. 108–109)

Here is another observation:

> [T]he person becomes confused and attributes inner experiences to the outer world, entering a state of transient psychosis. Dominant affects include despair, hatred, resentment, and helpless fury, often directed by youngsters toward a parent or parent-substitute ... The person ... longs to submit to an all-powerful, benevolent figure who can give absolution and restore order ... This experience is intensely emotional and may be followed by a sense of inner joy and peace.
>
> (Frank and Frank, 1991, p. 81)

Dramatic turning points, tied to external or internal events (e.g. traumatic events), lead to the re-assessment of one's life, and then to an identity change and a biographical break with the past. It is higher self-esteem, or self-love, which enables converts to claim a new identity. The source of self-reported rebirth is found in internal, conscious and unconscious, conflicts. They are solved and a balance is reached through an attachment to a set of beliefs, specific ritual acts, changes in everyday behavior and functioning, and support by a group structure. In addition, the convert has gone through internalizing a loved and loving imaginary object, which then supports the whole personality system. A similar process may take place in secular psychotherapy.

In some traditions, pilgrimage is similar to conversion in being a process of re-commitment to religious faith. Pilgrims often sought atonement through the ordeals of travel. At the end of the voyage, the pilgrim was ready for an ecstatic experience, growing out of being physically present near a concentration of *mana*.

Our thinking on conversion has been affected by the long list of celebrated individuals in history who were religious converts. In addition to the cases of Nichiren in thirteenth-century Japan, Chaityana in sixteenth-century India, or Ramakrishna in nineteenth-century India, there are classical Christian converts, starting with Augustine, Ramon Lull, St. Francis of Assisi (Yarom, 1992), Dante Allighieri, Ignatius of Loyola, and Martin Luther. A more recent list must include John Newton (author of "Amazing Grace"), the writer C. S. Lewis, the poet W. H. Auden, the writer Graham Greene, the poet and critic T. S. Eliot, the author Thomas Merton, and the African-American leader Malcolm X.

We are ready to take seriously the possibility of radical transformation and renewal in the context of religious ideation, but, since the beginning of the psychology of religion, attempts have been made to offer cogent psychological, and clearly non-religious, explanations for their occurrence.

Identity discontinuity

Just how common are religious transformations? A survey of 11,000 American adolescents in 1995–1996 found that only about 5 percent experienced either a radical increase (conversion) or a radical decrease (apostasy) in religiosity, and

154 Conversion and convert-dependent groups

adolescence is supposed to be the time for such changes (Regnerus and Uecker, 2006). The question before us is of accounting for the deviant minority who stray from the fold, as normal intergenerational transmission is subverted by crisis and rebellion. There are two kinds of discontinuity, one in which the person becomes less religious than his or her parents (apostasy, defection), and the other in which the person becomes more religious (conversion). The first kind appears to be much less dramatic, and has attracted much less scholarly attention. Individual secularization, as we might call apostasy, is perceived as calling for fewer explanations, while conversion is examined with a skeptical gaze.

Many conversions can easily be explained by looking at macro-social factors, arising from history, and micro-social ones, arising from proximate social networks. These conversions may be significant historically and socially, but not psychologically. They stem from situational factors and obvious secondary gains, or opportunism, in the absence of any real ego-involvement. Switching, or "circumstantial" conversion, may occur with migration or geographic mobility or for other reasons which are far from religious. Many millions of individuals have changed religious affiliation because of such happy occasions as marriage, or under duress and oppression. Millions of Dalits ("Untouchables") and members of other low-status groups in India have converted to Islam, Christianity, or Buddhism, trying to shake off the Hindu caste system (without much success).

The majority of believers, those who display intergenerational continuity but low ego-involvement, demonstrate the effects of "simple" social learning. Looking at the minority which displays a radical discontinuity, we assume that personality dynamics and early experiences, which determine the attachment to, or alienation from, family and community are at work. Normal social learning is automatic and without awareness or conscious processing (see Chapter 3). Conversions, often described as spontaneous, like religious experiences, result from another form of social learning. Without exposure to beliefs there are no dramatic apparitions, and converts to Islam do not appear out of nowhere in a Tibetan Buddhist monastery.

Under the heading of conversion we encounter two seemingly separate kinds of identity change. In the first, a nominal (often minimal) affiliation with a religious tradition becomes intensified, redefined commitment. This is the "born again" variety, where a nominal Presbyterian, Baptist, Jew, or Moslem proclaims a new commitment and changes life accordingly. In the second, an individual rejects his former religious affiliation in favor of a new one, and thus a Baptist may become a Jew, or vice versa. We naturally look first at external changes in identities and labels, but the important changes are internal and private. William James taught us that the distinctions between these two kinds are irrelevant to psychology and that all conversions fit his description of crisis and resolution, because the basic psychological process is identical.

What characterizes the convert is the high level of displayed commitment, emotion, and activity, tied to the religious transformation. The convert reports a cognitive illumination, a sudden apprehension and comprehension of a divine plan for the cosmos and for individual destiny. The emotional reactions accompanying such a momentous revelation can then be easily justified and accepted.

An individual-centered approach to conversion starts with individual motivation and is expressed in the concept of the convert as an active seeker, animated by an inner hunger (Beit-Hallahmi, 1992; Kääriäinen, 1999; Warburg, 2001). The self-initiated quest leads the individual to an encounter with alternative, but accessible, belief systems. Self-direction and emotional involvement lead to a narrative of metamorphosis and public identity change. The "pure" cases of conversion present a process which develops within a social network, but is the absolute opposite of switching because of social norms, coercion, colonial rule, marriage, or status gain. Conversion because of marriage is not pure, but conversion that occurs because of an "experience" or a vision is. When conversion is ritualized and normative in a culture (as illustrated by the popularity of the "born again" experience in the United States), its psychological meaning is unclear.

The notion of purely psychological, self-directed, conversions is operationally relative. There is a continuum from the pure, active, and self-directed, to the totally circumstantial (under pressure, recruitment, secondary gain) and passive. We may try to deconstruct the psychological processes involved by looking at individual cases and at systematic extensive studies. The subjective gain in happiness, reported by the convert, has to be accounted for in psychological terms.

Narratives and traditions

Conversion testimonials tell us of a miraculous transformation, from darkness to a great light, from being lost to being found. There is a sharp contrast between earlier suffering and current exhilaration. The conversion narrative always includes a wide gap between the past and the present, between corruption and redemption, and through this gap the power of transformation through enlightenment is decisively proven. A past of doubt and error is transformed into a present of wholeness in one great moment of insight, order, and certainty. It is a new birth, leading to a new life. Conversion starts at a low point, and the new birth often occurs after the lowest depths of despair are reached, and consists of (in the words of William James) "an unexpected life succeeding upon death ... the deathlike terminating of certain mental processes ... that run to failure, and in some individuals ... eventuate in despair" (James, 1900, p. 303). This creates a wider belief in "a world in which all is well, in spite of certain forms of death, indeed because of certain forms of death – death of hope, death of strength" (James, 1900, p. 305). The crisis leading to conversion could have other endings: "Self-destruction ... could also be an alternative for the individual whose life lacks meaning ... joining a labor union or a political party, consulting a psychiatrist, or using drugs or alcohol might be considered as functional alternatives" (Wallace, 1975, p. 346). What characterizes the convert when the crisis has been resolved is an intensity of commitment, emotion, and activity. A conscious self-transformation is openly proclaimed, and what was once fragmented and de-centered is made coherent, at least in its conscious center. The new self is not just triumphant but triumphalist, expecting us to follow its example. The religious by birth may look at converts with real envy, because of their enthusiasm about religion and their externalized commitment (Spero and Mester, 1988). The convert's emotional state reminds us of romantic love, which brings about exhilaration, euphoria, self-confidence, and intense energy (Fisher, 2004). The descriptions offered by James focus on the subjective report of identity change and conscious mood change, which follows one formula. There is another level, beyond the dramatic subjective "experience": objective reports which indicate a change in behavior and functioning, a true miracle cure, putting previously uncontrollable drives under reins.

Convert testimonials are not taken at face value, but are always interpreted by observers and researchers (Dawson, 1995). They need to be read in their cultural context. The conversion narrative can be regarded as a literary or folklore genre, based on a persuasive rhetorical formula so predictable we tend to doubt it. Some have suggested that biographical reconstruction is the essence of individual conversion (Staples and Mauss, 1987; Stromberg, 1993). The personal past is erased as one's autobiography is publicly restructured, and divided into before and after. Life until the moment of epiphany is often described as totally wasted. Every sin must be confessed so that the power of redemption is magnified (Arendt, 1979). Presenting the conversion testimonial is a real test for the new self. First, because it is a public confession, exposing sins and weaknesses, and then because it is a self-enforcing act of commitment ("bridge burning"; Hine, 1970).

This formula is connected to a death–rebirth fantasy, basic to initiation rites in tribal societies:

> Initiation is a transition rite through which the initiate passes from one condition to another. It is normally fashioned on the pattern of the greatest transition rite of all, namely, death; indeed, it is really a pre-enactment of death and of the rising which it is desired should follow death.
>
> (Elkin, 1938, p. 166; Eliade, 1965)

Death and resurrection are claimed by the convert as his path to salvation, and his movement closer towards the sacred realm. In Candomble, the Afro-Brazilian religion, the initiate is "sacrificed," only to return to life as the son or daughter of a pre-determined deity. An animal has to be sacrificed before they are reborn, as the price of a new life is another life.

The case of Max Jacob (1876–1944)

Here is an enigmatic story, full of contradictions, tragedies, and secrets. Fhima (2002) described Jacob's "symbiosis of paradoxical identities": Jew, avant-garde artist, homosexual, convert, Catholic writer, and Jewish martyr. Jacob is remembered as a painter, playwright, critic, a remarkable poet, and a member of an stunningly talented group. He is immortalized in portraits by Pablo Picasso

Conversion and convert-dependent groups **157**

(1881–1973) and Amadeo Modigliani (1884–1920), and in hundreds of photographs and film clips where he always appears next to Picasso.

In 1934, Jacob gave extended interviews which provide us with the best source for the way in which he conceived his own life (Guiette, 1934). What Jacob tells us about his childhood is heart-rending. He was physically abused by his parents and siblings, and tried to commit suicide three times. At age thirteen he was taken to Paris for treatment by the renowned neurologist Jean-Martin Charcot. At age twenty-four, he was slapped by his mother for the last time, for a spelling mistake. Jacob was a brilliant student, and his artistic talents were noted early. At age nineteen he went to Paris with 29 francs stolen from his mother. Trying his hand in various jobs and careers to survive, he graduated from law school, but chose painting as a career. In 1901 he met Pablo Picasso, and the two became inseparable. In 1905, they met the poet Guillaume Apollinaire (1880–1918), and made a threesome that stayed together till Apollinaire's death.

In the 1934 interview, Jacob denied his homosexuality and improbably reported a love affair with a married woman, using her real name. He stated that the only moments in his life he would like to relive were the first night with this lover, and the "sacred moment of God's first appearance to him, six years later" (p. 18). Heartlessly, he reveals that he arranged to have one painting exhibited at the Salon des Independants so that Mme. Germaine Pfeipfer would show up. When she did, he was in the company of Picasso and Georges Braque (1882–1963), who found her very pretty. He found her grotesque.

In 1909 came the apparition:

> There was somebody on the wall, "Truth, truth, tears of truth, joy of truth, unforgettable truth, the Divine Body is on the wall of this poor room… What beauty! elegance and delicacy, His shoulders, his bearing! He wears a yellow silk robe with blue cuffs. He turns and I see his peaceful and shining face. Six monks bring a cadaver into the room. A woman with snakes around her arms and hair is next to me.
>
> The angel: Innocent, you have seen god. You don't understand your happiness
> Me: Cry Cry I am a poor human beast
> The angel: the Devil has departed, He will come back
> Me; The Devil, yes"
>
> (quoted in Guiette, 1934, pp. 254–255)

While this happened in 1909, Jacob was baptized only on February 18, 1915, through the Order of Notre-Dame-de-Sion, founded by the Ratisbonne brothers, two nineteenth-century Jewish converts (James, 1902/1961). In 1921 Jacob escaped the temptations of the big city for the deserted monastery of Saint-Benoit-Sur-Loire, and spent much of his time there, continuing his literary activities. He also became a supporter of *Action Francaise*, a fascist, monarchist, anti-Semitic movement. This did not help when the Nazis came, and he had to wear the yellow star. Arrested in

February 1944, Jacob died the following month in the concentration camp at Drancy, near Paris, on his way to Auschwitz, where almost his whole family died.

Jacob's conversion was not rewarded in any way, except internally. It was not only a negation of his family, but of his social network as well. Some of his friends thought the whole thing was a joke, another game played by a surrealistic prankster. What we realize is that in the midst of all the Bohemian gaiety, Jacob was the sad clown, feeling as unloved and lonely as he did in childhood. His eyes had "all the sadness of the Jews," testified Daniel-Henry Kahnweiler, Picasso's (Jewish) agent (Warnod, 1975, p. 106). The conversion created center and balance, but Jacob, by his own admission, still had all the "evil" character traits found in him before 1909, just differently colored.

Transitions and destinations

The broadest frame of reference when discussing conversion is the common phenomenon of attempts to escape personal destiny and identity. This includes any attempt to redefine biography and identity against "objective" conditions that created them. Such attempts at rebirth through private salvation may be common in certain historical situations (Beit-Hallahmi, 1992).

Conversion experiences start with conversion dreams, and private salvation narratives appear in response to dreams of a new self. Fantasies about self-transformation and world-transformation, so common among humans, play a major role in the history of religious movements, and in secular adventures. Attempts to transcend one's biologically and historically assigned life through intentional self-development can be examined on the basis of context, content, or consequences.

The writer Susan Sontag (1933–2004), in an interview with the BBC, on May 22, 2000, said that the American dream is to reinvent yourself, be born again, but reinvention is not just an American idea, but a universal modern dream, and possibly a universal human dream (McAdams, 2006). Zarifian, in *Les Jardiniers de la Folie* (1988), has written about the common escape fantasy of middle-aged men, who want to give up their identities and their histories in favor of a new existence or a "new birth." Umberto Gallini of Milan, Italy, opened in 1992 a service for individuals who wished to disappear from the real world and start a new life under a new identity. His clients were middle-aged men who wanted to leave behind families and obligations. Mr. Gallini arranged for escapes to the Third World (Madagascar) with a new identity, provided you had $100,000 in savings.

Many people see their lives as a first draft and dream of being or becoming somebody else and something else, but escape is a minority option. Most of us do not dare to escape from destiny in such ways and will continue to cope normatively, realistically, possibly in quiet desperation. Some of our own salvation fantasies focus on converts. We envy their courage to take such a dramatic step in the midst of crisis, and we envy even more their enthusiasm, self-confidence, optimism, and strong convictions, once they have taken this step.

Conversion and convert-dependent groups **159**

The idea of individual choice and voluntary change is in itself startlingly novel, tied to secularization and individualism. The religious career of a seeker, or a convert, is a totally modern idea. Conversions and defections may be seen as accidents or minor problems in the great scheme of successful intergenerational transmission, but the historical process of secularization means that the ideal of freedom to choose and separation from parental tradition becomes prevalent or dominant (Cadge and Davidman, 2006). It now means the freedom to reject a received identity, choose an alternative one, or invent a brand new one.

The ability to change is considered a major achievement and an ideal in modern culture, which promotes the imaginary triumph of an authentic self. The common theme of reorganizing the self around a new center is recent, together with the (mostly imagined) freedom to choose or reconstruct one's identity. More recently, the search for a social utopia has been being replaced by the private utopia of the re-invented self. If we cannot change the world, we are told that we can change ourselves. Dreams about the revitalization of self and identity through metamorphosis can be either secular or religious. In the former, the triumph is that of the new, re-invented self, while in the latter it is the double triumph of both the new religious message and the individual that embraced it.

Any desire for change must stem from dissatisfaction with the present, and a desire for radical change must stem from a radical dissatisfaction. If we desire a new body, a new name, or a new self, we must be unhappy with the old ones. Viewing oneself as "incompetent, unattractive, immoral … stupid, clumsy, inadequate, unlovable" (Baumeister, 1991, p. 23) is a powerful motive. What Baumeister described as "escaping the self" motivates many converts, as "[e]xistence itself has become the problem and a fundamental change is called for" (Pargament, 1997, p. 248). Getting rid of devalued aspects of the self, or the whole self, is a powerful fantasy. "So the hated self, the self that has been causing such inner suffering and anguish, gets expelled from the body" (Capps, 1997, p. 169). Attempts at escaping the self include secular psychotherapy and a variety of magical gestures. Such gestures, which aim at reaching a conscious break with the past and the shedding of visible aspects of identity include name change, plastic surgery, and "sex change."

The psychological uniqueness of religious conversion is clear when it is carefully compared with apostasy or with such acts as name change or "sex change." Magical or symbolic gestures as part of an intentional script for self-invention are not usually sufficient for a real metamorphosis and do not bring about much exuberance; these intentional scripts often end in disappointment. A name change does not lead to personality change, and a new nose does not do it either. A "sex change" often fails to bring about happiness. A magical gesture may be the culmination of a long process, and constitute a public "bridge burning," but it is unlikely that it gives birth to a new self.

Observers react to convert testimonials in a mix of empathy, identification, idealization, and distance. Despite identification and fascination, any psychological stance is secular and skeptical, asking what could lie behind the event and the narrative. Pratt (1920, p. 128) stated "[t]hat conversion is a natural human phenomenon, independent alike of supernatural interference and of theological prepossession."

160 Conversion and convert-dependent groups

Converts tell us that they have been compelled to transform by the blinding light of truth coming to them from the outside. Public statements about hunger for truth or about events that triggered a quest for coherence are just one link in the causal chain behind any individual trajectory. Freud (1928) raised this issue, and no one can dispute its pertinence in all cases (see Freud's conversion case in Chapter 8).

Interpretations of changes in religious identity as resulting from a search for meaning have to account for the fact that while alienation and meaninglessness may be experienced by many, only a few choose a religious answer to their quest. Many suffer existential anxieties, but what causes individuals to reach high levels of ego-involvement in religion is, as converts tell us, vulnerability and deprivation, together with an openness to religious ideas (Merton, 1948). Seekers must possess a certain vulnerability or disposition, because only a small fraction of those exposed to a new or alternative religious message are ready to hear it. What has been called hunger, which pushes seekers forward, combines with various environmental stresses to lead to an openness or even commitment (Beit-Hallahmi, 1992). We know that many converts are pulled into groups by spouses, lovers, friends, or relatives (Beit-Hallahmi and Argyle, 1997). Similarly, in defections from NRMs, individuals follow their spouses or close friends (Wright, 1986).

In modern societies we find a population of seekers, individuals in crisis who are open (or vulnerable) to accepting new self-definitions (Beit-Hallahmi, 1992). Warburg (2001) showed that among converts in Denmark, 51 percent went outside their immediate social network and 31 percent responded to impersonal stimuli, such as advertisements. Some active seekers become serial, or habitual, converts (see the case of Zilboorg in Beit-Hallahmi, 1989). Zachary, a young, white South African during the last decade of the apartheid regime,

> has studied Hinduism and other Oriental mysticisms. He has been an adept of an Indian guru ... thought seriously of joining a Zen monastery ... has been involved in several spiritualist groups ... and has more recently been attending the services of a neognostic society whose members come from the wealthiest strata of Johannesburg's spiritually enlightened.
>
> (Crapanzano, 1985, p. 174)

Apostasy as conversion

Apostasy is defined as disaffection, defection, and alienation from a religious group. It is often considered a variety of conversion, involving both conscious and presumably unconscious changes (Rambo, 1993). Caplovitz and Sherrow (1977) stated that "[a]postasy indicates not only loss of religious faith, but rejection of a particular ascriptive community as a basis for self-identification" (p. 31). This may mean leaving behind a tradition and an identity, or a general disillusionment with religion. In both apostasy and conversion there is a rejection of parental identity and parental beliefs and apostasy "might well be symptomatic of familial strain and dissociation from parents ... a form of rebellion against parents" (Caplovitz and

Sherrow, 1977, p. 50). The alienation may be not just from the parents, but from the community of origin.

What we don't find in apostates is joy, because the process does not involve a new love for an imaginary object, but rather a loss that the person has to cope with. Apostasy is not just having doubts or deviating from official doctrine. Many believers have doubts and fluctuate in their commitment; and that is why we find such variance on measures of religiosity within the same tradition, but leaving a community of believers behind requires some anger and determination.

Discontinuity dynamics: distancing self from parents

Adolescence as a time of crystallization in religious identity development has been highlighted in numerous studies, and the connection between adolescence and conversion has long been recognized (Argyle and Beit-Hallahmi, 1975; Beit-Hallahmi and Argyle, 1997; Hyde, 1965). Some students of adolescence have suggested that it is intellectual development at that stage which contributes to a growing distance from religious tradition (Ausubel et al., 1977; Garrison, 1965). "The adolescent is an individual who begins to build 'systems' or 'theories' in the largest sense of the term" (Inhelder and Piaget, 1958, p. 339). This is taking place on a conscious level, of course.

Offering another approach, Erikson (1963, 1968) coined the term "identity crisis," denoting a stage when a coherent sense of self must be developed. This happens in adolescence, when a person must develop "some central perspective and direction" (Erikson, 1958, p. 14), and establish a stable ego ideal (i.e. conscious ideals for the self) and social roles. An identity crisis "can have a highly conscious (and, indeed, self-conscious) quality and yet remain, in its motivational aspects, quite unconscious and beset with the dynamics of conflict" (Erikson, 1975, p. 18). Erikson stated that adolescent identity formation involves a struggle to create distance from parents, siblings, and other social contacts, and that is essential to proper development. Adolescence is characterized by conversions that are most often experiences of personal recommitment to a familiar religious tradition, and less often involve the change from one religious tradition to another.

All identity changes create a distance between oneself and one's parents, because they so clearly constitute an active rejection of one's past and of those responsible for the old identity. When a young European, who grew up in an average family, turns into a "born-again" Christian or a Buddhist, he is declaring a revolt against his parents. In terms of individual and family dynamics, every identity change is a rebellion against one's parents, who usually created the earlier identity, and against one's past. Even when what is involved is a re-commitment to a nominal "old" identity, a rejection of parental teachings and parental authority is often involved. Often the new framework is more demanding than the religious practices of the parents, so that adolescents can denounce the apparently superficial religiosity of their families. A psychological analysis may direct us to noting that cases of re-commitment to the parents' religion actually represents a way of expressing hostility towards them.

On a collective, generational level, finding new identities is a total ideological rebellion. The new religious identities constitute in many cases a rejection of the faith of the parents, and of the parents' everyday lifestyle. Rebelling against tradition and family is complex and paradoxical. The degree of similarity found in most cases between adolescents and their parents reminds us that most young people still do not move very far away from the beliefs of their families. Even in cases of nonconformist, radical religious youth groups, research has shown much continuity with parents. Research on the "Jesus movement" in the United States in the 1970s has shown that most members of such groups came from fundamentalist Christian families (Richardson, Stewart and Simmonds, 1979). These adolescents were rebelling against their parents by internalizing their parents' religious beliefs, but then acting on them in a more radical way.

Generalizing across cultures and movements

In discussing converts and conversion, can we generalize across cultures and religions? Is this another case of cultural imperialism, where a Western notion growing out of the Christian orbit is being forced on other cultures? This is not a recent question, possibly born out of faddish multiculturalism. William James (1902/1961) advised caution, but felt it necessary to comment on Asian traditions. Pratt (1920) was already well aware of possible criticisms and described conversion in many cultures, citing ancient Greece, Rome, medieval Islam, India, and Buddhism.

The psychological study of conversion was never limited to mainstream religion. Pratt (1920) and Thouless (1923) discussed conversions to the Salvation Army, and Cantril (1941) described the Father Divine movement. Clark (1958) based his view of conversion on fifty-five converts to the Oxford Movement, once the world's best known NRM. Movements may be ephemeral, but the phenomenon of conversion and the processes leading to it are perennial.

Who are the twice-born?

Most research on converts has been retrospective, i.e. post-conversion, and very few studies use control groups. Still, we see a growing body of accumulating evidence which is highly consistent. In both individuals and societies, religious awakening is tied to crises and anxieties (see Chapter 4). Classical and recent sources report that conversion follows a stage of personal crisis, stress, and demoralization (Beit-Hallahmi, 1992; Beit-Hallahmi and Argyle, 1997; Davidman, 1991; Murken and Namini, 2007; Namini and Murken, 2009; Paloutzian, Richardson and Rambo, 1999; Rambo, 1993; Starbuck, 1899). Conversion narratives testify first and foremost to frustration, crisis, and conflict (Stromberg, 1993). Strozier (1994), in a study based on extensive interviews with members of apocalyptic communities, suggested that the transformation to fundamentalism, shared by millions, is a reaction to insecurity, fear, and rage. Downton (1980) uses the terms "disillusionment," "disenchantment," "discontent," "alienation,"

Conversion and convert-dependent groups **163**

"inadequacy," "aimlessness," "futility," and "meaninglessness" to describe the pre-conversion stage, while Cantril (1963) uses the term "ego weakness."

Galanter (1989) assessed converts and nonconverts prior to conversion and found higher levels of distress in converts. Kox, Meeus, and Hart (1991) compared a group of adolescent converts to controls, and found that two-thirds of converts and only one-fifth of non-converts reported personal problems during the preceding three to five years, and major personal losses just before conversion. Similar findings were reported by Poling and Kenney (1986), Ullman (1982), and Zinnbauer and Pargament (1998). In a sample of 2500 American women, Shaver, Lenauer, and Sadd (1980) found that converts reported an unhappy childhood, and showed a higher level of authoritarianism. Warburg (2001) reported alienation and lack of attachment among seekers (Nicholi, 1974). Beit-Hallahmi and Nevo (1987) found lower self-esteem and level of aspiration in converts. Those likely to report dramatic conversions are also likely to be socially isolated (Beit-Hallahmi and Argyle, 1997). Buxant *et al.* (2007) compared 113 converts to NRMs in Belgium to the general population and found an insecure attachment history, high need for closure, and depressive tendencies in the past combined with positive feelings about the present and future. One hundred and eighty converts to majority religions, when compared to the general population, reported high levels of insecurity in attachment to parents (especially the father), high levels of avoidance in adult attachment, and a high need for cognitive order (Buxant, Saroglou and Scheuer, 2009).

We know that parents are more influential than any other actors, including peers, in the formation of individual religiosity, whether in the case of continuity or in discontinuity (Beit-Hallahmi and Argyle, 1997). Hunsberger and Brown (1984) found that a lesser emphasis placed on religion in the home, especially by the mother, affected the rejection of family religiosity. Re-affiliation, i.e. coming back to the family's religious tradition, is also related to the influence of the family of origin (Wilson and Sherkat, 1994). In a survey of United States "baby boomers," born between 1946 and 1982, Roof (1993) found that 67 percent dropped out of their parents' religious denominations, but 37 percent later re-affiliated in their middle and late twenties. Becoming a parent was a major factor in re-affiliation, but it seems that only marriage, as opposed to cohabitation, or nonmarital sex, contributes to the return to the fold (Uecker, Regnerus and Vaaler, 2007). Psychoanalytic theorists have suggested that individuals past their adolescence (or in post-adolescence) experience a "superego victory" which means moving closer to their parents in significant ways (Beit-Hallahmi, 1977a).

Insecure ties with parents, as reported and remembered, predict the likelihood of seeking and being converted. What seekers or converts tell us about interactions with parents may be just their fantasies, but these are significant nevertheless, and young apostates report more distant relations with their parents (Caplovitz and Sherrow, 1977). Being raised in divorced families is tied to becoming an apostate later in life (Lau and Wolfinger, 2011; Lawton and Bures, 2001), but individuals raised in unaffiliated divorced families are more likely to become affiliated (Lau and Wolfinger, 2011).

164 Conversion and convert-dependent groups

The wounds and scars of childhood struggles, real and imagined, are repaired (or fail to be) through illusions of coherence and grandeur, including imaginary surrogates for the family, such as new religious movements (Jacobs, 1989). Whether a member in a new religious movement will remain in the group for long seems to be affected by relations with one's parents (Wright and Piper, 1986). Beit-Hallahmi and Nevo (1987) compared fifty-nine male converts to Orthodox Judaism to matched controls and found that converts reported significantly lower identification with their parents. Among 295 seekers in Israel, compared to controls, more traumatic events throughout life were reported, more problems in relations with their parents, and a lower percentage of secure attachments (Beit-Hallahmi, Levy-Israeli and Farahat, 2004).

Converts are more likely to have had fathers who were absent, passive or hostile, and mothers who were hostile, unstable, or overprotective, and recalled more traumatic childhood events (Allison, 1969; Buchbinder, Bilu and Witztum, 1997; Deutsch, 1975; Ullman, 1982). Kose (1996) found that the majority in a group of British converts to Islam reported father absence and an unhappy childhood. Individuals who described their mothers as cold and distant were more likely to have had conversions (Kirkpatrick, 2005). Oksanen (1994), after performing a meta-analysis of twenty-five studies covering 4513 converts, concluded that conversion should be viewed as a fantasy compensation for an attachment deficit (Granqvist and Kirkpatrick, 2004).

A burning desire for coherence and meaning is linked to past histories (or memories) of loss, especially the loss of fathers (Granqvist and Hagekull, 2001; Namini and Murken, 2008). Research on US members of ISKCON showed an identical pattern of parental loss or absence (Poling and Kenney, 1986). The painful histories and psychological triumphs of the twice-born virtuosi have made them the leaders, models, and creators of religious traditions. Parental loss is common in the early lives of converts and leaders. George Fox and Ann Lee are just two of the religious founders who were orphaned early in life. In a study of modern United States televangelists, an absent father, and admiration for one's mother, were uniformly reported in autobiographies (Lienesch, 1993).

Antecedents: psychopathology

Converts are likely to be more vulnerable and disturbed (Galanter, 1989; Kobler, 1964; Olsson, 1983; Spero, 1982), some having had prior psychiatric treatment and even hospitalization (Galanter, 1989; Luhrmann, 1989). "It is typical of conversion to be preceded by morbid feelings, which shade into the apathy of depression" (Ostow and Sharfstein, 1954, p. 102).

Among members of the Divine Light Mission and the Unification Church, between 30 and 40 percent had sought professional help before joining and 6 to 9 percent had been hospitalized (Galanter, 1989; Levine and Salter, 1976). In a survey of 103 members of ISKCON, 48 percent admitted to "feeling discouraged and/or anxious about life" before joining the group, while 37 percent had some psychological treatment (Rochford, Purvis and Eastman, 1989). Deutsch (1975) interviewed fourteen converts; one was diagnosed as manic-depressive and four as borderline schizophrenics (cf. Kiev and Francis, 1964). Simmonds, Richardson, and Harder (1976) assessed eighty-eight members of Shiloh, a Jesus People commune in Oregon, and found a "maladaptive" pattern. Peters *et al.* (1999) found that individuals belonging to new religious movements (Druids and ISKCON) scored significantly higher on incidence of delusional ideation than control groups (non-religious and Christian), but they did not differ significantly from psychotic in-patients. Day and Peters (1999) reported that the same group of NRM members scored higher on the Unusual Experiences factor of schizotypy, described as psychosis-proneness which does not interfere with normal functioning (Claridge, 1987).

In a follow-up study of 520 mental patients, hospitalized in the New York State Psychiatric Institute between 1963 and 1976, and diagnosed as borderline or psychotic, it was found that thirty-two (6 percent) had conversions by 1985, which is far more than expected for the general population (Stone, 1992). Manic depressive patients were found to have a higher incidence (52 percent) of "conversion" or "salvation," compared to a control group (20 percent) (Gallenmore, Wilson and Rhoads, 1969). Bowman *et al.* (1987) reported conversion experiences in six out of seven cases of "multiple personality," while Daly and Cochrane (1968) reported conversions as more prevalent among manic-depressive patients compared to controls.

Data from a community clinic in Israel showed that two-thirds of recent converts to Orthodox Judaism were "psychiatrically unwell" and highly overrepresented among referrals to mental health professionals. Of 561 referrals to the clinic in 1985–1986, seventy-one were recent converts. Compared to the control group of 490 non-converts, they had extremely high rates of schizophrenia, major depression, and personality disorders, and most of them had had serious problems before their conversions (Witztum, Greenberg and Dasberg, 1990). Data collected in 1986–1987 in the same clinic showed again an extreme over-representation of converts among serious cases, and a high rate of paranoid schizophrenia (Witztum, Greenberg and Buchbinder, 1990).

Substance abuse or addiction are indications of serious pathology, and many converts have been described as drug abusers or drug addicts. Poling and Kenney (1986) state that "[f]rom 1967 to approximately 1975, ISKCON functioned as a voluntary detoxification unit" and then from 1975 to 1986, it functioned "as a rehabilitation program analogous to Alcoholics Anonymous" with "a therapist-leadership composed primarily of detoxified, former addicts" (pp. 170–171).

Conversion as psychopathology

A conscious preoccupation with ideology and identity among adolescents, which leads up to conversion, indicates serious problems. Schimel (1973) stated that, the quest for identity and meaning can be seen as an index of pathology. When the processes of maturation that optimally go on outside of conscious awareness become a matter of continual conscious scrutiny, concern and implementation, there is the strong suggestion that something is amiss.

(Schimel, 1973, p. 407)

Erikson (1968) described severe identity confusion as a serious form of pathology, from which some recover successfully and creatively (instancing William James), while others do not, sinking further into psychosis. "Severe identity confusion" may lead to "the display of a total commitment to a *role fixation* ... as against a *free experimentation* with available roles" (1968, p. 184), or "an intense and even fanatic investment" (p. 181). In this kind of conversion, the outcome is likely to be negative.

Blos (1979), Christensen (1963), Linn and Schwartz (1958), and Saltzman (1953) argued that conversion may in itself be a symptom of serious disturbance and never a solution. Sargent (1957) claimed that conversion is a hysterical neurotic breakdown. Pruyser stated that sudden conversion is an indication of a severe psychological crisis, and, at the same time, a way of warding off a total breakdown, and urged that "sudden conversions in people whose religious traditions do not demand them ... must be carefully evaluated in the religiocultural background of the person" (quoted in Malony and Spilka, 1991, p. 128).

Boisen (1936, 1945) stated that both religious experiences and psychosis are capable of producing a dramatic change in the self, whether salvation or disintegration, and described cases where a religious conversion is closely followed by a psychotic breakdown. Pre-schizophrenic adolescents show a preoccupation with philosophical, religious, and metaphysical ideas (Moller and Husby, 2000). In most cases, this leads to a full-blown psychosis, sometimes combined with a self-defined conversion: "The initial ineffable self-transformation is being progressively infused with content, reflected by new interests in Buddhist thought and motivated by charismatic and eschatological concerns" (Parnas and Handest, 2003, p. 131). Wootton and Allen (1983) suggested that the early stages of both conversion and schizophrenic decompensation are identical. Reported conversions (or apostasy) in adolescence were tied to later occurrence of schizophrenia (Wilson, Larson and Meier, 1983) and religious delusions (Siddle *et al.*, 2002), as well as drug abuse (Moscati and Mezuk, 2014).

The consequences of metamorphosis

Converts usually want us to believe they have profoundly changed; this is part of what defines them. One change we must take seriously is self-reports about elevated self-esteem and mood. Even if what happens is only a change in self-presentation, such a change is highly significant. After all, spontaneous self-presentation is used in diagnosing depression or schizophrenia. James (1902) and Starbuck (1899) reported a period of elation in the wake of conversion that led to higher self-esteem, and this is supported by more recent research (Nicholi, 1974; Zinnbauer and Pargament, 1998). Ng (2002) studied individuals treated for drug addiction and found that conversion led to significant positive changes in self-esteem and self-perception. Converts reported changes in self-confidence (Ng, H.-Y., 2002; Zinnbauer and Pargament, 1998) as well as in the level of meaning in life (Paloutzian, 1981; Ng and Shek, 2001). In a study of fifty-eight members in three new religious movements in Germany, it was found that the fit between the members' needs for autonomy and relatedness and the groups' abilities to satisfy these needs predicted individual well-being (Namini *et al.*, 2010). Despite the evidence for higher self-esteem, better impulse control, and reduction in anomie, basic personality structures do not change, just as Max Jacob reported in 1934 (Levine, 1984; Paloutzian, Richardson and Rambo, 1999; Simmonds, 1977).

Relief from distress has been reported in many studies (Beit-Hallahmi and Argyle, 1997; Galanter, 1989). On specific measures of mental health, results are more ambiguous (Edmondson and Park, 2009; Ross, 1985; Weiss and Mendoza, 1990), but conversion may be helpful as a treatment for drug abuse (Galanter, 1989; Nicholi, 1974; Robbins and Anthony, 1972; Simmonds, 1977; Wilson, 1972). By invoking belief and reliance on a higher power and mobilizing strong group pressure, religious groups may create a motivation strong enough to put an end to the use of drugs, especially alcohol (Galanter, 1989).

Joining a new and supportive community of believers (whether an NRM, or an "old" congregation) may be therapeutic and one observer claimed that it was easy "to discern in all the ties with mystico-religious or philosophico-religious sects and communities the manifestations of distorted cures of all kinds of neuroses" (Freud, 1921, p. 132). This may be so because "[r]eligious communities can also provide a haven for those who are disturbed or do not cope well with the world" (Brown, 1988, p. 57). Joining a religious group may be therapeutic (Frank and Frank, 1991; Galanter, 1989; Namini and Murken, 2009). Levine (1981) reported on positive effects in disturbed converts, but in many cases this cannot prevent another breakdown (Witztum, Greenberg and Dasberg, 1990). Converts may exhibit difficulties after leaving a group, as they lose the structure that helped them establish balance in their lives. Assuming the therapeutic effect of group membership clearly implies earlier pathology. Otherwise there is no need for improvement.

The problem with psychological rebirth is its inherent instability. Individual conversion, as well as its effects, are rather precarious and susceptible to reversals (Bragan, 1977; Levin and Zegans, 1974; Levine, 1984). The individual convert is always in danger of reverting to the old self, because of internal or external factors. The illusion of rebirth may lead to positive outcomes, but is often insufficient to maintain balance inside a personality system long beset with disharmonies and imbalances. Following the dramatic events surrounding conversion, there must be a decline in excitement and gratification, and the new doctrines may be seen as no longer attractive (Seggar and Blake, 1970). Tavory and Wincheser (2012) observed an Orthodox Jewish community and a community of Moslem converts in the United States, and found the fervor following conversion tapering off.

168 Conversion and convert-dependent groups

A small minority within the small minority of the convert population consists of those whose conversion has been followed by dramatic changes for the better in their lives. How do we account for successful, stable conversions, which we might think of as "overachieving"? There are cases involving a real sea-change in actual behavior, as sinners become not always saints, but productive members of society, self-destructive behaviors are dropped, and a lifetime of failure and hate is changed into garden variety (or better) life course. In cases of true transformation, something important and far-reaching must be going on beneath the surface. The process is one of accepting authority, loving authority, or internalizing a loving and supportive (but still demanding) authority. What happens in these conversion miracles is an experience of love, both a giving and receiving of love. On a conscious level, this is the unconditional (or maybe conditional) love of a God. On an unconscious level, it may be the unconditional love of a father, a mother, or a comprehensive parental image. The imagined reconciliation with this love object brings about a dramatic mood change.

Prison conversions, where individuals declare a new religious identity while incarcerated, are regarded intuitively as cynical manipulations. Eshuys and Smallbone (2006) report that among the 111 sex offenders they studied, there were sixteen converts, and they had a criminal record that was worse than the rest and included non-sexual offenses. These conversions were interpreted as a sincere attempt at radical change. There have been some cases of publicly reported conversions by individuals involved in major crimes against humanity. Hans Michael Frank (1900–1946) was the Nazi governor of Poland during World War II. During the last year of his life, when he was on trial, he claimed a renewed faith in Catholicism, in which he had been raised, and some religious experiences. He was one of only two Nazi leaders to express remorse, and regarded his execution as an atonement for his crime (Gilbert, 1995). His public stance of remorse was doubted by his own son (Frank, 1991). Kang Kek Ieu (1942–) is a former Khmer Rouge leader, who was directly responsible for many of the atrocities committed by the regime, which killed hundreds of thousands between 1975 and 1979. After the fall of the regime he was living in hiding, and in 1995, at age fifty-three, he started attending Christian prayer meetings and was baptized the following year, joining a tiny minority of converts in Buddhist Cambodia (Gluck, 1999). In 1999 he surrendered to the authorities in Cambodia, was put in prison, and in 2009 tried for crimes against humanity. During the trial he expressed remorse and asked for forgiveness, being the only member of the Khmer Rouge leadership to do that. Follwing the trial and the appeal process he was sentenced in 2012 to life in prison. These two cases have naturally drawn much attention and controversy.

The drama of convert-dependent movements

Beyond the individual level conversion is a social phenomenon, playing a major role in the development of modern religious movements. We can observe two kinds of such movements. One is the revival or revitalization movement in a

Conversion and convert-dependent groups **169**

historical ("old") religion (see Chapter 4). The other is the creation of new religious movements. A new tradition has to establish its authority, power, and uniqueness. This leads to a valued identity, for individuals and for the whole group. The community of believers is united in accepting a particular authority, but it is naturally challenged.

The loyalty to the new identity, which withstands crisis, and is proven in rare cases by suicide or other forms of violence, but in most cases in hard work and obedience, is puzzling. How can such a powerful commitment develop in what seems like a short time? Hine (1970) described the process of "bridge burning" which creates strong commitments and consists of changes in self-image, cognitive restructuring and overt public acts, that set the individual apart. Still, all observers keep wondering about the secret behind an absolute and unshaken loyalty. We may find similar loyalties in love and politics, but they are still puzzling, especially when individuals demonstrate total resistance to disconfirmation of faith in the face of serious challenges. Such high intensity commitment, inspired by charismatic leaders, sometimes leads to exploitation, whether financial, sexual, or psychological.

The conditions of military defeat may be a source of relevant insights. Researchers who have studied the determination and tenacity of German military units towards the end of World War II reached the conclusion that personal attachments to leaders, rather than ideology, explained this puzzling phenomenon.

> When the individual's immediate group ... offered him affection and esteem ... supplied him with a sense of power and adequately regulated his relations with authority, the element of self-concern in battle, which would lead to disruption of the effective functioning of his primary group, was minimized.
> (Shils and Janowitz, 1948, p. 281)

New religions

What is supposed to make a religious group unique are its own distinct beliefs and practices, but much more important is authority structure and leadership. Quite often the group's history starts with a new claim to authority on the part of a lone prophet, who turns into a leader by recruiting followers and keeping their loyalty. As used here, the term new religions, or new religious movements (NRMs), refers to groups founded after the year 1750. In recent years, such movements have been examined under the rubrics of religious experimentation, marginal religions, or oppositionist religions.

Over the past 200 years, the world has seen the appearance (and disappearance) of thousands of new religions. This may actually be directly related to the decline in the authority and political power of major historical religions (see Chapter 9). Democracy and the idea of freedom in both religion and political expression creates a free market for religious entrepreneurs. While declaring oneself to be in possession of a new religious truth was, in most parts of the world, quite risky or fatal 300 years ago, secularization offers new religions unprecedented freedom to operate, together with unlimited competition.

Almost all NRMs are convert-dependent. This means that most or all members are first-generation believers, without intergenerational traditions and identity to rely on. The membership of such movements as the Bahais, the Mormons, or the Unification Church is mostly made up of converts, who have decided to give up a former identity. The quantitative and qualitative marginality of high-intensity religious movements and their membership is always evident. Being part of a belief minority is never easy. Starting a new belief minority means feeling vulnerability and threat. This is a great challenge to both leaders and members, as just surviving is a great achievement. NRMs are always struggling and seeking legitimacy, while internally preoccupied with issues of authority, leadership, and identity. NRMs suffer from high rates of defection, and many religious movements have been started through schisms in existing groups.

Popper (2001) described destructive NRM leaders as "hypnotic," and they are sometimes described as charismatic, but charisma is something that we may find hard to predict, and usually recognize after the fact. It is needed to attract new recruits to a small group and keep them, and to maintain the leader's authority. It may be the followers' fantasy created in response to the leader's personality, and then projected on him.

Research on brain processing of charismatic authority suggests that neural circuits supporting ideological commitments are similar to those activated during hypnotic suggestion. Beliefs about speakers' abilities were shown to change the evoked brain responses in secular and Christian participants. Christian participants deactivated parts of the prefrontal cortex in response to speakers who they believed had healing abilities. This deactivation predicted their subsequent ratings of the speaker's charisma (Schjøedt et al., 2011). The findings point to an important mechanism which facilitates charismatic influence.

Group formation involves a psychological investment by members in group beliefs, in the group leader, and in other members (Freud, 1921). In most cases, founders of NRMs have sufficient charisma to attract the number of followers necessary to keep the group alive. A new source of *mana* will start in some cases with the appearance of an individual with great personal charisma, who creates a new sacred authority. An effective leader, in this case and in others, creates a mutually empowering relationship with his followers, at least for a while. This leader can then transmit *mana* either by biological inheritance and descent, or by "apostolic" succession and anointment procedures.

A psychological perspective on NRMs must include an appreciation of the experiences of both members and leaders. New religions face both internal and external tensions as they struggle to achieve survival and stability in an environment that is always indifferent and non-supportive, and often hostile. This struggle, often marked by desperation as outside pressures mount, colors the evolution of the group, its members, and its leaders. A new group's claim to originality and uniqueness in its beliefs may lead to what the world around it perceives as criminal deviance, leading to friction and resistance. Leaders must experience times of pressure or panic, and most groups barely survive. A new religious movement, by its very nature, is in opposition to established authorities and structure. Members of such a movement are required to commit themselves and to be active and involved, otherwise the movement will disappear.

What defines the dynamics of many NRMs is the actual presence of the founder or founders and the founding generation of members. Most groups are relatively small and so relationships and activities are more intense and personal. Because members are converts and the group relatively young, we can observe high levels of ego involvement, which do not characterize most members of historically established religions. While in "old" religions personal involvement takes the form of an identity label and often little else, in NRMs belonging has serious consequences in terms of identity and action, and members typically devote much of their energy, time, and money to the group.

The special situation of NRMs as belief minorities in modern society dictates certain behaviors to the groups and their members. This means that NRMs are sometimes not completely truthful about their doctrines or practices out of concern for possible majority reactions. At other times, deception in fund-raising, practiced by some groups, may be justified in religious terms. Some NRMs create nice profits for their founders, who may be regarded as cynical, but there are wealthy entrepreneurs who support orthodoxies and old religions. Zaretsky and Leone (1974) described "spiritual leaders" as the last frontier for entrepreneurs in the "helping" professions, as no diplomas are necessary. Such entrepreneurs operate all over the world, making a living or becoming quite wealthy by offering salvation. Both "old" and "new" entrepreneurs claim that there is more to life than money, and that material possessions are a burden, and so they offer to shoulder this burden for their followers. Mark Twain, an observer of life in the United States in the nineteenth century, reported on the lucrative practices of "workin' camp-meetin's, and missionaryin' around" (Twain, 1884/1965, p. 107). Elmer Gantry (Lewis, 1927) seems to be reborn and technologically amplified in the shape of modern televangelists.

When dealing with NRMs, we have to explain not only recruitment and growth, but also disaffection and failure, which are quite common. Many religious groups survive, but fail to grow, because of their conflicts with society around them, which lead to their encapsulation. Another problem NRMs face is that the number of seekers, their potential recruits, who are motivated or open to identity change, is limited, for the social and psychological reasons described above.

Research on NRMs in crisis

NRMs have been viewed as laboratories or natural experiments for testing hypotheses about human behavior in general (Festinger, Riecken and Schachter, 1956), or about charismatic leadership and violence (Robbins and Palmer, 1997). One kind of crisis that has been investigated most often is the failure of prophecy,

172 Conversion and convert-dependent groups

especially the phenomenon of unaffected faith following the disconfirmation of major assertions and prophecies. Much research has focused on groups which experienced a direct disproof of predictions made by leaders. Such was the case of the group described by Festinger, Riecken, and Schachter, in *When Prophecy Fails* (1956). The group was founded by Dorothy Martin (named Marian Keech in the book), who claimed to have received messages about the coming end of the world from a space being named Sananda, a source that was both extraterrestrial and religious (described as Jesus of Christian mythology). On a specified date, which she announced to the world, all of humanity would perish, except for group members, who would be taken away in a spaceship. The date was announced (December 21, 1953), and group members expected the end of the world, and their own salvation by Sananda. After the prophecy failed, some of the group members maintained their faith. The group did not survive this crisis, but its disintegration was not immediate. The disconfirmation caused some committed members to proclaim their faith even more vigorously by proselytizing. Mrs. Martin claimed that the world was saved by their full faith. She also made additional predictions about various disasters, which also failed to materialize. These events took place in Chicago in 1953, but Dorothy Martin continued her activities leading various small groups and conveying messages from Sananda until her death in 1992.

A popular notion, derived from Festinger, Riecken, and Schachter (1956), is that disconfirmation leads to increased proselytizing, as a way of reducing members' cognitive dissonance. This proselytizing hypothesis has not been confirmed in other studies (Balch, Farnsworth and Wilkins, 1983; Hardyck and Braden, 1962; Sanada, 1979). Still, the typical case remains that of a group which manages to cope well with what outsiders consider a major disconfirmation of faith (Dawson, 1999). What happens when a group considers its leader the Messiah who is destined to rule the world and bring salvation and then that leader dies? The Hassidic Habad (Lubavitch) movement experienced such a predicament in 1994, when it lost its leader, M. M. Schneerson, widely proclaimed as the Messiah by many of his followers since the 1980s. There were dire predictions about the group's fate, especially because the leader left no heirs or successors. To the surprise of outsiders, the group has only grown in strength over the years. The missing leader is remembered (some might say worshipped), but his followers are still full of energy and confidence despite their loss (Dein, 2010; Shaffir, 1995).

There are cases where prophecy failures have not led to any visible crisis, possibly because the prophecies were only subject to disconfirmation in terms of timing. Thus, a prediction about the coming end of the world in 1984 may be re-interpreted as true in principle, and only temporarily delayed by other events. A belief system should be flexible enough to accommodate such failures (Singelenberg, 1989; Weiser, 1974; Zygmunt, 1970, 1972). Under these conditions, a challenge to the group is met by an affirmation of ideological loyalty. Balch *et al.* (1997) described a group that survived repeated disconfirmations over fifteen years.

It has been suggested that researchers have underestimated the power of faith and commitment: "Committed, as well as peripheral members, have a range of

Conversion and convert-dependent groups **173**

unfalsifiable beliefs they can draw upon in the maintenance of group reality" (Tumminia, 1998, p. 166). Weiser (1974) stated that "[p]rophecies cannot and do not fail for the committed" (p. 20), and the reason is that "[t]he prophet and his messianic belief are a necessity to the individual believer living with misfortune, offering to him the only remaining hope of obliterating the social and/or psychological malaise to which he has been subjected" (Weiser, 1974, p. 27).

This means that outsiders have failed to realize that what they regarded as a decisive challenge simply wasn't that. Zygmunt (1972) suggested that groups use three reactions to prophetic failure: adaptation, reaffirmation, and reappraisal. Melton (1985, p. 21) pointed out that "the denial of failure of prophecy is not just another option, but the common mode of adaptation of millennial groups following a failed prophecy," and proposed two additional reactions to seeming failure: cultural (spiritualization) and social (reaffirmation). Spiritualization means claiming that the prophecy has been fulfilled in an immaterial way in the spirit world. This means that,

> both conscious and at times unconscious deceptions are carried out by believers to renew both their own and their neighbor's faith, thereby quelling any doubt and dissonance preceding or subsequent to, the prophetic disproof. Any event may be manipulated as a sign of the success of the prophecy.
>
> (Melton, 1985, p. 25)

One way of recovering from a loss is the refusal to fully register events. There is nothing specifically religious about the normal denial of loss, which can be observed in countless individuals every day, and is a normal part of bereavement and mourning.

Wallace observed that "[a] great deal of doctrine in every movement ... is extremely unrealistic in that predictions of events made on the basis of its assumptions will prove to be more or less in error" (1956, pp. 278–279). That is why every movement must prepare in advance a "strategy of doctrinal modification" (p. 273) in order to cope with inevitable criticisms and challenges by outsiders. Such a strategy is vital for group survival, and in most cases proves itself. That is why in most cases groups have survived disconfirmation through some effort, but in other cases a direct disconfirmation of claims leads to crisis and sometimes decline or disintegration (Hazani, 1986; Palmer and Finn, 1992; van Fossen, 1988).

To an outsider, it appears that prophetic or messianic failure will lead the need to cope with shame and disgrace, and will be accompanied by loss of confidence and depression, but in many situations, individuals and groups are naturally capable of tolerating ambiguity and contradictions. It should be recalled that most humans do not lose sleep over contradictions in their beliefs or in their own behavior. Consistency is something that humans try to achieve only when reflective thinking is involved and some outside demand is felt. Schjøedt and Bulbulia (2011) point to the marginal role of consistency in religious belief systems and propose a brain pathway to the selective inattention so often used by believers (Schjøedt *et al.*,

174 Conversion and convert-dependent groups

2011). In some cases the failure of several predictions about apocalyptic events was simply ignored by members. It was probably considered less important than other aspects of group membership.

In the movement known as Osho Meditation and formerly known as Rajneesh Foundation International (RFI), founded by Bhagwan Sree Rajneesh (real name: Chandra Mohan, 1931–1990), there were many predictions of apocalyptic catastrophes. The movement became known for its emphasis on free sexual expression, but members were not allowed marriages or children. There was a belief in an expected cataclysm that would end life on earth. Only Rajneesh followers may survive, and even that was not certain. In 1983 Rajneesh predicted an earthquake that would devastate much of the United States' West Coast. In 1984 he announced that billions would die of AIDS within the next decade. In 1985, the group's official publications predicted floods, earthquakes, and nuclear war within the next decade (Beit-Hallahmi, 1998; Belfrage, 1981; Carter, 1990). The consistent disconfirmations of all predictions caused no dissension or doubt among followers. Apparently, such predictions were experienced by members as marginal, compared to other teachings, beliefs, and activities.

Apparently, what counts is the framing of an event. A prophecy by a leader may be perceived from the outside as central and experienced from the inside as marginal. Some believers may frame an event as irrelevant to their commitment, which remains stable despite outsiders' judgment. Holding on to a religious belief system, and other ideologies, is a constant process of disappointment and adjustment. Members will decide whether a disappointment is great or small. Identical processes may be observed in political groups, where loyalty is tested by repeated defeats.

Succession crises

A crisis that is more common than a failure of prophecy involves the loss of a leader, who in an NRM is often the founder. The International Society of Krishna Consciousness (ISKCON), popularly known as "Hare Krishna," was founded in 1966 by Swami Prabhupada in New York City and became one of the best known NRMs of the period. Before his death in 1977, the founder decided to create a collective leadership and appointed eleven gurus from among the membership. This has not stopped the group from going into what might be called a "post-charismatic decline" (Bryant and Ekstrand, 2004). After 1977 the movement has suffered a series of serious leadership crises, schisms, and disputes. Eight of the eleven trusted disciples were expelled from ISKCON. There have been many confirmed reports of drug abuse, physical and sexual abuse, and of criminal behavior, including murder, involving members and leaders, which led to serious attempts at reform and revitalization. ISKCON entered a phase which all NRMs wish for, and that is a second generation: children of members were expected to follow the faith, but educating them turned out to be a serious problem. In 1998 ISKCON issued an official report detailing abuses in its boarding schools and paid about $10 million to victims. In the twenty-first century, ISKCON in the United

Conversion and convert-dependent groups **175**

States has been experiencing a surprising rebirth, thanks to Indian immigrants who have joined its temples (Berg and Kniss, 2008: Bryant and Ekstrand, 2004; Rochford, 1989, 2007; Squarcini, 2000).

A crisis of succession and leadership which also involved one of the most shocking cases of sexual exploitation by a leader, took place in 1988–1993. Vajradhatu, a Western Tibetan Buddhist group, which has changed its name to Shambhala International, was founded in 1971 by Chogyam Trungpa, Rinpoche (1939–1986). Contrary to the widely held image of the Buddhist monk, Trungpa was visibly non-celibate, drank alcohol quite heavily, enjoyed meat and smoked tobacco (Clark, 1980), but objected to the use of marijuana.

In 1976 Trungpa named a successor, Thomas Rich, who took the name Osel Tendzin. Tendzin became the leader, or "dharma heir of Vidyadhara," upon Trungpa's death in 1987. Appointing a non-Tibetan as the successor to Trungpa set a highly unusual precedent, but the Vajra Regent, as he was known, was a man of charisma and ability. The movement seemed to be overcoming the succession crisis, but then came a predicament that very few had expected. It grew out of the leader's sexual practices: "Although married, the Regent was openly bisexual and known to have numerous sexual partners, an aspect that members tolerated without judgment" (Eldershaw, 2007, p. 79). Moreover, one source claimed that "it became a mark of prestige for a man, gay or straight, to have sex with the Regent, just as it had been for a woman to have sex with Rinpoche" (Kane, 1998, p. 154). This turned out to be a problem when the leader contracted AIDS and still continued to have sex with followers.

The movement tried to hide the problem for a while. This is the testimony of one member:

> I was very distressed that he and his entourage had lied to us for so long, always saying he did not have AIDS. I was even more distressed over the stories of how the Regent used his position … to induce "straight" students to have unprotected sex with him, while he claimed he had been tested for AIDS but the result was negative.
>
> (quoted by Eldershaw, 2004, p. 79)

In March 1989, Osel Tendzin was accused of having sexual relations with disciples, and of knowingly transmitting to them the AIDS virus. At that point he explained his behavior in public meetings and stated that it was his teacher, the movement's founder Trungpa, who had assured him that he had nothing to worry about regarding himself or his sex partners, thanks to "Vajrayana purification practices" and his enlightened state of being which protected him from any effects of the HIV virus (Bell, 1998; Butler, 1990; Butterfield, 1994; Kane, 1998). He was eventually asked to resign from his position, and died in 1990.

It should be noted that despite the crisis and disillusionment with the leadership, most members remained completely loyal, and the movement survived. Since 1993, the group's leader is the Sawang, Osel Mukpo, son of Chogyam Trongpa.

176 Conversion and convert-dependent groups

A visit to the Shambala International web page leads to the following description of Osel Tendzin:

> The Vajra Regent was both an inspiring teacher and an effective administrator. His example was powerful as well as provocative. Through his inspiration, joyful energy, and hard work many students encountered the teachings of Buddhism and Shambhala Training and embarked upon the practice of meditation. He played a vital role in the task of planting these profound spiritual teachings firmly in the Western world.

This statement proves how successfully the crisis has been overcome.

Apocalyptic dreams and tragedies

Since the late 1970s, discussions of active new religious movements (NRMs) have been taking place in the shadow of several well-publicized NRM tragedies, including the murders and terrorist attacks by Aum Shinrikyo in Japan, and mass killings in the Peoples Temple, the Branch Davidians, the Solar Temple, and Heaven's Gate (Beit-Hallahmi, 2001b). The victims often included dependents of group members, and not just members. Deviant and destructive groups such as Aum Shinrikyo and the Order of the Solar Temple must be viewed against a background of personal and social pathology, related to vulnerability and deprivation among members.

Religious dreams of world destruction and rebirth are common or almost universal, but will rarely lead to violence. In addition to the well-known end-of-times historical traditions, there have been several interesting cases of new religious movements, founded since 1800, where apocalyptic dreams have been prominent. In the Church of Jesus Christ of Latter Day Saints (Mormons) there is an expectation of upheavals and imminent disasters before the Second Coming, which would leave only the Mormons unharmed. Members are expected to have in storage one year's worth of food, in preparation for the coming global catastrophe.

Similar dreams have appeared in the Baha'i movement, started in the nineteenth century as a heterodox Moslem sect. Its founder, Baha'u'llah, is believed to be the Messiah long expected by Judaism, Christianity, Islam, Zoroastrianism, and Buddhism. With the coming of Baha'u'llah, the "Manifestation of God," a new era has begun, lasting 5,000 years. It will lead to the Baha'i Cycle, lasting 500,000 years, but this will happen only after a global catastrophe, and the disintegration of the present world order. Dissident Baha'i groups in the United States had predicted catastrophic floods and nuclear wars for 1963, 1980, and 1995 (Balch, Farnsworth and Wilkins, 1983; Smith, 1987).

One modern version of the end-of-times fantasy is the move to another planet, following the total destruction of all life on planet earth. This fantasy played a role in 1953 in Mrs. Martin's group (Festinger, Schachter and Riecken, 1956), but it also appeared in the tragedies of Heaven's Gate and the Solar

Temple, where the collective death ritual was believed to carry members on to a rebirth on another planet.

The tragedy of the Branch Seventh Day Adventists is well known. Originally, its members followed the teachings of Victor T. Houteff, who deviated from established Seventh Day Adventist teachings in the 1930s by predicting the coming of a Davidian kingdom in Palestine, preceding the Second Coming of Christ. In the 1960s, Ben Roden (1902–1978) renamed the group Branch Davidians, and was succeeded by his wife Lois (1915–1986). Their son George Roden (1938–) tried to become leader in the 1970s, but was then ousted by a new leader, Vernon Wayne Howell (1960–1993), known after 1990 as David Koresh. He joined the Branch Davidians in 1982, became the lover of Lois Roden, and then assumed the leadership in 1987, after she died.

David Koresh gathered a veritable arsenal in the 1990s, including 350 guns and two million rounds of ammunition, which attracted official attention. "When asked about the weapons ... Koresh defended them as part of the biblical understanding of the group" (Tabor and Gallagher, 1995, p. 65). On February 28, 1993, the group's Mount Carmel compound near Waco, Texas was raided by more than 100 agents of the United States Bureau of Alcohol, Tobacco, and Firearms (ATF), searching for illegal weapons. The Branch Davidians opened fire, and four agents, as well as six group members, died. This led to a fifty-one-day siege by the FBI and the ATF, around what the Davidians now called Ranch Apocalypse.

On April 19, 1993, as millions around the world watched the unfolding events on television, the Mount Carmel compound went up in flames. We know now that the fire was started by group members. Eighty-three group members and their dependents died, including seventeen children. Five of the children were believed to have been fathered by Koresh. Following the end of the siege, nine members of the group were sentenced to prison terms for their involvement, five of them for forty years (Beit-Hallahmi, 1998; Reavis, 1995; Wright, 1995).

The history of NRMs since 1750 introduces us to a variety of sexual control regimes, which include forbidding sex altogether, breaking up couples, and sexual monopoly by charismatic leaders. These regimes are accepted by most members without doubts about the leader's intentions. In the case of David Koresh, both sex and violence were heightened and visible, as was the prediction of the coming end. One aspect of the tragedy which has received some attention is the sexual exploitation and domination of group members and their children by the leader. In 1989 Koresh officially announced to the members his rights to all females, and some followers left because of this. "The sexual practices of the Branch Davidians involved a strange mixture of celibacy and polygamy" (Tabor and Gallagher, 1995, p. 66). This mixture, not so strangely and quite predictably, meant celibacy for all men in the group, and polygamy for David Koresh. Tabor and Gallagher (1995) even quote one member of the group as saying that "we as Branch Davidians aren't interested in sex. Sex is so assaultive, so aggressive. David has shouldered this burden for us" (p. 72). At age twelve, girls were moved to gender-segregated adult quarters, where they became available to Koresh.

178 Conversion and convert-dependent groups

Regarding the leader's sexual partners, Tabor and Gallagher (1995) report the following: after arriving in Mt. Carmel in 1981 Koresh had an affair with the sixty-seven- (or sixty-nine)-year-old Lois Roden, the Branch Davidian prophetess, and announced that she would soon give birth to the Messiah. In January 1984 he legally married fourteen-year-old Rachel Jones, the daughter of a long-time Branch Davidian, Perry Jones. In 1986 he announced his marriage to fourteen-year-old Karen Doyle, whose father was also a group member of long standing. Later that year Koresh "married" Michelle Jones, twelve-year-old sister of wife number one. The contact with Michelle started in what seemed like a rape (Ellison and Bartkowski, 1995).

Later he took at least three more wives, ages seventeen, sixteen, and twenty, who had children by him (Tabor and Gallagher, 1995). Later on there was another "wife," whose relations with Koresh started when she was thirteen. It is also clear that in some cases Koresh had sex with both a daughter and her mother. By 1993, there were more than a dozen women in the group who considered themselves wives to the leader. Tabor and Gallagher (1995) report that he had fathered at least twelve children in the group. "During the March 7 videotape, which the group sent out ... Koresh affectionately introduced all twelve of his children on camera and several of his wives ... he also held up photos of several of his 'wives' who had left the group. He had not always been so forthcoming. He realized that the practice of polygamy itself, not to mention sexual relations with girls as young as twelve or thirteen, could cause him serious legal problems" (p. 66). As a result, "he even arranged sham 'marriages' for his wives with selected male members" (p. 67). Most of the leader's contacts were instances of statutory rape, as the age of consent in Texas is seventeen.

There was evidence not only of violent potential, but of real murderous acts in Mt. Carmel long before the ATF got involved. In November 1987 David Koresh, fighting for the leadership of the Branch Davidians, was challenged by George Roden (the son of the two former leaders, whose mother Lois Roden was Koresh's lover) to a final showdown. Roden dug up the body of a Davidian who had been dead for twenty years and challenged Koresh to raise her from the dead. This led to a fotrty-five-minute gun battle, in which Roden was slightly wounded. Koresh and seven of his followers were charged with attempted murder. The seven followers were acquitted, while Koresh won a mistrial, and was never retried. George Roden left the group, and in 1989 shot his roommate and then cut the body to pieces. He was found innocent by reason of insanity by a court in Texas and hospitalized. In 1995 he escaped to New York, but was caught and returned to Texas.

The final confrontation between the Branch Davidians and law-enforcement agencies had nothing to do with religion, and everything to do with guns. As Fogarty (1995) wrote:

> They were defending their turf with guns, protecting their messiah with an
> arsenal. They seemed to have stockpiled their weapons with as much ease as

they stockpiled feed for their animals ... It does not take a prophet, or a psychologist ... to see that a little gun control might have gone a long way toward preventing this pending apocalyptic confrontation.

(Fogarty, 1995, p. 14)

In this tragic case, a deranged leader was able to take scores of followers and their helpless children to their deaths. The history of the Branch Davidians did not end in 1993. The group, which has always been small, survives and believers still hold on to the teachings of David Koresh.

The case of the Solar Temple

The Order of the Solar Temple (Ordre du Temple Solaire) was an international Rosicrucian-Christian group, started in the 1980s by Luc Jouret (1948–1994), a Belgian practitioner of homeopathy, and Joseph Di Mambro (1924–1994), a Canadian. The group was active in France and in French-speaking areas of Canada, Switzerland, and Belgium. Joseph Di Mambro and Luc Jouret had between them a wide repertoire of fraudulent practices, from bad checks to fake cures. The official belief system of the group, combining claims about "ancient Egypt," "energy fields," reincarnation, and the "Age of Aquarius," is so widely offered in hundreds of groups all over the world (Beit-Hallahmi, 1992) as to be banal and harmless. But this was a high-involvement group, not just a club built around a series of lectures.

This meant that members signed over their assets to the group, which according to some estimates had more than ninety million dollars. Jouret preached a coming apocalypse, for which members had to prepare by arming themselves. At the same time, there were promises of a "transition to the future," an afterlife for members on another planet near Sirius, the brightest star in the firmament.

In 1993, the Solar Temple became the target of police attention (for illegal weapon charges) and sensational media reports in both Canada and Australia. In July 1993, Jouret and two associates received light sentences from a judge in Quebec for their attempts to buy pistols with silencers. The most sensational media reports, calling the Solar Temple a "doomsday cult," turned out to be right on the mark. On October 4, 1994, forty-six members and four children were found dead in two locations in Granges-sur-Salvan, in Cheiry, Switzerland, and in one location in Morin, Quebec. The victims were shot and then set on fire; the leaders, who did the shootings, committed suicide. Five days earlier two former members and their infant son were murdered in Quebec.

On December 16, 1995, in a repetition of the same horror, thirteen more members and three children met their death, laid out in a star pattern in the Vercors region of eastern France. The ritual killings were explained on the basis of the group's beliefs in a new life after death on another planet. "We leave this earth to rediscover a Plane of Absolute Truth, far from the hypocrisy and oppression of this world," said a collective suicide note. Many of the dead at this going-away party were murdered, some for revenge, while others were willing victims (Hall and

Schuyler, 1997; Mayer, 1999). The murders in Quebec were explained as the result of the victims' disobedience to the leaders in having a baby without permission. It is possible that Di Mambro, terminally ill, wanted to take as many with him as he could.

Learning from NRMs

It is now unfortunately quite clear that without these horrendous tragedies the world would have never known about the reality of backstage life among the Branch Davidians, Solar Temple, the Peoples Temple, Aum Shinrikyo, and Heaven's Gate. Of course, most religious organizations are undemocratic by definition (and by claimed revelation), but in recent times not all have been totalitarian dictatorships. These groups were totalitarian organizations where exploitation and violence were inherent.

What have we learned about the dynamics of destructive dreams from the tragedies of the Branch Davidians or the Solar Temple? When and how do apocalyptic dreams and beliefs lead to action? In every case of NRM disaster over the past fifty years there was a hidden reality of madness and exploitation, with extremely narcissistic leaders being followed by a group of dependent, obedient individuals. Totalitarian leaders tested their power over the membership through many displays of sadism and exploitation. The feeling before the actual disaster is that the leadership, and the group, has reached the end of the road and is facing destruction or severe disruption by outside forces. For violence to appear, we need a totalitarian leadership and some real despair. The apocalypse may then follow. Suicide was the end of the world, because group members were the elect. Here the price of rebirth was actual, not imagined, death.

New religious movements in modern societies receive much attention, which is out of all proportion to their success in recruiting converts or their overall influence on society. The impact of NRMs is much narrower than often perceived. They are small and marginal, and touch the lives of fewer than 1 percent of all religious believers. A look at the history of twentieth-century NRMs is quite sobering in this respect. Movements that once seemed on the verge of becoming global powers are now remembered only by historians. Moral Rearmament (the "Oxford Movement"), the best-known NRM of the 1930s in Britain and the United States, is today almost forgotten (Eister, 1950; Sack, 2009). The Jesus Movement of the 1970s in the United States, with its hundreds of communes all over the country, has similarly disappeared from memory (Shires, 2007). Adolescence and the move into young adulthood and a return to the mainstream is more of a factor than has often been realized. When enthusiastic members get older, commitment wanes in favor of more conventional pursuits.

Looking at a particular religious group, our diagnostic and predictive efforts are severely hampered by the complexity of interactions between beliefs, individual members, leadership, and the surrounding environment. What we have learned over the years is that predicting the future fate of a religious movement, large or small, old or new, is impossible. Groups that today seem marginal may rise to prominence, while groups which are at the moment well-known decline into obscurity. The history of new religious movements is replete with such cases. Developments in religion today are not just international but global, and belief systems cross borders easily. A little known group in South America or Africa may gain followers in Europe or the United States. Failures in prediction and analysis on the part of scholars are immortalized in academic publications. A celebrated case involves a participant observation study of a small group of desperate believers in a messiah from Korea in the San Francisco Bay Area. The author was convinced that the group was destined to disappear and would be remembered only because of his research (Lofland, 1966). In reality, it was the first outpost of the Unification Church (Moonies) in the United States, which became well known in the 1970s and 1980s, and went into decline later on.

Nevertheless, like the phenomenon of conversion, NRMs deserve, and get, attention just because of their rarity and intensity. If it is suggested that individual conversion offers a direct view of the basic psychological dynamics of religion, looking at NRMs is a rare chance to observe how a budding religion develops in its early years. This is something that is not really known about historical religions such as Buddhism, Judaism, Christianity, or Islam. Historical circumstances are totally different for ISKCON, founded in New York City in 1966, and for Islam, started in the seventh century in Arabia, but there is reason to believe that the dynamics of belief, leadership, and group loyalty have been similar.

8

PSYCHOANALYSIS AND THE PSYCHOLOGICAL STUDY OF RELIGION

The work of Sigmund Freud is not really a part of academic psychology, because Freud and his followers have worked outside the academic world. Nevertheless, academic psychology, lacking a unifying paradigm, has always been open to ideas coming from the outside, and has been affected by Freudian ideas. The psychology of religion has been similarly influenced, but psychoanalytic theory has been called speculative, untested, or untestable, and psychoanalytic interpretations of religion have been severely criticized (Beit-Hallahmi, 1996, 2010). How justified, then, is a chapter that relies on Freud's original writings? The only reason to look at the theory is that it has inspired some interesting research and has drawn attention to significant phenomena which otherwise would have been neglected.

Sigmund Freud (1856–1939) remains one of the most cited authors in psychology textbooks and in psychology articles. He is an icon for psychology and psychiatry, but had little training in these fields. Actually, he was a well-respected neurologist, a man of enormous learning and huge talents, who developed a theory of human behavior known as psychoanalysis. The creation of psychoanalysis was meant to offer at once a theory of the human psyche, a proposed treatment system for the relief of its ills, and a method for the interpretation of culture and society. Freud insisted on trying to reinterpret virtually all social phenomena in the light of his new theory. He remains the best spokesman for the theory he created, and this chapter will rely mostly on his writings.

The theory

Sigmund Freud is popularly known for emphasizing the role of sexuality in development and for proposing the idea of an Oedipal stage or template. These will be discussed later in the chapter, because the first order of business is to present his general approach to religion. Psychoanalytic theory tries to explain both the origin of supernaturalist ideas in general and the specific form they may take in beliefs, narratives, and rituals (Beit-Hallahmi, 1996, 2010). Freud's theoretical explanation for the origin and existence of religion is based on presumed universal experiences and processes: the basic mechanism of projection, the universal experience of helplessness, the tendency for compensation through fantasy, and the impact of early relations with protective figures, which creates "the human lifelong yearning for a once-experienced security in the contact with a caring parent" (Belzen and Uleyn, 1992, p. 166), and becomes a central part of the supernaturalist pantheon: "the smiling face and the guiding voice of infantile parent images which religion projects onto the benevolent sky" (Erikson, 1958, pp. 265–266). Every individual is psychologically prepared by early universal experiences to accept the religious ideas transmitted by culture. Belief in omnipotent gods is a psychic reproduction of the universal state of helplessness in infancy. Like an idealized father, gods are projections of childish wishes for an omnipotent protector. Projection, the mechanism which was used to explain the content of religious beliefs, is similar to anthropomorphism, described in Chapter 2 and referred to by ancient and modern writers.

Jean Piaget, like Freud, found the roots of religion in actual childhood experiences and, just as importantly, in childhood fantasies. Both Freud and Piaget described anthropomorphism as leading to children's ideas about the gods. Piaget recorded what he called "artificialism" (see Chapter 2), which leads children to believe that the natural world is the product of human activities (Piaget, 1929). He also reported, in agreement with Freud, that young children believe that parents and adults in general are omniscient and omnipotent: "[T]he child in extreme youth is driven to endow its parents with all of those attributes which theological doctrines assign to their divinities – sanctity, supreme power, omniscience, eternity, and even ubiquity" (Piaget, 1929, p. 378). Both described the disillusionment children undergo on discovering their parents' human limitations.

Freud claimed that God is "an exalted father figure" as a result of projecting the imagined father of early childhood, protective and powerful (Freud, 1927), while Piaget expressed the notion that God is a parent who helps to account for the structure of this world:

> The child begins by attributing the distinctive qualities of the divinity— especially omniscience and almightiness—to his parents and thence to men in general. Then, as he discovers the limits of human capacity, he transfers to God, of whom he learns in his religious instruction, the qualities which he learns to deny to men.
>
> (Piaget, 1929, p. 268)

As Piaget correctly notes, this change is the result of social learning, and not of the child's own ideas (see Chapter 3). Piaget stated that at age six children come to see humans as fallible, subject to limitations, and thus distinct from God who retains the extraordinary properties bestowed earlier. This suggestion has been supported by research in many cultures.

184 Psychoanalysis and the psychological study of religion

The universal early experience of all humans, which consists of being totally dependent, should be considered as the psychological framework for the creation of significant supernatural agents. Childhood is a series of attachments and loves, but childhood means much insecurity and anxiety, which lead to some powerful religious images:

> Who are the gods who panic? Who are the monsters and were wolves, ogres and witches? Or the bogeys, vampires, and vultures who appear in dreams and mysteries and threaten one's life? Whence those fears and figments; the notion of fantastic beings and domains no human is able to fathom? ... They are an integral part of the vast repertoire of human imagination, nay, the human condition. Their supernatural craft stems from that inspiration which in one way or the other belongs inevitably to everyone's childlike sense of impending doom or disaster and only magic, ritual, or prayer can tame or dispel.
>
> (Muensterberger, 1972, p. ix)

Psychoanalysis has denied the separation between childishness and adult experience, as one's childhood remains alive forever. Maturity is not a natural state or stage, but an achievement, and a considerable one at that. It has to be kept at an effort, an ideal rather than reality. Infantile thinking and immaturity are universal and normal, and this explains the universal readiness to leave reality behind and switch to a fantasy world. Childhood persists, and behind the mask of adult maturity there hides a five-year-old, who still wonders about the confusing world of adulthood. In a similar vein, psychoanalytic theory regards the difference between pathology (tied to childishness) and normality (tied to maturity) as only quantitative, not qualitative.

The focus in interpretation has been on the actual content of beliefs and rituals, and the actual behavior of concrete believers and communities (Beit-Hallahmi, 1996, 2010). "Let us return to the common man and to his religion – the only religion which ought to bear that name" (Freud, 1930, p. 74). This approach to the study of religious beliefs and practices has been much closer to the experiences of the majority of humanity than of most psychologists and sociologists, who seem to avoid dealing with the substance of religion, such as the myths of the Virgin Birth of Krishna, Buddha, and Jesus.

Psychoanalysis has examined "existential" concerns that lead to religious commitment. Such concerns most often refer to death or to insecurity and uncertainty in life. Freud stated that religion is "born of the need to make tolerable the helplessness of man" (1927, p. 32) and that it "must exorcise the terrors of nature, they must reconcile men to the cruelty of Fate, particularly as it is shown in death" (1927, p. 22).

Freud in his own words

What follows is a carefully chosen collection of ideas. Those familiar with Freud's voluminous writings will notice that this selection focuses on possible contributions

Psychoanalysis and the psychological study of religion **185**

to the psychology of religion and ignores other materials. It starts with the way Freud described his attitude toward everyday experiences often tied to religion:

> To my regret I must confess that I am one of those unworthy people in whose presence spirits suspend their activity and the supernatural vanishes away, so that I have never been in a position to experience anything myself which might arouse a belief in the miraculous. Like every human being, I have had presentiments and experienced trouble, but the two failed to coincide with one another, so that nothing followed the presentiments, and the trouble came upon me unannounced.
>
> (Freud, 1901, p. 261)

Being Jewish by birth, Freud felt the effect of discrimination, which was quite official during his lifetime. In Austria, where Freud lived for almost his whole life, Jews were excluded from many positions in government and the academic world. One response chosen by many Jews was a conversion of convenience, which gave them an admission ticket to first-class citizenship. Freud's reaction to such acts was one of contempt and anger: "a Jew ought not to get himself baptized and attempt to turn Christian because it is essentially dishonest, and the Christian religion is every bit just as bad as the Jewish. Jew and Christian ought to meet on the common ground of irreligion and humanity" (Wortis, 1954, p. 144).

How was Freud's work related to his atheism? Becoming an atheist, or being an atheist, does not require any special knowledge or training, and certainly not a theory about religion. Freud did not become an atheist after developing a theory about religion, but at a young age. Later on, when he started theorizing about human behavior, he responded to the challenge of explaining why most of humanity clings to what he considered illusions and delusions.

In 1901, as soon as he was ready to present his novel theoretical approach to the world, Freud spelled out a theory of religion based on the mechanism of projection:

> I believe that a large part of the mythological view of the world, which extends a long way into the most modern religions, is nothing but psychology projected into the external world ... One could venture to explain in this way the myths of paradise and the fall of man, of God, of good and evil, of immortality, and so on, and to transform metaphysics into metapsychology.
>
> (Freud, 1901, pp. 258–259)

Then he offered a dynamic interpretation of negative beliefs:

> Superstition derives from suppressed hostile and cruel impulses. Superstition is in part the expectation of trouble; and a person who had harbored frequent evil wishes against others, but has been brought up to be good and has therefore repressed such wishes into the unconscious will be especially ready

186 Psychoanalysis and the psychological study of religion

to expect punishment for his unconscious wickedness in the form of trouble threatening him from without.

(Freud, 1901, p. 260)

Freud was a spokesman for Enlightenment humanism, promoting a vision of autonomy and freedom. Like others, he regarded religion as a roadblock to progress. He sounded like Karl Marx and other Enlightenment thinkers when, during a visit to Rome in 1901, he wrote: "I found almost intolerable the lie of salvation which rears its head so proudly to heaven" (Masson, 1985, p. 449). Religious salvation was a lie, and should be exposed as such. Even if it does bring temporal relief, for Freud and Marx it dooms humanity to eternal damnation, because progress must follow truth and nothing but the truth.

In 1907 Freud pointed to the similarity of religious ritual and obsessive symptoms:

> The complex of conscious and unconscious ideation around both individual obsessional neurosis and collective religious rituals seems to be identical. We have stereotypical acts, which must be performed meticulously, with much anxiety surrounding them. In both cases the emphasis is on performance rather than meaning, which is truly hidden. Both obsessional behavior and religious rituals are based on the repression of certain drives ... an obsessional neurosis furnishes a tragi-comic travesty of private religion ... a pathological counterpart to the formation of religion ... This neurosis can be regarded as a private religious system, and religion as a universal neurosis.
>
> (Freud, 1907, p. 126)

Similar observations were made in latter writings: "if he is left to himself, a neurotic ... creates his own world of imagination for himself, his own religion, his own system of delusions" (1921, p. 124–125). The ideas presented in the 1907 essay are still deemed relevant to students of ritual (Gay, 1979; Liénard and Boyer, 2006).

In 1910, Freud suggested that the images of both father and mother are projected on the heavens: "The almighty and just God, and kindly Nature, appear to us as grand sublimations of father and mother, or rather as revivals and restorations of the young child's ideas of them" (1910, p. 123).

By 1913 Freud started dealing with death as the main factor in the formation of religion. He first suggested that encounters with death, together with ambivalence about the departed, led to the invention of evil demons, which were the precursors of all divinities: "Spirits and demons ... are only projections of man's own emotional impulses. He turns his emotional cathexes [investments of psychic energy] into persons, he peoples the world with them and meets his internal mental processes again outside himself" (1913a, p. 92).

In the middle of World War I, Freud explained the beginning of religion as a defense against the reality of death:

It is beside the body of someone he loved that he invented spirits ... memory of the dead became the basis for assuming other forms of existence and gave him the conception of life continuing after apparent death ... What came into existence beside the dead body of the loved one was not only the doctrine of the soul, but the belief in immortality and a powerful source of man's sense of guilt.

(Freud, 1915, pp. 294–295)

Realizing the meaning of death leads to the creation of a belief system based on immortality, guilt, and restraints on violence. This becomes the transformative moment of humanity.

In *The Uncanny* (1919), Freud offers observations on childish ways of dealing with reality that stay with all adults:

the idea that the world was peopled by the spirits of human beings; by the subject's narcissistic over-valuation of his own mental processes; by the belief in the omnipotence of thoughts and the technique of magic based on that belief; by the attribution of various outside persons and things of carefully graded magical powers, or mana; as well as by all the other creations with the help of which man, in the unrestricted narcissism of the stage of development, strove to fend off the manifest prohibitions of reality.

(Freud, 1919, pp. 240–241)

In Freud's discussion of group dynamics (1921), religion is described as one example of a strongly cohesive group, united by love. One essential feature of a living religion is the community, the feeling of partnership and belonging, which brings about ecstasy in members. Freud here ties the excitement and communion to the leader, who is the common love object.

[A] religion, even if it calls itself the religion of love, must be hard and unloving to those who do not belong to it. Fundamentally indeed every religion is in the same way a religion of love for all those whom it embraces; while cruelty and intolerance towards those who do not belong to it are natural to every religion.

(Freud, 1921, p. 128)

This recognition of parochial altruism, confirmed by research, anticipates modern social identity theory and research on prejudice (Chapters 3 and 6).

The Future of an Illusion (1927) is written out of exasperation at the readiness of humans to embrace tempting fictions about a benevolent cosmic order guided by perfect parents. But exasperation is not an explanation. Freud emphasizes religion's infantile roots, its perpetuation of the child's dependence and submission to the omnipotent father in the form of God, and its irrational foundations, which cannot tolerate doubts. The aim is "to make helplessness tolerable," first childhood

188 Psychoanalysis and the psychological study of religion

helplessness and then the helplessness of adults facing nature and death. Childhood helplessness creates the need for protection by the powerful father, and the continuing experience of helplessness throughout life creates a need for a much stronger father, but humans cannot remain children forever. We have to go out into the cruel world and face its harsh realities.

Freud's description of perceptual projection echoes the way the mechanisms of animism and anthropomorphism have been discussed above (Chapter 2):

> Primitive man has no choice, he has no other way of thinking. It is natural to him, something innate, as it were, to project his existence outwards into the world and to regard every event which he observes as the manifestation of beings who at bottom are like himself. It is his only method of comprehension.
>
> (Freud, 1927, p. 27)

The power of religious ideas,

> will be found if we turn our attention to the psychical origin of religious ideas. These, which are given out as teachings, are not precipitates of experience or end results of thinking: they are illusions, fulfilments of the oldest, strongest and most urgent wishes of mankind. The secret of their strength lies in the strength of those wishes.
>
> (Freud, 1927, p. 45)

Could an illusion represent reality? One of Freud's comments about illusion has been quoted many times by religious apologists, but Farrell (1955) shows Freud to be simply inconsistent:

> When he defines an illusion in *The Future of an Illusion* he says … that "it need not necessarily be false". Yet on the very next page he says of religious illusions that "they do not admit of proof … just as they cannot be proved, neither can they be refuted". But the second remark obviously does not square with the first (that they need not necessarily be false); and it makes nonsense of Freud's demand that *all* illusions must be proved or disproved by independent evidence.
>
> (Farrell, 1955, p. 195)

It has been argued that Freud meant to say that illusion could be positive in some way. This would be hard to claim when he used such terms as delusion or lie (Beit-Hallahmi, 2010; Hill and Hood, 1999; Hood, 2010).

Freud believed that supernaturalist beliefs could not be just benign:

> Ignorance is ignorance, no right to believe anything can be derived from it. In other matters no sensible person will behave so irresponsibly or rest content

with such feeble grounds for his opinions and for the line he takes. It is only in the highest and most sacred things that he allows himself to do so.

(Freud, 1927, p. 32)

The British psychoanalyst D. W. Winnicott (1971) proposed a mechanism for the development of illusions:

the substance of *illusion*, that which is allowed to the infant, and which in adult life is inherent in art and religion, and yet becomes the hallmark of madness when an adult puts too powerful a claim on the credulity of others … We can share a respect for *illusory experience*, and if we wish we may collect together and form a group on the basis of the similarity of our illusory experiences.

(Winnicott, 1971, p. 3, italics in the original)

This originates in the child's play as "an intermediate area of experience which is not challenged (arts, religion, etc.). This intermediate area is in direct continuity with the play area of the small child who is 'lost' in play" (Winnicott, 1971, p. 13). Winnicott repeatedly places religion, like art, squarely in the realm of the imagination.

Winnicott actually borrowed from Freud, without acknowledgement, the idea of a half-way zone:

Art is a conventionally accepted reality in which, thanks to artistic illusion, symbols and substitutes are able to provoke real emotions. Thus art constitutes a region half-way between a reality which frustrates wishes and the wish-fulfilling world of the imagination—a region in which, as it were, primitive man's strivings for omnipotence are still in full force.

(Freud, 1913b, p. 188)

While denouncing the lie that religion is, Freud had no misconceptions about the impact of his own work. His writings posed no danger to the status quo, and will not corrupt the mind of any believers: "There is no danger of a devout believer's being overcome by my arguments and deprived of his faith" (1927, pp. 57–58). In 1930, Freud was still exasperated: "The whole thing is so patently infantile, so foreign to reality, that to anyone with a friendly attitude to humanity it is painful to think that the majority of mortals will never be able to rise above this view of life" (1930, p. 74).

Some of Freud's best known pronouncements on religion use a diagnostic rhetoric, polemically applying a variety of psychopathological labels, but also proposing interesting psychological analogies: "our work leads us to a conclusion which reduces religion to a neurosis of humanity and explains its enormous power in the same way as a neurotic compulsion in our individual patients" (Freud, 1939, p. 55). Later on he uses another term: "[t]he religions of mankind must be classed

190 Psychoanalysis and the psychological study of religion

among the mass delusions," but then offers an interesting comment: "the dogmas of religion ... bear the character of psychotic symptoms but ... as group phenomena, escape the curse of isolation" (Freud, 1939, p. 81). This means that the same ideas which would be considered psychotic in individuals should be treated differently when they are shared by a whole group. This idea has been widely accepted: "the most significant difference between a religion, as held by a person, and a state of systematized delusion resides in the element of social participation ... there is a community of assumptions" (Sullivan, 1964, p. 81).

Freud's conversion case, 1928

Looking at one case study is a good way of learning about Freud's approach to usual and unusual behavior. Offering a testimonial, an American physician wrote a letter to Freud, asking him to consider faith before it would be too late. According to Dr. X's account, in his last year of medical school:

> One afternoon while I was passing through the dissecting room my attention was attracted to a sweet-faced dear old woman who was being carried to a dissecting table. This sweet-faced woman made such an impression on me that a thought flashed through my mind: 'There is no God' ... if there were a God he would not have allowed this dear old woman to be brought into the dissecting-room.
>
> (Freud, 1928, p. 169)

The facts of nature-made suffering are referred to by religionists as "[t]he problem of evil." If God is omnipotent, omniscient, and benevolent, why are we surrounded by so much suffering? The standard response of believers is theodicy, the justification of the gods. Ever since the Biblical Book of Job (and earlier versions of this book in ancient West Asia) the answer has been that God's true purposes were inexplicable. In the eighteenth century the philosopher Leibnitz offered a long-range view of divine justice. "In the end all good is rewarded and all evil punished, if not actually in this form of life then in the later existences that begin after death" (Freud, 1927, p. 19).

Dr. X's crisis soon ended: "God made it clear to my soul that the Bible was His Word, that the teachings about Jesus Christ were true ... Since then God has revealed Himself to me by many infallible proofs" (p. 169). Like countless other believers before and after, Dr. X resolved his crisis and moved from disillusion to certainty through submission and reconciliation.

Freud's first reaction to the story was to challenge the notion that a medical student (or any man in his twenties) had to wait for this occasion to be shocked by evil and death. Most children learn about suffering and loss gradually and ever too early. Even if you are not a medical student, even with the most sheltered kind of existence, you should have discovered these horrors earlier.

God, as we know, allows horrors to take place of a kind very different from the removal to a dissecting-room of the dead body of a pleasant-looking old woman. This has been true at all times, and it must have been so while my American colleague was pursuing his studies. Nor, as a medical student, can he have been so sheltered from the world as to have known nothing of such evils.

(Freud, 1928, p. 170)

Dr. X's strong emotional reaction to this stimulus must raise questions. If this sight triggered a realization of "the question of evil," why wasn't this realization triggered by other instances of evil he must have witnessed before that day? Why did the process start at this point and not before or after? We must assume that the external, visible drama is a reflection of hypothetical internal processes.

Freud offered an interpretation because the story raises a simple question, which might not, nevertheless, occur to other observers. Freud's starting point in questioning the story is one of common sense. The next step is an interpretation which is counter-intuitive and speculative. We don't have to accept the interpretation in order to appreciate the basic question and the inquisitive attitude. Freud's convert reports that his trigger was seeing a woman's body on the way to dissection (which got him to think bitterly about God permitting such evil in this world). Freud asked why is it that "the problem of evil" serves as a trigger for change on particular occasions and not on others, while the presence of evil in our life is permanent. Freud's response to the reflection on "the problem of evil" should serve as an example for examining dramatic transformations, religious and secular. Anybody allegedly discovering for the first time either the harsh facts of life and death, or a great bliss in a brave new world, must be involved in more than just a sudden reaction to the environment. Triggers cannot appear out of nowhere, but must follow a process of latent incubation. Life-transforming moments should be scrutinized within the whole span of the transformed life.

What is it about a particular stimulus that activates and mobilizes metamorphosis, and how is it that the ensuing process leads to change despite opposing forces which must be present inside and outside any individual? Public statements about hunger for truth or about events that started a quest for coherence are just one link in the causal chain behind any individual trajectory. Stimuli for great moments of re-assessment and discovery are chosen, both consciously and unconsciously, through a complex individual process, which leads to a conscious determination to find the "meaning of life" or Truth. When this sense of urgency is accompanied by disillusionment, it may lead to deserting one's home, in every sense, and the invention of a new identity and sometimes a new family.

Freud's interpretation of this religious conversion, not surprisingly, assumed that the consequences of our early relations were behind disillusionment and compensatory salvation. Research on religious converts has indeed shown that they report more problems in their relationships with their parents, and have suffered more often the loss of a parent in childhood (Chapter 7). Asking questions

192 Psychoanalysis and the psychological study of religion

about the early experiences behind metamorphoses seems fully warranted, while interpretations of any specific cases must proceed with extreme caution (Beit-Hallahmi, 1989, 1996).

Using Freud's ideas

Freud's writings have been criticized for being vague and speculative, but for almost a century many scholars regarded them as a source of ideas to be tested. "Freud's writings should be taken as a series of observations, some of which are worth converting into testable hypotheses" (Bulbulia, 2013, p. 125). Testing these ideas has taken on many forms and has used many sources of data. Quite early on, Freud's ideas about personality development and psychosexual conflicts were taken up by historians in attempts to explore the biographies of religious leaders, such as Martin Luther (Smith, 1913).

If religion is a projection, and religions are cultural projective systems, then there should be a connection between the characteristic experiences in a culture and its projective system. Spiro and D'Andrade (1960) tested this hypothesis by using cross-cultural anthropological data. The findings showed a correlation between the treatment of children in a given culture, and the presumed benevolence or malevolence of deities in the same culture. Similarly, Lambert, Triandis, and Wolf (1959) found that beliefs in malevolent beings was found to be correlated with cruel socialization practices. Early experience was found to be projected onto the cosmos, in agreement with psychoanalytic predictions.

The idea of projection has been applied to varied cultural beliefs. The anthropologist Raymond Firth stated that,

> [c]oncepts of evil principles, of sorcery and witchcraft, of demons, provide more acceptable explanations of social failures than does the notion of human inadequacy. Reinforced by ideas of sacrifice and scapegoat, of the devil and of hell, they provide outlets for aggressive impulses which need not react physically on other members of the society ... The process of projection is therefore carried further, to concepts of divine entity.
>
> (Firth, 2004, p. 221)

Explanations using the psychoanalytic notion of projected parental images have appeared in the literature without explicit references to this concept, but, acknowledged or not, the connections are obvious. Thus, Goodenough (1981) noted the connection between beliefs about spirits and beliefs about senior relatives in the culture of Truk, and Carl Sagan (1979, pp. 132, 137) stated that "all gods are symbolic projections of what people think their parents are, or should be ... The gods do not exist; they take their shape from the shadow of our parents that fell on our lives."

The anthropologist Meyer Fortes claims that "all the concepts and beliefs we have examined are religious extrapolations of the experiences generated in the relationships between parents and children" (Fortes, 1959, p. 78). He refers to Freud's ideas when he states:

> I follow him only as far as to see in Tallensi totem animals a symbolic representation of paternity perpetuated in the lineage ... At the same time there is no denying that these taboos stand for unquestioning submission to ancestral, that is magnified paternal, authority.
>
> (Fortes, 1987, p. 142)

One researcher of spontaneous mystical experiences stated that "infantile memories of parental images (perhaps even perinatal representations proprioception), and ... images from before four to five years of age" are the building materials of such experiences (Persinger, 1983, p. 1260).

Mythology and the testing of psychoanalytic claims

One domain of human behavior which may allow for the testing of Freudian ideas is the content of religious narratives. When approaching mythology, the challenge is that of explaining local traditions. Tylor (1871) stated that myth reflected "the history of its authors, not of its subjects" (1, p. 416), and this is clearly true. The psychological history of those who have authored mythologies seems to contain a limited number of repeated themes and categories which appear across time and space, history and cultures.

If religious narratives are not related to childhood experiences, we need to account for the salience of family, parenting, and kinship themes in them. The centrality of kinship idioms may be related to evolution, which leads to kin loyalties, but there are unique patterns of family relations which play a central role in religious traditions, and one basic template is seemingly expressed through many specific narratives. This fantasy pattern seems to be universally attractive. Otherwise, why would the same stories be repeated in so many cultures?

Psychoanalysis offers an answer, and suggests that there is a kernel of truth in mythical stories, but it is solely psychological. The reason similar myths describe Jesus and Krishna as having a similar childhood lies in universal childhood experiences, shared by all. The constellation of both positive and negative wishes directed at parents is thought to be expressed in a well-known narrative formula, in which miraculous salvation from death is followed by bloody struggles, and triumph often precedes tragedy (Freud, 1915–1916).

The Oedipus story starts with a terrible prophecy, revealed to his parents, the royal couple Laius and Jocasta, before his birth: Their son would kill his father and have intercourse with his mother. When the child is born, the desperate parents try to get rid of him, but he is saved from death and raised in the court of another king. When Oedipus, a young prince, somehow hears of the prophecy, he leaves his parents trying to escape his fate. On the road he encounters a man, quarrels with him and kills him. He then reaches the city of Thebes, the place of his birth, still

194 Psychoanalysis and the psychological study of religion

mourning its slain king Laius. Oedipus then wins Queen Jocasta in marriage and becomes king. He has children by Jocasta, but then a terrible epidemic breaks out in the city. Tiresias, the same prophet that pronounced the original prophecy that sealed his fate, now tells Oedipus that the epidemic is the divine punishment for his sins, and the king then blinds himself and goes into exile.

Freud regarded the story as a reflection of the critical stage all humans go through between the ages of three and six, when the desire for one parent and the hostility for the other dominate the child's life. This developmental stage is a rehearsal for adult intimate relations. Freud's claims about the prevalence of the Oedipal stage have been criticized first because he collected his data, such as they were, from neurotics, and those neurotics came only from European culture (Horney, 1939).

The Oedipal plot may sound absurd, but its many versions are quite easily produced and entertained by the human imagination. Stories which get repeated thousands of times contain an important truth. What is it? It is not the truth of the narrative, but the truth of anxieties, desires, and imagined solutions. The eternal and universal fears of children are projected on parents and attributed to them as actions. Family tensions and conflicts, real and imagined, are at the center of most human narratives. Freud claimed that the Oedipal template, or an Oedipal master narrative, plays a central role in all cultures and all cultural products. This can be tested by assessing the frequency and prevalence of patterns repeatedly found in cultural traditions.

Oedipal motifs, involving conflict, competition, and violence are easily found in religious narratives. The stories about Krishna, Buddha, Jesus, and others demonstrate the predicted regularities, with certain motifs appearing together in consistent patterns. The Bible is filled with the theme of child sacrifice and of various ritual sacrifices. The binding of Isaac, the killing of all the firstborn in the land of Egypt, as well as the Crucifixion, represent related fantasies. The typical configuration combines an irregular, miraculous birth with violent intergenerational conflict and the hero's choice of the wrong love object. The asexual birth may be a triumphal way of starting life, but it is followed by mortal dangers. The father is pushed aside, but he is still a force.

Rank (1914), after looking at thirty-four myths from the Mediterranean basin and West Asia, offered a general formula, or "standard saga," which could be found in innumerable mythological stories and fits such well-known cases as those of Romulus and Remus, Krishna, Moses, Isaac, Oedipus, and Jesus. The mythological hero is the son of royal parents, born in a difficult birth (often after a long period of childlessness), prophesied to be a danger to the safety of his father, who banishes him (often by putting him in a basket and setting it afloat). The child is then saved by poor people or animals, and only upon maturity does he discover his real parents. He eventually gains the love and recognition of his people, achieves fame and greatness, and wreaks vengeance on his father, fulfilling the prophecy.

Rank's model was expanded into a hero's biographical template by Raglan (1936), who came up with a list of twenty-two elements which are part of the hero myth of all cultures: His mother is a royal virgin, his father is a king, and the circumstances of his conception are unusual, as he is also reputed to be the son of a god. At birth an attempt is made, usually by his father, uncle, or maternal grandfather to kill him, but he is spirited away, and reared by foster-parents in a far country. After a victory over the king and/or a giant, dragon, or wild beast, he marries a princess, often the daughter of his predecessor and becomes king. For a time he reigns uneventfully and prescribes laws, but later he loses favor with the gods and/or his subjects, and is driven from the throne and city, after which he meets with a mysterious death, often at the top of a hill. His body is not buried, but nevertheless, he has one or more holy sepulchers. What sounds like a rollercoaster may be related to ancient initiation practices and their symbols.

We should note that in Raglan's template the mother's virginity is the starting point of the hero's mythical biography. Not every hero narrative includes all twenty-two elements, but if we examine the traditions concerning mythological figures like Krishna, Moses, Romulus, Perseus, Jesus, Herakles, and Buddha, we find that at least fifteen elements are present in all. In the case of Krishna, the best match, twenty-one are present. Buddha, Krishna, Moses, and Jesus all share similar biographies in these myths (Dundes, 1981).

Even if not everybody is ready to adopt the psychoanalytic framework, the evidence for the recurrence and repetition of certain themes all over the world is incontrovertible (Beit-Hallahmi, 1996, 2010; Caldwell, 1989; Campbell, 1981; Carroll, 1986, 1989; Obeyesekere, 1991). Kluckhohn (1959) presented a survey of global mythology, with the following themes found in all cultures: creation, flood, slaying of monsters, incest, sibling rivalry, castration, hero myths, and "Oedipus-type myths." Ubiquitous themes in myths were said to "result from recurrent reactions of the human psyche to situations and stimuli of the same general order" (p. 268). Brown (1991), in his list of human universals, included religion, mythology, and the "Oedipus complex." Johnson and Price-Williams (1996) found Oedipal themes as globally ubiquitous.

Some Oedipal narratives do not even include any father. The Egyptian sun-god, Ra, was said to have been born of a virgin mother, Net (or Neith), and to have had no father. The Egyptian god Horus, in some accounts, was said to be the child of the Virgin Mother, Isis, with no father. In India, one story about the birth of Ganesha relates how the goddess Parvati, while bathing, created a boy out of the dirt of her body and assigned it to guard her bathroom door. When her husband, the god Shiva, returned, he was surprised to find this stranger at the door, and knocked off the boy's head. Parvati broke down in grief, and Shiva attached an elephant's head to the boy's body. The Ganesha story is a prime example of Oedipality, with no virgin mother but with parthenogenesis, eliminating the father completely. Ganesha was conceived without any male involvement, but the non-father still wants to kill his rival (Hershman, 1974).

Miracle birth narratives such as the Virgin Birth express one version of a decisive "Oedipal triumph," which eliminates the father. Thus, in Greek mythology, Cronos, who castrated his father Uranus and married his sister Rhea,

196 Psychoanalysis and the psychological study of religion

was told that his son would defeat him. He swallowed his first five children. The sixth, Zeus, was saved miraculously, raised by nymphs on Crete, and came back to defeat his father. Later on, Zeus himself received a similar warning about his children by his wife Metis, and so turned her into a fly and swallowed her. This led to Athena being born fully grown out of his head. In the Mahabrata, the story of Krishna's birth starts with a prophecy, in which king Kamsa is warned that his sister Devaki's future son will kill him. Kamsa killed the first six of Devaki's children. The seventh baby, Krishna, is saved by being smuggled to the home of foster parents. Eventually, Krishna returns, kills his uncle Kamsa, and has intercourse with his aunt Kubja (Campbell, 1981). If we look at themes of Biblical mythology, what we are struck by is the amount of irregularities in terms of sexual relations, birth, and kinship.

Why does the myth of the hero include such Oedipal elements? Heroes are known and admired for slaying monsters, saving their people from disasters, sometimes killing their fathers, uncles, and other relatives and non-kin in struggles over succession. Being born to a virgin or committing incest seems to us less vital to the hero biographical formula, but in reality most hero myths include such elements, thus proving the attraction of the Oedipal template. When we attribute divine paternity or a miraculous conception to a human hero, it is evidence of inherent superiority.

To the believers, the message in miracle birth narratives is exceptionality, divinity, uniqueness, and superiority. The events are presented as miraculous, characterized by interventions and communications coming from the spirit world. The canonized denial of conception, pregnancy, and normal birth is an assertion of uniqueness and superiority. The miraculous or immaculate birth is a stunning miracle. The psychoanalytic interpretation has been that these fantasies express the denial of sexual intercourse between the parents, and this is the only kind of intercourse one is really concerned about.

Claiming divine paternity implies strong and close contact with great spirits. How and why would a virgin birth add to other claims of superiority for kings, gods, and heroes? Victory over earthly paternity is decisive evidence of superiority, much stronger than other kinds of proof. A resurrection from death is a greater miracle than a virgin birth, but bypassing normal paternity is still a victory over nature and fate. The message in many of the narratives is that having been conceived without sexual intercourse and being born without passing through the vagina is the ideal way to start life, but only a few heroes and gods have experienced this privileged route.

Miracle birth narratives may reflect only a desire for purity and an aversion to sex, but if this were the most important or exclusive motivation, we would find discrete birth narratives expressing this wish. In reality, as we have seen, the asexual birth narrative appears always within a wider plot, which is clearly Oedipal. As significant as the purity ideal may be, it appears together with other motifs, part of the predictable conflict template. Bypassing parental intercourse in birth is followed by threats from fathers, grandfathers, uncles, or kings (as in the cases of Jesus and

Krishna). Confusion about sex and parents, and the desire for purity may be easily channeled to the unifying Oedipal template.

The Oedipal template is relevant not only to mythology, but to various practices as well. Genital mutilation, which is part of initiation rites which affect about 20 percent of humanity, are consciously interpreted in various cultures as completing the process of gaining a full sexual identity. We have to recall that genital mutilation is performed by father-figures, and for females by mother-figures (Bettelheim, 1954).

While is it possible to show that Oedipal themes are indeed universal, and play a major role in religious traditions, it still isn't clear what bearing this might have on Freud's claims about the psychosexual development of children between the ages of three and six.

The love object hypothesis

Wherever and whenever we look, women show a stronger commitment to religion than men (Chapter 5). Moreover, in addition to the overall general difference between the sexes, there are also variations, and it turns out that among Christian denominations, the Roman Catholic Church attracts more men, while all Protestant denominations enjoy the support of significantly more women. To explain these differences we can use the pantheon hypothesis, a derivative of parental projection.

According to psychoanalytic conceptions of the Oedipal period (age three to six), girls should have a positive attachment to fathers but boys should feel ambivalent about them. We find that images of God are similar to images of parents, particularly to opposite sex parents (Beit-Hallahmi and Argyle, 1997).

Freud's notions of paternal projection can provide an explanation for the greater sex differences found in membership ratios, especially in Protestant groups. If the culture carries an image of God as male, and as a father, this image should therefore appeal more to women. It has been found that Catholics experience God more like a mother (Rees, 1967) and the Virgin Mary and some female saints are prominent in Catholic worship. What about the image of the Virgin Mary? Carroll (1986) proposes that it offers men an Oedipal object, and for women an opportunity for identification and satisfaction of a common Oedipal fantasy, that of having a child by their father. Also relevant is the maleness of most of the clergy, who are addressed as "father" in many religious traditions.

For Protestants the main object of worship is Jesus, and this should be the same for women. Research on individual believers in the Christian sphere of culture has shown some support for the idea that Oedipality is involved in determining deity images. Larsen and Knapp (1964) found that the deity image as rated by females was more benevolent, while males rated it as more punitive. This was interpreted as supporting the Oedipal origins of the deity image.

Attitudes towards the Christian God are closer to attitudes towards the opposite sex parent. For women, the image of God, and attitudes to God, are more similar

198 Psychoanalysis and the psychological study of religion

to those towards their father, and for men for those towards their mother. Comparing women in different roles, it has been found that attitudes towards the Christian God image and father image were most similar for nuns (r=.65), followed by unmarried girls, and then by older women (Beit-Hallahmi and Argyle, 1997).

Another interesting piece of evidence: Since the middle of the twentieth century, there have been various attempts by feminists to develop Goddess religions, designed to serve the needs of women. These attempts have been utter failures. We may suggest that Goddess religions fail to attract women because the pantheon must be headed by a true and natural (Oedipal) love object.

Projections and conflicts

As we have read earlier in this chapter, Freud himself did not think that father projection had to be researched, "because this God–Creator is openly called father" (1933, p. 167), but many studies tried to assess how relations with parents affect various god images. Beit-Hallahmi and Argyle (1975) surveyed eleven academic studies which had attempted to assess the similarity between individual images of the parents and the perceived image of God. While most of the findings did not support a straightforward paternal projection hypothesis, they did support a parental projection explanation. In a study of 4660 French Catholic children, parental references to God were found to increase in both girls and boys between the ages of nine and fifteen. The image of God in boys was more often connected to the maternal image of the Virgin Mary and less often to the image of Jesus, while the opposite was true for girls (Deconchy, 1968). Three experiments with Swedish students showed a clear overlap between the attachment felt to one's parents and to the Christian God (Birgegard and Granqvist, 2004).

Dickie *et al.* (1997) studied two different samples of children, aged four to eleven, who rated their mother, father, and God on nurturance and on power. Children rated God like both parents. God was rated as nurturant when parents, and especially fathers, were rated as nurturant, and as powerful when parents, especially mothers, were perceived as powerful.

De Roos, Idedema, and Miedma (2004) tested individual differences in God concepts among 363 Dutch preschoolers (mean age=66 months) and 271 of their mothers. Differences in children's "punishing God" concept were explained by strict child-rearing practices, offering some support for projection theory. Dickie *et al.* (2006) found that mothers, more than fathers, contributed to sons' self-esteem through nurturance and discipline, which in turn contributed to seeing God as nurturing, feeling close to Him, and being more religious. For daughters, mothers and fathers affected the image of God as nurturing and powerful. Punishing/judging parents contributed to punishing/judging God images in young adults. Men perceived God to be more punishing/judging than did women, while women perceived God to be more nurturing.

Hood, Morris, and Watson (1991) tested a hypothesis proposed by Carroll (1986) about the dynamics of the Catholic cult of the Virgin Mary. The prediction was that a repressed attraction to the mother will push young males toward the Virgin Mary cult. They will also be pulled by images of the suffering Christ, which expresses guilt and punishment. The study measured early maternal bonding and preferences for iconic religious images. Seventy-one non-Catholic males, selected for religious commitment, had to respond to crucifixes and pictorial representations of the Virgin Mary. Each participant was taken into a room with four crucifixes and one cross which were ranked on the degree of expressing suffering, randomly displayed on a wall. He was asked to select the image that best expressed what Christ meant to him, and then was asked to choose a painting that expressed what Mary meant to him from among five images. As predicted, an operational interactive measure of early maternal care and protection, indicative of repression, and the Parental Bonding Instrument, best predicted selecting both a suffering Christ image and an erotic/nurturing Virgin Mary image. This was interpreted as relating to Oedipal dynamics, as suffering relieves guilt.

Conversion and the father

Freud's interpretation of a case of religious conversion (1928), presented above, leads to specific hypotheses regarding the connection between one's relations with the father and the occurrence of conversion or heightened commitment. The prediction would be that problems in the relations with one's father (absence, loss, bad relations) will increase the likelihood of involvement in religious conversions and a commitment to a religious career (as monks or clergy).

Ullman (1982) carried out intensive interviews with forty converts (to Catholicism, Orthodox Judaism, ISKCON, and Bahaism) and a control group of thirty non-converts (members of the same groups). Almost one-third of the converts reported the loss of their fathers by death or divorce before age ten, and about half reported unsatisfactory and stressful relations with them. Thus, the psychoanalytic prediction was clearly supported. It has also been supported by a significant amount of data from various cultures and settings (Beit-Hallahmi and Argyle, 1997). Masson (1976) reported that Indian ascetics have typically suffered one of three major childhood traumas: loss of a parent, seduction, or physical abuse.

Erotic imagery

Psychoanalytic theory would predict gender differences in descriptions of erotic and mystical experiences. Hood and Hall (1980) asked respondents to describe mystical and erotic experiences. As predicted, females used receptive terms to describe both erotic and mystical experiences. Males used agentive terms to describe erotic experiences, but not mystical experiences. This is interpreted in terms of the difficulty on the part of males to experience an imagined mystical union with a masculine god, because this would have meant a homosexual act.

Looking at a similar question of sexual imagery and its meaning, Bilu and Beit-Hallahmi (1989) explored cases of a Dybbuk, a traditional Jewish variant of spirit-possession, involving spirits of the dead. Manifestations of such supposed possessions have always been considered malevolent and treated by exorcism. Based on sixty-three documented cases (forty-one females and twenty-two males), specific psychoanalytically derived hypotheses were tested. The reality of the cases was found to fit well with the conceptualization of this phenomenon as a hysterical syndrome resulting from repressed impulses, primarily sexual. Fifty-eight of the spirits were described as male, and only five as female. There were no cases of a female spirit entering a male, five cases of females entering other females, twenty-two cases of male–male entry, and thirty-six cases of male spirits entering females. The interpretation seems straightforward, confirming psychoanalytically derived hypotheses concerning the dynamics of hysterical symptoms.

Obsessive actions and religious practices

Freud's observations (1907) about private obsessive symptoms and public religious rituals have led to some interesting surveys of clinical population. Obsessive compulsive disorder (OCD) has been found to be related to religiosity, as OCD sufferers often display religious obsessions (Tek and Ulug, 2001), and there is a connection between religiosity and obsessive traits (Lewis, 1994, 1998; Tek and Ulug, 2001; Tolin *et al.*, 2001).

Fiske and Haslam (1997) tested the hypothesis that the same actions and thoughts that are ego-dystonic (i.e. cause subjective distress) in OCD are positively valued when they are appropriately performed in socially legitimated rituals. This was tested by checking for the presence of forty-nine features of OCD and nineteen features of other pathologies in rituals occurring in fifty-two cultures. OCD features were more likely to appear as compared to other pathologies.

Current status

In the twenty-first century, Freud is still very much a presence in the study of religion, and specifically in the psychological study of religion. An interesting historical point to ponder is how psychoanalytic ideas, this time through the agency of Bowlby's attachment theory, continue to serve as a stimulus in the psychological study of religion (see Chapter 4).

Sigmund Freud's ideas about religion are of more than historical interest. They are still being read, re-read, and re-interpreted (Beit-Hallahmi, 2010; Belzen, 2010; Bulbulia, 2013; Faber, 2004; Hill and Hood, 1999; Hood, 1992, 1997, 2010; Ladd, Spilka and McIntosh, 2011; Wulff, 1997). Freud's lasting contribution may be his intriguing observations and questions. The answers and assertions offered are often less than satisfying, but the counter-intuitive examination of motives is still intriguing.

9

SECULARIZATION AND THE PERSISTENCE OF RELIGION

All the observations and generalizations about religion and religiosity presented here are being made within the historical context of secularization, a process through which both society and individuals have moved away from the dominance of religious institutions and religious ideation. Over hundreds of years, there has been a decline of supernaturalist organizations and ideologies, which meant that they were losing their power to command respect and obedience, together with a persistent impact of supernaturalist ideas. Secularization is the quantitative decline in the allocation of material and psychological resources to supernaturalism. It is gradual and relative, and does not mean that religious ideas disappear, but only that less energy is invested in them. This decrease in investment can be observed even among those who consciously and explicitly proclaim support for supernaturalism.

In traditional societies, religious ideas are pervasive, and affect all and everything.

> The point is that before these transformations every aspect of life had involved religious associations. Everywhere people looked they were reminded of another dimension in life. There was not yet a secular world to escape to, as there is today, where one can effectively forget about anything beyond what we take to be ordinary reality.
>
> (Sommerville, 2002, p. 367)

The great change in everyday discourse is the possibility of looking at religion from the outside, which used to be not just impossible but inconceivable before. Not all members of a given society can do that, but some can, and this is a momentous development.

Sociologists have described secularization in terms of the change in the interaction between religion and other institutions in society. Emile Durkheim, one of the founders of sociology, wrote (1893/1964):

> Originally religion pervades everything; everything social is religious; the two worlds are synonymous. Then, little by little, political, economic, scientific functions free themselves from the religious function, constitute themselves apart, and take on a more and more acknowledged temporal character. God, who was at first present in all human relations, progressively withdraws from them; he abandons the world to men and their disputes.
>
> (Durkheim, 1893/1964, p. 169)

More than a century later, this is how the process appeared:

> [T]he rise of individualism and egalitarianism, the growth of religious diversity, the separation of human rights from religious rectitude, the displacement of supernatural remedies by scientific-based technological solutions, and the growth of a positive view of human power and potential … have been accompanied … by such fundamental changes in the nature and place of religion as privatization and de facto relativism, which in turn have been accompanied by a marked decline in religious activities, religious institutions, and religious beliefs.
>
> (Bruce, 2012, pp. 533–534)

Roy (2010) described secularization as the separation between religion and culture, which creates a new form of religion, de-territorialized and globalized. Devoid of its historical roots, it can find new adherents all over the world. Globalization lets religions and believers, of many origins, travel easily. What travels most easily are religious ideas, which become part of a global market.

Mobility, spatial and social, education, and urbanization, weaken ties to communities and traditions. In this continuing process, religious commitment declines, belief systems are becoming fragmented, privatized, and reinterpreted. Secularization often entails the psychologizing of religion, which means emphasizing personal experience, or "inner experience" and personal faith, rather than communal experiences or meanings. Karl Marx described how religion has become "the abstract confession of a particular peculiarity, of private whim, of caprice" (quoted in Easton and Guddat, 1967, p. 227). It is the individual who is being offered salvation in modern religion, rather than the community or society as a whole. Rather than clear cosmological assertions and the promise of world transformation, religion now offers the believers notions of individual psychological change (Witten, 1993). This is evident in both traditional denominations and in many new religious movements (NRMs), which claim to ensure immediate individual happiness. Successful televangelists in North America offer mainly a secularized gospel of "health and wealth" (Bruce, 1990b). The promise of happiness in this world comes from both old and new religions.

One consequence of secularization is a new discourse of defense and rejection. On the one hand, a defense of generic religion and on the other, a total rejection of supernaturalism. In earlier times, and in many cultures today, both acceptance and rejection focused on specific religions. The thirty-fourth President of the United States, Dwight D. Eisenhower, declared: "Our government makes no sense, unless it is founded on a deeply felt religious faith—and I don't care what it is" (Hofstadter, 1963, p. 84). This ecumenical show of faith, often cited to demonstrate the centrality of religion in US culture, paradoxically reflects the extent of its weakness, which has allowed only such generic expressions.

The prominence of pragmatic arguments in terms of the benefits of religion in general and of specific religions is another reflection of secularization. Today one can often hear pragmatic claims about how religion supports morality, makes people happier, or helps overall adjustment (see Chapter 6).

The secularization of politics

This process in Western nations has been gradual. Ideas about divine rights and divine laws have been banished from public debate in modern democracies. Religious tolerance has appeared together with capitalism, science, and nationalism, which sought to unify different ethnic and religious communities under a new identity. In some cases, national identity has taken over as the prime way of classifying and separating individuals, replacing religion. Nationalism has been accepted as worthy of killing and dying for, as religion was losing that legitimacy.

The idea of banishing religion from politics, a momentous historical change, is at present a dominant point of view globally. Before the middle of the nineteenth century, Karl Marx already described the process through which religion was separated and isolated from other realms of life: "In a form and manner corresponding to its nature, the state as such emancipates itself from religion, that is, by recognizing no religion and recognizing itself simply as the state" (quoted in Easton and Guddat, 1967, p. 223).

Some nations still have an official state religion, most of them with Moslem majorities, but even Moslem-majority countries, such as Albania, Azerbaijan, Burkina Faso, Gambia, Kyrgyzstan, Mali, Niger, Senegal, Turkey, and Tajikistan do have a formal separation of state and religion. Other nations with formal separation include the United States, India, Australia, Canada, Mexico, Japan, Brazil, Spain, Norway, Sweden, and France.

A sea change in outlook is evident in the Universal Declaration of Human Rights (UNUDHR), adopted by the United Nations on December 10, 1948. This document is both a declaration of the triumph of the Enlightenment, and a political program for future action, which is bent on tearing down traditional human divisions. Religion is mentioned, but only as a potential source of discrimination against individuals.

> Everyone has the right to freedom of thought, conscience and *religion*; this right includes freedom to change his *religion* or belief, and freedom, either alone or in community with others and in public or private, to manifest his religion or belief in teaching, practice, worship and observance.
>
> (United Nations 2000/1948, italics inserted)

204 Secularization and the persistence of religion

As the Declaration was being drafted and debated in 1947–1948, there were attempts to introduce religion into its preamble, but they were successfully resisted (McFarland, 2011). Out of fifty-eight member states at the time, forty represented historically Christian nations, nine had a Moslem majority, and six were communist-led. The communist opposition to any mention of religion apparently gained support from many Western leaders, which is an indication of the degree of separation between politics and religion already in effect. The preamble is phrased in purely secular language and starts with: "recognition of the inherent dignity and of the equal and inalienable rights of all members of the human family is the foundation of freedom, justice and peace in the world."

The disappearance of religious justification for the social order has not brought about the disintegration of society and has not reduced human kindness. Just the opposite is true. Secularization means that humans no longer interpret misfortune as caused by gods or ancestors angry at human sins, and cope with natural disasters and disease without tying them to any imaginary moral calculus. The Enlightenment means that humans have come to think of injustice and of many forms of suffering as social arrangements, under human control and human consideration. The new public morality means a change from an emphasis on the idea of individual sin to concern about collective inequity and individual rights. The Enlightenment has led to a new, totally secular public discourse about morality, focusing on rights, equality, and human welfare, and dealing with impulse control as an individual problem. This language of rights, which today seems natural and familiar, has been created in a secular context, by secular individuals.

Embracing the language of rights has been a radical departure from the historical stances of world religions regarding individual rights and obligations. As a leading historian stated:

> Human rights—roughly the idea that all individuals everywhere are entitled to life, liberty and the pursuit of happiness on this earth—is a relatively modern proposition. Political orators like to trace this idea to religious sources, especially to the so-called Judeo-Christian tradition. In fact the great religious ages were notable for their indifference to human rights in the contemporary sense—not only for their acquiescence in poverty, inequality and oppression, but for their addiction to slavery, torture, wartime atrocities and genocide.
>
> (Schlesinger, 1978, p. 503)

Together with advances in the state of individual rights, organized violence, reduced in scope, is part of reality. The secularization of political violence is self-evident when we look at the events of what has become known as "the other 9/11." On September 11, 1973, about 3,000 people died in Santiago, Chile, during a military coup that ended the career, and the life, of the Chilean president Salvador Allende. If we examine media and scholarly reactions to this event at the time and later on, they were much more muted than those to the events of the more recent 9/11. That was not only because the anti-Allende coup was long in the making, and a United States CIA task force was working on it since September 1970. The discussion of the 1973 events, regardless of whether we cheered the coup, as the United States did, or deplored it, took place within the framework of normal, secular violence. The actors' behavior, on either side, did not require a specialized explanation. People killed other people, or were killed, demonstrating commitment, courage, cowardice, or cruelty, but in the modern context, there was nothing unusual to ponder. Both sides represented modern, secular interests. The other 9/11, of 2001, caused a shock not only because of the violence involved, but because it looked like a throwback to earlier, pre-modern times. The nineteen individuals who were the perpetrators saw themselves as martyrs. Did any of those who died on September 11, 1973 in Chile regard themselves that way?

Political violence, engaged in by only a minority of humans, always comes with a justification. It is always presented as an attempt to redress an imbalance and rectify an injustice. Such justifications sometimes are stated within a religious belief system. Sacralized violent death is given a cosmic meaning, while death in the service of a secular ideology, national or supra-national, can have only a historical meaning. Most of the committed victims of violence on both sides in Chile did not conceive of their death as part of a cosmic struggle for salvation. Whether on the right or the left, they could see their struggle as historical, human, and finite. It was part of secular life.

Looking back

Some historians suggest that the thirteenth century was a turning point in Western religiosity. Medieval Europe entered a time of relative prosperity, which reduced otherworldly concerns (Barber, 1992; Strayer, 1940). Later on, it was the Protestant Reformation, the coming of the nation-state and the rise of capitalism which were the milestones on the road to the end of religious domination (Bruce, 1990a, 1992; Sommerville, 2002). The transfer of ecclesiastical territory to the early modern nation-state, which demonstrated a decisive loss of political power, was another one (Wilford, 2010).

In 1784, Emanuel Kant described the Enlightenment as,

> the liberation of man from his self-caused state of minority. Minority is the incapacity of using one's understanding without the direction of another. The state of minority is self-caused when its source lies not in the lack of understanding, but in lack of determination and courage to use it without the assistance of another. *Sapere aude*. Dare to use your own understanding! That is the motto of Enlightenment.
>
> (cited in Manuel, 1983, p. viii)

Economic power gained by new classes gave rise to new ideas about equality, citizenship, and democracy, and to changes in the power of religious establishments.

Secularization is most clearly proven by the formalization of individual rights in the United States Constitution and the Bill of Rights (especially the First Amendment, 1791) and the French Declaration of the Rights of Man and Citizen of 1789. These documents signify the decline of monarchy and aristocracy, and made possible a secular society in which religion is a private matter, a matter of "conscience" and personal preference.

The Radical Enlightenment consists of a set of core values. They are "democracy, racial and sexual equality; individual liberty of lifestyle; full freedom of thought, expression, and the press; eradication of religious authority from the legislative process and education; and full separation of church and state" (Israel, 2010, p. vii–viii). Modernity defines itself as committed to the values of free inquiry, the centrality of the individual, and to basic individual freedoms. It,

> puts a greater emphasis on the nuclear family (as opposed to the extended family), on egalitarian relationships between the sexes; on status based on achievement ... (as opposed to status based on birth ... or other ascriptive characteristics); and on greater concern with individualism (rather than with doing what is prescribed by authority figures or by social groups).
>
> (Triandis, 1973, p. 165)

This has led to what might be called "expressive individualism." Self-actualization has become the dominant ideal, replacing commitments to the survival of family, community, and society. This new ideal is expressed through the modern institution of psychotherapy, which offers a humanist meaning system to secularized individuals (Beit-Hallahmi, 1992).

Measuring secularization

The notion of secularization as measurable starts with determining a date for comparison, when religiosity was at a high level, and then using the same measures at intervals over time. If we look at any society 100 years ago and today, the differences are striking. The global secularization hypothesis states that worldwide religiosity in the year 2020 would be lower on all measures than it was in 1800. Another version of this hypothesis is that religion will make less of a difference in individual and social behavior as the worldwide process of secularization continues. If we choose 1700 or 1600 or 1000 as the reference point, changes are even more striking. It is clear that humanity is investing much less in religious activities today compared to 1000 years ago, 500 years ago, 100 years ago, or 50 years ago.

This has been happening globally, with the status of religion as an institution radically changing in most of the world. It is in Europe, North America, and English-speaking settler colonies such as Australia and New Zealand that we can observe striking changes, but we can also find them in India, China, Korea, and Japan (Reader, 2012). The exception is the Islamic world, where secularization is limited. Evidence for change, where it has occurred, is found in all aspects of culture. A readership interest survey of 11,000 households in the United States in 1953 listed religion as the top interest for women, and the fifth-ranked for men. By 1983, based on a survey of 4547 households, religion has totally disappeared from the list of top ten interests. For women, fashions and clothes were number one, and for men business. Fifth place for men was science (Kidder, 1985). Wuthnow (1978) noted the decline in donations to religious organizations in the United States after 1961 and the parallel decline in the number of religious books as a percentage of all books published.

All measures used to assess religiosity can serve as quantitative indicators of secularization. The gradual historical decline when such measures are applied is the operationalization of the above hypotheses, and both hypotheses seem to be proven beyond dispute. The number of individuals who identify as having no religion (who are not necessarily agnostics or atheist, but still reject religious identity labels) has been growing worldwide (Roth and Kroll, 2007). In the course of the twentieth century, the number of non-believers skyrocketed from 3.2 million in 1900 to 918 million in 2000, or from 0.2 percent of world population in 1900 to 15.3 percent in 2000 (Barrett, Kurian and Johnson, 2001; Zuckerman, 2007).

Public rejections of supernaturalist beliefs are obviously the highlight of secularization. Atheism, the conscious rejection of all supernaturalism, has become an identity label for individuals and movements (Baker and Smith, 2009; LeDrew, 2012; Sherkat, 2008), and secular humanism has become an established point of view (Budd, 1977; Kurtz, 1989; Lamont, 1935/1990, 1949).

Pollack (2008) described a common switch from belief in a personal God to belief in a "higher power" in Europe. In 1994, 36 percent of Dutch respondents described themselves as atheists or agnostics, 16 percent believed in a "higher power," and 48 percent were believers (Lechner, 1996). Table 9.1 presents the results of a survey in the United Kingdom in November 2012, which shows that one-fifth believed in a "higher power," and 29 percent were atheists.

According to Abrams, Haley, and Wiener (2011), in the foreseeable future religious affiliation may be on the verge of extinction in Australia, Austria, Canada,

TABLE 9.1 Belief in supernatural entities

Choices presented to respondents	Overall yes	For men	For women
1. I believe there is a God.	37%	30%	43%
2. I do not believe in a God, but do believe there is some sort of spiritual higher power.	21%	18%	23%
3. I do not believe in any sort of God or higher spiritual power.	29%	37%	22%
4. I don't know.	13%	14%	13%

Source: All figures, unless otherwise stated are from YouGov Plc. The sample size was 1642 adults. Fieldwork was undertaken November 8–9, 2012. The survey was carried out online. The figures have been weighted and are representative of GB adults (aged 18+).

208 Secularization and the persistence of religion

the Czech Republic, Finland, Ireland, New Zealand, Switzerland, and the Netherlands. In March 1996 the prediction was made (by the church itself) that the Methodist Church in Britain, which has been part of history for almost three centuries, will become extinct in the following century.

The reality of secularization can be assessed along the dimensions of uniformity, collectivism, and pluralism. It is easy to prove that in all industrial societies today, religion, which was once uniform, collectivistic, public, ascribed, and inherited, is today pluralist, individualistic, privatized, and sometimes chosen (Singleton, 2012). Religious beliefs survive and are commonly expressed, but they are rarely tied to collective action. This leads to underestimating their ability to motivate public actions (Beit-Hallahmi, 2001a).

Sometimes, the effect of a particular tradition is expressed at the neural level. Some religions teach their followers an ideal of self-denial. How could we measure the effect of such an ideal on actual believers? Han *et al.* (2008) and Han *et al.* (2010) found that the conflicts and struggles around this idea were affecting brain processes in both Christians and Buddhists, and these religious individuals were indeed preoccupied with keeping their self-enhancement under control. Christensen *et al.* (2014) compared eleven Roman Catholics and thirteen atheists (all female) who responded to moral dilemmas. Different brain areas were activated as individuals in the two groups reached moral judgments. Sometimes a belief system may affect temperamental ideals and followers of Buddhism may be different from followers of Christianity in their declared "affective style" (Tsai, Miao and Seppala, 2007). With growing secularization and globalization, we may wonder whether such effects of tradition are going to grow weaker.

Many of the phenomena discussed in this book, such as changes in religious identity, disaffiliation, and NRMs (Chapter 7), are possible only in a secularized culture. The possibility of choice and preference, of identity change or joining an NRM, is a modern phenomenon, interpreted as a symptom of the decline of tradition. A study of conversion rates in forty nations showed a positive correlation with religious pluralism (Barro, Hwang and McCleary, 2010). Individuals are free to make choices only in a world where religion has lost its authority and its power: "persons are seen to be free to choose not only *which* religion will be theirs but also *whether* to choose any at all. It is the changeover of the church from being 'inherited' and to some extent therefore involuntary, to being completely a matter of individual choice" (Hammond, 1991, p. 517; Demerath, 1995).

When researchers have asked individuals directly how much God might be involved in hypothetical events, a general bias has been found toward attributing positive as opposed to negative events to God (Gorsuch and Smith, 1983; Lupfer, Brock, and DePaola 1992; Lupfer *et al.*, 1994). This bias was confirmed in personal letters related to "healing" (Williams and Watts, 2014). How often do individuals use religious ideas to explain real events in the world around them? With growing secularization, miracle stories were treated not only with skepticism, but with ridicule, and religious explanations which view disasters as divine punishment have been regarded as relics of ignorance. In the 1960s, an observer from India reported on the religion of the people of an American suburb, in contrast with Hinduism of rural as well as urban Bengal. He noted that "[t]he role of divine intervention in natural phenomena as well as in human problems such as economics, health, and litigation is very much attenuated" (Sinha, 1966, p. 195).

Natural disasters used to play a much bigger role in religious discourse, but the discussion of catastrophes as evidence of cosmic justice has become rare (Kelly, 2005). Misfortunes, disasters, disease, suffering, and death are explained in natural and naturalist terms (Steinberg, 2000; Chester, 2005), and spirits are less often invoked to explain storms, epidemics, or earthquakes. Supernaturalist beliefs are utilized in coping with what appear like random misfortunes such as business failures, unemployment, illness, and accidents. Reliance on supernaturalism in such cases is a function of the total other means available and the degree of possible human control (Ashforth, 1998; Harnischfeger, 2006; Stewart and Strathern, 2004). Sibley and Bulbulia (2012) assessed the religiosity in a representative sample of the inhabitants of Christchurch, New Zealand, which experienced a major earthquake which killed 185 people on February 22, 2011, before and after the quake. Those affected became more religious, as compared to the general population of the country, but this increase in individual religiosity did not improve subjective well-being. Stephens *et al.* (2013) found that victims of horrific natural disasters are likely to think about them in religious terms when their experiences were indeed unpredictable and uncontrollable. It seems obvious, and consistent with experimental findings (Kay *et al.*, 2010b) that resorting to religious explanations will persist as uncontrollable events (or events that appear beyond control) continue to occur around us. Nevertheless, for some humans, what seemed uncontrollable 300 years ago (epidemics, illnesses, earthquakes, storms) seems more manageable, if not preventable. With improvements in engineering and biomedicine, humans are better able to cope with catastrophes. Individuals in earthquake and flood-prone countries with more advanced economies are less likely to experience them as totally debilitating.

Formal explanations of secularization

Harrington (1983) stated that the family, religion, and community are undermined by the market and by the ideology of utilitarian individualism, urbanization, and industrialization. The family has changed from a unit of production, consumption, and socialization, to a unit of consumption and only some socialization. When discussing the psychological aspects of modernization in developing countries, Inkeles and Smith (1974) note that "religion ranks with the extended family as the institution most often identified both as an obstacle to economic development and as a victim of the same process" (p. 27). When Farrell (1955, p. 196) presented a blueprint for the eradication of religion, the first items had to do with economic and political security: "the achievement of external social security by the gradual control of inter-state relations and the maintenance of peace; the achievement of internal social security by means of ... an expanding economy with full employment."

Chapter 4 discussed in detail the situational factors leading to higher religiosity, mainly deprivation. Most explanations of secularization refer to situational changes, especially lower overall deprivation. Urbanization and industrialization are psychologically tied to an increase in self-confidence, with relatively more control over nature and circumstances (Norris and Inglehart, 2004). Universal education, exposure to other cultures, the development of technology and science, and the general eclipse of authority lead to individual empowerment. Non-belief emerges as a viable personal choice as existential security rises in modern industrialized societies (Norris and Inglehart, 2004; Zuckerman, 2009). It is easy to become an atheist when you enjoy economic prosperity and security (Diener, Tay and Myers, 2011). But if deprivation really accounts for higher religiosity, then the persistence of supernaturalism must be related to various forms of continuing deprivation and frustration, especially economic insecurity, but also psychological distress. Table 9.2 demonstrates the relationship between economic security and the persistence of religion.

McCleary and Barro (2006b) stated that their explanations of secularization are part of modernization theory, which covers the effects of economic development on society (Inglehart and Baker, 2000). They also acknowledged their debt to the economic determinism proposed by Karl Marx (1859/1913), who argued that economic structure determines the superstructure of social consciousness, which includes religion. Using data collected between 1985 and 2005 from 68 nations, they found that religiosity, measured through beliefs (belief in heaven, belief in hell, belief in after-life, belief in God in some form, self-definition as a religious person) and service attendance, declined with economic development and urbanization. Moreover, they argued that this relationship indicated causation and not just correlation.

In an alternative to the Marxian view, data on sixty beliefs and seventy-seven values, collected in 2002–2003 in a random sample of Canadians (n=1174), were used to explain secularization in terms of prevalent ideologies. The results showed that individualism ("believing it is up to the individual to decide what is right and wrong") together with materialism ("all that exists is physical; there is nothing

TABLE 9.2 Strength of religiosity by type of society (percent)

	Agrarian	Industrial	Post-industrial	Total
Believe in God	97	80	79	83
Believe in life after death	83	62	68	69
Religion "very important"	87	60	55	64
Identify as religious	73	58	59	61
Comfort from religion	74	51	46	54
Attend religious service regularly	47	45	21	28
Mean religiosity (0–100)	73	54	53	58

Source: Inglehart and Norris, 2003, p. 55

Secularization and the persistence of religion **211**

transcendent beyond matter itself") and support for the theory of evolution led to the movement away from religion (Hay, 2014).

A global overview of secularization

Even if secularization is not uniform on a global scale, high levels are a reality in large parts of the Northern hemisphere, with the most secular nations found in Northern Europe and in East Asia (China, Japan, and Korea). Halman and Draulans (2006) and Voas (2009) argued that secularization, reflected in declining support for religious beliefs and in dwindling ritual attendance, has been occurring all over Europe at different rates. Scandinavia has led the way in creating islands of humanism, characterized by a commitment to individualism and self-actualization and where religion became simply irrelevant (Tomasson, 1968). East Germany (the former German Democratic Republic), Estonia, and the Czech Republic seem to be the most secularized areas of the world (Pickel, 2009; Wohlrab-Sahr, 2009). It has been said that "[w]hat makes modern Europe unique is that it is the first and only civilization in which atheism is a fully legitimate option, not an obstacle to any public post" (Zizek, 2006, p. A23). This has become true of other nations. Australia has had at least three atheist prime ministers since 1970. In North America, Canada has experienced a "European" decline in religiosity since the 1960s (Eagle, 2011; Hay, 2014; O'Toole, 1996).

Even in traditionally Catholic countries, such as Spain and Poland, non-affiliation has been slowly growing (Requena and Stanek, 2013). Ireland has been showing dramatic changes. In the late 1960s, a study which compared practices in major cities in Bulgaria, Finland, Germany, and Ireland, found that Dublin was the most religious (Lüschen *et al.*, 1972), and Ireland was considered one of the exceptions to European secularization trends. This started changing in the late twentieth century, and accelerated in the twenty-first. By 2011, according to WIN-Gallup International (2012), the percentage of individuals defining themselves as a "religious person" was 47 percent, 44 percent defined themselves as "not a religious person," and 10 percent defined themselves as atheist. This put Ireland in forty-third place out of fifty-seven nations on religiosity. There was a 22 percent drop in the percentage of Irish who defined themselves as a "religious person" between 2005 (when it was 69 percent) and 2011. The term "post-Catholic Ireland" is encountered more and more often. Since 2000, Brazil, the most populous Catholic nation, has experienced a significant decline in all Catholic practices, and the lowering of fertility, with the number of non-believers constantly growing. Since 2000, Russia has been regarded as an exception to the European secularization trend (Evans and Northmore-Ball, 2012).

In Europe, some changes are especially dramatic against the background of the last millennium or even the past century. Since the end of World War II in 1945, the decline of religiosity in Europe has been accelerating. In 1945, 100 percent of Germans had a religious affiliation, equally divided between Roman Catholics and Protestants. In the twenty-first century, more than 30 percent of Germans are

212 Secularization and the persistence of religion

unaffiliated, and the rest equally divided between Catholics and Protestants (Wohlrab-Sahr, 2009). In the Netherlands, what has been described as "the cultural revolution" since the 1960s has resulted in a radical de-Christianization. In 1899, 97.7 percent of the population belonged to a church. By 1981, it was 55 percent, and by 2000, the number was down to 40 percent (Te Grotenhuis and Scheepers, 2001). Looking at data from 1979 up to 2005, de Graaf and Te Grotenhuis (2008) found that embracing beliefs of the traditional kind ("There is a God who concerns Himself with every individual personally") together with less traditional ones ("I believe in the existence of a Supreme Being") has declined over time. According to a 2011 poll, 36 percent of the French believed in God, 34 percent did not, and 30 percent were uncertain (United States Department of State, 2011).

One clear measure of secularization is the decline in reported ritual participation. In most Western countries, rates of participation in weekly religious services have been in decline ever since such measures have been taken. In England, attendance at Church of England weekly services had declined to 2.3 percent of the population by 1992 (Crockett and Voas, 2006). Rituals which were once at the center of one's religious identity, such as the obligatory confession in the Roman Catholic tradition, have become totally marginal, and most Catholics no longer go to confession. Any visitor to the cities of Europe can witness the effect of secularization. In the cityscape, churches which have served as the heart of communities since the Middle Ages are now locked-up relics. One encounters dilapidated churches surrounded by signs offering them to whomever will convert them to any socially useful purposes.

Decades of deliberations have led to the European Union constitutional documents, making up the Treaty of Lisbon (2009). During these long discussions, there have been attempts to include a reference to Christianity, as a source of inspiration and an essential part of European heritage, in the preamble to the constitution. These attempts have been defeated, and the preamble opens with the following statement: "Drawing inspiration from the cultural, religious and humanist inheritance of Europe, from which have developed the universal values of the inviolable and inalienable rights of the human person, freedom, democracy, equality and the rule of law." The European Charter of Fundamental Rights (2010) starts with the following: "Conscious of its spiritual and moral heritage, the Union is founded on the indivisible, universal values of human dignity, freedom, equality and solidarity; it is based on the principles of democracy and the rule of law." Putting the "humanist inheritance" on an equal footing with the religious one is in clear defiance of a millennium of European history when Christianity was at the center of European identity. The cross is still at the center of nineteen European national flags, reminding everyone of that history. The decline in the salience of religion is not just a matter of political deliberations, but is reflected in the views of all ordinary citizens.

The European Union has been carrying out mass surveys (Eurobarometer) which ask respondents to choose three from a list of twelve values. In November 2010, Europeans placed human rights first (47 percent), followed by peace (44 percent), respect for human life (41 percent), democracy (29 percent), individual freedom (23 percent), the rule of law (22 percent), equality (19 percent), solidarity (15 percent), tolerance (15 percent), self-fulfillment (10 percent), respect for other cultures (8 percent), and religion (6 percent). These results, for a population of more than 500 million, demonstrate a clear victory of Enlightenment values in one continent (European Union Eurobarometer, 2012).

The decline of the religious professions

Religions act through the clergy, specialists who sometimes devote their whole lives to religious acts, lead rituals and congregations, and take care of connections with the spirit world by officiating at rituals. The significant decline in the number, authority, and status of clergy is one of the clearest indicators of secularization. It can be measured through the ratio of clergy to population, which has declined over the past two centuries. In the Roman Catholic Church, the largest religious establishment globally, there has been a worldwide precipitous decline in the number of individuals who are ready to join religious orders and the priesthood since the middle of the twentieth century, despite the rise in total nominal membership, which by the end of the century passed one billion. In 1965, there were 180,000 Catholic nuns in the United States; in 2012, there were about 56,000, with the average age being seventy-four (Winerip, 2012).

The growing reluctance of individuals to commit themselves to religion as a full-time pursuit is striking. It may seem surprising today that in the nineteenth century the clergy in most Western countries were still a majority of the educated classes. Just as religion was identified with culture, so religious leaders in the community were the bearers of culture and education and leaders in their communities. In Britain or the United States, clergymen were members of the professional classes or the intellectual elite (Annan, 1978), but Western religious elites have been marginalized by other knowledge-workers (Hunter, 1987; Hunter and Hawdon, 1991). Being in the clergy today means playing a more pastoral role, not that of authority figures representing a higher order or a cosmic order. Another global change is the decline of missions from the First World to the Third World, a feature of Western history for hundreds of years.

Religious accommodation to change

Secularization means that religion itself is transformed: "The divorce of criminal law, family law, 'welfare,' artistic patronage, political decision-making, political symbolism, political theory, economic arrangements, ethical discussions, holidays, oaths, diplomacy, from religious considerations changes religion out of recognition" (Sommerville, 2002, p. 369).

What can easily be observed in the West is a significant change in the descriptions of the Christian spirit world. The pantheon has been partly depopulated. Hell or Satan are rarely invoked, and demons have disappeared, while angels or heaven are often recalled. If God used to be powerful, active and judgmental, now the images offered reflect benevolence and distance. The image of God as punishing sins, so important both individually and socially, has been fading, together with the rest of traditional cosmology. Studies in the United States show a gradual decline over time of the "all-seeing eye who watches us," and the "God of wrath and judgment" (Nelsen and Kroliczak, 1984).

Hunter (1983) found that the presentation of Evangelical Christian doctrine has changed since the nineteenth century. It has been "repackaged" to appear less offensive, and ideas about sin, hell, and damnation have been de-emphasized (this is not true, of course, in the case of the most traditional groups). Surveys have shown that among the general public, belief in hell has declined, but not belief in heaven or afterlife (Popp-Baier, 2010). Religious mythology has been transformed among more secular individuals into naturalistic events in ancient history. Thus, the Biblical Exodus myth is often presented as historical, and the mythical Moses is described as an ancient leader.

These changes in beliefs are connected to the weakening of most religious bodies. Johnson and Chalfant (1993) described religious organization in the United States as forced to cope with a secularized environment which may consider them "deviant." One strategy is the development of ecumenical alliances across denominational lines. Other strategies include "demographically sensitive church services, small groups in homes, parks, coffee shops, and workplaces, and continuously updated outreach programs" (Wilford, 2010, p. 341).

An article in the *New York Times*, titled "Building Congregations Around Art Galleries and Cafes as Spirituality Wanes" reports on the creative efforts of church leaders in the United States to attract congregants:

> Inside there are the trappings of a revitalization project, including an art gallery, a yoga studio and a business incubator, sharing the building with a coffee shop and a performance space. But it is, in fact, a church … part of a wave of experimentation around the country by evangelicals to reinvent "church" in an increasingly secular culture. They house exercise studios and coffee shops to draw more traffic. Many have even cast aside the words "church" and "church service" in favor of terms like "spiritual communities" and "gatherings," with services that do not stick to any script. One Sunday before Easter, the pastor at the Relevant Church in Tampa, Fla., wearing a rabbit suit, whisked the unsuspecting congregation away on chartered buses to a nearby park to build enthusiasm for the coming service.
>
> (O'Leary, 2012, p. A14)

Nevertheless, there is some evidence of religious militancy even in secularized countries. Using 1998 data from the International Social Survey Program (ISSP) in eighteen Western countries, Achterberg *et al.* (2009) found that Christian demands for a stronger public role of religion were stronger in countries where Christianity was in steeper decline. Data from the Netherlands collected during 1970–1996 showed the same activist trend, challenging the privatization of religion.

Pluralism

Pluralism has been defined as "the coexistence in the society of different worldviews and value systems under conditions of civic peace and under conditions where people interact with each other" (Berger, 2006, p. 153). The presence of many competing points of view, which undermines religious authority, is a reality that is hard to avoid. It creates a "crisis of credibility" for all religions, as more religious alternatives compete (Berger, 1967). Students of new religious movements (Stark and Bainbridge, 1985; Robbins, Anthony and Richardson, 1978) have stated that their rise is tied to the decline of old religious traditions and takes place at their expense. Montgomery (2003) demonstrated that pluralism is tied to lower rates of religious participation.

The accelerated globalization of economy and culture leads to a relativistic stance regarding cultures and identities. Improvements in transportation and communication, and growing literacy, have brought about exposure to other cultures and religions. This may lead individuals to confront their own beliefs, and must create an epistemological relativism regarding authority and revelation. Religions claim similar miracles, and tell similar stories, while still claiming absolute truth and superiority. Individuals realize that there are other possible identities and that cultural differences are arbitrary. The normal reaction (cultural in-group bias) is not to take foreign traditions seriously, but observing the power of devotion eventually must create doubts regarding one's own culture. Once you accept the idea that culture is humanly and arbitrarily constructed, a more skeptical view of your own traditions may appear (Chadwick, 1975).

If we take seriously the absolutist and exclusive claims of religion, any religion, and we know that some adherents take them quite seriously, we will have a war of all against all. Today life in most modern nations is free of religious conflict only because these claims are not taken seriously. Pluralism is made possible by minimizing loyalties, which reduces conflicts.

The 1893 Parliament of the World's Religions, held in Chicago, with representatives of both Eastern and Western religions, already offered evidence of this modern trend, as representatives of Islam, Buddhism, Hinduism, Jainism, and other groups were hosted by the Christian organizers of the event. Western fascination with Asian religions from Buddhism to Zoroastrianism was evident at least from the seventeenth century, reflecting a certain loss of confidence in the old ways of Christianity (Clarke, 1997).

In recent decades, the rise of official inter-religious dialogues among world religions and the ecumenical movement among Christian denominations are striking instances of the weakening of traditions. Such ecumenism reflects growing tolerance and the absence of emphasis on uniqueness and superiority, in a radical departure from millennia of religious conflicts. Of course, not all religious individuals are ready for dialogue, but there is some evidence for everyday acceptance of de facto sharing. In the twenty-first century one encounters multi-faith prayer spaces at international airports and other public places, proving both secularization and persistent supernaturalism.

The secularization of culture and consciousness

Only a few centuries ago, most of what we think of as basic cultural activities, such as reading, writing, art, music, or drama used to take place within a religious context. Literacy itself was tied to religion, but over the past few centuries religion has been separated from learning, cultural production, and the arts. In most cultures, the first written works were scriptures, and most materials published before the nineteenth century had to do with religion. Today only a small proportion of printed matter is religious in nature. Modern fiction, an art form developed together with secularization, has been called "the enemy of superstition, the slayer of religions" (Wood, 1999, p. vii).

The majority of artworks produced throughout history had religious subjects, but today religious art is simply a rarity. An analysis of paintings at the Metropolitan Museum of Art in New York City showed a gradual process of secularization in the depicted materials, with a precipitous drop in religious themes since 1800 (Silverman, 1989). On the other hand, religious objects taken from Christian churches in Europe are on display in the same museum, together with an Egyptian temple built more than 2,000 years ago. They are appreciated for their artistic qualities, but are devoid of any *mana*, which they once had. On display, Christian objects are treated just like the ancient Egyptian temple dedicated to Isis and Osiris, expressing a totally secular attitude. While religious art aimed at reinforcing and celebrating tradition, Enlightenment art became individualistic and self-expressive, and artists have become critics or rebels. Expressing the reverence with which modernity treats art, museums, in which the objects are mostly secular-themed or desacralized, have been referred to as temples (Steffensen-Bruce, 1998). In large cities, the locales (or temples) of high and low culture, such as museums, theatres and stadiums, among other leisure activities, compete successfully for popular attention with religious services (Barro and McCleary, 2003).

The desacralization of culture means that religious symbols, language, and references are abandoned, or used without reference to their original meaning. There is no better way of illustrating the process than language itself. Greenfield (2013) examined the frequencies of specific words in approximately 1,160,000 books published in the United States and 350,000 books published in the United Kingdom between 1800 and 2000. The importance of obedience, social relationships, and religion in everyday life has decreased, as reflected in the declining use of words such as "obedience," "authority," "belong," and "pray." Another survey found that in the 1500s and 1600s words such as "baptized," "hymns," "God," "Christ," and "Pope," were among the most common, together with the expressions "baptized in the name of" or "God forbid it should be." By the 1800s, the above words and phrases were being used less and less often (Petersen *et al.*, 2012). These findings reflect a profound transformation of consciousness. Because the process is historical and relative, language everywhere still contains many religious terms. Religious exclamations may still be heard, but have lost their original power.

Western folklore used to be filled with witches, spirits, and trolls, but over the past couple of centuries it has become naturalized. Supernaturalist motifs have been transformed into real objects and creatures (Simpson, 1981). A similar transformation has taken place in the content of psychotic delusions. Whereas in the mid-nineteenth century religious ideas were common in delusions and hallucinations, a hundred years later they had been replaced by ideas about electrical and electronic forces. Klaf and Hamilton (1961) reported data from Britain, showing that religious content in schizophrenic ideation went down over a century from 65 percent around 1850 to 23 percent around 1950. Religious ideas persist, and appear in a minority of delusions and hallucinations, but for many individuals the content of psychotic ideation is dominated by the electronic media. Thus, a person may claim to be controlled by radio messages, or to be the real topic of reports on television. In more traditional populations, religious ideation in schizophrenia is still common (Ndetei and Vadher, 1985).

Education and knowledge systems

The decline of religion as a social institution has been connected to the rise of the sciences. Merton (1970) reports on the shift of interests among the British elite between 1601 and 1700, as the percentage of those interested in religion as a vocation declined from 7 percent to 1.9 percent, while the percentage of those interested in science and medicine rose from 2.8 percent to 6.2 percent. For the past 500 years, the natural sciences have been replacing religion's traditional cosmology with a secular one, and biological sciences have demolished the view of humanity as unique in the natural world. The process of the decline of religion and the rise of science has been eloquently described by Frazer (1922, p. 546): "For ages the army of spirits, once so near, has been receding farther and farther from us, banished by the magic wand of science from hearth and home." The course of the struggle between science and religion is unidirectional and consistent. As Wallace (1966) states, "In these contests, whenever the battle is fully joined, and both parties commit themselves to the struggle, science *always* wins."

Historically, higher education (and education in general) was dominated by religion. Universities in both medieval Europe and the Islamic world started as religious institutions. They produced the clergy, among other professionals and scholars, and used to be dominated by theology. Over the past two centuries, theology, which was once the "queen of the sciences," has been relegated to oblivion, banished from most research universities. The battle over secularization in the academic world has been fought and won (Hollinger, 1996; Marsden, 1996; Smith, 2003; White, 1896/1993). In the United States, leading institutions such as Harvard, Yale, Princeton, and Columbia, were founded as religious colleges. Today they are totally secular institutions. In the United States, the actions of the secularized academic elite have had a far-reaching effect on society, with religious messages disappearing from public education at all levels. The skirmishes over school prayer and the teaching of evolution over the past fifty years are all part of

218 Secularization and the persistence of religion

the continuing secularization war in the United States. Almost every encounter between the secular elite and the forces of tradition ends up with a victory for the former, with a series of uninterrupted defeats in the courts starting in 1925 in Kansas with the famous Scopes trial (Hofstadter, 1963; Smith, 2003).

The struggle over religious activities in public schools should be recalled to appreciate this process. A major historical struggle for secularizing all public school systems in the United States ended with triumph on June 17, 1963. In *Engel v. Vitale* (1962), the Supreme Court ruled that the New York Board of Regents could not require the daily recitation of prayers in schools. In *Abington School District v. Schempp* (1963), the Supreme Court ruled that any Bible reading in public schools was unconstitutional. Before the 1963 *Schempp* decision, Bible readings and organized prayers were common in public schools, and not only in the "Bible belt." *Engel* and *Schempp* had to do with a New York City suburb and a Philadelphia suburb, respectively. It should be pointed out that a majority of Americans still favor prayer in public schools, despite the judicial rulings which clearly represent an elite view, even though this support has been declining (to 56 percent) as secularization reaches downward (Schwadel, 2013).

Biology is part of the challenge to religious cosmology when it offers a theory of the development of species, including mankind. Geology and astrophysics present another challenge when they account for the creation of the universe. Evolution has become the most potent symbol of science without animism or teleology as the ruling paradigm in biology. The assumptions of the evolution paradigm are a threat to all religions, beyond the account of human descent from other species. It assumes no design, no intentionality, and no guiding hand, but rather randomality and purposelessness, with events only subject to the impersonal, natural laws of physics and chemistry. The resulting humanist worldview was expressed by a leading scientist: "man knows at last that he is alone in the universe's unfeeling immensity, out of which he emerged only by chance. His destiny is nowhere spelled out, nor is his duty" (Monod, 1971, p. 180).

The debate over evolution is indeed about an anthropocentric or an impersonal, non-anthropocentric universe. The idea that human fortune and misfortune are the result of random, impersonal events is totally counter-intuitive, as humans naturally find meaning in imaginary sequences of design, intention, purpose, reward, and punishment. All academic fields, from anthropology to zoology, practice methodological atheism, i.e. any supernaturalist explanations are excluded from discussion. Academics do not assume purpose or design, whether in nature, or in history beyond human intentions. A researcher may privately believe in divine purpose explanations, but trying to include them in any academic publication will lead to ridicule. The subversive idea of the creation of life without any consciousness being involved has been correctly judged as tolling the bell for supernaturalism. Graffin (2004; Graffin and Provine, 2007) reported the responses of 149 prominent evolutionary scientists, members of twenty-eight national academies worldwide, to a questionnaire on evolution and religion. The majority of researchers could see no conflict between religion and evolution, simply because

Secularization and the persistence of religion **219**

they regarded the former as another product of the latter, and so it could be studied and understood with the help of standard evolutionary theories (see Chapter 2).

The human sciences are a threat to religion inasmuch as they study changes in culture over time and space, and show time and again that beliefs and customs, including religious ones, are relative and culturally conditioned, and because they treat religion as a natural phenomenon, and not as a representation of a special reality or a special mode of knowledge. Any scholarly discussion of religion is an affront to the believers. It is subversive, deconstructive, and reductive, a most serious threat (Segal, 1989). The psychological study of religion is clearly predicated on intensive secularization. Ideas about psychological factors and individual differences in religiosity, which are basic to the psychology of religion, are a reflection of this process. This would have been inconceivable only a couple of centuries ago.

Religious reactions to the image of science

The image of science in the private and public imaginations has been tied to visions of power and superiority (Preston and Epley, 2009). Over the past two centuries, there have been numerous examples of religionists feeling a strong need to obtain legitimacy from the power of the new social institution which rose in prestige above revelation. The rising authority of science has led religionists to claim it in the most direct and magical way. Since the nineteenth century, we have seen the founding of hundreds of religious movements, using the term science in their official names and claiming a unity of science and religion. The best known is the "healing" movement of Christian Science, founded in 1879 by Mary Baker Eddy (1821–1910), as the First Church of Christ, Scientist. Eddy's ideas were totally animistic, of course, and the science label reflected her magical thinking about the power of words, and the desire to appear powerful (Bloom, 1992). Christian Science was followed by Divine Science, Religious Science, and Jewish Science. A little-known early version of African-American Islam was founded in Newark, New Jersey in 1913, as the Moorish Science Temple of America (Fauset, 1944). The magical gesture of using the term "science" had little effect on the fortunes of these movements.

Advances in the natural sciences and technologies have led to fantasies about proving the existence of the eternal soul by mechanical means. The modern movement to establish "scientifically" the existence of the soul is a case in point. This started in the heyday of spiritualism, and led to the founding of the Society for Psychical Research (SPR) in London in 1882. The Society, led by such luminaries as Henri Bergson, William James, and Arthur James Balfour, was seeking physical evidence for the existence of the soul through the investigation of "psychics" and "paranormal" events, which always turned out to be hoaxes. So-called psychical research "restored the hope of immortality and alleviated the fear of 'spiritual extinction'" (Hearnshaw, 1964, p. 157). This elite version of spiritualism in turn brought about the development of "parapsychology" in the United States (Mauskopf and McVaugh, 1980; Moore, 1977).

220 Secularization and the persistence of religion

The great inventor Thomas Alva Edison (1847–1931), whose work gave the world the light bulb, recorded music, and movies, was speculating in 1920 how he could build a machine that would prove the existence of spirits: "I have been thinking for some time of a machine or apparatus which could be operated by personalities which have passed onto other existence or sphere … I am inclined to believe that our personality does affect matter" (Lescarboura, 1920, p. 446).

The enormous prestige of modern physics has created a minor industry of authors who attempt to use its arcane theories in defense of religion. For a century, religious apologists have been using the concepts of modern physics such as relativity, the uncertainty principle, and quantum mechanics in hundreds of books and articles. This is designed to impress non-experts, and proves how much (imagined) physics has become a source of knowledge and authority, and how the prestige of (imagined) science has surpassed that of (experienced and lived) religion.

Science, "science," and human confidence

Against the historical background of supernaturalism, science denotes naturalism, materialism, and the rejection of dualism. The term "science" is an abstraction, and the equations of physics or chemistry are remote and inaccessible to most of humanity, but the consequences of progress in the sciences have touched all of us. Technologies derived from scientific advances have led to enormous gains in human health and longevity, in freedom from hard labor, in mobility, communication, and culture. This has led to a sense of empowerment, with technology moving humans closer to controlling nature actively, whether it is through curing diseases or exploiting minerals.

The technology of medicine has done much to decrease, if not eliminate, much deprivation and hardship. "[A]pplied science has made it possible to remove unnecessary suffering from a billion individual human lives – to remove suffering of a kind which, in our own privileged society, we have largely forgotten, suffering so elementary that it is not genteel to mention it. For example, we *know* how to heal many of the sick: to prevent children dying in infancy and mothers in childbirth: to produce enough food to alleviate hunger … All this we *know* how to do" (Snow, 1965, p. 78).

Biomedicine has changed the way humans experience the boundary points of existence, birth, and death, which used to be beyond any human control. It has led first to a revolution in human death. Immunization, clean water, sanitation, and effective medical care have created a reality in which the typical death in modern societies is no longer in childhood from infectious disease, but in old age from degenerative illnesses. The decline in mortality rates in modern times has made death less of a presence than it was in earlier times, and so death may be denied more easily without any help from religion.

Biomedicine has brought about another dramatic development in human self perception and self-determination: so-called "sex change" or sex reassignment medical procedures. The idea of sex change is a fantasy, because chromosomal sex

Secularization and the persistence of religion **221**

can never be changed. What can be changed, with surgery and hormonal treatment, is external appearance. A man may be made to look like a woman through a suppression of male secondary sex characteristics, but he will have to keep using hormones for life. Naturally, religious establishments have been horrified by the phenomenon, regarded as an open rebellion against nature and the gods.

The biomedical revolutions and religion: controlling reproduction

Conception, pregnancy, and birth used to be mysteries no smaller than death. Pregnancy and childbirth were intimately tied to dying, because of the many cases of mother or baby dying at birth or soon after. Like other natural events, conception, pregnancy, and birth were believed to be under the control of the spirit world. Progress in knowledge of the physiological processes involved brought about one of the most radical changes in human history. Throughout history, women have been occupied in their reproductive and nurturant role, being always, first and foremost pregnant or taking care of children. The separation of sexuality from procreation through effective contraception and the reduction in the number of pregnancies experienced by women throughout their lives is one of the most significant revolutions in history and human biology. It has liberated those women with access to biomedicine from these biological constraints and changed their social status and everyday life.

After separating sex from pregnancy, the next achievement of the new reproductive technology has been that of separating sex from birth. Infertility used to be interpreted as divine punishment, but progress in science has led to procreation under human control. In vitro fertilization (IVF) has meant that egg or sperm are taken from parents (or donors) and may later be frozen. This has brought about posthumous parenting, where frozen eggs and sperm may be used years after the death of the bodies that produced them. The fertilized egg, carrying the genetics of dead parents, may be implanted in the womb of a surrogate, who will carry the fetus to term, but will be genetically unrelated to the baby. IVF will even make it possible to create babies with genetic material coming from three or four people.

Opposition to advances in reproductive technology (both contraception and the facilitation of pregnancy) has united various religious establishments, the best known of which is the Roman Catholic Church, which on this issue found a common ground with Islam. This broad religious opposition has been defeated in most cases. The Roman Catholic Church has been adamant in its proscription of any contraceptive measures. Still, self-identified Roman Catholics in huge numbers acted contrary to official teachings as soon as effective contraception became available. In the late 1990s, Spain, along with Italy, two Catholic countries with traditionally large families, had the lowest birthrates in the history of humankind.

The practice of IVF has faced strict opposition from the Catholic Church on the grounds that it breaks the God-given connection between sex and procreation, but it has been allowed in Italy since 2004. In many countries with Catholic majorities, such as Italy, Spain, and the Philippines, church opposition has been defeated only

222 Secularization and the persistence of religion

in the twenty-first century. It should be recalled that in the United States, contraceptives were illegal in many jurisdictions until 1965. These historical changes have been connected to a total transformation of the dominant discourse about sexual practices, with an emphasis on individual rights and personal gratification, autonomy, and individualism (Boonin, 2013). They have also been connected with the transformation of the family.

Because women are the main supporters of religion (Chapter 5), changes in their status are a major factor in the decline of religion: "the transformation in women's lives in modern societies during the twentieth century, generated by widening opportunities in education, the workforce, and public affairs … the home, and modern lifestyles, has contributed to this dramatic decline in religiosity" (Inglehart and Norris, 2003, p. 57).

The New Family

In the twenty-first century, the institution of the family in the Western world is being transformed, together with sexuality. Public discourse about sexuality has been transformed, and the emphasis has shifted from historical prohibitions to ideals of self-expression and pleasure. Cohabitation before marriage is becoming a majority practice, and formal matrimony comes at a later age, often in a civil ceremony. Fewer children are born, sometimes to older mothers helped by medical technology, and motherhood without marriage is socially accepted.

Changes in the Western conception of the family, the ideals of marriage, and the status of women are all undoubtedly related to secularization. The New Family expresses ideals that run counter to religious traditions. The desacralization of marriage and divorce has been a process that took several centuries (Stone, 1991). In earlier times, religion was an active party to marriage, which was regarded as a sacrament. Now this third party has been removed with the coming of "no fault" divorce with only the partners involved (McRae, 1978). The Italians (1974), the Argentinians (1990), and the Irish (1995) have abolished the prohibition on divorce, connected to the historical dominance of the Roman Catholic Church, and adopted the superiority of civil law in marital questions.

Nothing expresses better the coming of the New Family than same-sex marriage, an astounding reversal of history and biology which has become accepted in more and more nations. Same-sex marriage joins the list of earlier upheavals in reproduction and the family, which have taken place over the opposition of historical religions (Evans, 2010). Same-sex marriages have become legal in Argentina, Brazil, Portugal, Spain, and Uruguay, as well as some parts of Mexico, historically dominated by Roman Catholicism.

The combination of same-sex marriage and reproductive technology creates family constellations that would have been inconceivable not long ago. Thus, a couple made up of two lesbian women, Sandy and Sarah, is raising two children, born with the help of donor sperm. Katy was born from Sandy's egg, implanted in Sarah's womb. Jimmy was born from Sarah's egg, implanted in Sandy's womb.

These genetic and social combinations have created a new kinship constellation, which would still look bizarre to most of humanity.

Here is another striking example of a New Family, the result of unlimited individualism and technology: Robert, a sixty-year-old man used his own sperm and donated eggs for an IVF procedure. The fertilized eggs were carried to term by a surrogate mother, and he became the proud father of twins, Mickey and Joey.

To appreciate the significance of recent historical changes, one has only to go back to a novel such as *Jude the Obscure*, by Thomas Hardy, which was published in 1895 and describes the height of Victorian "family values." To readers today, Hardy's world may seem like the Middle Ages, but it simply demonstrates the distance traveled in one century from domination by tradition to expressive individualism.

The decline of endogamy

Homogamy, marrying a mate of the same religion, has been the historical rule in religious communities. One social consequence of secularization is the lowering or elimination of boundaries between religious groups, leading to a rise in intermarriage. A comparison of marriage data for the Netherlands in 1938, 1963, and 1983, showed a consistent decline in religious homogamy (Hendrickx, Lammers and Ultee, 1991), and similar findings have been reported in the United States (Sherkat, 2004).

The increase in intermarriage, or "interfaith marriage," means that traditional identities carry less meaning and lower salience. Rokeach (1960) showed that the likelihood of inter-denominational marriage was directly related to the perception of their similarity. If intermarriage does occur between individuals from denominations which seem quite similar, with secularization we might say that all religions appear more similar.

Matches which were once unlikely are more prevalent today, and the combinations are varied. In some cases one partner claims no religious affiliation while the other is clearly committed. In other cases partners may come from two traditions which have been historically quite remote, or even antagonistic. In some cases a couple may choose civil marriage and a non-religious wedding, while in others members of the clergy representing more than one religion officiate. Such hybrid rituals are practiced in other life cycle celebrations, such as name-giving to babies. High intermarriage rates demonstrate a lessening of bigotry, a rise in individualism, and an increase in social interaction across historical boundaries. They may lead to hybrid individual identities as a result of growing up with two kinds of practices and teachings.

The secularization of death

The secularization of death in the modern world has been another momentous historical change. In traditional societies, physical death is ever present, together

224 Secularization and the persistence of religion

with the human imaginative response of a belief in immortality and attendant rituals. In modern societies, death may be conceived as the true extinction of the self or as a way station on the road to ultimate salvation. Secularization has meant privatizing and marginalizing all religious messages, including those dealing with death.

Secularization has affected what is regarded as one of the last bastions of religion: funerals (Badone, 1989; McManners, 1975; Wojtkowiak and Venbrux, 2009). The creation of large cemeteries in Paris in the eighteenth century was an expression of the Enlightenment spirit (Etlin, 1986), and the de-Christianization of the West (McLeod, 1981). In most traditional cultures the dead were buried not far from their living relatives. In Europe this meant parish churches, but large urban cemeteries meant that burial was becoming more anonymous.

The rhetoric of secularized funerals (Dickinson, 2012; Caswell, 2011) focuses on the personal life and relationships of the deceased, marginalizing religious ideas about death and the afterlife (Caswell, 2011; Garces-Foley and Holcomb, 2006). Composing the texts to be read publicly for funerals (or weddings) is an expression of individualism and confidence, with individuals demonstrating no need for traditional authorities.

Choosing when and how to die has been the latest stage in the emancipation from religious traditions. More and more jurisdictions around the world allow euthanasia under medical supervision. In Switzerland, clinics where individuals are provided with lethal medication have operated legally since 1998. In Belgium and the Netherlands euthanasia or suicide are allowed when a patient decides that life is unbearable, and the request is supported by a physician. In December 2012, two Belgian twins, forty-five years old, who had been born deaf and were losing their eyesight, committed suicide with the full permission and support of the authorities. Euthanasia is an act of human defiance against nature, which leaves behind all beliefs about decisions made by gods or ancestors.

The persistence of religious identities and beliefs

In Western nations, the meaning of membership in a religious congregation has changed dramatically over the past two centuries. Religious identities and denominations tend to survive, but the meaning of being a Roman Catholic or a Methodist changes radically. There has been a growing tendency among those who regard themselves as members of religious denominations to ignore the ideals and prescriptions of their own tradition. The "identity shell" is preserved, tied to minimal ritual participation, and without adherence to any explicit norms. In France in 2005, 76 percent considered themselves Roman Catholics, but only 5 percent attended church regularly. A French survey in 2006 interviewed individuals who identified as Catholics. To the question "Why are you a Catholic?", 55 percent replied that it was a matter of birth in a Catholic family, and only 21 percent said it was a matter of faith. In this group of French Catholics, only 26 percent believed in God (Roy, 2010).

In Italy in 2005, 97 percent considered themselves Catholic, but only 30 percent attended church, and only a few followed church teachings on birth control. Individuals seem to be saying: "We are Catholic, but we use birth control, and we don't go to confession." Terms such as "cultural Christian," "cultural Moslem," or "cultural Hindu" express the reality of secularization, where labels imply family descent, but not any practices. The loyalty to the religious identity label has been explained by Hout and Greeley (1987) by comparing it with the loyalty to national label. The most radical dissent from national goals and policies will rarely lead a Briton or a Spaniard to disown the nationality label.

Not only identity labels, but supernaturalist beliefs and practices persist in many ways. First, the traditional forms of religion have survived all over the world. There are islands of traditionality, untouched by secularization, especially in the Islamic world, which cover large parts of Asia and Africa. Elsewhere, even in the secularized West, forms of supernaturalist commitment are evident together with secularization. Some of those supporting the right to abortions in Ireland may still believe in the Virgin Birth. The lesbian couple mentioned above, Sandy and Sarah, may be another good example of persistence. Despite the fact that their family could be regarded as a triumph of secular forces, which dared to challenge religious orthodoxy on both marriage rules and reproductive technology, Sandy and Sarah may be devout Roman Catholics, or Evangelicals, or followers of various "New Age" practices. In addition to the survival of traditional practices and beliefs, new forms of individualized religiosity have become known under the labels of "New Age" and spirituality.

Gellner (1974) argued that despite the sweeping economic and social changes brought about by modernization,

> serious cognition need not pervade all aspects of daily life. On the contrary, the insulation of various spheres of life ... makes it easier to permit any degree of fantasy in those aspects of life which are distinct from the serious business of knowledge ... It is only in the residual sphere, where nothing very serious is at stake, that the scientific vision has become optional ... The concepts which are part of the serious business of real knowledge constitute one strand, and the many other styles, whose virtues are different—such as to be jolly, entertaining, homely, or comforting—constitute another.
>
> (Gellner, 1974, p. 193)

This makes possible the co-existence of astrology and astro-physics, both flourishing in the same culture.

The persistence of religion: "New Age"

The term "New Age" refers to the emergence of a large-scale, decentralized religious subculture with roots in the nineteenth century, often inspired by sources outside of Western traditions. This broad range of beliefs and practices has become popular and visible since the late twentieth century. Most of these beliefs and practices are not new, but their popularity clearly is. What marks the "New Age" is the wide variety of ideas involved, from a discourse that claims to be tied to theories in modern physics, to miraculous cures through "energies," sounds and colors, to claims about uncovering ancient wisdom. In individuals, what is observed is an openness to any presumed authority, transmitted informally by peers and the mass media. A comprehensive definition of "New Age" refers to "non-traditional medicine, psychics, fortune tellers, horoscopes, Ouija boards, UFOs, ghosts, astrology, and mysterious animals, such as Bigfoot" (Driskell and Lyon, 2011, p. 389). The modern movement reflects what was presented in Chapter 1 under the heading of para-religious beliefs (Beit-Hallahmi, 1992; Champion, 1990; Höllinger and Smith, 2002; Rice, 2003).

Roof (1993) described "New Age" activities among 1599 "baby boomers" who had defected from established religions, and regarded this as an expression of growing religious personalization. A survey in the 1990s among Texans found that the purchase of "New Age" materials was common and evenly distributed across social space. The strongest predictor of such consumption was being in interpersonal networks composed of other devotees (Mears and Ellison, 2000).

"New Age" beliefs and practices have been covered by mass surveys for decades.

> Since 1982, the International Social Survey Programme (ISSP) has added a package of four questions in order to assess non-church religiosity: whether good luck charms sometimes do bring good luck, whether some fortune tellers really can foresee the future, whether some faith healers do have God-given healing powers, and whether a person's horoscope can affect the course of his or her future.
>
> (Pollack and Pickel, 2007, p. 610)

Other items frequently used deal with "the effectiveness of Zen meditation and Yoga, reincarnation, magic, spiritualism, occultism, astrology, faith-healers or spiritual healers" (Pollack and Pickel, 2007, p. 611).

Some religious individuals are drawn to "New Age" beliefs. This has been found to be true across cultures (Canetti-Nisim and Beit-Hallahmi, 2007; Mencken, Bader and Kim, 2009). In Russia, those identifying as members of the Russian Orthodox Church are likely to follow "New Age" beliefs and practices (Titarenko, 2008). Belyaev (2011) described heterodox beliefs as those that do not originate either in secular education or in established religion. Surveying 1600 individuals, a representative sample of the Russian population, he found that 52 percent believed in "healers" who could cure the incurable, 49 percent believed in the connection between zodiac signs and personality, and 44 percent believed in "telepathy."

The overlap between "New Age" and old supernaturalism is obvious. If you believe in reincarnation or "karma," it is clear that you assume the existence of a spirit world. Belief in reincarnation is common, possibly universal, and has been mentioned in religious writings for millennia. Belief in karma also assumes the existence of a power controlling the destiny of humans. Communicating with the dead, traditionally called spiritualism and today known as channeling, which is mentioned as representing "New Age" beliefs, is implied or expected in many traditions, as a corollary of the belief in souls and the afterlife. Another modern progeny of spiritualism is known as "past-life therapy" (Weiss, 1988).

There is much evidence of the prevalence of "New Age" beliefs worldwide. Surveys in Russia in the 1990s showed that while only 40 percent said they believe in God, and 12 percent believed in heaven and hell, 66 percent believed in "telepathy," 56 percent believed in astrology, 67 percent believed in "the evil eye and the stealing of bio-energy," and 37 percent believed in "the abominable snowman" (Kääriäinen, 1999; Vorontsova and Filatov, 1994). Findings presented by Haraldsson and Houtkooper (1996) show a similar situation in various industrialized countries. Thus, in Italy 41 percent believed in "telepathy," in Iceland 41 percent, and in the United States 54 percent.

Titarenko (2008, p. 244) states that "Europe in general experiences religious eclecticism ... the majority of believers combine some traditional (Christian) beliefs with some non-traditional and non-Christian beliefs. This is a tendency to individualize beliefs on the basis of personal preferences." According to Titarenko, this tendency unites all developed nations, and is part of the individualizing process in Europe and North America (Ester, Halman and de Moor, 1994). This individualistic bent has little to do with dissenting from majority norms, and is quite conformist (Höllinger, 2004).

Most "New Age" consumers are dabblers, and most "New Age" activities are commercial ventures, initiated by small entrepreneurs, fortune-tellers of all kinds, mediums, and "healers." "The New Age is eclectic to an unprecedented degree and ... is ... dominated by the principle that the sovereign consumer will decide what to believe" (Bruce, 2002, p. 105). Most modern religious awakenings are private, informal, and often don't involve stable commitments, but they are experienced by masses of individuals. Here is a description of "New Age" activities, correctly put in the context of consumption:

> They consume products for gathering and enhancing sensations. They can visit a "New Age" healing centre for a few days, participate in a "vision quest" and be initiated in shamanism, buy crystals and indigenous paraphernalia, and learn astrology ... Many conventional book and music shops often have a stall specifically for "New Age" books and recordings.
>
> (Possamai, 2003, p. 31)

Astrology, considered part of the "New Age," flourishes in every modern society, because it is highly accessible and uses natural language (cf. Adorno, 1974, 1978). Here is one interpretation of its power: "The real absurdity is reproduced in the astrological hocus-pocus, which adduces the impenetrable connections of alienated elements—nothing more alien than the stars—as knowledge about the subject"

(Adorno, 1978, p. 241). In 1975 and again in 1986, the American Humanist Association, a leading secular organization, published statements against astrology signed by prominent academic researchers and intellectuals (www.americanhumanist. org/about/astrology.html). This has hardly been noticed. Astrology today involves little investment of resources and is consumed mostly in private. It is not tied to identity, and some of its Western proponents will use non-animistic explanations in its defense. Similarly, some believers in "extrasensory perception" will offer naturalist theories in its support, despite its historical origins in nineteenth-century spiritualism. This reflects another advance for modernity and secularization, and a step back for animism. What started with belief in the human soul in the case of "extrasensory perception," and with the idea of consciousness in the planets in the case of astrology, must now rely on (unconvincing) naturalist arguments.

The "New Age" phenomenon reflects both secularization and the persistence of supernaturalism, because it combines supernaturalist thinking with privatization and low investment, in most cases, but through this privatization, supernaturalism survives. It does not take the place of old religion in terms of the investment of resources, and does not neutralize non-religiosity (Houtman and Mascini, 2002), because religious individualization is a component of the predominant secularization process (Pollack and Pickel, 2007).

Studies of "New Age" consumers in terms of personality traits have reported that they differ from traditional religious and non-religious people by their high level of individualism (Houtman and Mascini, 2002), insecure parental attachment (Granqvist and Hagekull, 2001; Granqvist et al., 2007), and schizotypal personality traits (Farias, Claridge and Lalljee, 2005).

The persistence of religion: spirituality

Until the twentieth century, the terms "religious" and "spiritual" were treated as synonymous, but over the past fifty years, the idea of spirituality as separate from religion has become eminently fashionable, first in the mass media, and then in academic publications. Hill et al. (2000) report that "[d]uring the 1960s and 1970s … spirituality began to acquire more distinct meanings and more favorable connotations separate from religion" (p. 58).

In some research projects, attempts have been made to "widen the definition of religion to include questions about the meaning of life, the purpose of mankind's existence, the future of the planet and man's responsibilities to his fellow man and to the earth itself " (Davie, 1990, p. 462). This widening of the operational definition for religion was actually known long before the 1960s, and was even then regarded as apologetic. Sigmund Freud stated that it was a mistake to describe

> as 'deeply religious' anyone who admits to a sense of man's insignificance or impotence in the face of the universe. The man who goes no further, but humbly acquiesces in the small part which human beings play in the

great world – such a man is, on the contrary, irreligious in the truest sense of the word.

(Freud, 1927, p. 28)

Spirituality is being promoted in various "self-help" books, which promise a yield of identifiable virtues: "mindfulness or awareness, acceptance and equanimity, gratitude and generosity, compassion, and loving connection to other people, nature, and God" (Gottlieb, 2013, p. 23). The rhetoric of "spirituality" has been described as follows: "Spirituality also came to mean the 'superior side' of religion, as the individual experience of the divine uncontaminated by its social and organized forms, its traditions and institutions (which represented the 'inferior side' of religion)" (Popp-Baier, 2010, p. 42). Another observer has stated:

Religion is primarily characterized by its traditional forms, rituals, institutions and orthodox teachings, uninspired rigidity, lack of feeling, obsolescence, reactionary attitude, moralizing, etc. In contrast, spirituality has come to mean something new, interesting, spontaneous, informal, creative, and universal.

(Říčan, 2004, p. 136)

Some consider "ecstasies during sexual union or artistic activities" as spirituality (Říčan, 2004, p. 144).

One sociologist described it as "everything from an interest in angels, crystals, psychic readings, and other forms of so-called 'New Age' spirituality, to the more charismatic born-again Evangelical movements within Christianity" (Bradley, 2009, p. 205). Walter (2012, p. 132), following Heelas (2002), offers the following description: "Spirituality entails the individual using whatever ideas, beliefs and practices feel right to the individual, and the authority of religious institutions, especially those of the world religions, is distrusted." Hill *et al.* (2000), Roof (1993), and Zinnbauer *et al.* (1997) show that the most important characteristic of the new spirituality is extreme individualism, and this hallmark was noted as it spread globally. Howell (2005, p. 477) described "the popularization of the notion of non-denominational, eclectic "spirituality" that can be appropriated from diverse sources to enhance one's declared religion or adapted as a primary commitment over which the practitioner asserts autonomous control." What is significant is that this description refers to a small minority in Indonesia, the most populous Moslem nation. This personalization of beliefs reflects secularization, whether in Indonesia, where it is minimal, France, or Britain (Wood, 2009).

In academic publications, spirituality has been defined as "people's search for meaning, in relation to the big existential question," which can be "expressed by atheists and agnostics, by people deeply engaged in ecology and other idealistic endeavors, and by people inspired by religious impulses not easily understood by classic religious concepts (e.g. sacredness)" (Stiffos-Hanssen, 1999, p. 28). The eminent psychologist Albert Bandura stated:

> Most people acknowledge a spiritual aspect to their lives, in the sense of seeking meaning and social connectedness to something greater than oneself without being tied to a formal religion or deity. In such instances, they embrace spirituality but not religiosity.
>
> (Bandura, 2003, p. 170)

Schwartz (1992) tested the concept of spirituality with 8,000 respondents in thirteen cultures, and concluded that it was not in any way universal, but limited to some cultures. In the United States, "spirituality" has become part of the discourse about the proper training for medical professionals. The Association of American Medical Colleges formed a task force on "Spirituality, Cultural Issues, and End of Life Care" whose conclusions were included in the 1999 Medical Schools Objectives Project (MSOP) Report III (Berlinger, 2004, pp. 683–684). The report stated that "spirituality" is "found in all cultures and societies" and "is expressed in an individual's search for ultimate meaning through participation in religion and/or belief in God, family, naturalism, rationalism, humanism, and the arts" (AAMC, 1999, p. 25).

In 2009, a Consensus Conference on "spiritual care as a dimension of palliative care" stated that spirituality can be defined as "the aspect of humanity that refers to the way individuals seek and express meaning and purpose, and the way they experience their connectedness to the moment, to self, to others, to nature and to the significant or sacred" (Puchalski *et al.*, 2009, p. 887). In some studies, there has been an effort to use the most inclusive definitions and measures: "Traditionally, spirituality was used to describe the deeply religious person, but it has now expanded to include the superficially religious person, the religious seeker, the seeker of well-being and happiness, and the completely secular person" (Koenig, 2008b, p. 349).

What should be of interest is not only these ways of offering the broadest possible definition, but the lack of distinction between supernaturalism and spirituality. Hill *et al.* (2000) emphasized the spirituality–religion connection, stating: "The criteria discussed above suggest that spirituality is a central and essential function of religiosity" (p. 70) and "the significant sociological and psychological overlap among religion and spirituality" (p. 71). This umbilical cord will not be severed because in the majority of cases individuals describe themselves as both religious and spiritual, and atheists are unlikely to be found among them. Houtman and Aupers (2007) surveyed "post-Christian spirituality" in fourteen Western countries between 1981 and 2000, and found that followers of both "New Age" and spirituality hold traditional supernaturalist beliefs in God and the afterlife. Discussions of spirituality usually go back to the "sacred," "transcendent" or other synonyms (or euphemisms) for religion. Spirituality and "New Age" are labels for privatized, low-orthodoxy supernaturalism (Marler and Hadaway, 2002).

In a nationally representative sample of 1422 adults in the United States in 1998, respondents were asked to rate themselves on spirituality and religiosity. The options were spiritual but not religious, religious but not spiritual, both spiritual and religious, and neither spiritual nor religious. Self-perceptions of spirituality were positively correlated with being female, higher education, and having no religion. The spiritual and religious group was more likely to be involved in public and private religious activities. They were also more intolerant than either of the non-religious groups and similar on intolerance to the religious-only group (Shahabi *et al.*, 2002). Most spirituality scales include items that reflect positive thinking and kindness, such as "I accept others even when they do things I think are wrong," "I feel that life is a positive experience," or "It is easy for me to admit that I am wrong" (Koenig, 2008b, p. 352). Such scales have been used with various samples, and the most curious findings showed spirituality to be positively correlated with sexual satisfaction in two groups of women: one included lesbian and bisexual women (Smith and Horne, 2008) and the other included actresses in pornographic films who were matched controls (Griffith *et al.*, 2012).

The term "spiritual but not religious," which means less involvement in public activities together with loyalty to supernaturalist beliefs, has gained popularity. In terms of beliefs and practices, the "spiritual but not religious" group described by Zinnbauer *et al.* (1997) is very similar to the "New Age" seekers described by Roof (1993).

Jang and Franzen (2013) looked at a sample of 14,322 young adults, with an average age of 21.8. In terms of self-identification, they were: spiritual but not religious, 11.5 percent; religious but not spiritual, 6.8 percent; both spiritual and religious, 37.9 percent; and neither spiritual nor religious, 43.8 percent. "Spiritual but not religious" were more likely to commit property crimes than those who identify themselves as either "religious and spiritual" or "religious but not spiritual." Neither spiritual nor religious were less likely to commit property crimes than the "spiritual but not religious" individuals, but no difference was found between the two groups when it came to violent crimes. The conclusion was that "spiritual but not religious" tend to have lower self-control than those who are religious.

The transition from "New Age" rhetoric to spirituality discourse is in evidence in the writings of researchers who in the 1990s reported on a "New Age" revolution and ten years later on a spiritual one (Heelas, 1996, 2002; Heelas and Woodhead, 2005). The radical change is indeed in the extent of individualization, as both "New Age" and spirituality offer personalized supernaturalism (Streib and Hood, 2011). This is an aspect of secularization, where "religion becomes privatized, which means that every individual … might create his own cocktail of Christian devotion, Buddhism, and belief in astrology" (Tschannen, 1991, p. 401). It has been called a "bricolage of personal beliefs" (Pollack and Pickel, 2007, p. 605), "pastiche" (Roof, 1993, 2000), "a la carte," "idiosyncratic," "eclectic" (Singleton, 2012), or "the religion of your choice" (Wilson, 1976, p. 96).

Explaining change and stability

The theoretical explanations for the origins of religion presented above (Chapter 2) predict the persistence of religion, because they assume invariant human

232 Secularization and the persistence of religion

capacities and psychological mechanisms, which propel humans towards religion and religiosity. If indeed there is a neurophysiological basis for all religious behaviors, as we assume, then we should not expect any decline in their prevalence.

As suggested in Chapter 2, humans will always think animistically, teleologically, and anthropomorphistically, despite the institutional decline of religion. Stark and Bainbridge (1985) suggest that secularization is merely a change in the organizational and ideological forms of belief in supernatural compensators, which remain constant, because of a human need for illusions and delusions. But at the same time, religious ideas may become marginal. It means that in addition to the psychological mechanisms pulling humans forcefully towards religion, other, opposing, forces are at work. When it comes to high involvement religiosity, the situation is clear. As reported above, fewer people are ready to devote their lives to religion in the ranks of the clergy. Those who still believe in the tenets of supernaturalism but do not participate in public worship obviously invest less (time, money, and mental energy) than those who believe and worship.

While the trend towards secularization is driven by economic and existential security, levels of religiosity may remain stable in the world overall because of low birth rates in secularized societies (Norris and Inglehart, 2004). Decline in religious affiliation leads to low birth rates in both Europe and in East Asia (Kaufmann, Goujon and Skirbekk, 2012). Immigration of more religious populations to secularized nations has also been contributing to overall stability. The tendency of women, who are a majority in most populations, to invest more in supernaturalism under any conditions, is another causal factor.

CONCLUDING REMARKS
The new psychology of religion

This book has described some of the advances made in understanding both religious beliefs and religious believers. It has combined theoretical innovations appearing since the 1980s, and known as the cognitive-evolutionary approach, with established approaches to studying the social and behavioral correlates of religiosity, and the classics in the psychological study of religion such as James and Freud. It has examined first the basic psychological processes leading to religious thinking, the background for individual variations in religiosity resulting from identity, personality, and biology, and then looked at religion in historical and cultural contexts. It did not attempt a complete integration of research directions, which is impossible, but has focused on non-trivial and non-obvious findings, together with psychological explanations that deserve to be broadly shared and discussed.

Still, they may not satisfy many of those looking for answers about religion. The most common questions about religion can rarely be answered. Often we are asked about how particular religions got started, how particular ideas first appeared, or how rituals and identity markers first developed. These questions are intriguing and will always keep people curious, but discovering the reasons why particular miracle stories were created or why certain groups avoid some foods requires the kind of historical reconstruction that is beyond our reach. We may have some general hunches about food taboos (Simoons, 1994) or genital mutilation (Bettelheim, 1954), but no answers about specific cases. All we can safely know is that particular myths, taboos, or rituals became identity markers, but in most cases the actual process of their formation will remain unknown.

How did the phenomenon of religion (i.e. thinking about supernatural agents, their minds, and their actions) first get started? Romantic fantasies about ancient founders who had mystical visions, ate psychedelic mushrooms, and formulated myths which started particular traditions are often encountered. All we can do is use the help of archaeological finds going back more than 100,000 years that

234 Concluding remarks

demonstrate the practice of significant investment in burials. We can imagine the first funeral, a truly dramatic event, one of the most important in the history of *homo sapiens*, described by Sigmund Freud (1913, 1915) and Bronislaw Malinowski (1925) as the starting point of religion. Since that modest, but dramatic, beginning, started a tradition of thinking about death and afterlife. The proliferation of thousands of local and global religions, sharing a common denominator, which we are all aware of, came much later.

Religion is studied by talking to believers, not reading scriptures, and the psychology of religion is the reality of believers and their beliefs. What Buddhists or Moslems or Jews believe is what they tell us. We have some ideas about the rules of the religious imagination, which creates souls, gods, angels, and devils. The brain mechanisms that create such ideas were there when our ancestors first buried their dead, and they are still with us today. The same basic cognitive mechanisms have led to all religious belief systems. These mechanisms are universal, and the process that develops religious ideas through them is totally normal. This is an anti-romantic turn of mind, which still emphasizes the often dramatic activity of the human imagination.

A non-trivial fact that is often ignored is the social learning of religion. Individuals believe in Krishna, Jesus, or Jehovah only because their parents taught them these specific beliefs. Religious identity has nothing to do with choice or deliberation and everything to do with the accidents of birth and history. Another important fact about religion, which in this book has received the attention it deserves, is that women, rather than men, are those who are responsible for the persistence and survival of religious traditions. The study of religious believers is the study of women. This is a secret to most of the world, and our responsibility is to make it known.

If religion is natural and universal, as proposed above, how has secularization taken place? Secularization can be viewed as part of the variations in religiosity across time and space, and the many ways religion may be lived, but it is much more than that. For many individuals, secularization has meant the possibility of radical privatization. Religious individualism and individualization became possible only with the weakening of historical authority, as every individual can determine how she deals (or doesn't deal) with the spirit world. The ideals of expressive individualism and self-actualization reflect this new reality. Religious traditions and authorities do not disappear, but become weak or marginal in some societies. This marginalization is tied to the decline of collectivism and group loyalties, such as nationalism. Its most direct manifestation is public declarations of atheism, the total rejection of supernaturalism.

Most research on religiosity and its correlates has been carried out in the United States. This raises not only the issue of generalizing from findings that may reflect a particular cultural constellation and economic conditions, but whether we are all prisoners of a unique mindset produced by the history of one country, long known for its unique pattern of religiosity (de Tocqueville, 1835/1994). Because the field was started in the United States, we owe the pioneers a great deal (Beit-Hallahmi,

1974). Over the past few decades, the field has become significantly internationalized. The basic strategy to assess the effects of religiosity, followed by countless studies, has been to correlate religiosity, as a continuous variable, with other continuous psychological, sociological, and biological variables. Higher religiosity is compared with lower religiosity in terms of personality variables, health, or well-being. Galen and Kloet (2011) challenged this strategy and argued that only a comparison of believers with atheists will make possible real tests of the effects of religiosity. If most studies are done in the United States, it is difficult to recruit atheists, a small minority there: "Belief in God is so common in the United States ... that there is virtually no one who can be effectively contrasted to religious believers" (Froese and Bader, 2008, p. 693). This is another reason to carry out more studies in more countries.

The fact that findings and ideas are produced in the United States means not only that it reflects a particular cultural outlook, but not less significantly, that it is likely to reflect a religionist bias more than research done in other countries. Even though academic psychologists in the United States are highly secular, those interested in the study of religion have been, for many years, likely to be religious themselves (Beit-Hallahmi, 1989).

The field may still be negatively affected by religious influences. In its early days in the United States, as Beit-Hallahmi (1974) pointed out, most psychologists involved showed "deference and reverence" to religion in their writings (p. 86). Pinker (1997, p. 555) stated that "the psychology of religion has been muddied by scholars' attempts to exalt it while understanding it." A similar trend has been noted in the sociology of religion (Kohn, 1989). Wulff (2003, 2007) described the psychology of religion in the United States as hampered by the agenda of religious psychologists, committed to promoting a religious tradition. Assertions about the vital role of religion in the survival of the social order and in providing better lives for individuals are part of a wider discourse of pragmatic apologetics promising believers earthly rewards. Most of this research has been guided by the desire to prove that religion is a force for the good in individuals and societies, and most of those who try to convince us of the benefits of religion do not mention any specific tradition but imply that any supernaturalist beliefs will help (Cadge, 2009; Smilde and May, 2010). This is a reflection of secularization. Religions have always promised worldly benefits, and not just otherworldly salvation, but such promises were not backed by statistics and always specified only one tradition which produced the desired and miraculous effects.

It is possible to find more and more first-rate psychological research which is not burdened by religious apologetics. This turn of events was not always regarded as inevitable. Orlo Strunk Jr. (1925–2013) was one of the leaders in the pastoral psychology movement, which has attempted to combine secular psychotherapy and religion, and contribute to the functioning of religious congregations. He was also a great scholar who knew well the psychology of religion. Writing in 1957, Strunk tried to predict the future of the psychology of religion, and suggested that the most likely development was that the field "might simply be engulfed by

236 Concluding remarks

pastoral psychology or become a relatively insignificant appendage of that applied field" (Strunk, 1957, p. 290). Strunk was writing with real concern. That was not a development he wished for, quite the opposite. His vision for the field was that of becoming a "branch of general psychology which attempts to understand, control, and predict human behavior ... which is perceived as being religious by the individual" (1957, p. 291). Fortunately, the prediction was wrong and the vision was much closer to actual developments over the past few decades. Nevertheless, there are still those who refer to an applied psychology of religion, a telltale signal of a religionist agenda.

Since the 1990s, the field has been undergoing a reframing and a rebirth. The book has tried to keep pace with these developments, which represent, if not a utopian golden age, an exciting time. Real progress is being made when questions about religion are anchored in general psychological theories. This basic research is carried out by psychologists who have not been identified with the psychology of religion as a research specialty, and study religious behavior in the context of broad psychological theories. They may also feel fascinated and challenged by the phenomenon of religion, and that is even better. In recent years, developmental psychologists, cognitive psychologists, social psychologists, and social neuroscience researchers have been involved in studying religion and changing the vocabulary used in discussing religion. There will always be a psychology of religion, like the psychology of the arts. The reason is that academic psychology pursues research on basic processes, and religion does not involve unique processes, but a unique content. Nevertheless, the field will enjoy more attention than the psychology of the arts because of the historical centrality of religion in culture.

Basic research relevant to psychological questions is also produced by sociologists, economists, anthropologists, and researchers in other disciplines, and progress is tied to developments in the social sciences and the life sciences. The new psychology of religion, emerging in the twenty-first century, is no longer segregated, but multidisciplinary and accessible. The future will usher in more research from diversified settings, where all hypotheses and hunches still need to be tested and re-tested.

REFERENCES

Aarnio, K., & Lindeman, M. (2005). Paranormal beliefs, education, and thinking styles. *Personality and Individual Differences, 39*, 1227–1236.

Aarts, O., Grotenhuis, H. F., Need, A., & de Graaf, N. D. (2010). Does duration of deregulated religious markets affect church attendance? Evidence from 26 religious markets in Europe and North America between 1981 and 2006. *Journal for the Scientific Study of Religion, 49*, 657–672.

Abdel-Khalek, A. M. (2006). Happiness, health and religiosity: Significant relations. *Mental Health, Religion and Culture, 9*, 85–97.

Abdel-Khalek, A. M. (2010). Religiosity, subjective well-being, and neuroticism. *Mental Health, Religion & Culture, 13*, 67–79.

Abdel-Khalek, A. M., & Eid, G. K. (2011). Religiosity and its association with subjective well-being and depression among Kuwaiti and Palestinian Muslim children and adolescents. *Mental Health, Religion & Culture, 14*, 117–127.

Abdel-Khalek, A. M., & Naceur, F. (2007). Religiosity and its association with positive and negative emotions among college students from Algeria. *Mental Health, Religion & Culture, 10*, 159–170.

Aboud, F. E. (2003). The formation of in-group favoritism and out-group prejudice in young children: Are they distinct attitudes? *Developmental Psychology, 39*, 48–60.

Abrams, D. M., Haley, A. H., & Wiener, R. J. (2011). A mathematical model of social group competition with application to the growth of religious non-affiliation. *Physical Review Letters 107*(8), 088701.

Achterberg, P., Houtman, D., Aupers, S., Koster, W. D., Mascini, P. & Waal, J.V.D. (2009). A Christian cancellation of the secularist truce? Waning Christian religiosity and waxing religious deprivatization in the West. *Journal for the Scientific Study of Religion, 48*, 687–701.

Adams, H. (1905/1931). *The Education of Henry Adams*. New York: Random House.

Adams, J., Easthope, G., & Sibbritt, D. (2003). Exploring the relationship between women's health and the use of complementary and alternative medicine. *Complementary Therapies in Medicine, 11*, 156–158.

238 References

Adorno, T. W. (1974). "The Stars Down to Earth": The Los Angeles Times astrology column. *Telos, 19,* 13–90.

Adorno, T. W. (1978). *Minima Moralia: Reflections from Damaged Life.* London: Verso.

Adorno, T. W., Frenkel-Brunswik, E., Levinson, D. J., & Sanford, R. N. (1950). *The Authoritarian Personality.* New York: Harper & Row.

Ahern, E. M. (1973). *The Cult of the Dead in a Chinese Village.* Stanford: Stanford University Press.

Ahmed, A. M. (2009). Are religious people more prosocial? A quasi-experimental study with Madrasah pupils in a rural community in India. *Journal for the Scientific Study of Religion, 48,* 368–374.

Ahmed, A. M., & Salas, O. (2009). Is the hand of God involved in human cooperation? *International Journal of Social Economics, 36,* 70–80.

Ahmed, A. M., & Salas, O. (2013). Religious context and prosociality: An experimental study from Valparaíso, Chile. *Journal for the Scientific Study of Religion, 52,* 627–637.

Albrecht, S., Chadwick, B., & Alcorn, D. (1977). Religiosity and deviance: Application of an attitude-behavior contingent consistency model. *Journal for the Scientific Study of Religion, 16,* 263–274.

Alcantara, C., & Gone, J. P. (2007). Reviewing suicide in Native American communities: Situating risk and protective factors within a transactional-ecological framework. *Death Studies, 31,* 457–477.

Alcorta, C. S., & Sosis, R. (2005). Ritual, emotion, and sacred symbols: The evolution of religion as an adaptive complex. *Human Nature, 16,* 323–359.

Alexander, R. D. (1987). *The Biology of Moral Systems.* New York: Aldine De Gruier.

Allison, J. (1969). Religious conversion: Regression and progression in an adolescent experience. *Journal for the Scientific Study of Religion, 8,* 23–38.

Allotey, P., & Reidpath, D. (2001). Establishing the causes of childhood mortality in Ghana: the 'spirit child'. *Social Science and Medicine, 52,* 1007–1012.

Allport, G. W. (1958). *The Nature of Prejudice.* New York: Anchor Books.

Ament, W. S. (1927). Religion, education, and distinction. *School and Society, 26,* 399–406.

Anderson, B. (1991). *Imagined Communities: Reflections on the Origin and Spread of Nationalism.* London: Verso.

Anderson, J. (1993). Out of the kitchen, out of the temple: Religion, atheism and women in the Soviet Union. In S. P. Ramet (Ed.), *Religious Policy in the Soviet Union* (pp. 206–228). Cambridge: Cambridge University Press.

Anderson, L. R., & Mellor, J. M. (2009). Religion and cooperation in a public goods experiment. *Economics Letters, 105,* 58–60.

Anderson, L. R., Mellor, J., & Milyo, J. (2010). Did the Devil make them do it? The effects of religion in public goods and trust games. *Kyklos, 63,* 163–175.

Andrade, C., & Radhakrishnan, R. (2009). Prayer and healing: A medical and scientific perspective on randomized controlled trials. *Indian Journal of Psychiatry, 51,* 247–253.

Andresen, J. (Ed.) (2000). *Religion in Mind: Cognitive Perspectives on Religious Belief, Ritual and Experience.* Cambridge: Cambridge University Press.

Annan, N. (1978). "Our age": Reflections on three generations in England. *Deadalus, 107,* 81–109.

Ano, G. G., & Vasconcelles, E. B. (2005). Religious coping and psychological adjustment to stress: A meta-analysis. *Journal of Clinical Psychology, 61,* 1–20.

Antai, D. (2009). Faith and child survival: the role of religion in childhood immunization in Nigeria. *Journal of Biosocial Science, 41,* 57–76.

Antonovsky, A. (1979). *Health, Stress, and Coping.* San Francisco: Jossey-Bass.

References **239**

Arendt, H. (1979). *Love and Saint Augustine*. Chicago: University of Chicago Press.

Argyle, M. (1958). *Religious Behaviour*. London: Routledge & Kegan Paul.

Argyle, M., & Beit-Hallahmi, B. (1975). *The Social Psychology of Religion*. London: Routledge & Kegan Paul.

Arzy, S., Seeck, M., Ortigue, S., Spinelli, L., & Blanke, O. (2006). Induction of an illusory shadow person. *Nature, 443*, 287.

Ashforth, A. (1998). Reflections on spiritual insecurity in a modern African city (Soweto). *African Studies Review, 41*, 39–67.

Ashforth, A. (2001). An epidemic of witchcraft? The implications of AIDS for the post-apartheid state. In H. Moore & T. Sanders (Eds.), *Magical Interpretations, Material Realities* (pp. 184–225). London: Routledge.

Asp, E., Ramchandran, K., & Tranel, D. (2012). Authoritarianism, religious fundamentalism, and the human prefrontal cortex. *Neuropsychology, 26*, 414–421.

Asser, S. M., & Swan, R. (1998). Child fatalities from religion-motivated medical neglect. *Pediatrics, 101*, 625–629.

Assimeng, M. (1986). *Saints and Social Structures*. Tema: Ghana Publishing Corporation.

Assimeng, M. (1989). *Religion and Social Change in West Africa*. Accra, Ghana: Ghana Universities Press.

The Associated Press (2014). Snake-handling pastor dies after bite. *The New York Times*, February 16, p. A10.

Association of American Medical Colleges (1999, October). *Medical schools objectives project report III: Contemporary issues in medicine: Communication in medicine*. Washington, DC: Association of American Medical Colleges.

Astuti, R., & Harris, P. L. (2008). Understanding mortality and the life of the ancestors in Madagascar. *Cognitive Science, 32*, 713–740.

Atkinson, Q. D., & Bourrat, P. (2011). Beliefs about God, the afterlife and morality support the role of supernatural policing in human cooperation. *Evolution and Human Behavior, 32*, 41–49.

Atran, S. (2002). *In Gods We Trust: The Evolutionary Landscape of Religion*. New York: Oxford University Press.

Atran, S., & Ginges, J. (2012). Religious and sacred imperatives in human conflict. *Science, 336*, 855–857.

Atran, S., & Henrich, J. (2010). The evolution of religion: How cognitive by-products, adaptive learning heuristics, ritual displays, and group competition generate deep commitments to prosocial religions. *Biological Theory, 5*, 18–30.

Aune, K., Sharma, S., & Vincett, G. (Eds.). (2009). *Women and Religion in the West: Challenging Secularization*. Aldershot, UK: Ashgate.

Ausubel, D. P. (1977). *Theories and Problems of Adolescent Development*. New York: Grune & Stratton.

Auyeung, B., Baron-Cohen, S., Ashwin, E., Knickmeyer, R., Taylor, K., Hackett, G., & Hines, M. (2009). Fetal testosterone predicts sexually differentiated childhood behavior in girls and in boys. *Psychological Science, 20*, 144–148.

Axelrod, R., & Hamilton, W. D. (1981). The evolution of cooperation. *Science, 211*, 1390–1396.

Aydin, N., Fischer, P., & Frey, D. (2010). Turning to God in the face of ostracism: Effects of social exclusion on religiousness. *Personality and Social Psychology Bulletin, 36*, 742–753.

Azari, N. P., Nickel, J., Wunderlich, G., Niedeggen, M., Hefter, H., Tellmann, L., Herzog, H., Stoerig, P., Birnbacher, D., & Seitz, R. J. (2001). Neural correlates of religious experience. *European Journal of Neuroscience, 13*, 1649–1652.

240 References

Back, C. W., & Bourque, L. B. (1970). Can feelings be enumerated? *Behavioral Science, 15*, 487–496.

Bader, C. (2003). Supernatural support groups: Who are the UFO abductees and ritual abuse survivors? *Journal for the Scientific Study of Religion, 42*, 669–678.

Bader, C., Mencken, F. C., & Parker, J. (2006). Where have all the communes gone? Factors influencing the success and failure of religious and non-religious communes. *Journal for the Scientific Study of Religion, 45*, 73–85.

Bader, C. D., Desmond, S. A., Mencken, F. C., & Johnson, B. R. (2010). Divine justice: The relationship between images of God and attitudes toward criminal punishment. *Criminal Justice Review, 35*, 90–106.

Bader, C. D., Baker, J. O., & Molle, A. (2012). Countervailing forces: Religiosity and paranormal belief in Italy. *Journal for the Scientific Study of Religion, 51*, 705–720.

Badone, E. (1989). *The Appointed Hour: Death, Worldview and Social Change in Britanny.* Berkeley: University of California Press.

Baethge, C. (2002). Grief hallucinations: True or pseudo? Serious or not? An inquiry into psychopathological and clinical features of a common phenomenon. *Psychopathology, 35*, 296–302.

Baetz, M., Griffin, R., Bowen, R., & Marcoux, G. (2004). Spirituality and psychiatry in Canada: Psychiatric practice compared with patient expectations. *Canadian Journal of Psychiatry, 49*, 265–271.

Baier, C. J., & Wright, B. R. (2001). If you love me, keep my commandments: A meta-analysis of the effect of religion on crime. *Journal of Research in Crime and Delinquency, 38*, 3–21.

Bailey, R., & Doriot, P. (1985). Perceptions of professionals who express religious beliefs. *Social Behavior and Personality, 13*, 167–170.

Bailey, R., & Young, M. (1986). The value and vulnerability of perceived religious involvement. *Journal of Social Psychology, 126*, 693–694.

Bainbridge, W. S. (1989). The religious ecology of deviance. *American Sociological Review, 54*, 288–295.

Baker, J. O. (2008a). Who believes in religious evil? An investigation of sociological patterns of belief in Satan, Hell, and demons. *Review of Religious Research, 50*, 206–220.

Baker, J. O. (2008b). An investigation of the sociological patterns of prayer frequency and content. *Sociology of Religion, 69*, 169–185.

Baker, J. O. (2009). The variety of religious experiences. *Review of Religious Research, 51*, 39–54.

Baker, J. O., & Smith, B. (2009). None too simple: Examining issues of religious nonbelief and nonbelonging in the United States. *Journal for the Scientific Study of Religion, 48*, 719–733.

Baker, P., & Cruickshank, J. (2010). I am happy in my faith: The influence of religious affiliation, saliency, and practice on depressive symptoms and treatment preference. *Mental Health, Religion & Culture, 12*, 339–357.

Baker-Sperry, L. (2001). Passing on the faith: The father's role in religious transmission. *Sociological Focus, 34*, 185–198.

Balch, R. W., Farnsworth, G., & Wilkins, L. (1983). When the bombs drop: Reactions to disconfirmed prophecy in a millennial sect. *Sociological Perspectives, 26*, 58–137.

Balch, R. W., Domitrovich, J., Mahnke, B., & Morrison, V. (1997). Fifteen years of failed prophecy: Coping with cognitive dissonance in a Baha'i sect. In T. Robbins, & S. Palmer (Eds.), *Millennium, Messiahs, and Mayhem*. London: Routledge.

References **241**

Baldwin, M. W., Carrell, S. E., & Lopez, D. F. (1990). Priming relationship schemas: My advisor and the pope are watching me from the back of my mind. *Journal of Experimental Social Psychology, 26,* 435–454.

Bandura, A. (2003). On the psychosocial impact and mechanisms of spiritual modeling. *International Journal for the Psychology of Religion, 13,* 167–173.

Banerjee, K., & Bloom, P. (2012). Would Tarzan believe in God? Conditions for the emergence of religious belief. *Trends in Cognitive Sciences, 17,* 7–8.

Bao, W., Whitbeck, L. B., Hoyt, D. R., & Conger, R. D. (1999). Perceived parental acceptance as a moderator of religious transmission among adolescent boys and girls. *Journal of Marriage and the Family, 61,* 362–375.

Barash, D., & Lipton, J. (2001). *Gender Gap: The Biology of Male-Female Differences.* New Brunswick, NJ: Transaction Publishers.

Barber, M. (1992). *The Two Cities: Medieval Europe 1050–1320.* London: Routledge.

Barber, N. (2013). Country religiosity declines as material security increases. *Cross-Cultural Research, 47,* 42–50.

Barkan, S. E. (2006). Religiosity and premarital sex in adulthood. *Journal for the Scientific Study of Religion, 45,* 407–417.

Barker, D. C., Hurwitz, J., & Nelson, T. L. (2008). Of crusades and culture wars: "Messianic" militarism and political conflict in the United States. *Journal of Politics, 70,* 307–322.

Barkun, M. (1986). *Crucible of the Millennium: The Burned-Over District of New York in the 1840s.* Syracuse: Syracuse University Press.

Baron-Cohen, S. (2003). *The Essential Difference: Male and Female Brains and the Truth about Autism.* New York: Basic Books.

Baron-Cohen, S., & Wheelwright, S. (2004). The Empathy Quotient: An investigation of adults with Asperger syndrome or high functioning autism, and normal sex differences. *Journal of Autism and Developmental Disorders, 34,* 163–175.

Baron-Cohen, S., Lutchmaya, S., & Knickmeyer, R. (2004). *Prenatal Testosterone in Mind: Amniotic Fluid Studies.* Cambridge, MA: MIT Press.

Barrett, D. B., Kurian, G., & Johnson, T. (Eds.). (2001). *World Christian Encyclopedia: A Comparative Survey of Churches and Religions in the Modern World.* New York: Oxford University Press.

Barrett, J. B., Pearson, J., Muller, C., & Frank, K. A. (2007). Adolescent religiosity and school contexts. *Social Science Quarterly, 88,* 1024–1037.

Barrett, J. (2004). *Why Would Anyone Believe in God?* Lanham, MD: Altamira.

Barrett, J. L. (1998). Cognitive constraints on Hindu concepts of the divine. *Journal for the Scientific Study of Religion, 37,* 608–619.

Barrett, J. L., & Keil, F. C. (1996). Anthropomorphism and God concepts: Conceptualizing a non-natural entity. *Cognitive Psychology, 31,* 219–247.

Barrett, J. L., Richert, R. A., & Driesenga, A. (2001). God's beliefs versus mother's: The development of nonhuman agent concepts. *Child Development, 72,* 50–65.

Barrett, J. L., Newman, R. M., & Richert, R. A. (2003). When seeing is not believing: Children's understanding of humans' and nonhumans' use of background knowledge in interpreting visual displays. *Journal of Cognition and Culture, 3,* 91–108.

Barro, R., & McCleary, R. (2003). Religion and economic growth across countries. *American Sociological Review, 68,* 760–781.

Barro, R., Hwang, J., & McCleary, R. (2010). Religious conversion in 40 countries. *Journal for the Scientific Study of Religion, 49,* 15–36.

Bartels, A., & Zeki, S. (2004). The neural correlates of maternal and romantic love. *NeuroImage, 21,* 1155–1166.

242 References

Bartov, O., & Mack, P. (Eds.). (2001). *In God's Name: Genocide and Religion in the Twentieth Century*. Oxford & New York: Berghahn Books.

Batson, C. D. (2011). *Altruism in Humans*. New York: Oxford University Press.

Batson, C. D., & Gray, R. A. (1981). Religious orientation and helping behavior: Responding to one's own or the victim's needs? *Journal of Personality and Social Psychology, 40,* 511–520.

Batson, C. D., & Stocks, E. L. (2004). Religion: Its core psychological functions. In T. Pyszczynski, S. L. Koole, & J. Greenberg (Eds.), *Handbook of Experimental Existential Psychology: An Emerging Synthesis* (pp. 141–155). New York: Guilford.

Batson, C. D., Naifeh, S. J., & Pate, S. (1978). Social desirability, religious orientation, and racial prejudice. *Journal for the Scientific Study of Religion, 17,* 31–41.

Batson, C. D., Oleson, K. C., Weeks, J. L., Healy, S. P., Reeves, P. J., Jennings, P., & Brown, T. (1989). Religious prosocial motivation: Is it altruistic or egoistic? *Journal of Personality and Social Psychology, 57,* 873–884.

Batson, C. D., Schoenrade, P., & Ventis, W. L. (1993). *Religion and the Individual: A Social-Psychological Perspective*. New York: Oxford University Press.

Baumeister, R. F. (1991). *Escaping the Self: Alcoholism, Spirituality, Masochism, and Other Flights from the Burden of Selfhood*. New York: Basic Books.

Baumeister, R. F., & Exline, J. J. (1999). Virtue, personality, and social relations: self-control as the moral muscle. *Journal of Personality, 67,* 1165–1194.

Bax, M. (1995). *Medjugorje: Religion, Politics, and Violence in Rural Bosnia*. Amsterdam: VU University Press.

Beard, G. M. (1879). The psychology of spiritism. *North American Review, 129,* 65–80.

Bearman, P. S., & Brückner, H. (2001). Promising the future: Virginity pledges and the transition to first intercourse. *American Journal of Sociology, 106,* 859–912.

Beck, A. T. (1983). Cognitive therapy of depression: New perspectives. In P. J. Clayton, & J. E. Barrett (Eds.), *Treatment of Depression: Old Controversies and New Approaches*. New York: Raven Press.

Becker, E. (1973). *The Denial of Death*. New York: Macmillan.

Becker, G. (1996). *Accounting for Taste*. Cambridge, MA: Harvard University Press.

Becker, G., Xander, C. J., Blum, H. E., Lutterbach, J., Momm, F., Gysels, M., & Higginson, I. J. (2007). Do religious or spiritual beliefs influence bereavement? A systematic review. *Palliative Medicine, 21,* 207–217.

Begue, L. (2002). Beliefs in justice and faith in people: just world, religiosity and interpersonal trust. *Personality and Individual Differences, 32,* 375–382.

Beit-Hallahmi, B. (1974). Psychology of religion 1880–1930: The rise and fall of a psychological movement. *Journal of the History of the Behavioral Sciences, 10,* 84–90.

Beit-Hallahmi, B. (1977a). Identity integration, self-image crisis, and "Superego Victory" in post adolescent university students. *Adolescence, 12,* 57–69.

Beit-Hallahmi, B. (1977b). Curiosity, doubt, and devotion: The beliefs of psychologists and the psychology of religion. In H. Newton Maloney (Ed.), *Perspectives in the psychology of religion* (pp. 381–391). Grand Rapids, MI: Wm. B. Eerdmans.

Beit-Hallahmi, B. (1985). Dangers of the vagina. *British Journal of Medical Psychology, 58,* 351–356.

Beit-Hallahmi, B. (1989). *Prolegomena to the Psychological Study of Religion*. Lewisburg, PA: Bucknell University Press.

Beit-Hallahmi, B. (1992). *Despair and Deliverance: Private Salvation in Contemporary Israel*. Albany, NY: SUNY Press.

Beit-Hallahmi, B. (1993). *Original Sins: Reflections on the History of Zionism and Israel*. Brooklyn, NY: Interlink.

Beit-Hallahmi, B. (1996). *Psychoanalytic Studies of Religion: Critical Assessment and Annotated Bibliography*. Westport, CT: Greenwood Press.

Beit-Hallahmi, B. (1997). Biology, destiny and change: Women's religiosity and economic development. *Journal of Institutional and Theoretical Economics, 153*, 166–178.

Beit-Hallahmi, B. (1998). *The Illustrated Encyclopedia of Active New Religions, Sects, and Cults* (revised edition). New York: Rosen Publishing.

Beit-Hallahmi, B. (2001a). Explaining religious utterances by taking seriously supernaturalist (and naturalist) claims. In G. Hon, & S. Rakover (Eds.), *Explanation: Philosophical Essays*. Dordrecht: Kluwer.

Beit-Hallahmi, B. (2001b). 'O truant muse': collaborationism and research integrity. In B. Zablocki, & T. Robbins (Eds.), *Misunderstanding Cults*. Toronto: University of Toronto Press.

Beit-Hallahmi, B. (2003). Religiosity and religion among Nobel Laureates. Unpublished.

Beit-Hallahmi, B. (2006–2007). Triggers and transformations: Freud and Siddhartha. *Annual of Psychoanalysis, Religion and Spirituality: Psychoanalytic Perspectives, 34–35*, 151–163.

Beit-Hallahmi, B. (2007). Atheists: A psychological profile. In M. Martin (Ed.), *The Cambridge Companion to Atheism* (pp. 300–313). Cambridge, UK: Cambridge University Press.

Beit-Hallahmi, B. (Ed.) (2010). *Psychoanalysis and Theism: Critical Reflections on the Grünbaum Thesis*. Lanham, MD: Jason Aronson.

Beit-Hallahmi, B. (2012). Fear of the dead, fear of death: Is it biological or psychological? *Mortality, 17*, 322–337.

Beit-Hallahmi, B., & Argyle, M. (1975). God as a father projection: The theory and the evidence. *British Journal of Medical Psychology, 48*, 71–75.

Beit-Hallahmi, B., & Argyle, M. (1997). *The Psychology of Religious Behavior, Belief and Experience*. London: Routledge.

Beit-Hallahmi, B., & Nevo, B. (1987). Born-again Jews in Israel: The dynamics of an identity change. *International Journal of Psychology, 22*, 75–81.

Beit-Hallahmi, B., Levi-Israeli, E., & Farahat, M. (2004). Looking at seekers: A psychological profile of individuals in search of a new religious identity. Unpublished.

Bekker, M.H.J. (2001). Stressing the female side: Do women react differently to stress by nature? *Psychology, Evolution & Gender, 3*, 265–271.

Belenky, M. F., Clinchy, B. M., Goldberger, N. R., & Tarule, J. M. (1986). *Women's Ways of Knowing: The Development of Self, Voice, and Mind*. New York: Basic Books.

Belfrage, S. (1981). *Flowers of Emptiness*. New York: Dial.

Bell, S. (1998). "Crazy Wisdom," charisma, and the transmission of Buddhism in the United States. *Nova Religio: The Journal of Alternative and Emergent Religions, 2*, 55–75.

Bellah, R. N. (1975). *The Broken Covenant*. New York: The Seabury Press.

Belle, D. (1982). The stress of caring: Women as providers of social support. In L. Goldberger, & S. Breznitz (Eds.), *Handbook of Stress: Theoretical and Clinical Aspects* (pp. 496–505). New York: Free Press.

Bellemare, C. and Kröger, S. (2007). On representative social capital. *European Economic Review, 51*, 183–202.

Bello, F. (1954). The young scientists. *Fortune, 49*, 142–143.

Belyaev, D. (2011). Heterodox religiousness in today's Russia: Results of an empirical study. *Social Compass, 58*, 353–372.

Belzen, J. (1996). Beyond a classic? Hjalmar Sunden's role theory and contemporary narrative psychology. *International Journal for the Psychology of Religion, 6*, 181–200.

Belzen, J. A. (2010). Beyond Freud in psychoanalytic psychology of religion? On the discussion of religion as projection. *Journal of Religion in Europe, 3*, 1–33.

244 References

Belzen, J. A., & Geels, A. (2003). *Mysticism: A Variety of Psychological Perspectives*. Amsterdam: Rodopi.

Belzen, J. A., & Uleyn, A.J.R. (1992). What is real? Speculations on Hood's implicit epistemology and theology. *International Journal for the Psychology of Religion, 2*, 165–169.

Benda, B., & Corwyn, R. F. (1997). Religion and delinquency: The relationship after considering family and peer influences. *Journal for the Scientific Study of Religion, 36*, 81–92.

Bengtson, V. L., Copen, C. E., Putney, N. M., & Silverstein, M. (2009). A longitudinal study of the intergenerational transmission of religion. *International Sociology, 24*, 325–345.

Benjamin, D. J., Choi, J. J., & Fisher, G. W. (2010). Religious identity and economic behavior. *NBER Working Paper* 15925; www.nber.org/papers/w15925.

Benjamins, M. R., Musick, M. A., Gold, D. T., & George, L. K. (2003). Age-related declines in activity level: the relationship between chronic illness and religious activities. *Journal of Gerontology: Series B, Psychological Sciences and Social Sciences, 58*, S377–385.

Ben-Ner, A., & Kramer, A. (2011). Personality and altruism in the dictator game: Relationship to giving to kin, collaborators, competitors, and neutrals. *Personality and Individual Differences, 51*, 216–221.

Ben-Ner, A., McCall, B. P., Stephane, M., & Wang, H. (2009). Identity and in-group/out-group differentiation in work and giving behaviors: Experimental evidence. *Journal of Economic Behavior & Organization, 72*, 153–170.

Benson, P. L. (1992). Religion and substance abuse. In J. F. Shumaker (Ed.), *Religion and Mental Health* (pp. 211–220). New York: Oxford University Press.

Benson, P. L., Donahue, M. J., & Erickson, J. A. (1989). Adolescence and religion: A review of the literature from 1970 to 1986. *Research in the Social Scientific Study of Religion, 1*, 151–179.

Benson, P. L., Masters, K. S., & Larson, D. B. (1997). Religious influences on child and adolescent development. In N. E. Aless (Ed.), *Varieties of Development* (Vol. 4, pp. 206–219). New York: Wiley.

Berg, T. V., & Kniss, F. (2008). ISKCON and immigrants: The rise, decline, and rise again of a New Religious Movement. *The Sociological Quarterly, 49*, 79–104.

Berger, P. L. (1967). *The Sacred Canopy: Elements of a Sociological Theory of Religion*. New York: Doubleday.

Berger, P. L. (2006). An interview with Peter L. Berger. *The Hedgehog Review, 8*, 152–162.

Berggrena, N., & Bjornskov, C. (2011). Is the importance of religion in daily life related to social trust? Cross-country and cross-state comparisons. *Journal of Economic Behavior & Organization, 80*, 459–480.

Bering, J. M. (2006). The folk psychology of souls. *Behavioral and Brain Sciences, 29*, 453–462.

Bering, J. M. (2011). *The Belief Instinct: The Psychology of Souls, Destiny, and the Meaning of Life*. New York, NY: Norton.

Bering, J. M., McLeod, K., & Shackelford, T. K. (2005). Reasoning about dead agents reveals possible adaptive trends. *Human Nature, 16*, 360–381.

Berkel, J., & de Waard, F. (1983). Mortality pattern and life expectancy of Seventh-Day Adventists in the Netherlands. *International Journal of Epidemiology, 12*, 455–459.

Berkley Center (2008). *Inspired by Faith: A Background Report 'Mapping' Social Economic Development Work in the Muslim World*. Washington, DC: Georgetown University, Berkley Center for Religion, Peace and World Affairs.

Berlinger, N. (2004). Spirituality and medicine: Idiot-proofing the discourse. *Journal of Medicine and Philosophy, 29*, 681–695.

Bernardi, L., Sleight, P., Bandinelli, G., Cencetti, S., Fattorini, L., Wdowczyc-Szulc, J., & Lagi, A. (2001). Effect of rosary prayer and yoga mantras on autonomic cardiovascular rhythms: Comparative study. *British Medical Journal, 325*, 1446–1449.

References 245

Bernhard, H., Fischbacher, U., & Fehr, E. (2006). Parochial altruism in humans. *Nature*, *442*, 912–915.

Berry, J. (1976). *Human Ecology and Cognitive Style*. New York: Wiley.

Berryman, E. (2001). Medjugorje living icons: Making spirit matter (for sociology). *Social Compass*, *48*, 593–610.

Bettelheim, B. (1954). *Symbolic Wounds; Puberty Rites and the Envious Male*. Glencoe, IL: Free Press.

Bhugra, D. (2005). Sati: A type of nonpsychiatric suicide. *Crisis*, *26*, 73–77.

Billings, D. B. (1990). Religion as opposition: A Gramscian analysis. *American Journal of Sociology*, *96*, 1–31.

Bilu, Y., & Beit-Hallahmi, B. (1989). Dybbuk possession as a hysterical symptom: Psychodynamic and social considerations. *Israel Journal of Psychiatry*, *26*, 138–149.

Birgegard, A., & Granqvist, P. (2004). The correspondence between attachment to parents and God: three experiments using subliminal separation cues. *Personality and Social Psychology Bulletin*, *30*, 1122–1135.

Birnbaum, N. (1973). *Toward A Critical Sociology*. New York: Oxford University Press.

Bjork, J. M., Smith, A. R., Chen, G., & Hommer, D. W. (2011). Psychosocial problems and recruitment of incentive neurocircuitry: exploring individual differences in healthy adolescents. *Developmental Cognitive Neuroscience*, *27*, 4839–4849.

Bjork, J. P., & Cohen, L. M. (1993). Coping with threats, losses and challenges. *Journal of Social and Clinical Psychology*, *12*, 56–72.

Blaine, B. E., Trivedi, P., & Eshleman, A. (1998). Religious belief and the self-concept: Evaluating the implications for psychological adjustment. *Personality and Social Psychology Bulletin*, *24*, 1040–1052.

Blake, W. (1804/1905). *Poems of William Blake*. London: Routledge.

Blanke, O., Landis, T., Spinelli, L., & Seeck, M. (2003). Out-of-body experience and autoscopy of neurological origin. *Brain*, *127*, 243–258.

Blatt, S. J. (1990). Interpersonal relatedness and self definition: Two personality configurations and their implication for psychopathology and psychotherapy. In J. Singer (Ed.), *Repression and Dissociation: Implications for Personality Theory, Psychopathology and Health* (pp. 299–335). Chicago: University of Chicago Press.

Blaydes, L., & Linzer, D. A. (2008). The political economy of women's support for fundamentalist Islam. *World Politics*, *60*, 576–609.

Block, J. H. (1976). Issues, problems, and pitfalls in assessing sex differences: A critical review of "The psychology of sex differences." *Merrill-Palmer Quarterly*, *22*, 283–308.

Block, J., & Robins, R. W. (1993). A longitudinal study of consistency and change in self-esteem from early adolescence to early adulthood. *Child Development*, *64*, 909–923.

Blogowska, J., Lambert, C., & Saroglou, V. (2013). Religious prosociality and aggression: It's real. *Journal for the Scientific Study of Religion*, *52*, 524–536.

Bloodgood, J. M., Turnley, W. H., and Mudrack, P. (2008). The influence of ethics instruction, religiosity, and intelligence on cheating behavior. *Journal of Business Ethics*, *82*, 557–571.

Bloom, H. (1992). *The American Religion: The Making of a Post-Christian Nation*. New York: Simon & Schuster.

Bloom, P. (2004). *Descartes' Baby*. New York, NY: Basic Books.

Bloom, P. (2007). Religion is natural. *Developmental Science*, *10*, 147–151.

Blos, P. (1979). *The Adolescent Passage*. New York: International Universities Press.

246 References

Blumenthal, J. A., Babyak, M. A., Ironson, G., Thoresen, C., Powell, L., Czajkowski, S. M., Burg, M. M., Keefe, F. J., Steffen, P. R., & Catellier, D. (2007). Spirituality, religion, and clinical outcomes in patients recovering from an acute myocardial infarction. *Psychosomatic Medicine, 69*, 501–508.

Boisen, A. (1936). *The Exploration of the Inner World*. New York: Harper.

Boisen, A. (1945). *Religion in Crisis and Custom*. New York: Harper & Row.

Bonger, W. A. (1943). *Race and Crime*. New York, NY: Columbia University Press.

Boonin, D. (2013). *Reductio ad Absurdum* objections and the disintegration argument against merely instrumental sex. *Journal of Social Philosophy, 44*, 233–249.

Booth, J. N., & Persinger, M. A. (2009). Discrete shifts within the theta band between the frontal and parietal regions of the right hemisphere and the experiences of a sensed presence. *The Journal of Neuropsychiatry and Clinical Neurosciences, 21*, 279–283.

Borg, J., Andree, B., Soderstrom, H., & Farde, L. (2003). The serotonin system and spiritual experiences. *American Journal of Psychiatry, 160*, 1965–1969.

Borg, M. B. (1988). The problem of nihilism. *Sociological Analysis, 49*, 1–16.

Borras, L., Mohr, S., Brandt, P.-Y., Gillieron, C., Eytan, A., & Huguelet, P. (2007). Religious beliefs in schizophrenia: Their relevance for adherence to treatment. *Schizophrenia Bulletin, 33*, 1238–1246.

Bottoms, B. L., Shaver, P. R., Goodman, G. S., & Qin, J. J. (1995). In the name of God: A profile of religion-related child abuse. *Journal of Social Issues, 51*, 85–111.

Bottoms, B. L., Nielsen, M. E., Murray, R., & Filipas, H. (2004). Religion-related child physical abuse: Characteristics and psychological outcome. *Journal of Aggression, Maltreatment and Trauma, 8*, 87–114.

Bouchard, T. J., Jr. (2009). Authoritarianism, religiousness, and conservatism: Is "obedience to authority" the explanation for their clustering, universality and evolution? In E. Voland, & W. Schiefenhövel (Eds.), *The Biological Evolution of Religious Mind and Behavior* (pp. 165–180). Berlin: Springer-Verlag.

Boulware, L. E., Ratner, L. E., Cooper, L. A., Sosa, J. A., LaVeist, T. A., & Powe, N. R. (2002). Understanding disparities in donor behavior: Race and gender differences in willingness to donate blood and cadaveric organs. *Medical Care, 40*, 85–95.

Bourget, D., & Chalmers, D. (2013). What do philosophers believe? *PhilPapers*, May 13.

Bowlby, J. (1969). *Attachment and Loss*. London: Hogarth Press.

Bowlby, J. (1973). *Separation: Anxiety and Anger*. London: Hogarth Press.

Bowman, E., Coons, P., Jones, R., & Oldsrom, M. (1987). Religious psychodynamics in multiple personalities. *American Journal of Psychotherapy, 41*, 542–554.

Boyer, P. (2001). *Religion Explained: The Evolutionary Origins of Religious Thought*. New York: Basic Books.

Bradley, C. (2009). The interconnections between religious Fundamentalism, spirituality and the four dimensions of empathy. *Review of Religious Research, 51*, 201–219.

Bradley, M. M., Codispoti, M., Sabatinelli, D., & Lang, P. J. (2001). Emotion and motivation II: Sex differences in picture processing. *Emotion, 1*, 300–319.

Bradshaw, M., & Ellison, C. G. (2008). Do genetic factors influence religious life? Findings from a behavior genetic analysis of twin siblings. *Journal for the Scientific Study of Religion, 47*, 529–544.

Bradshaw, M., & Ellison, C. G. (2009). The nature-nurture debate is over, and both sides lost! Implications for understanding gender differences in religiosity. *Journal for the Scientific Study of Religion, 48*, 241–251.

Bradshaw, M., Ellison, C. G., & Flannelly, K. J. (2008). Prayer, God imagery, and symptoms of psychopathology. *Journal for the Scientific Study of Religion, 47*, 644–659.

Bragan, K. (1977). The psychological gains and losses of religious conversion. *The Journal of Medical Psychology, 50,* 80–117.

Brainerd, E. (2001). Economic reform and mortality in the former Soviet Union: A study of the suicide epidemic in the 1990s. *European Economic Review, 45,* 1007–1019.

Braithwaite, J. J., Hulleman, J., Samson, D., & Apperly, I. (2011). Cognitive correlates of the spontaneous out-of-body experience in the psychologically normal population: Evidence for a role of temporal-lobe disturbance, body-distortion processing, and impairments in own-body transformations. *Cortex, 47,* 839–853.

Brandt, M. J., & Henry, P. J. (2012). Psychological defensiveness as a mechanism explaining the relationship between low socioeconomic status and religiosity. *The International Journal for the Psychology of Religion, 22,* 321–332.

Brasher, B. (1998). *Godly Women: Fundamentalism and Female Power.* New Brunswick, NJ: Rutgers University Press.

Braun, W. (2008). Sallekhana: The ethicality and legality of religious suicide by starvation in the Jain religious community. *Medical Law Review, 27,* 913–924.

Brenner, P. S. (2011). Identity importance and the overreporting of religious service attendance: Multiple imputation of religious attendance using the American Time Use Study and the General Social Survey. *Journal for the Scientific Study of Religion, 50,* 103–115.

Brenner, R. R. (1980). *The Faith and Doubt of Holocaust Survivors.* New York: Macmillan.

Brewer, M. B. (1979). In-group bias in the minimal intergroup situation: A cognitive-motivational analysis. *Psychological Bulletin, 86,* 307–324.

Brink, J., & Mencher, J. (Eds.). (1997). *Mixed Blessings: Gender and Religious Fundamentalism Cross Culturally.* London: Routledge.

Britton, W. B., & Bootzin, R. R. (2004). Near-death experiences and the temporal lobe. *Psychological Science, 15,* 254–258.

Brodzinsky, D. M., & Rubien, J. (1976). Humor production as a function of sex of subject, creativity, and cartoon content. *Journal of Consulting and Clinical Psychology, 14,* 597–600.

Brown, D. E. (1991). *Human Universals.* New York, McGraw-Hill.

Brown, L. B. (1988). *The Psychology of Religion: An Introduction.* London: SPCK.

Bruce, S. (1990a). *A House Divided: Protestantism, Schism, and Secularization.* New York: Routledge.

Bruce, S. (1990b). *Pray TV: Televangelism in America.* London: Routledge.

Bruce, S. (1992). *Religion and Modernization: Sociologists and Historians Debate The Secularization Thesis.* Oxford: Oxford University Press.

Bruce, S. (2002). *God is Dead: Secularization in the West.* Oxford: Blackwell.

Bruce, S. (2012). Patronage and secularization: social obligation and church support. *The British Journal of Sociology, 63,* 533–552.

Brunvand, J. H. (1999). *Too Good to Be True: The Colossal Book of Urban Legends.* New York: Norton.

Bryant, A. N. (2007). Gender differences in spiritual development during the college years. *Sex Roles, 56,* 835–846.

Bryant, E. F., & Ekstrand, M. L. (2004). *The Hare Krishna Movement: The Postcharismatic Fate of a Religious Transplant.* New York: Columbia University Press.

Buchbinder, J. T., Bilu, Y., & Witztum, E. (1997). Ethnic background and antecedents of religious conversion among Israeli Jewish outpatients. *Psychological Reports, 81,* 187–202.

Budd, S. (1977). *Varieties of Unbelief.* London: Heinemann.

Buddenbaum, J. (1981). Characteristics and media related needs of the audience for religious television. *Journalism Quarterly, 58,* 266–272.

248 References

Bulbulia, J. (2005). Are there any religions? *Method and Theory in the Study of Religion, 17,* 71–100.

Bulbulia, J. (2013). *Classical Social Theory and the Cognitive Science of Religion.* Durham, UK: Acumen Publishing.

Bulbulia, J., & Mahoney, A. (2008). Religious solidarity: The hand grenade experiment. *Journal of Cognition and Culture, 8,* 3–4.

Burling, J. W. (1993). Death concerns and symbolic aspects of the self: The effects of mortality salience on status concern and religiosity. *Personality and Social Psychology Bulletin, 19,* 100–105.

Burridge, K. (1975). *New Heaven, New Earth: A Study of Millenarian Activities.* New York: Schocken.

Burris, C. T., & Petrican, R. (2011). Hearts strangely warmed (and cooled): Emotional experience in religious and atheistic individuals. *The International Journal for the Psychology of Religion, 21,* 183–197.

Burris, C. T., Branscombe, N. R., & Jackson, L. M. (2000). "For god and country": Religion and the endorsement of national selfstereotypes. *Journal of Cross-Cultural Psychology, 31,* 517–527.

Bushman, B. J., Ridge, R. D., Das, E., Key, C. W., & Busath, G. L. (2007). When God sanctions killing: Effect of scriptural violence on aggression. *Psychological Science, 18,* 204–207.

Butler, K. (1990). Encountering the shadow in Buddhist America. *Common Boundary, 8* (May/June), 14–22.

Butler, P. M., McNamara, P., & Durso, R. (2010). Deficits in the automatic activation of religious concepts in patients with Parkinson's disease. *Journal of the International Neuropsychology Society, 16,* 252–261.

Butterfield, S. T. (1994). *The Double Mirror: A Skeptical Journey into Buddhist Tantra.* Berkeley: North Atlantic Books.

Buxant, C., Saroglou, V., Casalfiore, S., & Christians, L.-L. (2007). Cognitive and emotional characteristics of New Religious Movements members: New questions and data on the mental health issue. *Mental Health, Religion, and Culture, 10,* 219–238.

Buxant, C., Saroglou, V., & Scheuer, J. (2009). Contemporary conversions: Compensatory needs or self-growth motives? *Research in the Social Scientific Study of Religion, 20,* 47–68.

Byrd, K. R. & Boe, A. D. (2001). The correspondence between attachment dimensions and prayer in college students. *International Journal for the Psychology of Religion, 11,* 9–24.

Byrnes, J. P., Miller, D. C., & Schafer, W. D. (1999). Gender differences in risk taking: A meta-analysis. *Psychological Bulletin, 125,* 367–383.

Cadge, W. (2004). Gendered religious organizations: The case of Theravada Buddhism in America. *Gender and Society, 18,* 777–793.

Cadge, W. (2009). Saying your prayers, constructing your religions: Medical studies of intercessory prayer. *The Journal of Religion, 89,* 299–327.

Cadge, W., & Davidman, L. (2006). Ascription, choice, and the construction of religious identities in the contemporary United States. *Journal for the Scientific Study of Religion, 45,* 23–38.

Cahill, L., Uncapher, M., Kilpatrick, L., Alkire, M. T., & Turner, J. (2004). Sex-related hemispheric lateralization of amygdala function in emotionally influenced memory: An fMRI investigation. *Learning and Memory, 11,* 261–266.

Caldwell, R. (1989). *The Origin of the Gods.* New York: Oxford University Press.

Cameron, N. (1963). *Personality Development and Psychopathology: A Dynamic Approach.* Boston: Houghton Mifflin.

Campbell, A. (2002). *A Mind of Her Own: The Evolutionary Psychology of Women.* Oxford: Oxford University Press.

Campbell, J. (1981). *The Mythic Image.* Princeton: Princeton University Press.

Canetti-Nisim, D., & Beit-Hallahmi, B. (2007). Effects of authoritarianism, religiosity, and "New Age" beliefs on support for democracy: Unraveling the strands. *Review of Religious Research, 48,* 369–384.

Cantril, H. (1941). *The Psychology of Social Movements.* Hoboken, NJ: John Wiley & Sons.

Caplovitz, D., & Sherrow, F. (1977). *The Religious Drop-Outs: Apostasy Among College Graduates.* Beverly Hills: Sage.

Caporael, L. A. (1986). Anthropomorphism and mechanomorphism: Two faces of the human machine. *Computers in Human Behavior, 2,* 215–234.

Capps, D. (1992). Religion and child abuse: Perfect together. *Journal for the Scientific Study of Religion, 31,* 1–14.

Capps, D. (1997). *Men, Religion, and Melancholia.* New Haven: Yale University Press.

Caprara, G. V., Schwartz, S. H., Capanna, C., Vecchione, M., & Barbaranelli, C. (2006). Personality and politics: Values, traits, and political choice. *Political Psychology, 27,* 1–28.

Cárdenas, R. A., Harris, L. J., & Becker, M. W. (2013). Sex differences in visual attention toward infant faces. *Evolution and Human Behavior, 34,* 280–287.

Carey, B. (2006). Long-awaited medical study questions the power of prayer. *The New York Times,* March 31, p. C1.

Carrazana, E., DeToledo, J., Tatum, W., Rivas-Vasquez, R., Rey, G., & Wheeler, S. (1999). Epilepsy and religious experiences: Voodoo possession. *Epilepsia, 40,* 239–241.

Carroll, M. P. (1975). Revitalization movements and social structure: Some quantitative tests. *American Sociological Review, 40,* 389–401.

Carroll, M. P. (1979). The sex of our gods. *Ethos, 7,* 37–50.

Carroll, M. P. (1986). *The Cult of the Virgin Mary: Psychological Origins.* Princeton: Princeton University Press.

Carroll, M. P. (1989). *Catholic Cults and Devotions.* Montreal: McGill-Queens University Press.

Carter, L. F. (1990). *Charisma and Control in Rajneeshpuram: The Role of Shared Values in the Creation of a Community.* New York: Cambridge University Press.

Cassibba, R., Granqvist, P., and Costantini, A. (2013). Mothers' attachment security predicts their children's sense of God's closeness. *Attachment and Human Development, 15,* 51–64.

Caswell, G. (2011). Personalisation in Scottish funerals: Individualised ritual or relational process? *Mortality, 16,* 242–258.

Cavalli-Sforza, L. L. (1993). How are values transmitted? In M. Hechter, L. Nadel, & R. E. Michod (Eds.), *The Origin of Values* (pp. 304–318). Hawthorne, NY: AldineTransaction.

Cha, K. Y., Wirth, D. P., & Lobo, R. A. (2001). Does prayer influence the success of in vitro fertilization-embryo transfer? Report of a masked, randomized trial. *Journal of Reproductive Medicine, 46,* 781–787.

Chadwick, O. (1975). *The Secularization of the European Mind in the Nineteenth Century.* Cambridge: Cambridge University Press.

Chafets, Z. (2006). Preaching to Wall Street. *The New York Times Magazine,* December 17, pp. 15–22.

Chaiken, S., & Trope, Y. (1999). *Dual-Process Theories in Social Psychology.* New York: Guilford Press.

Chalfant, H. P., Beckley, R. E., & Palmer, C. E. (1981). *Religion in Contemporary Society.* Sherman Oaks, CA: Alfred Publishing Co.

250 References

Chamberlain, K., & Zika, S. (1988). Religiosity, life meaning and wellbeing: Some relationships in a sample of women. *Journal for the Scientific Study of Religion, 27,* 411–420.

Champion, F. (1990). La nébuleuse mystique-ésotérique. Orientations psychoreligieuses des courants mystiques et ésotériques contemporains. In F. Champion, and D. Hervieu-Léger (Eds.), *De l'émotion en religion: Renouveaux et traditions* (pp. 17–69). Paris: Centurion.

Chan, M., Rogers, K. H., Parisotto, K. L., & Biesanz, J. S. (2011). Forming first impressions: The role of gender and normative accuracy in personality perception. *Journal of Research in Personality, 45,* 117–120.

Chaves, M. (2010). Rain dances in the dry season: Overcoming the religious congruence fallacy. *Journal for the Scientific Study of Religion, 49,* 1–14.

Chen, H., Cheal, K., McDonel, Herr E., Zubritsky, C., & Levkoff, S. (2007). Religious participation as a predictor of mental health status and treatment outcomes in older adults. *International Journal of Geriatric Psychiatry, 22,* 144–153.

Chester, D. K. (2005). Volcanoes, society and culture. In J. Marti, & G. J. Ernst (Eds.), *Volcanoes and the Environment* (pp. 404–439). Cambridge: Cambridge University Press.

Christensen, C. W. (1963). Religious conversion. *Journal of Nervous and Mental Disease, 9,* 207–223.

Christensen, J. F., Flexas, A., de Miguel, P., Cela-Conde, C. J., & Munar, E. (2014). Roman Catholic beliefs produce characteristic neural responses to moral dilemmas. *Social Cognitive and Affective Neuroscience, 9,* 240–249.

Claridge, G. (1985). *Origins of Mental Illness.* Oxford: Blackwell.

Claridge, G. A. (1987). "The schizophrenias as nervous types" revisited. *British Journal of Psychiatry, 151,* 735–743.

Claridge, G. (1997). Schizotypy: Theoretical background and issues. In G. Claridge (Ed.), *Schizotypy: Implications for Illness and Health* (pp. 3–18). Oxford: Oxford University Press.

Clark, C. A., Worthington, E. L., & Danser, D. B. (1988). The transmission of religious beliefs and practices from parents to firstborn early adolescent sons. *Journal of Marriage and the Family, 50,* 463–472.

Clark, E. T. (1965). *The Small Sects in America.* New York: Abingdon Press.

Clark, T. (1980). *The Great Naropa Poetry Wars.* Santa Barbara: Cadmus Editions.

Clark, W. H. (1958). *The Psychology of Religion.* New York: Macmillan.

Clark, W. H. (1969). *Chemical Ecstasy: Psychedelic Drugs and Religion.* New York: Sheed and Ward.

Clarke, G. (2007). Agents of transformation? Donors, faith-based organisations and international development. *Third World Quarterly, 28,* 77–96.

Clarke, G., Jennings, M., & Shaw, T. (Eds.). (2008). *Development, Civil Society and Faith-Based Organizations: Bridging the Sacred and the Secular.* Basingstoke: Palgrave Macmillan.

Clarke, J. J. (1997). *Oriental Enlightenment: The Encounter between Asian and Western Thought.* London: Routledge.

Cnaan, R. A., & Helzer, A. L. (2004). Women in congregations and social service provision: Findings from the Philadelphia census. *Social Thought, 23,* 25–43.

Cochran, J., & Akers, R. (1989). Beyond hellfire: An exploration of the variable effects of religiosity on adolescent marijuana and alcohol use. *Journal of Research in Crime and Delinquency, 26,* 198–225.

Cohen, A. B., Shariff, A. F., & Hill, P. C. (2008). The accessibility of religious beliefs. *Journal of Research in Personality, 42,* 1408–1417.

Cohen, B.-Z. (1999). Measuring the willingness to seek help. *Journal of Social Service Research, 26,* 67–79.

Cohn, N. (1975). *Europe's Inner Demons.* New York: Basic Books.

Colby, A., & Damon, W. (1992). *Some Do Care: Contemporary Lives of Moral Commitment.* New York: Free Press.

Cole, L. (1942). *Psychology of Adolescence.* New York: Rinehart & Co.

Colzato, L. S., van Beest, I., van den Wildenberg, W.P.M., Scorolli, C., Dorchin, S., Meiran, N., Borghi, A. M., & Hommel, B. (2010). God: Do I have your attention? *Cognition, 117,* 87–94.

Conklin, B. A. (2001). *Consuming Grief: Mortuary Cannibalism in an Amazonian Society.* Austin, TX: University of Texas Press.

Conroy, S. J., & Emerson, T.L.N. (2004). Business ethics and religion: Religiosity as a predictor of ethical awareness among students. *Journal of Business Ethics, 74,* 383–396.

Coyne, J. C., Stefanek, M., & Palmer, S. C. (2007). Psychotherapy and survival in cancer: The conflict between hope and evidence. *Psychological Bulletin, 133,* 367–394.

Coyne, J. C., Thombs, B. D., Stefanek, M., & Palmer, S. C. (2009). Time to let go of the illusion that psychotherapy extends the survival of cancer patients: Reply to Kraemer, Kuchler, and Spiegel (2009). *Psychological Bulletin, 135,* 179–182.

Cragun, R. T., & Lawson, R. (2010). The secular transition: The worldwide growth of Mormons, Jehovah's Witnesses, and Seventh-day Adventists. *Sociology of Religion, 71,* 349–373.

Cramer, P. (1991). *The Development of Defense Mechanisms: Theory, Research, and Asessment.* New York: Springer-Verlag.

Crapanzano, V. (1985). *Waiting: The Whites of South Africa.* New York: Random House.

Crockett, A., & Voas, D. (2006). Generations of decline: Religious change in 20th-century Britain. *Journal for the Scientific Study of Religion, 45,* 567–584.

Cromer, A. H. (1993). *Uncommon Sense: The Heretical Nature of Science.* New York: Oxford University Press.

Csibra, G., and Gergely, G. (2009). Natural pedagogy. *Trends in Cognitive Sciences, 13,* 148–153.

Curlin, F. A., Chin, M. H., Sellergren, S. A., Roach, C. J., & Lantos, J. D. (2006). The association of physicians' religious characteristics with their attitudes and self-reported behaviors regarding religion and spirituality in the clinical endeavor. *Medical Care, 44,* 446–453.

Curlin, F., Odell, S., Lawrence, R., Chin, M., Lantos, J., Meador, K., & Koenig, H. (2007a). The relationship between psychiatry and religion among U.S. physicians. *Psychiatric Services, 58,* 1193–1198.

Curlin, F. A., Sellergren, S. A., Lantos, J. D., & Chin, M. H. (2007b). Physicians' observations and interpretations of the influence of religion and spirituality on health. *Archives of Internal Medicine, 167,* 649–654.

Curry, E. W., Koch, J. R., & Chalfant, H. P. (2004). Concern for God and concern for society: Religiosity and social justice. *Sociological Spectrum, 24,* 651–666.

Cyrus, V. (1993). *Experiencing Race, Class, and Gender in the United States.* Mountain View, CA: Mayfield Publishing Company.

Dacey, A. (2008). *The Secular Conscience: Why Belief Belongs in Public Life.* Amherst, NY: Prometheus Books.

Dafni, A. (2002). Why are rags tied to the sacred trees of the Holy Land? *Economic Botany, 56,* 315–327.

Dalbert, C., Lipkus, I. M., Sallay, H., & Goch, I. (2001). A just and an unjust world: Structure and validity of different world beliefs. *Personality and Individual Differences, 30,* 561–577.

Dalton, R. J. (2006). *Citizen Politics: Public Opinion and Political Parties in Advanced Industrial Democracies.* Washington, DC: Congressional Quarterly Press.

252 References

Daly, R. J., & Cochrane, C. M. (1968). Affective disorder taxonomies in middle-aged females. *British Journal of Psychiatry, 14*, 1295–1297.

Danielson, A. J., & Holm, H. J. (2007). Do you trust your brethren? Eliciting trust attitudes and trust behavior in a Tanzanian congregation. *Journal of Economic Behavior and Organization, 62*, 255–271.

Darwin, C. (1839/1965). *The Voyage of the Beagle.* London: Dent.

Darwin, C. (1887/2004). *The Autobiography of Charles Darwin.* New York: Totem Books.

Davidman, L. (1991). *Tradition in a Rootless World: Women Turn to Orthodox Judaism.* Berkeley: University of California Press.

Davidson, J. D. (2008). Religious stratification: Its origins, persistence, and consequences. *Sociology of Religion, 69*, 371–395.

Davie, G. (1990). Believing without belonging: Is this the future of religion in Britain? *Social Compass, 37*, 455–469.

Davis, K. (1948). *Human Society.* New York: Macmillan.

Davis, N. J., & Robinson, R. V. (1996). Are the rumors of war exaggerated? Religious orthodoxy and moral progressivism in the United States. *American Journal of Sociology, 102*, 756–787.

Davis, N. J., & Robinson, R. V. (1999a). Religious cosmologies, individualism, and politics in Italy. *Journal for the Scientific Study of Religion, 38*, 339–353.

Davis, N. J., & Robinson, R. V. (1999b). Their brothers' keepers? Orthodox religionists, modernists and economic justice in Europe. *American Journal of Sociology, 104*, 1631–1665.

Davis, N. J., & Robinson, R. V. (2001). Theological modernism, cultural libertarianism and *laissez-faire* economics in contemporary European societies. *Sociology of Religion, 62*, 23–50.

Davis, N. J., & Robinson, R. V. (2006). The egalitarian face of Islamic orthodoxy: Support for Islamic law and economic justice in seven Muslim-majority nations. *American Sociological Review, 71*, 167–190.

Dawkins, R. (2006). *The God Delusion.* Boston: Houghton Mifflin.

Dawson, L. L. (1995). Accounting for accounts: How should sociologists treat conversion stories? *International Journal of Comparative Religion and Philosophy, 1*, 51–68.

Dawson, L. L. (1999). When prophecy fails and faith persists: A theoretical overview. *Nova Religio: The Journal of Alternative and Emergent Religions, 3*, 60–82.

Day, S., & Peters, E. R. (1999). Incidence of schizotypy in New Religious Movements. *Personality and Individual Differences, 27*, 44–56.

Decety, J., & Batson, C. D. (2009). Empathy and morality: Integrating social and neuroscience approaches. In J. Braeckman, J. Verplaetse, and J. De Schrijver (Eds.), *The Moral Brain* (pp. 109–127). Berlin: Springer Verlag.

Dechesne, M., Pyszczynski, T., Arndt, J., Ransom, S., Sheldon, K. M, van Knippenberg, A., & Janssen, J. (2003). Literal and symbolic immortality: The effect of evidence of literal immortality on self-esteem striving in response to mortality salience. *Journal of Personality and Social Psychology, 84*, 722–737.

Deconchy, J. P. (1968). God and parental images: the masculine and feminine in religions free association. In A. Godin (Ed.), *From Cry to Word* (pp. 85–94). Brussels: Lumen Vitae.

de Graaf, N. D., & te Grotenhuis, M. (2008). Traditional Christian belief and belief in the supernatural: Diverging trends in the Netherlands between 1979 and 2005? *Journal for the Scientific Study of Religion, 47*, 585–598.

Dein, S. (2010). *Lubavitcher Messianism: What Really Happens When Prophecy Fails?* New York: Continuum.

References   253

Deka, N., & Broota, K. D. (1988). Relation between level of religiosity and principled moral judgment among four religious communities in India. *Journal of Personality and Clinical Studies, 4,* 151–156.

Delamontagne, R. G. (2010). High religiosity and societal dysfunction in the United States during the first decade of the twenty-first century. *Evolutionary Psychology, 8,* 617–657.

De La O, A. L., & Rodden, J. A. (2008). Does religion distract the poor? Income and issue voting around the world. *Comparative Political Studies, 41,* 437–476.

Del Giudice, M., Booth, T., & Irwing, P. (2012). The distance between Mars and Venus: Measuring global sex differences in personality. *PLOS ONE, 7*(1), e29265.

Demerath, J. (1995). Rational paradigms, a-rational religion and the debate over secularization. *Journal for the Scientific Study of Religion, 34,* 105–112.

Demertzi, A., Lie, C., Ledoux, D., Bruno, M.-A., Sharpe, M., Laureys, S., & Zeman, A. (2009). Dualism persists in the science of mind. *Annals of the New York Academy of Sciences, 1157,* 1–9.

Demoulin, S., Saroglou, V., & Van Pachterbeke, M. (2008). Infra-humanizing others, supra-humanizing gods: The emotional hierarchy. *Social Cognition, 26,* 235–247.

Dennett, D. C. (1989). *The Intentional Stance.* Cambridge, MA: MIT Press.

Denniston, G. C., Grassivaro Gallo, P., Hodges, F. M., Milos, M. F., & Viviani, F. (Eds.). (2006). *Bodily Integrity and the Politics of Circumcision: Culture, Controversy, and Change.* New York: Springer.

Depression Guideline Panel (1993). *Depression in Primary Care: Vol. 1. Diagnosis and Detection.* Rockville, MD: Department of Health and Human Services.

De Roos, S. A., Idedema, J., & Miedma, S. (2001). Attachment, working models of self and others, and God concept in kindergarten. *Journal for the Scientific Study of Religion, 40,* 607–618.

De Roos, S. A., Idedema, J., & Miedma, S. (2004). Influence of maternal denomination, God concepts, and child-rearing practices on young children's God concepts. *Journal for the Scientific Study of Religion, 43,* 519–535.

Dervic, K., Oquendo, M. A., Grunebaum, M. F., Ellis, S., Burke, A. K., & Mann, J. J. (2004). Religious affiliation and suicide attempts. *The American Journal of Psychiatry, 161,* 2303–2308.

De Tocqueville, A. (1835/1994). *Democracy in America.* London: Fontana.

Deutsch, A. (1975). Observations on a sidewalk ashram. *Archives of General Psychiatry, 32,* 166–175.

Devinsky, O. (2003). Religious experiences and epilepsy. *Epilepsy & Behavior, 4,* 76–77.

Devinsky, O., & Lai, G. (2008). Spirituality and religion in epilepsy. *Epilepsy & Behavior, 12,* 636–643.

Dewhurst, K., & Beard, A. W. (1970). Sudden religious conversions in temporal lobe epilepsy. *British Journal of Psychiatry, 117,* 497–507.

Dickie, J. R., Eshleman, A. K., Merasco, D. M., Shepard, A., Vander Wilt, M., & Johnson, M. (1997). Parent-child relationships and children's images of God. *Journal for the Scientific Study of Religion, 36,* 25–43.

Dickie, J. R., Lindsey V., Ajega, J. R. Kobylak, K., & Nixon, M. (2006). Mother, father, and self: Sources of young adults' God concepts. *Journal for the Scientific Study of Religion, 45,* 57–71.

Dickinson, G. E. (2012). Diversity in death: Body disposition and memorialization. *Illness, Crisis & Loss, 20,* 141–158.

Diener, E., & Clifton, D. (2002). Life satisfaction and religiosity in broad probability samples. *Psychological Inquiry, 13,* 206–209.

254 References

Diener, E., Kahneman, D., & Helliwell, J. (2010). *International Differences in Well-Being*. New York: Oxford University Press.

Diener, E., Tay, L., & Myers, D. G. (2011). The religion paradox: If religion makes people happy, why are so many dropping out? *Journal of Personality and Social Psychology, 101,* 1278–1290.

Diesendruck, G., & haLevi, H. (2006). The role of language, appearance, and culture in children's social category-based induction. *Child Development, 77,* 539–553.

Dijksterhuis, A., Preston, J., Wegner, D. M., & Aarts, H. (2008). Effects of subliminal priming of self and God on self-attribution of authorship for events. *Journal of Experimental Social Psychology, 44,* 2–9.

Dittes, J. E. (1969). Psychology of religion. In G. Lindzey, & E. Aronson (Eds.), *The Handbook of Social Psychology*. Reading, MA: Addison-Wesley.

Dodds, E. R. (1951). *The Greeks and the Irrational*. Berkeley: University of California Press.

Doering, S., Muller, E., Kopche, W., Pietzcher, A., Gaebel, W., Linden, M., Müller, P., Müller-Spahn, F., Tegeler, J., & Schüssler, G. (1998). Predictors of relapse and rehospitalization in schizophrenia and schizoaffective disorder. *Schizophrenia Bulletin, 24,* 87–98.

Dogan, M. (2002). Accelerated decline of religious beliefs in Europe. *Comparative Sociology, 1,* 127–149.

Donahue, M. J., & Benson, P. L. (1995). Religion and the well-being of adolescents. *Journal of Social Issues, 51,* 145–160.

Donahue, M. J., & Nielsen, M. E. (2005). Religion, attitudes, and social behavior. In R. F. Paloutzian, & C. L. Park (Eds.), *Handbook of the Psychology of Religion and Spirituality* (pp. 274–291). New York: Guilford.

Dossey, L. (2000). Prayer and medical science: A commentary on the prayer study by Harris et al. and a response to critics. *Archives of Internal Medicine, 160,* 1735–1737.

Dossey, L., & Hufford, D. J. (2005). Are prayer experiments legitimate?: Twenty criticisms. *EXPLORE: The Journal of Science and Healing, 1,* 109–117.

Dostoyevsky, F. (1880/1999). *The Brothers Karamazov*. New York: Penguin Group USA.

Douvan, E., & Adelson, J. (1966). *The Adolescent Experience*. New York: Wiley.

Downton, J. V. Jr. (1980). An evolutionary theory of spiritual conversion and commitment: The case of Divine Light Mission. *Journal for the Scientific Study of Religion, 19,* 381–396.

Driskell, R. L., & Lyon, L. (2011). Assessing the role of religious beliefs on secular and spiritual behavior. *Review of Religious Research, 52,* 386–404.

Dundes, A. (1981). The hero pattern and the life of Jesus. *Psychoanalytic Study of Society, 9,* 49–84.

Dundes, A. (1991). The ritual murder or blood libel legend: A study of anti-Semitic victimization through projective inversion. In A. Dundes (Ed.), *The Blood Libel Legend: A Casebook in Anti-Semitic Folklore* (pp. 336–367). Madison: University of Wisconsin Press.

Dunham, Y., & Emory, J. (2014). Of affect and ambiguity: The emergence of preference for arbitrary ingroups. *Journal of Social Issues, 70,* 81–98.

Dunham, Y., Baron, A. S., & Carey, S. (2011). Consequences of "minimal" group affiliations in childhood. *Child Development, 82,* 793–811.

Dunham, Y., Srinivasan, M., Dotsch, R., & Barner, D. (2013). Religion insulates ingroup evaluations: the development of intergroup attitudes in India. *Developmental Science,* 1–9.

Durante, K. M., Rae, A., & Griskevicius, V. (2013). The fluctuating female vote: Politics, religion, and the ovulatory cycle. *Psychological Science, 24,* 1007–1016.

Duriez, B. (2004). Taking a closer look at the religion-empathy relationship: Are religious people nicer people? *Mental Health, Religion & Culture, 7,* 249–254.

Duriez, B., Soenens, B., & Beyers, W. (2004). Personality, identity styles, and religiosity: An integrative study among late adolescents in Flanders (Belgium). *Journal of Personality, 72*, 877–908.

Durkheim, É. (1893/1964). *The Division of Labor in Society*. New York: The Free Press.

Durkheim, É. (1912/1995). *The Elementary Forms of Religious Life*. New York: The Free Press.

Duschinsky, R. (2012). Fundamentalism and the changing religious field. *Social Compass, 59*, 21–32.

Eagle, D. E. (2011). Changing patterns of attendance at religious services in Canada, 1986–2008. *Journal for the Scientific Study of Religion, 50*, 187–200.

Eagly, A. H. (1978). Sex differences in influenceability. *Psychological Bulletin, 85*, 86–116.

Eagly, A. H. (1995). The science and politics of comparing women and men. *American Psychologist, 50*, 145–158.

Earle, J. R., Knudsen, D. D., & Shriver, D. W., Jr. (1976). *Spindles and Spires. A Re-study of Religion and Social Change in Gastonia*. Atlanta: John Knox Press.

Easton, L., & Guddat, K. (Eds.) (1967). *The Writings of Young Marx*. Garden City, NY: Doubleday.

Eckel, C. C., & Grossman, P. J. (2004). Giving to secular causes by the religious and nonreligious: An experimental test of the responsiveness of giving to subsidies. *Nonprofit and Voluntary Sector Quarterly, 33*, 271–289.

Ecklund, E. H., & Park, J. Z. (2009). Conflict between religion and science among academic scientists? *Journal for the Scientific Study of Religion, 48*, 276–292.

Ecklund, E. H., & Scheitle, C. P. (2007). Religion among academic scientists: Distinctions, disciplines, and demographics. *Social Problems, 54*, 289–307.

Ecklund, E. H., Park, J. Z., & Veliz, P. T. (2008). Secularization and religious change among elite scientists: A cross-cohort comparison. *Social Forces, 86*, 805–840.

Edgell, P., & Tranby, E. P. (2007). Religious influences on understandings of racial inequality in the United States. *Social Problems, 54*, 263–288.

Edgell, P., Gerteis, J., & Hartmann, D. (2006). Atheists as "other": Moral boundaries and cultural membership in American society. *American Sociological Review, 71*, 211–234.

Edmondson, D., & Park, C. (2009). Shifting foundations: Religious belief change and adjustment in college students. *Mental Health, Religion & Culture, 12*, 289–302.

Eibl-Eibesfeldt, I. (1989). *Human Ethology*. New York: Aldine de Gruyter.

Eichhorn, J. (2011). Happiness for believers? Contextualizing the effects of religiosity on life-satisfaction. *European Sociological Review, 28*, 583–593.

Eiduson, B. (1962). *Scientists: Their Psychological World*. New York: Basic Books.

Eiduson, B., & Beckman, L. (Eds.). (1973). *Science as a Career Choice: Theoretical and Empirical Studies*. New York: The Russell Sage Foundation.

Eisinga, R., Konig, R., & Scheepers, P. (1995). Orthodox religious beliefs and anti-Semitism: A replication of Glock and Stark in the Netherlands. *Journal for the Scientific Study of Religion, 34*, 214–223.

Eister, A. W. (1950). *Drawing-Room Conversation: A Sociological Account of the Oxford Group Movement*. Durham, NC: Duke University Press.

Eldershaw, L. P. (2007). Collective identity and the post-charismatic fate of Shambhala International. *Nova Religio: The Journal of Alternative and Emergent Religions, 10*, 72–102.

Eliade, M. (1965). *Rites and Symbols of Initiation*. New York: Harper & Row.

Elkin, A. P. (1938). *The Australian Aborigines*. Sydney: Angus and Robertson.

Ellenberger, H. F. (1970). *The Discovery of the Unconscious: The History and Evolution of Dynamic Psychiatry*. New York: Basic Books.

Ellison, C. G. (1991). Religious involvement and subjective well-being. *Journal of Health and Social Behavior, 32*, 80–99.

Ellison, C. G. (1996). Conservative Protestantism and the corporal punishment of children: Clarifying the issues. *Journal for the Scientific Study of Religion, 35,* 1–16.

Ellison, C. G., & Anderson, K. L. (2001). Religious involvement and domestic violence among U.S. couples. *Journal for the Scientific Study of Religion, 40,* 269–287.

Ellison, C. G., & Bartkowski, J. P. (1995). "Babies were being beaten." In S. A. Wright (Ed.), *Armageddon in Waco* (pp. 111–149). Chicago: University of Chicago Press.

Ellison, C. G., & Fan, D. (2008). Daily spiritual experiences and psychological well-being among U.S. adults. *Social Indicators Research, 88,* 247–271.

Ellison, C. G., & George, L. K. (1993). Religious involvement, social ties, and social support in a southeastern community. *Journal for the Scientific Study of Religion, 33,* 46–61.

Ellison, C. G., & Levin, J. S. (1998). The religion-health connection: Evidence, theory, and future directions. *Health Education & Behavior, 25,* 700–720.

Ellison, C. G., & Sherkat, D. E. (1993). Obedience and autonomy: Religion and parental values reconsidered. *Journal for the Scientific Study of Religion, 32,* 313–329.

Ellison, C. G., Bartkowski, J. P., & Anderson, K. L. (1999). Are there religious variations in domestic violence? *Journal of Family Issues, 20,* 87–133.

Ellison, C. G., Bartkowski, J. P., & Segal, M. L. (1996). Do conservative Protestant parents spank more often? Further evidence from the national survey of families and households. *Social Science Quarterly, 77,* 663–673.

Ellison, C. G., Bradshaw, M., Kuyel, N., & Marcum, J. P. (2012). Attachment to God, stressful life events, and changes in psychological distress. *Review of Religious Research, 53,* 493–511.

Ellison, C. G., Burr, J. A., & McCall, P. L. (1997). Religious homogeneity and metropolitan suicide rates. *Social Forces, 76,* 273–299.

Ellwood, R. (1979). *Alternative Altars: Unconventional and Eastern Spirituality in America.* Chicago: University of Chicago Press.

Emmons, C. F., & Sobal, J. (1981). Paranormal beliefs: Testing the marginality hypothesis. *Sociological Focus, 14,* 49–56.

Enstrom, J. E., & Breslow, L. (2008). Lifestyle and reduced mortality among active California Mormons, 1980–2004. *Preventive Medicine, 46,* 133–136.

Epley, N., Waytz, A., & Cacioppo, J. T. (2007). On seeing human: A three-factor theory of anthropomorphism. *Psychological Review, 114,* 864–886.

Epley, N., Akalis, S., Waytz, A., & Cacioppo, J. T. (2008). Creating social connection through inferential reproduction: Loneliness and perceived agency in gadgets, gods, and greyhounds. *Psychological Science, 19,* 114–120.

Epley, N., Converse, B. A., Delbosc, A., Monteleone, G. A., & Cacioppo, J. T. (2009). Believers' estimates of God's beliefs are more egocentric than estimates of other people's beliefs. *Proceedings of the National Academy of Sciences of the United States of America, 106,* 21533–21538.

Erickson, J. A. (1992). Adolescent religious development and commitment: A structural equation model of the role of family, peer group, and educational influences. *Journal for the Scientific Study of Religion, 31,* 131–152.

Erikson, E. H. (1958). *Young Man Luther.* New York: Norton.

Erikson, E. H. (1963). *Childhood and Society* (2nd ed.). New York: Norton.

Erikson, E. H. (1964). Identity and uprootedness in our time. In *Insight and Responsibility: Lectures on the Ethical Implications of Psychoanalytic Insight.* New York: Norton.

Erikson, E. H. (1968). *Identity: Youth and Crisis.* New York: Norton.

Erikson, E. H. (1975). *Life History and the Historical Moment.* New York: Norton.

Eriksson, K., & Funcke, A. (2014). Religiosity and the better-than-average effect. *Social Psychological and Personality Science, 5,* 76–83.

Eshuys, D., & Smallbone, S. (2006). Religious affiliations among adult sexual offenders. *Sex Abuse, 18*, 279–288.

Ester, P., Halman, L., & de Moor, R. A. (Eds.). (1994). *The Individualizing Society: Value Change in Europe and North America.* Tilburg: Tilburg University Press.

Etlin, R. A. (1986). *The Architecture of Death: The Transformation of the Cemetery in Eighteenth-Century Paris.* Cambridge, MA: MIT Press.

European Union Eurobarometer (2012). See http://ec.europa.eu/public_opinion/archives/eb/eb74/eb74_publ_en.pdf at page.

Evans, C. J. (2008). *The Burden of Black Religion.* New York: Oxford University Press.

Evans, G., & Northmore-Ball, K. (2012). The limits of secularization? The resurgence of orthodoxy in post-Soviet Russia. *Journal for the Scientific Study of Religion, 51*, 795–808.

Evans, J. H. (2010). *Contested Reproduction: Genetic Technologies, Religion, and Public Debate.* Chicago: University of Chicago Press.

Evans, T. D., Cullen, F. T., Dunaway, R. G., & Burton, V. S. (1995). Religion and crime re-examined: the impact of religion, secular controls, and social ecology on adult criminality. *Criminology, 33*, 195–224.

Evans-Pritchard, E. E. (1970). *Nuer Religion.* Oxford: Clarendon Press.

Everhart, D. E., Shucard, J. L., Quatrin, T., & Shucard, D. W. (2001). Sex-related differences in ERPs, face recognition, and facial affect processing in prepubertal children. *Neuropsychology, 15*, 329–341.

Exline, J. J., Yali, A. M., & Sanderson, W. C. (2000). Guilt, discord, and alienation: The role of religious strain in depression and suicidality. *Journal of Clinical Psychology, 56*, 1481–1496.

Faber, M. D. (2004). *The Psychological Roots of Religious Belief: Searching for Angels and the Parent-God.* Amherst, NY: Prometheus.

Farias, M., Claridge, G., & Lalljee, M. (2005). Personality and cognitive predictors of New Age practices and beliefs. *Personality and Individual Differences, 39*, 979–989.

Farrell, B. A. (1955). Psychological theory and the belief in God. *International Journal of Psycho-Analysis, 36*, 187–204.

Fauset, A. F. (1944). *Black Gods of the Metropolis.* Philadelphia: University of Pennsylvania Press.

Fehr, E., Fischbacher, U., Schupp, J., von Rosenbladt, B., & Wagner, G. G. (2002). A nationwide laboratory examining trust and trustworthiness by integrating behavioural experiments into representative surveys. *Schmollers Jahrbuch, 122*, 519–542.

Feigelman, W., Gorman, B. S., & Varacalli, J. A. (1992). Americans who give up religion. *Sociology and Social Research, 76*, 138–144.

Feingold, A. (1994). Gender differences in personality: A meta-analysis. *Psychological Bulletin, 104*, 429–456.

Feist, G. J. (2006). *The Psychology of Science and the Origins of the Scientific Mind.* New Haven, CT: Yale University Press.

Feist, G. J., & Gorman, M. E. (1998). The psychology of science: Review and integration of a nascent discipline. *Review of General Psychology, 2*, 3–47.

Fergusson, D. M., Horwood, L. J., Kershaw, K. L., & Shannon, F. T. (1986). Factors associated with reports of wife assault in New Zealand. *Journal of Marriage and the Family, 48*, 407–412.

Fernandez, J. W. (1982). *Bwiti: An Ethnography of the Religious Imagination in Africa.* Princeton: Princeton University Press.

Ferraro, K. F., & Kelley-Moore, J. A. (2000). Religious consolation among men and women: Do health problems spur seeking? *Journal for the Scientific Study of Religion, 39*, 220–234.

258 References

Ferriman, K., Lubinski, D., & Benbow, C. P. (2009). Work preferences, life values, and personal views of top math/science graduate students and the profoundly gifted: Developmental changes and sex differences during emerging adulthood and parenthood. *Journal of Personality and Social Psychology, 97*, 517–532.

Ferriss, A. L. (2002). Religion and quality of life. *Journal of Happiness Studies, 3*, 199–215.

Fershtman, C., Gneezy, U., & Verboven, F. (2005). Discrimination and nepotism: The efficiency of the anonymity rule. *Journal of Legal Studies, 34*, 371–394.

Festinger, L., Riecken, H. W., & Schachter, S. (1956). *When Prophecy Fails: A Social and Psychological Study of a Modern Group that Predicted the Destruction of the World.* Minneapolis, MN: University of Minnesota Press.

Fhima, C. (2002). Max Jacob ou la symbiose des identités paradoxales. *Archives juives, 35*, 77–101.

Fichter, J. H. (1973). *Sociology* (2nd ed.). Chicago: University of Chicago Press.

Field, A. (2001). *Altruistically Inclined? The Behavioral Sciences, Evolutionary Theory, and The Origins of Reciprocity.* Ann Arbor, MI: University of Michigan Press.

Fielder, R. L., Walsh, J. L., Carey, K. B., & Carey, M. P. (2013). Predictors of sexual hookups: a theory-based, prospective study of first-year college women. *Archives of Sexual Behavior, 42*, 1425–1441.

Fincher, C. L., & Thornhill, R. (2012). Parasite-stress promotes in-group assortative sociality: The cases of strong family ties and heightened religiosity. *Behavioral and Brain Sciences, 35*, 61–79.

Fink, B., Manning, J. T., & Neave, N. (2004). Second to fourth digit ratio and the big five personality factors. *Personality and Individual Differences, 37*, 495–503.

Finke, R., & Adamczyk, A. (2008). Cross-national moral beliefs: The influence of national religious context. *Sociological Quarterly, 49*, 617–652.

Finkelstein, M. J. (1984). *The American Academic Profession: A Synthesis of Social Scientific Inquiry Since World War II.* Columbus: Ohio State University Press.

Firth, R. W. (1981). *Elements of Social Organization.* London: Routledge.

Firth, R. W. (2004). *Social Change in Tikopia.* London: Routledge.

Fisher, H. (2004). *Why We Love: The Nature and Chemistry of Romantic Love.* New York: Henry Holt.

Fishman, A. (1992). *Judaism and Modernization on the Religious Kibbutz.* Cambridge: Cambridge University Press.

Fishman, A., & Goldschmidt, Y. (1990). The Orthodox kibbutzim and economic success. *Journal for the Scientific Study of Religion, 29*, 505–511.

Fiske, A. P., & Haslam, N. (1997). Is obsessive-compulsive disorder a pathology of the human disposition to perform socially meaningful rituals? Evidence of similar content. *Journal of Nervous and Mental Disease, 185*, 211–222.

Fiske, S. T., & Taylor, S. E. (2013). *Social Cognition.* Thousand Oaks, CA: Sage.

Flannelly, K. J., Koenig, H. G., Ellison, C. G., & Galek, K. C. (2006). Belief in an afterlife and mental health: findings from a national survey. *Journal of Nervous and Mental Disease, 194*, 524–529.

Flor, D. L., & Knapp, N. F. (2001). Transmission and transaction: Predicting adolescents' internalization of parental religious values. *Journal of Family Psychology, 15*, 627–645.

Flora, C. B. (1973). Social dislocation and pentecostalism: A multivariate analysis. *Sociological Analysis, 34*, 296–307.

Fogarty, R. S. (1995). An age of wisdom, an age of foolishness. In S. A. Wright (Ed.), *Armageddon in Waco.* Chicago: University of Chicago Press.

Folkman, S., & Lazarus, R. S. (1980). An analysis of coping behavior in a middle-aged community sample. *Journal of Health and Social Behavior, 21*, 219–239.

References **259**

Fonnebo, V. (1992). Mortality in Norwegian SDAs 1962–1986, *Journal of Clinical Epidemiology, 45*, 157–167.

Forster, P. G. (1998). Religion, magic, witchcraft, and AIDS in Malawi. *Anthropos, 93*, 537–545.

Fortes, M. (1959). *Oedipus and Job in West African Religion.* Cambridge: Cambridge University Press.

Fortes, M. (1961). Pietas in Ancestor Worship. *The Journal of the Royal Anthropological Institute of Great Britain and Ireland, 91*, 166–191.

Fortes, M. (1987). *Religion, Morality and the Person: Essays on Tallensi Religion.* Cambridge: Cambridge University Press.

Foster, G. M. (1976). Disease etiologies in non-Western medical systems. *American Anthropologist, 78*, 773–782.

Francis, L. J. (1991). The personality characteristics of Anglican ordinands: feminine men and masculine women? *Personality and Individual Differences, 12*, 1133–1140.

Francis, L. J. (1997). The psychology of gender differences in religion: a review of empirical research. *Religion, 27*, 81–96.

Francis, L. J., & Wilcox, C. (1996). Religion and gender orientation. *Personality and Individual Differences, 15*, 43–59.

Francis, L. J., & Wilcox, C. (1998). Religiosity and femininity: Do women really hold a more positive attitude toward Christianity? *Journal for the Scientific Study of Religion, 37*, 462–469.

Francis, L. J., Jones, S. H., Jackson, C. J., & Robbins, M. (2001). The feminine personality profile of male Anglican clergy in Britain and Ireland: A study employing the Eysenck Personality Profiler. *Review of Religious Research, 43,* 14–23.

Francis, L. J., Williams, E., & Robbins, M. (2009). Christianity, paranormal belief and personality: A study among 13- to 16-year-old pupils in England and Wales. *Archive for the Psychology of Religion, 31*, 337–344.

Francis, L. J., Flere, S., Klanjšek, R., Williams, E., & Robbins, M. (2013). Attitude towards Christianity and New Age beliefs among undergraduate students in Slovenia: A study in implicit religion. *Mental Health, Religion & Culture, 16*, 953–963.

Frank, J. D., & Frank, J. B. (1991). *Persuasion and Healing: A Comparative Study of Psychotherapy.* Baltimore: The Johns Hopkins University Press.

Frank, N. (1991). *In the Shadow of the Reich.* New York: Knopf.

Frankenberry, N. K. (2002). Preface. In N. K. Frankenberry (Ed.), *Radical Interpretation in Religion* (pp. xiii–xv). Cambridge: Cambridge University Press.

Franklin, M. D., Sclundt, D. J., McClellan, L., Kinebrew, T., Sheats, J., Belue, R., Brown, A., Smikes, D., Patel, K., & Hargreaves, M. (2007). Religious fatalism and its association with health behaviors and outcomes. *American Journal of Health Behavior, 31*(6), 563–572.

Frazer, J. G. (1922). *The Golden Bough.* New York: Macmillan.

Frazer, J. G. (1933–1936). *The Fear of the Dead in Primitive Religion.* London: Macmillan.

French, D. C., Eisenberg, N., Vaughan, J., Purwono, U., & Suryanti, T. A. (2008). Religious involvement and the social competence and adjustment of Indonesian Muslim adolescents. *Developmental Psychology, 44*, 597–611.

Freud, S. (1901). The psychopathology of everyday life. In *The Standard Edition of the Complete Psychological Writings of Sigmund Freud, 6*, 1–290. London: The Hogarth Press.

Freud, S. (1907). Obsessive actions and religious practices. In *The Standard Edition of the Complete Psychological Works of Sigmund Freud, 9*, 116–129. London: The Hogarth Press.

Freud, S. (1910). Leonardo da Vinci and a memory of his childhood. In *The Standard Edition of the Complete Psychological Works of Sigmund Freud, 11*, 59–137. London: The Hogarth Press.

Freud, S. (1913a). Totem and taboo. In *The Standard Edition of the Complete Psychological Works of Sigmund Freud*, *13*, 1–164. London: The Hogarth Press.

Freud, S. (1913b). The claims of psycho-analysis to scientific interest. In *The Standard Edition of the Complete Psychological Works of Sigmund Freud*, *8*, 165–192. London: The Hogarth Press.

Freud, S. (1915). Thoughts for the times on war and death. In *The Standard Edition of the Complete Psychological Works of Sigmund Freud*, *14*, 274–301. London: The Hogarth Press.

Freud, S. (1915–1916). Introductory lectures on psycho-analysis (Parts I and II). In *The Standard Edition of the Complete Psychological Works of Sigmund Freud*, *15*, 1–390. London: The Hogarth Press.

Freud, S. (1919). The uncanny. In *The Standard Edition of the Complete Psychological Works of Sigmund Freud*, *17*, 219–256. London: The Hogarth Press.

Freud, S. (1921). Group psychology and the analysis of the ego. In *The Standard Edition of the Complete Psychological Works of Sigmund Freud*, *18*, 65–144. London: The Hogarth Press.

Freud, S. (1927). The future of an illusion. In *The Standard Edition of the Complete Psychological Works of Sigmund Freud*, *21*, 3–56. London: The Hogarth Press.

Freud, S. (1928). A religious experience. In *The Standard Edition of the Complete Psychological Work of Sigmund Freud*, *21*, 167–174. London: The Hogarth Press.

Freud, S. (1930). Civilization and its discontents. In *The Standard Edition of the Complete Psychological Works of Sigmund Freud*, *21*, 57–146. London: The Hogarth Press.

Freud, S. (1933). New introductory lectures on psychoanalysis. In *The Standard Edition of the Complete Psychological Works of Sigmund Freud*, *22*, 1–182. London: The Hogarth Press.

Freud, S. (1939). Moses and monotheism. In *The Standard Edition of the Complete Psychological Works of Sigmund Freud*, *23*, 1–138. London: The Hogarth Press.

Friedman, M., & Rholes, W. S. (2007). Successfully challenging fundamentalist beliefs results in increased death awareness. *Journal of Experimental Social Psychology*, *43*, 794–801.

Froese, P. (2005). Secular Czechs and devout Slovaks: Explaining religious differences. *Review of Religious Research*, *46*, 269–283.

Froese, P., & Bader, C. (2008). Unraveling religious worldviews: The relationship between images of God and political ideology in a cross-cultural analysis. *The Sociological Quarterly*, *49*, 689–718.

Froese, P., & Mencken, F. C. (2009). An American Holy War? The connection between religious ideology and neo-conservative Iraq War attitudes. *Social Science Quarterly*, *90*, 103–116.

Froese, P., Bader, C. D., & Smith, B. (2008). Political tolerance and God's wrath in the United States. *Sociology of Religion*, *69*, 29–44.

Fromm, F. (1961). *Marx's Concept of Man*. New York: Frederick Ungar.

Fuller, T. (2013). Extremism rises among Myanmar Buddhists. *The New York Times*, June 20, 2013, p. A1.

Fumagalli, M., Ferrucci, R., Mameli, F., Marceglia, S., Mrakic-Sposta, S., Zago, S., Lucchiari, C., Consonni, D., Nordio, F., Pravettoni, G., Cappa, S., & Priori, A. (2009). Gender-related differences in moral judgments. *Cognitive Processing*, *11*, 219–226.

Fumagalli, M., Vergari, M., Pasqualetti, P., Mameli, F., Ferrucci, R., Mrakic-Sposta, S., Zago, S., Sartori, G., Pravettoni, G., Barbieri, S., Cappa, S., & Priori, A. (2010). Brain switches utilitarian behavior: does gender make the difference? *PLOS ONE*, *5*(1), 1–9.

Funder, D. C. (2003). Why study religion? *Psychological Inquiry*, *13*, 213–214.

Funk, C. L., Smith, K. B., Alford, J. R., Hibbing, M. V., Eaton, N. R., Krueger, R. F., Eaves, L. J., & Hibbing, J. R. (2013). Genetic and environmental transmission of political orientations. *Political Psychology*, *34*, 805–819.

Furnham, A. (2003). Belief in a just world: Research progress over the past decade. *Personality and Individual Differences, 34,* 795–817.

Furnham, A., & Ribchester, T. (1995). Tolerance of ambiguity: A review of the concept, its measurement and applications. *Current Psychology, 14,* 179–199.

Furrow, J. L., King, P. E., & White, K. (2004). Religion and positive youth development: Identity, meaning, and pro-social concerns. *Applied Developmental Science, 8,* 17–26.

Furseth, I. (2005). From 'everything has a meaning' to 'I want to believe in something': religious change between two generations of women in Norway. *Social Compass, 52,* 157–168.

Gabriel, S., & Gardner, W. L. (1999). Are there 'his' and 'hers' types of interdependence? The implications of gender differences in collective versus relational interdependence for affect, behavior, and cognition. *Journal of Personality and Social Psychology, 77,* 642–655.

Galanter, M. (1989). *Cults, Faith Healing, and Coercion.* New York: Oxford University Press.

Galanter, M., Larson, D. B., & Rubenstone, E. (1991). Christian psychiatry: The impact of evangelical belief on clinical practice. *American Journal of Psychiatry, 148,* 90–95.

Galek, K., Krause, N., Ellison, C. G., Kudler, T., & Flannelly, K. J. (2007). Religious doubt and mental health across the lifespan. *Journal of Adult Development, 14,* 16–25.

Galen, L. W. (2012). Does religious belief promote prosociality? A critical examination. *Psychological Bulletin, 138,* 876–906.

Galen, L. W., & Kloet, J. (2011). Personality and social integration factors distinguishing non-religious from religious groups: The importance of controlling for attendance and demographics. *Archive for the Psychology of Religion, 33,* 205–228.

Galen, L. W., & Miller, T. R. (2011). Perceived deservingness of outcomes as a function of religious fundamentalism and target responsibility. *Journal of Applied Social Psychology, 41,* 2144–2164.

Gallenmore, J .L. Jr., Wilson, W. P., & Rhoads, J. M. (1969). The religious life of patients with affective disorders. *Diseases of the Nervous System, 30,* 483–487.

Gallup, G., & Lindsay, D. M. (1999). *Surveying the Religious Landscape: Trends in U.S. Beliefs.* Harrisburg, PA: Morehouse Publishing.

Galton, F. (1872). Statistical inquiries into the efficacy of prayer. *Fortnightly Review, 12,* 125–135.

Gans, H. J. (1972). The positive functions of poverty. *The American Journal of Sociology, 78,* 275–289.

Garces-Foley, K., & Holcomb, J. S. (2006). Contemporary American funerals: Personalizing tradition. In K. Garces-Foley (Ed.), *Death and Religion in a Changing World* (pp. 207–227). New York and London: M. E. Sharpe.

Garner, R. (2000). Safe sects? Dynamic religion and AIDS in South Africa. *The Journal of Modern African Studies, 38,* 41–69.

Garrison, K. C. (1965). *Psychology of Adolescence.* Englewood Cliffs, NJ: Prentice-Hall.

Gay, D. A., & Ellison, C. G. (1993). Religious subcultures and political tolerance: Do denominations still matter? *Review of Religious Research, 34,* 311–332.

Gay, V. P. (1979). *Freud on Ritual: Reconstruction and Critique.* Atlanta, GA: American Academy of Religion.

Gearing, R. E., Alonzo, D., Smolak, A., McHuge, K., Harmon, S., & Baldwin, S. (2011). Association of religion with delusions and hallucinations in the context of schizophrenia: Implications for engagement and adherence. *Schizophrenia Research, 126,* 150–163.

Geary, D. C. (1998). *Male, Female: The Evolution of Human Sex Differences.* Washington, DC: American Psychological Association.

Gebauer, J. E., & Maio, G. R. (2012). The need to belong can motivate belief in God. *Journal of Personality, 80,* 466–501.

262 References

Gebauer, J. E., Paulhus, D. L., & Neberich, W. (2013). Big Two personality and religiosity across cultures: Communals as religious conformists and agentics as religious contrarians. *Social Psychological and Personality Science, 4*, 21–30.

Gebauer, J. E., Sedikides, C., & Neberich, W. (2012). Religiosity, social self-esteem, and psychological adjustment: On the cross-cultural specificity of the psychological benefits of religiosity. *Psychological Science, 23*, 158–160.

Gebauer, J. E., Nehrlich, A. D., Sedikides, C., & Neberich, W. (2013). The psychological benefits of income are contingent on individual-level and culture-level religiosity. *Social Psychological and Personality Science, 4*, 569–578.

Gee, G. K. (1995). Geography, nationality, and religion in Ukraine. *Journal for the Scientific Study of Religion, 34*, 383–390.

Geertz, A. W., & Markússon, G. I. (2010). Religion is natural, atheism is not: On why everybody is both right and wrong. *Religion, 40*, 152–165.

Geertz, C. (1960). *The Religion of Java*. Chicago: University of Chicago Press.

Geertz, C. (1966). Religion as a cultural system. In M. Banton (Ed.), *Anthropological Approaches to the Study of Religion* (pp. 1–46). London: Tavistock.

Geertz, C. (1973). *The Interpretation of Cultures: Selected Essays*. New York: Basic Books.

Gellner, E. (1974). *Legitimation of Belief*. Cambridge: Cambridge University Press.

George, L. K., Ellison, C. G., & Larson, D. B. (2002). Explaining the relationship between religious involvement and health. *Psychological Inquiry, 13*, 190–200.

George, M. S., Ketter, T. A., Parekh, P. I., Herscovitch, P., & Post, R. M. (1996). Gender differences in regional cerebral blood flow during transient self-induced sadness or happiness. *Biological Psychiatry, 40*, 859–871.

Gerber, A. S., Huber, G. A., Doherty, D., Dowling, C. M., & Ha, S. E. (2010). Personality and political attitudes: Relationships across issue domains and political contexts. *American Political Science Review, 104*, 111–133.

Gershoff, E. T., Miller, P. C., & Holden, G. W. (1999). Parenting influences from the pulpit: Religious affiliation as a determinant of parental corporal punishment. *Journal of Family Psychology, 13*, 307–320.

Gervais, W. M., & Henrich, J. (2010). The Zeus problem: Why representational content biases cannot explain faith in gods. *Journal of Cognition and Culture, 10*, 383–389.

Gervais, W. M., & Norenzayan, A. (2012a). Like a camera in the sky? Thinking about God increases public self-awareness and socially desirable responding. *Journal of Experimental Social Psychology, 48*, 298–302.

Gervais, W. M., & Norenzayan, A. (2012b). Analytic thinking promotes religious disbelief. *Science, 336*, 493–496.

Gervais, W. M., Shariff, A. F., & Norenzayan, A. (2011). Do you believe in atheists? Distrust is central to anti-atheist prejudice. *Journal of Personality and Social Psychology, 101*, 1189–1206.

Gervais, W. M., Willard, A., Norenzayan, A., & Henrich, J. (2011). The cultural transmission of faith: Why natural intuitions and memory biases are necessary, but insufficient, to explain religious belief. *Religion, 41*, 389–410.

Gibson-Cline, J. (Ed.) (1996). *Adolescence: From Crisis to Coping – A Thirteen Nation Study*. Oxford: Butterworth-Heinemann.

Gilbert, D. T. (1991). How mental systems believe. *American Psychologist, 46*, 107–119.

Gilbert, D. T., Krull, D. S., & Malone, P. S. (1990). Unbelieving the unbelievable: some problems in the rejection of false information. *Journal of Personality and Social Psychology, 59*, 601–613.

Gilbert, D. T., Tafarodi, R. W., & Malone, P. S. (1993). You can't not believe everything you read. *Journal of Personality and Social Psychology, 65*, 221–233.

References **263**

Gilbert, D. T., Brown, R., Pinel, E., & Wilson, T. (2000). The illusion of external agency. *Journal of Personality and Social Psychology, 79*, 690–700.

Gilbert, G. M. (1995). *Nuremberg Diary*. New York: De Capo Press.

Gill, A., & Lundsgaarde, E. (2004). State welfare spending and religiosity: A cross-national analysis. *Rationality and Society, 16*, 399–436.

Gillin, J. L. (1910). A contribution to the sociology of sects. *American Journal of Sociology, 16*, 236–252.

Gillings, V., & Joseph, S. (1996). Religiosity and social desirability: impression management and self-deceptive positivity. *Personality and Individual Differences, 21*, 1047–1050.

Gillum, R. F., & Holt, C. L. (2010). Associations between religious involvement and behavioral risk factors for HIV/AIDS in American women and men in a national health survey. *Annals of Behavioral Medicine, 40*, 284–293.

Gimenez-Dasi, M., Guerrero, S., & Harris, P. L. (2005). Intimations of omniscience and immortality in early childhood. *European Journal of Developmental Psychology, 2*, 285–297.

Ginges, J., Hansen, I., & Norenzayan, A. (2009). Religion and support for suicide attacks. *Psychological Science, 20*, 224–230.

Glass, J., Bengtson, V. L., & Dunham, C. C. (1986). Attitude similarity in three-generation families: socialization, status inheritance, or reciprocal influence? *American Sociological Review, 51*, 685–698.

Glendinning, T. (2006). Religious involvement, conventional Christian, and unconventional nonmaterialist beliefs. *Journal for the Scientific Study of Religion, 45*, 585–595.

Glendinning, T., and Bruce, S. (2006). New ways of believing or belonging: is religion giving way to spirituality? *The British Journal of Sociology, 57*, 399–414.

Glik, D. C. (1986). Psychosocial wellness among spiritual healing participants. *Social Science and Medicine, 22*, 579–586.

Glock, C. Y. (1962). On the study of religious commitment. *Religious Education, 57*, S98–S109.

Glock, C. Y. (1964). The role of deprivation in the origin and evolution of religious groups. In R. Lee, & M. E. Marty (Eds.), *Religion and Social Conflict* (pp. 24–36). New York: Oxford University Press.

Glock, C. Y., & Stark, R. (1965). *Religion and Society in Tension*. Chicago: Rand McNally.

Glock, C. Y., & Stark, R. (1966). *Christian Beliefs and Anti-Semitism*. New York: Harper and Row.

Glock, C. Y., Ringer, B. R., & Babbie, E. R. (1967). *To Comfort and to Challenge: A Dilemma of the Contemporary Church*. Berkeley, CA: University of California Press.

Gluck, C. (1999). The killer and the pastor. *Time*, July 12, p. 24.

Goldschmidt, W. R. (1954). *Ways of Mankind: Thirteen Dramas of Peoples of the World and How They Live*. Boston: Beacon Press.

Goldsen, R. K., Rosenberg, M., Williams, R. M. Jr., & Suchman, E. A. (1960). *What College Students Think*. Princeton: Van Nostrand.

González, A. L. (2011). Measuring religiosity in a majority Muslim context: Gender, religious salience, and religious experience among Kuwaiti college students—A research note. *Journal for the Scientific Study of Religion, 50,* 339–350.

Goodenough, W. (1981). On describing religion in Truk: An anthropological dilemma. *Proceedings of the American Philosophical Society, 125,* 411–415.

Gorer, G. (1955). *Exploring English Character*. London: Cresset.

Gorin, S. S. (2010). Theory, measurement, and controversy in positive psychology, health psychology, and cancer: Basics and next steps. *Annals of Behavioral Medicine, 39*, 43–47.

Gorsuch, R. L., & Smith, C. S. (1983). Attributions of responsibility to God: An interaction of religious beliefs and outcomes. *Journal for the Scientific Study of Religion, 22*, 340–352.

264 References

Gottlieb, R. S. (2013). *Spirituality: What It Is and Why It Matters*. New York: Oxford University Press.

Gould, S. J., & Lewontin, R. C. (1979). The spandrels of San Marco and the Panglossian paradigm: A critique of the adaptationist programme. *Proceedings of the Royal Society London B, 1161,* 581–598.

Graffin, G. (2004). *Evolution, Monism, Atheism, and the Naturalistic World-View*. Ithaca, NY: Polypterus Press.

Graffin, G. W., & Provine, W. B. (2007). Macroscope: Evolution, religion and free will. *American Scientist, 95,* 294–297.

Gramzow, R. H., & Gaertner, L. (2005). Self-esteem and favoritism toward novel in-groups: The self as an evaluative base. *Journal of Personality and Social Psychology, 88,* 801–815.

Granger, M. D., & Price, G. N. (2007). The tree of science and original sin: Do Christian religious beliefs constrain the supply of scientists? *Journal of Socio-Economics, 36,* 144–160.

Granqvist, P. (2002). Attachment and religiosity in adolescence: Cross-sectional and longitudinal evaluations. *Personality and Social Psychology Bulletin, 28,* 260–270.

Granqvist, P., & Hagekull, B. (1999). Religiousness and perceived childhood attachment: Profiling socialized correspondence and emotional compensation. *Journal for the Scientific Study of Religion, 38,* 254–273.

Granqvist, P., & Hagekull, B. (2000). Religiosity, adult attachment, and why "singles" are more religious. *International Journal for the Psychology of Religion, 10,* 111–123.

Granqvist, P., & Hagekull, B. (2001). Seeking security in the New Age: On attachment and emotional compensation. *Journal for the Scientific Study of Religion, 40,* 527–545.

Granqvist, P., & Hagekull, B. (2003). Longitudinal predictions of religious change in adolescence: Contributions from the interaction of attachment and relationship status. *Journal of Social and Personal Relationships, 20,* 793–817.

Granqvist, P., & Kirkpatrick, L. A. (2004). Religious conversion and perceived childhood attachment: A meta-analysis. *The International Journal for Psychology of Religion, 14,* 223–250.

Granqvist, P., Ivarsson, T., Broberg, A. G., & Hagekull, B. (2007). Examining relations among attachment, religiosity, and new age spirituality using the Adult Attachment Interview. *Developmental Psychology, 43,* 590–601.

Granqvist, P., Mikulincer, M., & Shaver, P. R. (2010). Religion as attachment: Normative processes and individual differences. *Personality and Social Psychology, 14,* 49–60.

Grasmick, H. G., Bursik, R. J., & Kimpel, M. (1991). Protestant fundamentalism and attitudes toward corporal punishment for children. *Violence and Victims, 6,* 283–298.

Grasmick, H. G., Morgan, C. S., & Kennedy, M. B. (1992). Support for corporal punishment in the schools: A comparison of the effects of socioeconomic status and religion. *Social Science Quarterly, 73,* 177–187.

Gray, K., & Wegner, D. M. (2010). Blaming God for our pain: Human suffering and the divine mind. *Personality and Social Psychology Review, 14,* 7–16.

Gray, H. M., Gray, K., & Wegner, D. M. (2007). Dimensions of mind perception. *Science, 315,* 619.

Greeley, A. M. (1975). *The Sociology of the Paranormal*. London: Sage.

Greeley, A. M. (1987). Hallucinations among the widowed. *Sociology and Social Research, 71,* 258–265.

Greeley, A. M. (1988). Evidence that a maternal image of God correlates with liberal politics. *Sociology and Social Research, 72,* 150–154.

Greeley, A. M. (1989). *Religious Change in America*. Cambridge, MA: Harvard University Press.

Greeley, A. M. (1991). Religion and attitudes towards AIDS policy. *Sociology and Social Research, 75*, 126–132.

Greeley, A. M. (1993). Religion and attitudes toward the environment. *Journal for the Scientific Study of Religion, 32*, 19–28.

Greenaway, K. H., Louis, W. R., & Hornsey, M. J. (2013). Loss of control increases belief in precognition and belief in precognition increases control. *PLOS ONE, 8*(8), e71327.

Greenberg, J., Pyszczynski, T., & Solomon, S. (1986). The causes and consequences of self-esteem: A terror-management theory. In R. F. Baumeister (Ed.), *Public Self and Private Self* (pp. 189–212). New York: Springer-Verlag.

Greenberg, J., Pyszczynski, T., Solomon, S., Rosenblatt, A., Veeder, M., Kirkland, S., & Lyon, D. (1990). Evidence for terror-management theory II: The effects of mortality salience on reactions to those who threaten or bolster the cultural worldview. *Journal of Personality and Social Psychology, 58*, 308–318.

Greenberg, J., Simon, L., Porteus, J., Pyszczynski, T., & Solomon, S. (1995). Evidence of a terror management function of cultural icons: The effects of mortality salience on the inappropriate use of cherished cultural symbols. *Personality and Social Psychology Bulletin, 21*, 1221–1228.

Greenberg, J., Solomon, S., & Arndt, J. (2008). A basic but uniquely human motivation: Terror management. In J. Y. Shah, & W. L. Gardner (Eds.), *Handbook of Motivation Science* (pp. 114–134). New York: Guilford Press.

Greenfield, P. M. (2013). The changing psychology of culture from 1800 through 2000. *Psychological Science, 24*, 1722–1731.

Greven, P. (1991). *Spare the Child: The Religious Roots of Punishment and the Psychological Impact of Physical Abuse.* New York: Knopf.

Gries, P., Su, J., & Schak, D. (2012). Toward the scientific study of polytheism: beyond forced-choice measures of religious belief. *Journal for the Scientific Study of Religion, 51*, 623–637.

Griffith, J. D., Mitchell, S., Hart, C. L., Adams, L. T., & Gu, L. L. (2012). Pornography actresses: An assessment of the damaged goods hypothesis. *Journal of Sex Research, 49*, 1–12.

Griffiths, J. G. (1980). *The Origins of Osiris and His Cult.* Leiden: E. J. Brill.

Gross, N., & Simmons, S. (2006). Americans' attitudes toward academic freedom and liberal "bias" in higher education. Working paper.

Gross, N., & Simmons, S. (2009). The religiosity of American college and university professors. *Sociology of Religion, 70*, 101–129.

Groth-Marnat, G., & Summers, R. (1998). Altered beliefs, attitudes, and behaviors following near-death experiences. *Journal of Humanistic Psychology, 38*, 110–112.

Gruenais, M. E. (1999). Does religion protect from AIDS? Congolese religious congregations face pandemic HIV-infection. *Cahiers d'Etudes Africaines, 39*, 253–270.

Guiette, R. (1934). Vie de Max Jacob. *La Nouvelle Revue Française, 22*, 5–19, 248–259.

Guillem, F., & Mograss, M. (2005). Gender differences in memory processing: Evidence from event-related potentials to faces. *Brain & Cognition, 57*, 84–92.

Guimond, S., Chatard, A., Martinot, D., Crisp, R. J., & Redersdorff, S. (2006). Social comparison, self-stereotyping, and gender differences in self-construals. *Journal of Personality and Social Psychology, 90*, 221–242.

Guiso, L., Sapienza, P., & Zingales, L. (2003). People's opium? Religion and economic attitudes. *Journal of Monetary Economics, 50*, 225–282.

Guiso, L., Sapienza, P., & Zingales, L. (2006). Does culture affect economic outcomes? *Journal of Economic Perspectives, 20*, 23–48.

266 References

Gunn, T. J. (2003). The complexity of religion and the definition of "Religion" in international law. *Harvard Human Rights Journal, 16*, 189–215.

Gunnoe, M. L., & Moore, K. A. (2002). Predictors of religiosity among youth aged 17–22: A longitudinal study of the National Survey of Children. *Journal for the Scientific Study of Religion, 41,* 613–622.

Guthrie, S. (1993). *Faces in the Clouds: A New Theory of Religion.* Oxford: Oxford University Press.

Guttman, J. (1984). Cognitive morality and cheating behavior in religious and secular school children. *Journal of Educational Research, 77,* 249–254.

Hackney, C. H., & Sanders, G. S. (2003). Religiosity and mental health: A meta-analysis of recent studies. *Journal for the Scientific Study of Religion, 42,* 43–55.

Hadaway, C. K. (1989). Identifying American apostates: A cluster analysis. *Journal for the Scientific Study of Religion, 28,* 201–215.

Hadaway, C. K., & Roof, W. C. (1979). Those who stay religious 'nones' and those who don't: A research note. *Journal for the Scientific Study of Religion, 18,* 194–200.

Hadaway, C. K., Marler, P. L., & Chaves, M. (1998). Overreporting church attendance in America: Evidence that demands the same verdict. *American Sociological Review, 63,* 122–130.

Hadnes, M., & Schumacher, H. (2012). The Gods are watching: An experimental study of religion and traditional belief in Burkina Faso. *Journal for the Scientific Study of Religion, 51,* 689–704.

Haidt, J. (2012). *The Righteous Mind: Why Good People Are Divided by Politics and Religion.* New York: Pantheon.

Haidt, J., & Bjorklund, F. (2008). Social intuitionists answer six questions about moral psychology. In W. Sinnott-Armstrong (Ed.), *Moral Psychology, Volume 2: The Cognitive Science of Morality: Intuition and Diversity* (pp. 181–217). Cambridge, MA: MIT Press.

Halbwachs, M. (1992). *On Collective Memory.* Chicago: University of Chicago Press.

Hall, D., Matz, D., & Wood, W. (2010). Why don't we practice what we preach? Social-cognitive motives behind religious racism. *Personality and Social Psychology Review, 14,* 126–139.

Hall, J. R., & Schuyler, P. (1997). The mystical apocalypse of the Solar Temple. In T. Robbins, & S. J. Palmer (Eds.), *Millennium, Messiahs, and Mayhem.* New York: Routledge.

Halloy, A. (2012). Gods in the flesh: Learning emotions in the Xangô possession cult (Brazil). *Ethnos: Journal of Anthropology, 77,* 177–202.

Halloy, A., & Naumescu, V. (2012). Learning spirit possession: An introduction. *Ethnos: Journal of Anthropology, 77,* 155–176.

Halman, L., & Draulans, V. (2006). How secular is Europe? *British Journal of Sociology, 57,* 263–288.

Hammond, P. E. (1991). The third disestablishment: A symposium. *Journal for the Scientific Study of Religion, 30,* 516–518.

Han, S., Gu, X., Mao, L., Ge, J., Wang, G., & Ma, Y. (2010). Neural substrates of self-referential processing in Chinese Buddhists. *Social Cognitive and Affective Neuroscience, 5,* 332–339.

Han, S., Mao, L., Gu, X., Zhu, Y., Ge, J., & Ma, Y. (2008). Neural consequences of religious belief on self-referential processing. *Social Neuroscience, 3,* 1–15.

Hanke, L. (1974). *All Mankind Is One: A Study of the Disputation between Bartolomé de Las Casas and Juan Gines de Sepulveda in 1550 on the Intellectual and Religious Capacity of the American Indians.* DeKalb, IL: Northern Illinois University Press.

Hansen, L. K. (2010). Divine intervention in mental health. *The Psychiatric Bulletin, 34,* 258–259.

Hanson, G. H., & Xiang, C. (2013). Exporting Christianity: Governance and doctrine in the globalization of US denominations. *Journal of International Economics, 91,* 301–320.

Haraldsson, E., & Houtkooper, J. (1996). Traditional Christian beliefs, spiritualism and the paranormal: An Icelandic-American Comparison. *International Journal for the Psychology of Religion, 6,* 51–64.

Hardacre, H. (1991). *Shinto and the State, 1868–1988.* Princeton: Princeton University Press.

Hardacre, H. (1993). The impact of Fundamentalisms on women, the family, and interpersonal relations. In M. E. Marty, & R. S. Appleby (Eds.), *Fundamentalisms and Society: Reclaiming the Sciences, the Family, and Education* (pp. 129–150). Chicago: University of Chicago Press.

Hardin, R. (1997). The economics of religious belief. *Journal of Institutional and Theoretical Economics, 153,* 259–278.

Hardy, K. R. (1974). Social origins of American scientists and scholars. *Science, 185,* 497–506.

Hardy, S. A., & Raffaelli, M. (2003). Adolescent religiosity and sexuality: An investigation of reciprocal influences. *Journal of Adolescence, 26,* 731–739.

Hardyck, J. A., & Braden, M. (1962). Prophecy fails again: A report of a failure to replicate. *Journal of Abnormal and Social Psychology, 65,* 136–141.

Harner, M. (1973). *Hallucinogens and Shamanism.* New York: Oxford University Press.

Harnischfeger, J. (2006). State decline and the return of occult powers: The case of Prophet Eddy in Nigeria. *Magic, Ritual and Witchcraft, 1,* 56–78.

Harrell, A. (2012). Do religious cognitions promote prosociality? *Rationality and Society, 24,* 463–482.

Harrell, D. E., Jr. (1985). *Oral Roberts: An American Life.* Bloomington, IN: Indiana University Press.

Harrington, M. (1983). *The Politics At God's Funeral: The Spiritual Crisis of Western Civilization.* New York: Holt, Rinehart and Winston.

Harris, M. (1981). *America Now: The Anthropology of a Changing Culture.* New York: Simon & Schuster.

Harris, P. L. (2011a). Death in Spain, Madagascar, and beyond. In V. Talwar, P. L. Harris, & M. Schleifer (Eds.), *Children's Understanding of Death.* New York: Cambridge University Press.

Harris, P. L. (2011b). Conflicting thoughts about death. *Human Development, 54,* 160–168.

Harris, P. L., & Giménez, M. (2005). Children's acceptance of conflicting testimony: The case of death. *Journal of Cognition and Culture, 5,* 143–164.

Harris, P. L., & Koenig, M. (2006). Trust in testimony: How children learn about science and religion. *Child Development, 77,* 505–524.

Harris, P. L., Pasquini, E. S., Duke, S., Asscher, J. J., & Pons, F. (2006). Germs and angels: The role of testimony in young children's ontology. *Developmental Science, 9,* 76–96.

Harris, S., Kaplan, J. T., Curiel, A., Bookheimer, S. Y., Iacoboni, M., *et al.* (2009). The neural correlates of religious and nonreligious belief. *PLOS ONE, 4*(10), e7272.

Harris, W. H., Gowda, M., Kolb, J. W., Strychacz, C. P., Vacek, J. L., Jones, P. G., Forker, A., O'Keefe, J. H., & McCallister, B. D. (1999). A randomized, controlled trial of the effects of remote, intercessory prayer on outcomes in patients admitted to the coronary care unit. *Archives of Internal Medicine, 159,* 2273–2278.

Harter, S. (1999). *The Construction of the Self: A Developmental Perspective.* New York: Guilford Press.

Hartman, H., & Hartman, M. (2011). Jewish identity and the secular achievements of American Jewish men and women. *Journal for the Scientific Study of Religion, 50*, 133–153.

Hay, D. (1982). *Exploring Inner Space*. Harmondsworth: Penguin.

Hay, D. A. (2014). An investigation into the swiftness and intensity of recent secularization in Canada: Was Berger right? *Sociology of Religion, 75*, 136–162.

Hayes, B. C. (1996). Gender differences in religious mobility in Great Britain. *British Journal of Sociology, 47*, 643–656.

Hayward, R. D., & Elliott, M. (2009). Fitting in with the flock: Social attractiveness as a mechanism for well-being in religious groups. *European Journal of Social Psychology, 39*, 592–596.

Hazani, M. (1986). When prophecy fails: Leaders die, followers persevere. *Genetic, Social, and General Psychology Monographs, 112*, 245–271.

Hearnshaw, L. S. (1964). *A Short History of British Psychology, 1840–1940*. London: Methuen.

Heelas, P. (1996). *The New Age Movement: The Celebration of the Self and the Sacralization of Modernity*. Oxford and Cambridge, MA: Blackwell.

Heelas, P. (2002). The spiritual revolution: from 'religion' to 'spirituality'. In L. Woodhead, P. Fletcher, H. Kawanami, & D. Smith (Eds.), *Religions in the Modern World. Traditions and Transformations* (pp. 357–377). London and New York: Routledge.

Heelas, P., & Woodhead, L. (2005). *The Spiritual Revolution: Why Religion is Giving Way to Spirituality*. Oxford: Blackwell.

Hegel, G.W.F. (1832/1962). *Lectures on the Philosophy of Religion*. London: Routledge & Kegan Paul.

Heiphetz, L., Spelke, E. S., & Banaji, M. R. (2014). The formation of belief-based social preferences. *Social Cognition, 32*, 22–47.

Helson, R., & Wink, P. (1992). Personality change in women from the early 40s to the early 50s. *Psychology and Aging, 7*, 46–55.

Hendrickx, J., Lammers, J., & Ultee, W. (1991). Religious assortative marriage in the Netherlands, 1938–1983. *Review of Religious Research, 33*, 123–145.

Henrich, J. (2009). The evolution of costly displays, cooperation, and religion: Credibility enhancing displays and their implications for cultural evolution. *Evolution and Human Behaviour, 30*, 244–260.

Henrich, N. S., & Henrich, J. (2007). *Why Humans Cooperate: A Cultural and Evolutionary Explanation*. Oxford: Oxford University Press.

Herman, D. M. (1996). An investigation of the relationship between androgyny and spirituality. *Dissertation Abstracts International: Section B: The Sciences and Engineering, 57*(6-B), 4074.

Hershman, P. (1974). Hair, sex and dirt. *Man, 9*, 274–298.

Hewstone, M., Rubin, M., & Willis, H. (2002). Intergroup bias. *Annual Review of Psychology, 53*, 575–604.

Hill, P. C., & Hood, R.W., Jr. (1999). Affect, religion, and unconscious processes. *Journal of Personality, 67*, 1015–1046.

Hill, P. C., Pargament, K. I., Hood, R. W., McCullough, M. E., Swyers, J. P., Larson, D. B., & Zinnbauer, B. J. (2000). Conceptualizing religion and spirituality: Points of commonality, points of departure. *Journal for the Theory of Social Behaviour, 30*, 51–77.

Hills, P., Francis, L. J., Argyle, M., & Jackson, C. J. (2004). Primary personality trait correlates of religious practice and orientation. *Personality and Individual Differences, 36*, 61–73.

Hinckley, G. B. (2001). Messages of inspiration from President Hinckley. LDS Church News, published by the *Deseret News*, November 2, 2002.

Hinde, R. A. (1999). *Why Gods Persist: A Scientific Approach to Religion*. London: Routledge.

Hine, V. H. (1970). Bridge burners: Commitment and participation in a religious movement. *Sociological Analysis, 31*, 61–66.

Hines, M. (2004). *Brain Gender*. New York: Oxford University Press.

Hodge, D. R. (2007). A systematic review of the empirical literature on intercessory prayer. *Research on Social Work Practice, 17*, 174–187.

Hoffman, M. L. (2000). *Empathy and Moral Development: Implications for Caring and Justice*. Cambridge: Cambridge University Press.

Hoffmann, R. (2013). The experimental economics of religion. *Journal of Economic Surveys, 27*(5), 813–845.

Hofstadter, R. (1963). *Anti-Intellectualism in American Life*. New York: Knopf.

Hoge, D. R., & Keeter, L. G. (1976). Determinants of college teachers' religious beliefs and participation. *Journal for the Scientific Study of Religion, 15*, 221–235.

Hogg, M. A., Adelman, J. R., & Blagg, R. D. (2010). Religion in the face of uncertainty: An uncertainty-identity theory account of religiousness. *Personality and Social Psychology Review, 14*, 72–83.

Holahan, C. K., & Sears, R. R. (1995). *The Gifted Group in Later Maturity*. Stanford, CA: Stanford University Press.

Hollinger, D. A. (1996). *Science, Jews, and Secular Culture: Studies in Mid-Twentieth Century American Intellectual History*. Princeton: Princeton University Press.

Höllinger, F. (2004). Does the counter-cultural character of new age persist? Investigating social and political attitudes of new age followers. *Journal of Contemporary Religion, 19*, 289–309.

Höllinger, F., & Smith, T. B. (2002). Religion and esotericism among students: A cross-cultural comparative study. *Journal of Contemporary Religion, 17*, 229–249.

Höllinger, F., Haller, M., & Valle-Höllinger, A. (2007). Christian religion, society and the state in the modern world. *Innovation: The European Journal of Social Science Research, 20*, 133–157.

Holm, N. G. (1991). Pentecostalism: conversion and charismata. *International Journal for the Psychology of Religion, 1*, 135–151.

Holmes, O. W. (1872). *The Poet at the Breakfast Table*. Boston: J. R. Osgood and Company.

Homan, R. (1986). Nineteenth century missions in South-East England: The organizational response to the French Revolution. *Archives de Sciences Sociales des Religions, 31*, 151–160.

Hood, R. W., Jr. (1975). The construction and preliminary validation of a measure of reported mystical experience. *Journal for the Scientific Study of Religion, 14*, 29–41.

Hood, R. W., Jr. (1992). Mysticism, reality, illusion and the Freudian critique of religion. *The International Journal for the Psychology of Religion, 2*, 141–164.

Hood, R. W., Jr. (1997). Psychoanalysis and fundamentalism: A lesson from feminist critiques of Freud. In J. L. Jacobs, & D. Capps (Eds.), *Religion, Society, and Psychoanalysis* (pp. 42–67). Boulder, CO: Westview.

Hood, R. W., Jr. (2010). Another epistemic evaluation of Freud's Oedipal theory of religion. In Beit-Hallahmi, B. (Ed.), *Psychoanalysis and Theism: Critical Reflections on the Grünbaum Thesis* (pp. 137–156). Lanham, MD: Jason Aronson.

Hood, R. W. Jr., & Chen, Z. (2013). Mystical, spiritual, and religious experiences. In R. F. Paloutzian, & C. L. Park (Eds.), *Handbook of the Psychology of Religion and Spirituality* (2nd ed.) (pp. 422–440). New York: Guilford.

Hood, R. W., Jr., & Hall, J. R. (1980). Gender differences in the description of erotic and mystical experiences. *Review of Religious Research, 21*, 195–207.

Hood, R. W., Jr., & Williamson, P. (2008). *Them That Believe: The Power and Meaning of the Christian Serpent-Handling Tradition*. Berkeley: University of California Press.

Hood, R. W., Jr., Morris, R. J., & Watson, P. J. (1991). Male commitment to the cult of the Virgin Mary and the passion of Christ as a function of early maternal bonding. *International Journal for the Psychology of Religion, 1*, 221–231.

Hopcroft, R. L., & Bradley, D. B. (2007). The sex difference in depression across 29 countries. *Social Forces, 85*, 1483–1507.

Horney, K. (1939). *New Ways in Psychoanalysis.* New York: Norton.

Horwitz, R. H. (1986). *The Moral Foundations of the American Republic.* Charlottesville, VA: University of Virginia Press.

Hout, M., & Fischer, C. S. (2002). Explaining the rise of Americans with no religious preference: Politics and generation. *American Sociological Review, 67*, 165–190.

Hout, M., & Greeley, A. M. (1987). The center doesn't hold: Church attendance in the United States, 1940–1984. *American Sociological Review, 52*, 325–345.

Houtman, D., & Aupers, S. (2007). The spiritual turn and the decline of tradition: The spread of post-Christian spirituality in 14 Western countries, 1981–2000. *Journal for the Scientific Study of Religion, 46*, 305–320.

Houtman, D., & Mascini, P. (2002). Why do churches become empty, while New Age grows? Secularization and religious change in the Netherlands. *Journal for the Scientific Study of Religion, 41*, 455–473.

Hoverd, W. J., & Sibley, C. G. (2013). Religion, deprivation and subjective wellbeing: Testing a religious buffering hypothesis. *International Journal of Wellbeing, 3*, 182–196.

Howell, J. D. (2005). Muslims, the New Age and marginal religions in Indonesia: Changing meanings of religious pluralism. *Social Compass, 52,* 473–493.

Huang, J., Napolitano, L. A., Wu, J., Yang, Y., Xi, Y., Li, Y., and Li, K. (2014). Childhood experiences of parental rearing patterns reported by Chinese patients with borderline personality disorder. *International Journal of Psychology, 49*, 38–45.

Hughes, R. A. (1990). Psychological perspectives on infanticide in a faith healing sect. *Psychotherapy, 27*, 107–115.

Hughes, R. A. (2004). The death of children by faith-based medical neglect. *Journal of Law and Religion, 20*, 247–265.

Huguelet, P., Mohr, S., Brandt, P-Y., Borras, L., & Gillieron, C. (2006). Spirituality and religious practices in outpatients with schizophrenia or schizo-affective disorders and their clinicians. *Psychiatric Services, 57*, 366–372.

Hume, D. (1757/1875). *Essays Literary, Moral, and Political.* London: Longmans Green.

Hummer, R. A., Rogers, R. G., Nam, C. B., & Ellison, C. G. (1999). Religious involvement and U.S. adult mortality. *Demography, 36*, 273–285.

Hunsberger, B., & Brown, L. B. (1984). Religious socialization, apostasy, and the impact of family background. *Journal for the Scientific Study of Religion, 23*, 239–251.

Hunsberger, B., & Jackson, L. (2005). Religion, meaning, and prejudice. *Journal of Social Issues, 61*, 807–826.

Hunsberger, B., Owusu, V., & Duck, R. (1999). Religion and prejudice in Ghana and Canada: Religious fundamentalism, right-wing authoritarianism, and attitudes toward homosexuals and women. *The International Journal for the Psychology of Religion, 9*, 181–194.

Hunsberger, B., Pratt, M., & Pancer, S. M. (2001). Religious versus nonreligious socialization: Does religious background have implications for adjustment? *The International Journal for the Psychology of Religion, 11*, 105–128.

Hunter, J. D. (1983). *American Evangelicalism: Conservative Religion and the Quandary of Modernity.* New Brunswick: Rutgers University Press.

Hunter, J. D. (1987). Religious elites in advanced industrial society. *Comparative Studies in Society and History, 29*, 360–374.

Hunter, J. D., & Hawdon, J. E. (1991). Religious elites in advanced capitalism: The dialectic of power and marginality. In W. C. Roof (Ed.), *World Order and Religion* (pp. 39–63). Albany: State University of New York Press.

Huntington, S. P. (1993). If not civilizations, what? Paradigms of the post-Cold War world. *Foreign Affairs, 72*, 185–207.

Hyde, K. E. (1965). *Religious Learning in Adolescence* (University of Birmingham Institute of Education Monograph Number 7). London: Oliver and Boyd.

Iannaccone, L. R. (1990). Religious practice: A human capital approach. *Journal for the Scientific Study of Religion, 29*, 297–314.

Iannaccone, L. R. (1994). Why strict churches are strong. *American Journal of Sociology, 99*, 1180–1211.

Iannaccone, L. R. (1998). Introduction to the economics of religion. *Journal of Economic Literature, 36*, 1465–1496.

Idler, E. L., & Kasl, S. V. (1997). Religion among disabled and non-disabled elderly persons: II. Attendance at religious services as a predictor of the course of disability. *Journal of Gerontology Series B – Psychological Sciences and Social Sciences, 52B*, S306–S316.

Ilfeld, F. W. (1980). Coping styles of Chicago adults: Description. *Journal of Human Stress*, June 2–10.

Inagaki, K., & Hatano, G. (1987). Young children's spontaneous personification as analogy. *Child Development, 58*, 1013–1020.

Inglehart, R., & Baker, W. E. (2000). Modernization, cultural change, and the persistence of traditional values. *American Sociological Review, 65*, 19–51.

Inglehart, R., & Norris, P. (2003). *Rising Tide: Gender Equality and Cultural Change around the World*. New York: Cambridge University Press.

Inglis, T. (2007). Catholic identity in contemporary Ireland: Belief and belonging to tradition. *Journal of Contemporary Religion, 22*, 205–220.

Ingram, R. E., Cruet, D., Johnson, B., & Wisnicki, K. (1988). Self-focused attention, gender, gender-role, and vulnerability to negative affect. *Journal of Personality and Social Psychology, 55*, 967–978.

Inhelder, B., & Piaget, J. (1958). *The Growth of Logical Thinking from Childhood to Adolescence*. New York: Basic Books.

Inkeles, A., & Smith, D. H. (1974). *Becoming Modern: Individual Change in Six Developing Countries*. Cambridge, MA: Harvard University Press.

Inzlicht, M., & Tullett, A. M. (2010). Reflecting on God: Religious primes can reduce neurophysiological response to errors. *Psychological Science, 21*, 1184–1190.

Inzlicht, M., Tullett, A. M., & Good, M. (2011). The need to believe: A neuroscience account of religion as a motivated process. *Religion, Brain & Behavior, 1*, 192–212.

Inzlicht, M., McGregor, I., Hirsh, J. B., & Nash, K. (2009). Neural markers of religious conviction. *Psychological Science, 20*, 385–392.

Isaac, S., Bailey, R., & Isaac, W. (1995). Perceptions of religious and nonreligious targets who participate in premarital sex. *Social Behavior and Personality, 23*, 229–233.

Islam, M. R., & Hewstone, M. (1993). Dimensions of contact as predictors of intergroup anxiety, perceived out-group variability, and out-group attitude: An integrative model. *Personality and Social Psychology Bulletin, 19*, 700–710.

Israel, J. I. (2010). *A Revolution of the Mind: Radical Enlightenment and the Intellectual Origins of Modern Democracy*. Princeton: Princeton University Press.

Jackson, M. (1997). Benign schizotypy? The case of spiritual experience. In G. Claridge (Ed.), *Schizotypy: Implications for Illness and Health* (p. 227–250). Oxford: Oxford University Press.

272 References

Jacobs, J. L. (1989). *Divine Disenchantment: Deconverting from New Religions*. Bloomington: Indiana University Press.

Jacobson, C. K. (1999). Denominational and racial and ethnic differences in fatalism. *Review of Religious Research, 41*, 9–20.

Jahoda, G. (1969). *The Psychology of Superstition*. London: Allen Lane.

James, W. (1897/1956). *The Will to Believe*. New York: Dover Publications.

James, W. (1900/1943). *Radical Empiricism and a Pluralistic Universe*. London: Longmans, Green.

James, W. (1902/1961). *The Varieties of Religious Experience*. New York: Collier.

Jang, S. J., & Franzen, A. B. (2013). Is being 'spiritual' enough without being religious? A study of violent and property crimes among emerging adults. *Criminology, 51*, 595–627.

Jegede, A. S. (2007). What led to the Nigerian boycott of the polio vaccination campaign? *PLOS Medicine, 4*, 0417-0422.

Jelen, T. G., & Wilcox, C. (1995). *Public Attitudes Toward Church and State*. Armonk, NY: M. E. Sharpe.

Jennings, M. K., & Niemi, R. (1974). *The Political Character of Adolescence*. Princeton, NJ: Princeton University Press.

Jensen, G. F. (2006). Religious cosmologies and homicide rates among nations. *The Journal of Religion and Society, 8*, 1–13.

Jessor, R., Turbin, M. S., & Costa, F. M. (1998). Risk and protection in successful outcomes among disadvantaged adolescents. *Applied Developmental Science, 2*, 194–208.

Ji, C. H., & Ibrahim, Y. (2007). Islamic religiosity in right-wing authoritarian personality: The case of Indonesian Muslims. *Review of Religious Research, 49*, 128–146.

Jindal, B. (1994). Beating a demon: Physical dimensions of spiritual warfare. *New Oxford Review, 36*(10), 15–23.

Johansson-Stenman, O., Mahmud, M., &. Martinsson, P. (2009). Trust and religion: Experimental evidence from rural Bangladesh. *Economica, 76*, 462–485.

Johnson, A. W., & Price-Williams, D. (1996). *Oedipus Ubiquitous: The Family Complex in World Folk Literature*. Stanford: Stanford University Press.

Johnson, B. R., Jang, S. J., Larson, D. B., & Li, S. D. (2001). Does adolescent religious commitment matter? A reexamination of the effects of religiosity on delinquency. *Journal of Research in Crime and Delinquency, 38*, 22–44.

Johnson, D. D. P. (2005). God's punishment and public goods: a test of the supernatural punishment hypothesis in 186 world cultures. *Human Nature, 16*, 410–464.

Johnson, D. D. P., & Bering, J. M. (2006). Hand of God, mind of man: Punishment and cognition in the evolution of cooperation. *Evolutionary Psychology, 4*, 219–233.

Johnson, D. P., & Chalfant, H. P. (1993). Contingency theory applied to religious organizations. *Social Compass, 40*, 75–81.

Johnson, M. K., Rowatt, W. C., & LaBouff, J. P. (2010). Priming Christian religious concepts increases racial prejudice. *Social Psychological and Personality Science, 1*, 119–126.

Johnson, M. K., Rowatt, W. C., & LaBouff, J. (2012). Religiosity and prejudice revisited: Ingroup favoritism, outgroup derogation, or both? *Psychology of Religion and Spirituality, 4*, 154–168.

Joiner, T. E., Perez, M., & Walker, R. L. (2002). Playing devil's advocate: Why not conclude that the relation of religiosity to mental health is reduced to mundane mediators? *Psychological Inquiry, 13*, 214–216.

Jonason, P. K., Li, N. P., & Czarna, A. Z. (2013). Quick and dirty: Some psychosocial costs associated with the Dark Triad in three countries. *Evolutionary Psychology, 11*, 172–185.

Jong, J., Halberstadt, J., & Bluemke, M. (2012). Foxhole atheism, revisited: The effects of mortality salience on explicit and implicit religious belief. *Journal of Experimental Social Psychology, 48*, 983–989.

Joshi, S. T. (2003). *God's Defenders: What They Believe and Why They Are Wrong*. Amherst, NY: Prometheus Books.

Junisbai, A. K. (2010). Understanding economic justice attitudes in two countries: Kazakhstan and Kyrgyzstan. *Social Forces, 88*, 1677–1702.

Kääriäinen, K. (1999). Religiousness in Russia after the collapse of communism. *Social Compass, 46*, 35–46.

Kahneman, D. (2003). A perspective on judgment and choice: Mapping bounded rationality. *American Psychologist, 58*, 697–720.

Kalb, C. (2003). Faith and healing. *Newsweek*, November 17, pp. 47–55.

Kaldor, P. (1994). *Winds of Change*. Homebush West, NSW: Anze.

Kalichman, S. C., & Simbayi, L. (2004). Traditional beliefs about the cause of AIDS and AIDS-related stigma in South Africa. *AIDS Care, 16*, 572–580.

Kalish, R. A., & Reynolds, D. K. (1973). Phenomenological reality and post-death contact. *Journal for the Scientific Study of Religion, 12*, 209–221.

Kanazawa, S., & Still, M. C. (2000). Why men commit crimes (and why they desist). *Sociological Theory, 18*, 434–447.

Kane, S. (1998). *AIDS Alibis: Sex, Drugs, and Crime in the Americas*. Philadelphia: Temple University Press.

Kaplan, B. H. (1965). The structure of adaptive sentiments in lower class religious groups in Appalachia. *Journal of Social Issues, 21*, 126–141.

Kapogiannis, D., Barbey, A. K., Su, M., Zamboni, G., Krueger, F., & Grafman, J. (2009). Cognitive and neural foundations of religious belief. *Proceedings of National Academy of Sciences, 106*, 4876–4881.

Karakoç, E., & Baskan, B. (2012). Religion in politics: How does inequality affect public secularization? *Comparative Political Studies, 45*, 1510–1541.

Karlan, D. S. (2005). Using experimental economics to measure social capital and predict financial decisions. *American Economic Review, 95*, 1688–1699.

Katnik, A. (2002). Religion, social class, and political tolerance: A cross-national analysis. *International Journal of Sociology, 32*, 14–38.

Kaufmann, E., Goujon, A., & Skirbekk, V. (2012). The end of secularization in Europe? A socio-demographic perspective. *Sociology of Religion, 73*, 69–91.

Kay, A. C., Moscovitch, D. A., & Laurin, K. (2010). Randomness, attributions of arousal, and belief in God. *Psychological Science, 21*, 216–218.

Kay, A. C., Gaucher, D., McGregor, I., & Nash, K. (2010). Religious belief as compensatory control. *Personality and Social Psychology Review, 14*, 37–48.

Kay, A. C., Whitson, J., Gaucher, D., & Galinsky, A. D. (2009). Compensatory control: In the mind, in our institutions, in the heavens. *Current Directions in Psychological Science, 18*, 264–268.

Kay, A. C., Gaucher, D., Napier, J. L., Callan, M. J., & Laurin, K. (2008). God and the government: Testing a compensatory control mechanism for the support of external systems. *Journal of Personality and Social Psychology, 95*, 18–35.

Kay, A. C., Shepherd, S., Blatz, C. W., Chua, S. N., & Galinsky, A. D. (2010c). For God (or) country: The hydraulic relation between government instability and belief in religious sources of control. *Journal of Personality and Social Psychology, 99*, 725–739.

Kay, W. K., & Francis, L. J. (1996). *Drift from the Churches: Attitude Toward Christianity during Childhood and Adolescence*. Cardiff: University of Wales Press.

274 References

Kehoe, A. B., & Giletti, D. H. (1981). Women's preponderance in possession cults: The calcium-deficiency hypothesis extended. *American Anthropologist, 83*, 549–561.

Keister, L. A. (2008). Conservative Protestants and wealth: How religion perpetuates asset poverty. *American Journal of Sociology, 113*, 1237–1271.

Kelemen, D. (1999). Why are rocks pointy? Children's preference for teleological explanations of the natural world. *Developmental Psychology, 35*, 1440–1453.

Kelemen, D. (2004). Are children "intuitive theists"? Reasoning about purpose and design in nature. *Psychological Science, 15,* 295–301.

Kelemen, D., & DiYanni, C. (2005). Intuitions about origins: Purpose and intelligent design in children's reasoning about nature. *Journal of Cognition and Development, 6*, 3–31.

Kelemen, D., & Rosset, E. (2009). The human function compunction: Teleological explanation in adults. *Cognition, 111,* 138–143.

Kelemen, D., Rottman, J., & Seston, R. (2013). Professional physical scientists display tenacious teleological tendencies: Purpose-based reasoning as a cognitive default. *Journal of Experimental Psychology: General, 142*, 1074–1083.

Kelly, J. (2005). *The Great Mortality: An Intimate History of the Black Death, the Most Devastating Plague of All Times.* New York: Harper.

Kelley, J., & De Graaf, N. D. (1997). National context, parental socialization, and religious belief: Results from 15 nations. *American Sociological Review, 62*, 639–659.

Kelley, M. M., & Chan, K. T. (2012). Assessing the role of attachment to God, meaning, and religious coping as mediators in the grief experience. *Death Studies, 36*, 199–227.

Kellner, M., & Wellman, B. (1997). Health care and consumer choice: medical and alternative therapies. *Social Science and Medicine, 45*, 203–212.

Kenrick, D. T., Neuberg, S. L., Griskevicius, V., Becker, D. V., & Schaller, M. (2010). Goal-driven cognition and functional behavior: The fundamental motives approach. *Current Directions in Psychological Science, 19*, 63–67.

Kent, S. A. (1994). Lustful prophet: A psychosexual historical study of the Children of God's leader, David Berg. *Cultic Studies Journal, 11*, 135–188.

Kerley, K. R., Allison, M. C., & Graham, R. D. (2006). Investigating the impact of religiosity on emotional and behavioral coping in prison. *Journal of Crime and Justice, 29*, 71–96.

Kerley, K. R., Matthews, T. L., & Blanchard, T. C. (2005). Religiosity, religious participation, and negative prison behaviors. *Journal for the Scientific Study of Religion, 44*, 443–457.

Kerr, J. H., & Vlaminkx, J. (1997). Gender differences in the experience of risk. *Personality and Individual Differences, 22*, 293–295.

Kersten, L. (1971). *The Lutheran Ethic: The Impact of Religion on Laymen and Clergy.* Detroit: Wayne State University Press.

Keysar, A. (2007). Who are America's atheists and agnostics? In B. Kosmin, & A. Keysar (Eds.), *Secularism and Secularity: Contemporary International Perspectives* (pp. 33–39). Hartford, CT: Institute for the Study of Secularism in Society and Culture.

Keysar, A., & Kosmin, B. A. (2008). International Survey: Worldviews and Opinions of Scientists. Retrieved from prog.trincoll.edu/ISSSC/INDIAN_SURVEY_WEBSITE/, August 30, 2013.

Khalifa, N., Hardie, T., Latif, S., Jamil, I., & Walker, D. M. (2011). Beliefs about Jinn, black magic and Evil Eye among Muslims: Age, gender and first language influences. *International Journal of Culture and Mental Health, 4*, 68–77.

Kidder, R. M. (1985). Watching for the trends that swirl about one's feet. *The Christian Science Monitor*, May 6, p. 31.

Kiev, A., & Francis, J. L. (1964). Subud and mental illness: Psychiatric illness in a religious sect. *American Journal of Psychotherapy, 18*, 66–78.

Kildahl, J. P. (1972). *The Psychology of Speaking in Tongues*. New York: Harper and Row.

Kim, J., Lee, Y., Son, J., & Smith, T. W. (2009). Trends of religious identification in Korea: Changes and continuities. *Journal for the Scientific Study of Religion, 48*, 789–793.

King, P. E., & Furrow, J. L. (2004). Religion as a resource for positive youth development: Religion, social capital, and moral outcomes. *Developmental Psychology, 40*, 703–713.

King, P. M., Wood, P. K., & Mines, R. A. (1990). Critical thinking among college and graduate students. *Review of Higher Education, 13*, 167–186.

Kirby, J. P. (1997). White, red and black: Colour classification and illness management in northern Ghana. *Social Science and Medicine, 44*, 215–230.

Kirkpatrick, L. A. (1997). A longitudinal study of changes in religious belief and behavior as a function of individual differences in adult attachment style. *Journal for the Scientific Study of Religion, 36*, 207–217.

Kirkpatrick, L. A. (1998). God as a substitute attachment figure: A longitudinal study of adult attachment style and religious change in college students. *Personality and Social Psychology Bulletin, 24*, 961–973.

Kirkpatrick, L. A. (2005). *Attachment, Evolution, and the Psychology of Religion*. New York: Guilford.

Kirkpatrick, L. A. (2008). Religion is not an adaptation: Some fundamental issues and arguments. In R. Sosis, J. Bulbulia, E. Harris, C. Genet, R. Genet, and K. Wyman (Eds.), *The Evolution of Religion: Studies, Theories, and Critiques* (pp. 47–52). Santa Margarita, CA: Collins Foundation Press.

Kirkpatrick, L. A., & Shaver, P. R. (1992). An attachment-theoretical approach to romantic love and religious belief. *Personality and Social Psychology Bulletin, 18*, 266–275.

Kirkpatrick, L. A., Shillito, D. J., & Kellas, S. L. (1999). Loneliness, social support, and perceived relationship with God. *Journal of Social and Personal Relationships, 16*, 513–522.

Kitagawa, J. M. (1961). Ainu bear festival (Iyomante). *History of Religions, 1*, 95–151.

Kitzinger, S. (1969). Protest and mysticism: The Rastafari cult of Jamaica. *Journal for the Scientific Study of Religion, 8*, 240–262.

Klaf, F. C., & Hamilton, J. G. (1961). Schizophrenia – a hundred years ago and today. *Journal of Mental Science, 107*, 819–827.

Kling, K. C., Hyde, J. S., Showers, C. J., & Buswell, B. N. (1999). Gender differences in self-esteem: A meta-analysis. *Psychological Bulletin, 125*, 470–500.

Kluckhohn, C. (1959). Recurrent themes in myths and myth-making. *Daedalus, 88*, 268–279.

Knight, D. A., Woods, R. H. Jr., & Jindra, I. W. (2005). Gender differences in the communication of Christian conversion narratives. *Review of Religious Research, 47*, 113–134.

Knight, N., Sousa, P., Barrett, J. L., & Atran, S. (2004). Children's attributions of beliefs to humans and God: Cross-cultural evidence. *Cognitive Science, 28*, 117–126.

Kobler, F. (Ed.) (1964). *Casebook in Psychopathology*. New York: Alba House.

Koenig, H. G. (2002). The connection between psychoneuroimmunology and religion. In H. G. Koenig, & H. J. Cohen (Eds.), *The Link Between Religion and Health: Psychoneuroimmunology and the Faith Factor* (pp. 11–30). New York: Oxford University Press.

Koenig, H. G. (2008a). Religion and mental health: what should psychiatrists do? *Psychiatric Bulletin, 32*, 201–303.

Koenig, H. G. (2008b). Concerns about measuring "Spirituality" in research. *The Journal of Nervous and Mental Disease, 196*, 349–355.

Koenig, H. G., & Larson, D. B. (2001). Religion and mental health: Evidence for an association. *International Review of Psychiatry, 13,* 67–78.

Koenig, H. G., McCullough, M. E., & Larson, D. B. (2001). *Handbook of Religion and Health.* New York: Oxford University Press.

Koenig, H. G., Zaben, F., & Al Khalifa, D. A. (2012). Religion, spirituality and mental health in the West and the Middle East. *Asian Journal of Psychiatry, 5,* 180–182.

Koenig, H. G., Ford, S., George, L. K., Blazer, D. G., & Meador, K. G. (1993). Religion and anxiety disorder: An examination and comparison of associations in young, middle-aged, and elderly adults. *Journal of Anxiety Disorders, 7,* 321–342.

Koenig, L. B., McGue, M., Krueger, R. F., & Bouchard, T. J., Jr. (2005). Genetic and environmental influences on religiousness: Findings for retrospective and current religiousness ratings. *Journal of Personality, 73,* 471–488.

Koenig, L. B., McGue, M., Krueger, R. F., & Bouchard, T. J., Jr. (2007). Religiousness, antisocial behavior, and altruism: Genetic and environmental mediation. *Journal of Personality, 75,* 265–290.

Kohlberg, L. (1981). *The Philosophy of Moral Development. Moral Stages and the Idea of Justice.* San Francisco: Harper & Row.

Kohn, R.L.E. (1989). The return of religious sociology. *Method & Theory in the Study of Religion, 1,* 135–159.

Konig, R., Eisinga, R., & Scheepers, P. (2000). Explaining the correlation between religion and anti-Semitism. *Review of Religious Research, 41,* 373–393.

Koole, S. L., McCullough, M. E., Kuhl, J., & Roelofsma, P.H.M.P. (2010). Why religion's burdens are light: From religiosity to implicit self-regulation. *Personality and Social Psychology Review, 14,* 95–107.

Koppel, M., Argamon, S., & Shimoni, A. (2003). Automatically categorizing written texts by author gender. *Literary and Linguistic Computing, 17,* 401–412.

Köse, A. (1996). Religious conversion: Is it an adolescent phenomenon? The case of native British converts to Islam. *International Journal for the Psychology of Religion, 6,* 253–262.

Kosmin, B. A., & Keysar, A. (2009). *American Religious Identification Survey (ARIS 2008) Summary Report.* Hartford, CT: Institute for the Study of Secularism in Society & Culture.

Kox, W., Meeus, W., & Hart, H. (1991). Religious conversion of adolescents: Testing the Lofland and Stark model of religious conversion. *Sociological Analysis, 52,* 227–240.

Krause, N. (2003). Religious meaning and subjective well-being in late life. *Journal of Gerontology: Social Sciences, 58B,* S160–S170.

Krause, N. (2006a). Religious doubt and psychological well-being: A longitudinal investigation. *Review of Religious Research, 47,* 287–302.

Krause, N. (2006b). Exploring the stress-buffering effects of church-based social support and secular social support on health in late life. *Journal of Gerontology: Social Sciences, 61,* S35–S43.

Krause, N. (2008). The social foundations of religious meaning in life. *Research on Aging, 30,* 395–427.

Krause, N. (2010). Religious involvement, humility, and self-rated health. *Social Indicators Research, 98,* 23–39.

Krause, N., & Wulff, K. M. (2004). Religious doubt and health: Exploring the potential dark side of religion. *Sociology of Religion, 65,* 35–56.

Krause, N., & Wulff, K. M. (2005). Church-based social ties, a sense of belonging in a congregation, and physical health status. *International Journal for the Psychology of Religion, 15,* 73–93.

References **277**

Krause, N., Ellison, C. G., & Wulff, K. M. (1998). Church-based emotional support, negative interaction, and psychological well-being: Findings from a national sample of Presbyterians. *Journal for the Scientific Study of Religion, 37*, 725–741.

Krauss, S. W., Streib, H., Keller, B., & Silver, C. (2006). The distinction between authoritarianism and fundamentalism in three cultures: Factor analysis and personality correlates. *Archive for the Psychology of Religion, 28*, 341–348.

Krebs, D. L. (2011). *The Origins of Morality: An Evolutionary Account.* New York: Oxford University Press.

Kris, E. (1952). *Psychoanalytic Explorations in Art.* New York: International Universities Press.

Kristol, I. (1949). God and the psychoanalysts: Can Freud and religion be reconciled? *Commentary, 8*, 434–443.

Kroh, M., & Selb, P. (2009). Inheritance and the dynamics of party identification. *Political Behavior, 31*, 559–574.

Kruglanski, A. (1989). *Lay Epistemics and Human Knowledge: Cognitive and Motivational Bases.* New York: Plenum Press.

Kurpis, L. V., Beqiri, M. S., & Helgeson, J. G. (2008). The effects of commitment to moral self-improvement and religiosity on ethics of business students. *Journal of Business Ethics, 80*, 447–463.

Kurtz, P. (1989). *Eupraxophy: Living Without Religion.* Buffalo: Prometheus.

La Barre, W. (1970). *The Ghost Dance: The Origins of Religion.* New York: Doubleday and Company.

LaBouff, J. P., Rowatt, W. C., Johnson, M. K., & Finkle, C. (2011). Differences in attitudes towards out-groups in religious and non-religious contexts in a multi-national sample: A situational context priming study. *International Journal for the Psychology of Religion, 22*, 1–9.

la Cour, P., Avlund, K., & Schultz-Larsen, K. (2006). Religion and survival in a secular region: A twenty year follow-up of 734 Danish adults born in 1914. *Social Science and Medicine, 62*, 157–164.

Ladd, K. L., Spilka, B., & McIntosh, D. N. (2011). Religion and the paranormal: Assessing Freudian hypotheses. *INTERAÇÕES – Cultura e Comunidade / Uberlândia, 6* (jan./jun), 105–120.

Lambert, W. W., Triandis, H. M., & Wolf, M. (1959). Some correlates of beliefs in the malevolence and benevolence of supernatural beings: A cross societal study. *Journal of Abnormal and Social Psychology, 57*, 162–168.

Lamont, C. (1935/1990). *The Illusion of Immortality.* New York: Half-Moon Foundation.

Lamont, C. (1949). *The Philosophy of Humanism.* New York: Philosophical Library.

Lanternari, V. (1963). *The Religions of the Oppressed. A Study of Modern Messianic Cults.* New York: Knopf.

Larsen, L., & Knapp, R. H. (1964). Sex differences in symbolic conceptions of the deity. *Journal of Projective Techniques and Personality Assessment, 28*, 303–306.

Larson, E. J., & Witham, L. (1997). Scientists are still keeping the faith. *Nature, 386*, 435–436.

Larson, E. J., & Witham, L. (1998). Leading scientists still reject God. *Nature, 394*, 313.

Lau, H. H., & Wolfinger, N. H. (2011). Parental divorce and adult religiosity: evidence from the General Social Survey. *Review of Religious Research, 53*, 85–103.

Laubach, M. (2004). The social effects of psychism: Spiritual experience and the construction of privatized religion. *Sociology of Religion, 65*, 239–263.

Laungani, P. (2007). Counseling the dead. *Counselling Psychology Quarterly, 20*, 81–95.

Laurin, K., Kay, A. C., & Moscovitch, D. A. (2008). On the belief in God: Towards an understanding of the emotional substrates of compensatory control. *Journal of Experimental Social Psychology, 44*, 1559–1562.

Laurin, K., Shariff, A. Z., Henrich, J., & Kay, A. C. (2012). Outsourcing punishment to God: Beliefs in divine control reduce earthly punishment. *Proceedings of the Royal Society B, 279*, 3272–3281.

Lavric, M., & Flere, S. (2008). The role of culture in the relationship between religiosity and psychological well-being. *Journal of Religion & Health, 47*, 164–175.

Law, S. (2006). *The War for Children's Minds.* London: Routledge.

Lawrence, R. J. (2002). The witches' brew of spirituality and medicine. *Annals of Behavioral Medicine, 24*, 74–76.

Lawton, L. E., & Bures, R. (2001). Parental divorce and the 'switching' of religious identity. *Journal for the Scientific Study of Religion, 40*, 99–111.

Lazarus, R. S., & Folkman, S. (1984). *Stress, Appraisal, and Coping.* New York: Springer.

Le, T. N., Tov, W., & Taylor, J. (2007). Religiousness and depressive symptoms in five ethnic adolescent groups. *The International Journal for the Psychology of Religion, 17*, 209–232.

Lechner, F. J. (1996). Secularization in the Netherlands? *Journal for the Scientific Study of Religion, 35*, 252–264.

LeDrew, S. (2012). The evolution of atheism: Scientific and humanistic approaches. *History of the Human Sciences, 25*, 70–87.

Lee, S. A., Roberts, L. B., & Gibbons, J. A. (2013). When religion makes grief worse: negative religious coping as associated with maladaptive emotional responding patterns. *Mental Health, Religion & Culture, 16*, 291–305.

Legare, C. H., & Gelman, S. A. (2008). Bewitchment, biology, or both: The co-existence of natural and supernatural explanatory frameworks across development. *Cognitive Science: A Multidisciplinary Journal, 32*, 607–642.

Legare, C. H., Evans, E. M., Rosengren, K. S., & Harris, P. L. (2012). The coexistence of natural and supernatural explanations across cultures and development. *Child Development, 83*, 779–793.

Lehman, H. C., & Witty, P. A. (1931). Scientific eminence and church membership, *Scientific Monthly, 33*, 544–549.

Lenski, G. E. (1963). *The Religious Factor.* New York: Doubleday.

Lerner, G. (1986). *The Creation of Patriarchy.* New York: Oxford University Press.

Lerner, M. J. (1980). *The Belief in a Just World: A Fundamental Illusion.* New York: Plenum Press.

Lescarboura, A. C. (1920). Edison's views on life and death. *Scientific American, 123*, 446.

Lesniak, K. T. (2006). The effect of intercessory prayer on wound healing in nonhuman primates. *Alternative Therapies in Health and Medicine, 12*, 42–48.

Lester, D., Aldridge, M., Aspenberg, C., Boyle, K., Radsniak, P., & Waldon, C. (2002). What is the afterlife like? Undergraduate beliefs about the afterlife. *Omega: Journal of Death and Dying, 44*, 113–126.

Leuba, J. H. (1916). *Belief in God and Immortality: A Psychological, Anthropological and Statistical Study.* Boston: Sherman, French & Co.

Leuba, J. H. (1934). Religious beliefs of American scientists. *Harper's Magazine, 169*, 291–300.

Leuba, J. H. (1937). The making of a psychologist of religion. In V. Ferm (Ed.), *Religion in Transition* (pp. 173–200). New York: Macmillan.

Levin, J. S., Taylor, R. J., & Chatters, L. M. (1994). Race and gender differences in religiosity among older adults: Findings from four national surveys. *Journal of Gerontology, 49*, S137–S145.

Levin, T. M., & Zegans, L. S. (1974). Adolescent identity crisis and religious conversion: Implications for psychotherapy. *British Journal of Medical Psychology, 47*, 73–81.

Levine, S. V. (1981). Cults and mental health: Clinical conclusions. *Canadian Journal of Psychiatry, 16*, 534–539.

Levine, S. V. (1984). *Radical Departures*. New York: Harcourt Brace Jovanovich.

Levine, S. V., & Salter, N. E. (1976). Youth and contemporary religious movements: Psychosocial findings. *Canadian Psychiatric Association Journal, 21*, 411–420.

Levitt, M. (2003). Where are the men and boys? The gender imbalance in the Church of England. *Journal of Contemporary Religion, 18*, 61–75.

Lewis, C. A. (1994). Religiosity and obsessionality: The relationship between Freud's "religious practices." *Journal of Psychology, 128*, 189–196.

Lewis, C. A. (1998). Cleanliness is next to godliness: Religiosity and obsessiveness, *Journal of Religion and Health, 37*, 49–61.

Lewis, I. M. (1966). Spirit possession and deprivation cults. *Man, 1*, 307–329.

Lewis, S. (1927). *Elmer Gantry*. New York: Harcourt.

Lewis-Hall, F., Williams, T. S., Panetta, J. A., & Herrera, J. M. (Eds.) (2002). *Psychiatric Illness in Women: Emerging Treatments and Research*. Washington, DC: American Psychiatric Association.

Lewis-Williams, D., & Pearce, D. (2005). *Inside the Neolithic Mind: Consciousness, Cosmos and the Realm of the Gods*. London: Thames and Hudson.

Lewy, G. (1964). *The Catholic Church and Nazi Germany*. New York: McGraw-Hill.

Li, L.M.W., & Bond, M. H. (2010). Does individual secularism promote life satisfaction? The moderating role of societal development. *Social Indicators Research, 99*, 443–453.

Li, Y. J., Cohen, A. B., Weeden, J., & Kenrick, D. T. (2010). Mating competitors increase religious beliefs. *Journal of Experimental Social Psychology, 46*, 428–431.

Lieberman, M. D. (2000). Intuition: a social cognitive neuroscience approach. *Psychological Bulletin, 126*, 109–137.

Lieberman, M. D. (2009). What makes big ideas sticky? In M. Brockman (Ed.), *What's Next? Dispatches on The Future of Science* (pp. 90–103). New York: Vintage Books.

Liénard, P., & Boyer, P. (2006). Whence collective rituals? A cultural selection model of ritualized behavior. *American Anthropologist, 108*, 814–827.

Lienesch, M. (1993). *Redeeming America: Piety and Politics in the New Christian Right*. Chapel Hill: University of North Carolina Press.

Lim, C., & Putnam, R. D. (2010). Religion, social networks, and life satisfaction. *American Sociological Review, 75*, 914–933.

Lincoln, C. E. (1961). *The Black Muslims in America*. Boston: Beacon Press.

Lindeman, M., & Aarnio, K. (2007). Superstitious, magical, and paranormal beliefs: An integrative model. *Journal of Research in Personality, 41*, 731–744.

Linn, L., & Schwartz, L. W. (1958). *Psychiatry and Religious Experience*. New York: Random House.

Lippa, R. A. (2005). *Gender, Nature, and Nurture*. Hillsdale, NJ: Lawrence Erlbaum Associates.

Lipset, S. M. (1982). The academic mind at the top: The political behavior and values of faculty elites. *Public Opinion Quarterly, 46*, 143–168.

Liu, E. Y. (2010). Are risk-taking persons less religious? Risk preference, religious affiliation, and religious participation in Taiwan. *Journal for the Scientific Study of Religion, 49*, 172–178.

Livingston, K. (2005). Religious practice, brain, and belief. *Journal of Cognition and Culture*, *5*, 75–117.

Lizardi, D., & Gearing, R. E. (2009). Religion and suicide. *Journal of Religion and Health*, *48*, 332–341.

Locke, J. (1689/1983). *A Letter Concerning Toleration*. Indianapolis: Hackett Publishing.

Lodi-Smith, J., & Roberts, B. W. (2007). Social investment and personality: A meta-analysis of the relationship of personality traits to investment in work, family, religion, and volunteerism. *Personality and Social Psychology Review*, *11*, 68–88.

Loewenthal, K. M. (2007). *Religion, Culture and Mental Health*. Cambridge: Cambridge University Press.

Loewenthal, K. M., MacLeod, A. K., Goldblatt, V., Lubitsh, G., & Valentine, J. D. (2000). Comfort and joy? Religion, cognition, and mood in Protestants and Jews under stress. *Cognition and Emotion*, *14*, 355–374.

Loewenthal, K. M., MacLeod, A. K., & Cinnirella, M. (2002). Are women more religious than men? Evidence from a short measure of religious activity applicable in different religious groups in the UK. *Personality and Individual Differences*, *32*, 133–139.

Lofland, J. (1966). *Doomsday Cult: A Study of Conversion, Proselytization and Maintenance of Faith*. Englewood Cliffs, NJ: Prentice-Hall.

Logan, M., & Romans, S. (2002). Spiritual beliefs in bipolar affective disorder: Their relevance for illness management. *Journal of Affective Disorders*, *75*, 247–257.

Long, B. C. (1990). Relation between coping strategies, sex-type traits, and environmental characteristics: A comparison of male and female managers. *Journal of Counseling Psychology*, *37*, 185–194.

Lubinski, D., Schmidt, D. B., & Benbow, C. P. (1996). A 20-year stability analysis of the Study of Values for intellectually gifted individuals from adolescence to adulthood. *Journal of Applied Psychology*, *81*, 443–451.

Luckert, K. W. (1975). *The Navajo Hunter Tradition*. Tucson, AZ: University of Arizona Press.

Luhrmann, T. M. (1989). *Persuasions of the Witch's Craft: Ritual Magic in Contemporary England*. Oxford: Basil Blackwell.

Luhrmann, T., Nusbaum, H., & Thisted, R. (2010). The absorption hypothesis: learning to hear God in evangelical Christianity. *American Anthropologist*, *112*, 66–78.

Lun, V.M.C., & Bond, M. H. (2013). Examining the relation of religion and spirituality to subjective well-being across national cultures. *Psychology of Religion and Spirituality*, *5*, 304–315.

Lunn, J., Klay, R., & Douglass, A. (2001). Relationships among giving, church attendance, and religious belief: The case of the Presbyterian Church (USA). *Journal for the Scientific Study of Religion*, *40*, 765–775.

Lupfer, M. B., Brock, K. F., & DePaola, S. J. (1992). The use of secular and religious attributions to explain everyday behavior. *Journal for the Scientific Study of Religion*, *31*, 486–503.

Lupfer, M. B., DePaola, S. J., Brock, K. F., & Clement, L. (1994). Making secular and religious attributions: the availability hypothesis revisited. *Journal for the Scientific Study of Religion*, *33*, 162–171.

Lüschen, G., Staikof, Z., Heiskanen, V. S., & Ward, C. (1972). Family, ritual and secularization: A cross-national study conducted in Bulgaria, Finland, Germany and Ireland. *Social Compass*, *19*, 519–536.

Lutzky, H. (2008). Mourning and immortality: Ritual and psychoanalysis compared. In W. B. Parsons (Ed.), *Mourning Religion* (pp. 141–155). Charlottesville: University of Virginia Press.

McAdams, D. P. (2006). *The Redemptive Self: Stories Americans Live By*. New York: Oxford University Press.

McCann, S.J.H. (1999). Threatening times and fluctuations in American church memberships. *Personality and Social Psychology Bulletin, 25*, 325–336.

McCauley, R. N. (2012). *Why Religion is Natural and Science is Not*. New York: Oxford University Press.

McCleary, R. M., & Barro, R. J. (2006a). Religion and economy. *Journal of Economic Perspectives, 20*, 49–72.

McCleary, R. M., & Barro, R. J. (2006b). Religion and political economy in an international panel. *Journal for the Scientific Study of Religion, 45*, 149–175.

McConnell, K. M., Pargament, K. I., Ellison, C. G., and Flannelly, K. J. (2006). Examining the links between spiritual struggles and symptoms of psychopathology in a national sample. *Journal of Clinical Psychology, 62*, 1469–1484.

McCrae, R. R. (1996). Social consequences of experiential openness. *Psychological Bulletin, 120*, 323–337.

McCrae, R. R. (1999). Mainstream personality psychology and the study of religion. *Journal of Personality, 67*, 1209–1218.

McCreery, C. (1993). Schizotypy and out-of-the-body experiences. Unpublished D. Phil. thesis, University of Oxford.

McCullers, C. (1940). *The Heart is a Lonely Hunter*. Boston: Houghton Mifflin.

McCullough, M. E., & Willoughby, B.L.B. (2009). Religion, self-regulation, and self-control: Associations, explanations, and implications. *Psychological Bulletin, 135*, 69–93.

McCullough, M. E., Tsang, J., & Brion, S. (2003). Personality traits in adolescence as predictors of religiousness in early adulthood: Findings from the Terman longitudinal study. *Personality and Social Psychology Bulletin, 29,* 980–991.

McCullough, M. E., Enders, C. K., Brion, L. S., & Jain, A. R. (2005). The varieties of religious development in adulthood: a longitudinal investigation of religion and rational choice. *Journal of Personality and Social Psychology, 89*, 78–89.

McCullough, M. E., Hoyt, W. T., Larson, D. B., Koenig, H. G., & Thoresen, C. (2000). Religious involvement and mortality: A meta-analytic review. *Health Psychology, 19*, 211–222.

MacDonald, W. L. (1992). Idionecrophanies: The social construction of perceived contact with the dead. *Journal for the Scientific Study of Religion, 31*, 215–223.

MacDonald, W. L. (1994). The popularity of paranormal experiences in the United States. *Journal of American Culture, 17*, 35–42.

McFarland, H. N. (1967). *The Rush Hour of the Gods*. New York: Macmillan.

McFarland, S. (2011). The slow creation of humanity. *Political Psychology, 32*, 1–20.

McFarland, S., Brown, D., & Webb, M. (2013). Identification with all humanity as a moral concept and psychological construct. *Current Directions in Psychological Science, 22*, 194–198.

McGowan, A. (1994). Eating people: Accusations of cannibalism against Christians in the second century. *Journal of Early Christian Studies, 2*, 413–442.

McGregor, I., Nash, K., & Prentice, M. (2010). Reactive approach motivation (RAM) for religion. *Journal of Personality and Social Psychology, 99*, 148–161.

McGuire, W. G. (1969). The nature of attitudes and attitude change. In G. Lindzey, & E. Aronson (Eds.), *Handbook of Social Psychology*. Reading, MA: Addison-Wesley.

McIntosh, D. N., Silver, R. C., & Wortman, C. B. (1993). Religion's role in adjustment to a negative life event: Coping with the loss of a child. *Journal of Personality and Social Psychology, 65*, 812–821.

282 References

McLeod, H. (1981). *Religion and the People of Western Europe, 1789–1970*. Oxford: Oxford University Press.

McLoughlin, W. G. (1970). *The Meaning of Henry Ward Beecher: An Essay on the Shifting Values of Mid-Victorian America 1840–1870*. New York: Knopf.

McManners, J. (1975). *Reflections at the Death Bed of Voltaire*. Oxford: Oxford University Press.

McNamara, P. (2009). *The Neuroscience of Religious Experience*. New York: Cambridge University Press.

MacPherson, J. S., & Kelly, S. W. (2011). Creativity and positive schizotypy influence the conflict between science and religion. *Personality and Individual Differences, 50,* 446–450.

McRae, J. A. (1978). The secularization of divorce. In B. Duncan, and O. D. Duncan (Eds.), *Sex Typing and Social Roles*. New York: Academic Press.

Maccoby, E. E. (1988). Gender as a social category. *Developmental Psychology, 24,* 755–765.

Mahalik, J. R., & Lagan, H. D. (2001). Examining masculine gender role conflict and stress in relation to religious orientation and spiritual well-being. *Psychology of Men and Masculinity, 2,* 24–33.

Maher, R. F. (1961). *New Men of Papua: A Study of Culture Change*. Madison, WI: University of Wisconsin Press.

Mahmood, S. (2005). *Politics of Piety: The Islamic Revival and the Feminist Subject*. Princeton: Princeton University Press.

Mahoney, A., & Tarakeshwar, N. (2005). Religion's role in marriage and parenting in daily life and during family crises. In R. F. Paloutzian, & C. L. Park (Eds.), *Handbook of the Psychology of Religion and Spirituality* (pp. 177–195). New York: Guilford.

Mahoney, A., Pargament, K. I., Tarakeshwar, N., & Swank, A. (2001). Religion in the home in the 80s and 90s: A meta-analytic review and conceptual analysis of religion, marriage, and parenting. *Journal of Family Psychology, 15,* 559–596.

Mahoney, A., Carels, R., Pargament, K. I., Wachholtz, A., Edwards Leeper, L., Kaplar, M., & Frutchey, R. (2005). The sanctification of the body and behavioral health patterns of college students. *The International Journal for the Psychology of Religion, 15,* 221–238.

Mahoney, A., Pargament, K. I., Jewell, T., Swank, A. B., Scott, E., Emery E., *et al.* (1999). Marriage and the spiritual realm: The role of proximal and distal religious constructs in marital functioning. *Journal of Family Psychology, 13,* 1–18.

Majid, S. (2010). Women with borderline personality disorder: Aetiology, assessment, and prognosis. In D. Kohen (Ed.), *Oxford Textbook of Women and Mental Health* (pp. 115–126). New York: Oxford University Press.

Major, B., Sciacchitano, A. M., & Crocker, J. (1993). In-group versus outgroup comparisons and self-esteem. *Personality and Social Psychology Bulletin, 19,* 711–721.

Ma-Kellams, C., & Blascovich, J. (2013). Does "Science" make you moral? The effects of priming science on moral judgments and behavior. *PLOS ONE, 8*(3), e57989.

Malhotra, D. (2010). (When) are religious people nicer? Religious salience and the 'Sunday effect' on pro-social behavior. *Judgment and Decision Making, 5,* 138–143.

Malinowski, B. (1925). Magic science and religion. In J. Needham (Ed.), *Science, Religion and Reality* (pp. 18–94). London: The Sheldon Press.

Malony, H. M., & Spilka, B. (Eds.) (1991). *Religion in Psychodynamic Perspective: The Contributions of Paul W. Pruyser*. New York: Oxford University Press.

Manglos, N. D., & Trinitapoli, J. (2011). The third therapeutic system: faith healing strategies in the context of a generalized AIDS epidemic. *Journal of Health and Social Behavior, 52,* 107–122.

Manuel, F. (1983). *The Changing of the Gods*. London: University Press of New England.

References **283**

Marini, M. M., Fan, P. L., Finley, E., & Beutel, A. M. (1996). Gender and job values. *Sociology of Education, 69*, 49–65.

Markle, G. E., Petersen, J. C., & Wagenfeld, M. O. (1978). Notes from the cancer underground: Participation in the Laetrile movement. *Social Science and Medicine, 12*, 31–57.

Marler, P. L., & Hadaway, C. K. (2002). "Being religious" or "Being spiritual" in America: A zero-sum proposition? *Journal for the Scientific Study of Religion, 41*, 289–300.

Marsden, G. M. (1996). *The Soul of the American University: From Protestant Establishment to Established Nonbelief.* New York: Oxford University Press.

Martinez, J. S. (2012). *The Slave Trade and the Origins of International Human Rights Law.* New York: Oxford University Press.

Martinot, D., Redersdorff, S., Guimond, S., & Dif, S. (2002). In-group vs. out-group comparisons and self-esteem: The role of group status and in-group identification. *Personality and Social Psychology Bulletin, 28*, 1586–1600.

Marx, K. (1859/1913). *A Contribution to the Critique of Political Economy.* Chicago: Kerr.

Marx, K. (1964). *Early Writings.* New York: McGraw-Hill.

Maselko, J., & Buka, S. (2008). Religious activity and lifetime prevalence of psychiatric disorder. *Social Psychiatry and Psychiatric Epidemiology, 43*, 18–24.

Maselko, J., Gilman, S., & Buka, S. (2009). Religious service attendance and spiritual well-being are differentially associated with risk of major depression. *Psychological Medicine, 39*, 1009–1017.

Maslow, A. H. (1970). *Motivation and Personality.* New York: Harper & Row.

Masson, J. M. (1976). The psychology of the ascetic. *Journal of Asian Studies, 35*, 611–625.

Masson, J. M. (Ed.) (1985). *The Complete Letters of Sigmund Freud to Wilhelm Fliess, 1887–1904.* Cambridge, MA: Harvard University Press.

Masters, K. S., & Spielmans, G. I. (2007). Prayer and health: Review, meta-analysis, and research agenda. *Journal of Behavioral Medicine, 30*, 329–338.

Matsuba, M. K., & Walker, L. J. (2004). Extraordinary moral commitment: Young adults involved in social organizations. *Journal of Personality, 72*, 413–436.

Matthiessen, P. (1962). *Under the Mountain Wall: A Chronicle of Two Seasons in the Stone Age.* New York: Viking.

Matthews, D. A., McCullough, M. E., Larson, D. B., Koenig, H. G., Swyers, J. P., & Milano, M. G. (1998). Religious commitment and health status: A review of the research and implications for family medicine. *Archives of Family Medicine, 7*, 118–124.

Mauskopf, S. H., & McVaugh, M. (1980). *The Elusive Science: Origins of Experimental Psychical Research.* Baltimore: Johns Hopkins University Press.

Mauss, A. L. (1968). Mormon Semitism and anti-Semitism. *Sociological Analysis, 29*, 11–27.

Mayer, J.-F. (1999). Les chevaliers de l'apocalypse: L'Ordre de Temple Solaire et ses adeptes. In F. Champion, & M. Cohen (Eds.), *Sectes et Societe.* Paris: Seuil.

Mears, D. P., & Ellison, C. G. (2000). Who buys New Age materials? An examination of sociodemographic, religious, network, and contextual factors. *Sociology of Religion, 61*, 289–313.

Meier, B. P., Hauser, D. J., Robinson, M. D., Friesen, C. K., & Schjeldahl, K. (2007). What's "up" with God? Vertical space as a representation of the divine. *Journal of Personality and Social Psychology, 93*, 699–710.

Melton, J. G. (1985). Spiritualization and reaffirmation: What really happens when prophecy fails. *American Studies, 26*, 17–29.

Mencken, F. C., Bader, C., & Embry, E. (2009). In God we trust: Images of God and trust in the United States among the highly religious. *Sociological Perspectives, 52*, 23–38.

Mencken, F. C., Bader, C. D., & Kim, Y. J. (2009). Round trip to Hell in a flying saucer: The relationship between conventional Christian and paranormal beliefs in the United States. *Sociology of Religion, 70,* 65–85.

Mencken, H. L. (1930). *Treatise on the Gods.* New York: Knopf.

Mercer, C., & Durham, T. W. (1999). Religious mysticism and gender orientation. *Journal for the Scientific Study of Religion, 38,* 175–182.

Mercer, J. (2013). Deliverance, demonic possession, and mental illness: some considerations for mental health professionals. *Mental Health, Religion & Culture, 16,* 595–611.

Mernissi, F. (1977). Women, saints, and sanctuaries. *Signs, 3,* 101–112.

Merrill, R. M. (2004). Life expectancy among LDS and non-LDS in Utah. *Demographic Research, 10,* 61–82.

Merton, M. (1948). *The Seven-Story Mountain.* New York: Harcourt Brace.

Merton, R. K. (1970). *Science, Technology & Society in Seventeenth Century England.* New York: H. Fertig.

Miguel, E. (2005). Poverty and witch killing. *Review of Economic Studies, 72,* 1153–1172.

Millar, W. J. (1997). Use of alternative health care practitioners by Canadians. *Canadian Journal of Public Health, 88,* 154–158.

Miller, A. S. (1992). Predicting non-conventional religious affiliation in Tokyo: A control theory application. *Social Forces, 71,* 397–410.

Miller, A., & Stark, R. (2002). Gender and religiousness: Can socialisation explanations be saved? *American Journal of Sociology, 107,* 1399–1423.

Miller, L., & Gur, M. (2002). Religiousness and sexual responsibility in adolescent girls. *Journal of Adolescent Health, 31,* 401–406.

Mobbs, D., & Watt, C. (2011). There is nothing paranormal about near-death experiences. *Trends in Cognitive Neuroscience, 16,* 446–448.

Mochon, D., Norton, M. I., & Ariely, D. (2008). Getting off the hedonic treadmill, one step at a time: The impact of regular religious practice and exercise on well-being. *Journal of Economic Psychology, 29,* 632–642.

Mochon, D., Norton, M. I., & Ariely, D. (2011). Who benefits from religion? *Social Indicators Research, 101,* 1–15.

Moffitt, A. R., Kramer, M., & Hoffmann, R. F. (Eds.). (1993). *The Functions of Dreaming.* Albany, NY: SUNY Press.

Moffitt, T. E., Caspi, A., Rutter, M., & Silva, P. A. (2001). *Sex Differences in Antisocial Behaviour.* Cambridge: Cambridge University Press.

Moller, P., & Husby, R. (2000). The initial prodrome in schizophrenia: Searching for naturalistic core dimensions of experience and behavior. *Schizophrenia Bulletin, 26,* 217–232.

Mondak, J. J., Hibbing, M. V., Canache, D., Seligson, M. A., & Anderson, M. R. (2010). Personality and civic engagement: An integrative framework for the study of trait effects on political behavior. *American Political Science Review, 104,* 85–110.

Monod, J. (1971). *Chance and Necessity.* London: Collins.

Montgomery, J. D. (2003). A formalization and test of the religious economies model. *American Sociological Review, 68,* 782–809.

Mooney, J. (1965). *The Ghost Dance Religion and the Sioux Outbreak of 1890.* Chicago: University of Chicago Press.

Mooney, J. (1973). *The Ghost Dance Religion and Wounded Knee.* New York: Dover.

Moore, B., Jr. (1983). *Privacy: Studies in Social and Cultural History.* Armonk, NY: M. E. Sharpe.

Moore, B., Jr. (2000). *Moral Purity and Persecution in History.* Princeton: Princeton University Press.

Moore, R. L. (1977). *In Search of White Crows: Spiritualism, Parapsychology, and American Culture*. New York: Oxford University Press.

Morewedge, C. K., & Clear, M. E. (2008). Anthropomorphic God concepts engender moral judgment. *Social Cognition, 26,* 181–188.

Moscati, A., & Mezuk, B. (2014). Losing faith and finding religion: Religiosity over the life course and substance use and abuse. *Drug and Alcohol Dependence, 136,* 127–134.

Mourao, P. R. (2011). Determinants of the number of Catholic priests to Catholics in Europe – An economic explanation. *Review of Religious Research, 52,* 427–438.

Muensterberger, W. (1972). The sources of belief. Introduction to G. Roheim, *The Panic of the Gods* (pp. vi–x). New York: Harper.

Mulac, A., Giles, H., Bradac, J. J., & Palomares, N. A. (2013). The gender-linked language effect: an empirical test of a general process model. *Language Sciences, 38,* 22–31.

Mullick, M.S.I., Khalifa, N., Nahar, J. S., & Walker, D. M. (2013). Beliefs about Jinn, black magic and evil eye in Bangladesh: the effects of gender and level of education. *Mental Health, Religion & Culture, 16,* 719–729.

Munson, H. (2005). Religion and violence. *Religion, 35,* 223–246.

Murdock, G. P. (1980). *Theories of Illness: A World Survey*. Pittsburgh: University of Pittsburgh Press.

Murken, S., & Namini, S. (2007). Childhood familial experiences as antecedents of adult membership in new religious movements: A literature review. *Nova Religio: The Journal of Alternative and Emergent Religions, 10,* 17–37.

Murphy, P. E., Ciarrocchi, J. W., Piedmont, R. L., Cheston, S., Peyrot, M., & Fitchett, G. (2000). The relation of religious belief and practices, depression, and hopelessness in persons with clinical depression. *Journal of Consulting and Clinical Psychology, 68,* 1102–1106.

Myers, D. G. (2012a). Reflections on religious belief and prosociality: Comment on Galen (2012). *Psychological Bulletin, 138,* 913–917.

Myers, D. G. (2012b). Religious engagement and well-being. In S. David, I. Boniwell, & A. C. Ayers (Eds.). *Oxford Handbook of Happiness* (pp. 88–100). Oxford: Oxford University Press.

Myers, D. G., & Diener, E. (1995). Who is happy? *Psychological Science, 6,* 10–19.

Myers, S. M. (1996). An interactive model of religiosity inheritance: The importance of family context. *American Sociological Review, 61,* 858–866.

Namini, S., & Murken, S. (2008). Familial antecedents and the choice of a new religious movement: Which person in which religious group? *Nova Religio, 11,* 83–103.

Namini, S., & Murken, S. (2009). Self-chosen involvement in new religious movements (NRMs): well-being and mental health from a longitudinal perspective. *Mental Health, Religion & Culture, 12,* 561–585.

Namini, S., Appel, C., Jürgensen, R., & Murken, S. (2010). How is well-being related to membership in new religious movements? An application of person-environment fit theory. *Applied Psychology: An International Review, 59,* 181–201.

Natchwey, J., & Tessler, M. (1999). Explaining women's support for political Islam: contributions from feminist theory. In M. Tessler (Ed.) *Area Studies and Social Science: Strategies for Understanding Middle East Politics* (pp. 46–69). Bloomington, IN: Indiana University Press.

Navarrete, C. D., McDonald, M. M., Mott, M. L., Cesario, J., & Sapolsky, R. (2010). Fertility and race perception predict voter preference for Barack Obama. *Evolution and Human Behavior, 31,* 394–399.

Navon, D. (1977). Forest before trees: The precedence of global features in visual perception. *Cognitive Psychology, 9,* 353–383.

Ndetei, D. M., & Vadher, A. (1985). Cross cultural study of religious phenomenology in psychiatric in-patients. *Acta Psychiatrica Scandinavica, 72,* 59–62.

Neeleman, J., & King, M. B. (1993). Psychiatrists' religious attitudes in relation to their clinical practice: a survey of 231 psychiatrists. *Acta Psychiatrica Scandinavica, 88,* 420–424.

Nelsen, H. M., & Kroliczak, A. (1984). Parental use of the threat "God will punish": Replication and extension. *Journal for the Scientific Study of Religion, 23,* 267–277.

Nelsen, H. M., Cheek, N. H., & Hau, P. (1985). Gender differences in images of God. *Journal for the Scientific Study of Religion, 24,* 396–402.

Nelson, G. K. (1972). The membership of a cult: The Spiritualist National Union. *Review of Religious Research, 13,* 170–177.

Nelson, L. D. (1988). Disaffiliation, desacralization, and political values. In D. G. Bromley (Ed.), *Falling from the Faith. Causes and Consequences of Religious Apostasy* (pp. 122–139). Newbury Park, CA: Sage.

Neuberg, S. L., Warner, C. M., Mistler, S. A., Berlin, A., Hill, E. D., Johnson, J. D., Filip-Crawford, G., Millsap, R. E., Thomas, T.,Winkelman, M., Broome, B. J., Taylor, T. J., & Schober, J. (2014). Religion and intergroup conflict: Findings from the Global Group Relations Project. *Psychological Science, 25,* 198–206.

Newman, M. L., Groom, C. J., Handelman, L. D., & Pennebaker, J. W. (2008). Gender differences in language use: An analysis of 14,000 text samples. *Discourse Processes, 45,* 211–236.

Ng, E.M.L. (2002). Pedophilia from the Chinese perspective. *Archives of Sexual Behavior, 31,* 491–492.

Ng, H.-Y. (2002). Drug use and self-organization: A personal construct study of religious conversion in drug rehabilitation. *Journal of Constructivist Psychology, 15,* 263–278.

Ng, H., & Shek, D. T. (2001). Religion and therapy: Religious conversion and the mental health of chronic heroin-addicted people. *Journal of Religion and Mental Health, 40,* 399–410.

Nicholi, A. (1974). A new dimension of the youth culture. *American Journal of Psychiatry, 131,* 396–401.

Nicholson, A., Rose, R., & Bobak, M. (2009). Association between attendance at religious services and self-reported health in 22 European countries. *Social Science & Medicine, 69,* 519–528.

Nicholson, A,. Rose, R., & Bobak, M. (2010). Associations between different dimensions of religious involvement and self-rated health in diverse European populations. *Health Psychology, 29,* 227–235.

Nickerson, R. S. (1999). How we know—and sometimes misjudge—what others know: Imputing one's own knowledge to others. *Psychological Bulletin, 125,* 737–759.

Nielsen, M. E. (2003). Appalling acts in God's name. *Society,* March/April, pp. 16–19.

Niemi, R. G., Ross, R. D., & Alexander, J. (1978). The similarity of political values of parents and college-age youths. *Public Opinion Quarterly, 42,* 503–520.

Nilsson, K. W., Damberg, M., Ohrvik, I., Leppert, J., Lindstrom, L., Anckarsater, H., & Oreland, L. (2007). Genes encoding for AP-2beta and the Serotonin Transporter are associated with the Personality Character Spiritual Acceptance. *Neuroscience Letters, 411,* 233–237.

Nolen-Hoeksema, S. (2003). *Women Who Think Too Much: How to Break Free of Overthinking and Reclaim your Life.* New York: Holt.

Norenzayan, A., & Gervais, W. M. (2012). The cultural evolution of religion. In E. Slingerland & M. Collard (Eds.), *Creating Consilience: Integrating Science and the Humanities* (pp. 243–265). Oxford: Oxford University Press.

Norenzayan, A., & Hansen, I. G. (2006). Belief in supernatural agents in the face of death. *Personality and Social Psychology Bulletin, 32*, 174–187.

Norenzayan, A., & Shariff, A. F. (2008). The origin and evolution of religious prosociality. *Science, 322*, 58–62.

Norenzayan, A., Gervais, W. M., & Trzesniewski, K. H. (2012). Mentalizing deficits constrain belief in a personal God. *PLOS ONE, 7*, e36880.

Norris, P., & Inglehart, R. (2004). *Sacred and Secular: Religion and Politics Worldwide.* Cambridge: Cambridge University Press.

Nucci, L. (2001). *Education in the Moral Domain.* Cambridge: Cambridge University Press.

Nukunya, G. (1992). *Tradition and Change in Ghana: An Introduction to Sociology.* Accra, Ghana: Ghana Universities Press.

Nunn, C. Z. (1964). Child control through a 'coalition with God'. *Child Development, 35*, 417–432.

Oatley, K. (2004). *Emotions: A Brief History.* Oxford: Blackwell.

Obadare, E. (2005). A crisis of trust: history, politics, religion and the polio controversy in northern Nigeria. *Patterns of Prejudice, 39*, 265–284.

Obeyesekere, G. (1991). *The Work of Culture: Symbolic Transformation In Psychoanalysis and Anthropology.* Chicago: University of Chicago Press.

Offer, J. (Ed.) (1994). *Herbert Spencer: Political Writings.* Cambridge: Cambridge University Press.

Ohtsuki, H., Hauert, C., Lieberman, E., & Nowak, M. A. (2006). A simple rule for the evolution of cooperation on graphs and social networks. *Nature, 441*, 502–505.

Oksanen, A. (1994). *Religious Conversion: A Meta-Analytical Study.* Lund: Lund University Press.

Okulicz-Kozaryn, A. (2010). Religiosity and life satisfaction across nations. *Mental Health, Religion & Culture, 13*, 155–169.

Okulicz-Kozaryn, A. (2011). Does religious diversity make us unhappy? *Mental Health, Religion & Culture, 14*, 1063–1076.

O'Leary, A. (2012). Building congregations around art galleries and cafes as spirituality wanes. *The New York Times,* December 29, p. A14.

Oliner, S. P., & Oliner, P. M. (1988). *The Altruistic Personality: Rescuers of Jews in Nazi Europe.* New York: Free Press.

Olson, J. M., Vernon, P. A., & Harris, J. A. (2001). The heritability of attitudes: A study of twins. *Journal of Personality and Social Psychology, 80*, 845–860.

Olsson, P. A. (1983). Adolescent involvement with the supernatural and cults. In D. A. Halperin (Ed.), *Psychodynamic Perspectives on Religion, Sect, and Cult* (pp. 235–256). Boston: John Wright.

Oman, D., Kurata, J. H., Strawbridge, W. J., & Cohen, R. D. (2002). Religious attendance and cause of death over 31 years. *International Journal of Psychiatric Medicine, 32*, 69–89.

Orbell, J., Goldman, M., Mulford, M., & Dawes, R. (1992). Religion, context and constraint towards strangers. *Rationality and Society, 4*, 291–307.

Osarchuk, M., & Tatz, S. (1973). Effect of induced fear of death on belief in an afterlife. *Journal of Personality and Social Psychology, 27*, 256–260.

Ostow, M., and Sharfstein, B. (1954). *The Need to Believe.* New York: International Universities Press.

O'Toole, R. (1996). Religion in Canada: Its development and contemporary situation. *Social Compass, 43*, 119–134.

Owens, J., Cook, E., & Stevenson, I. (1990). Features of "near-death experience" in relation to whether or not patients were near death. *Lancet, 347*, 1175–1177.

Ozorak, E. W. (1996). The power but not the glory: How women empower themselves through religion. *Journal for the Social Scientific Study of Religion, 35,* 17–29.

Pacini, R., & Epstein, S. (1999). The relation of rational and experiential information processing styles to personality, basic beliefs and the ratio-bias phenomenon. *Journal of Personality and Social Psychology, 76,* 972–987.

Paldam, M. (2001). Corruption and religion: Adding to the economic model. *Kyklos, 54,* 383–414.

Palmer, S. J., & Finn, N. (1992). Coping with apocalypse in Canada: Experiences of endtime in la Mission de l'Esprit Saint and the Institute of Applied Metaphysics. *Sociological Analysis, 53,* 397–415.

Paloutzian, R. F. (1981). Purpose in life and value changes following conversion. *Journal of Personality and Social Psychology, 41,* 1153–1160.

Paloutzian, R. F., & Kirkpatrick, L. A. (1995). The scope of religious influences on personal and societal well-being. *Journal of Social Issues, 51,* 1–11.

Paloutzian, R. F., Richardson, J. T., & Rambo, L. R. (1999). Religious conversion and personality change. *Journal of Personality, 67,* 1047–1079.

Parboteeah, K. P., & Cullen, J. B. (2002). Managers' justifications of unethical behaviors: A 28 nation social institutions approach. *Academy of Management Proceedings,* (Meeting Abstract Supplement), D1–D6.

Parboteeah, K. P., Hoegl, M., & Cullen, J. B. (2008). Ethics and religion: An empirical test of a Multidimensional Model. *Journal of Business Ethics, 80,* 387–398.

Parboteeah, K. P., Hoegl, M., & Cullen, J. (2009). Religious dimensions and work obligation: A country institutional profile model. *Human Relations, 62,* 119–148.

Pargament, K. I. (1997). *The Psychology of Religion and Coping: Theory, Research, Practice.* New York: Guilford Press.

Pargament, K. I. (2002). The bitter and the sweet: An evaluation of the costs and benefits of religiousness. *Psychological Inquiry, 13,* 168–181.

Pargament, K. I., Smith, B. W., Koenig, H. G., & Perez, L. (1998). Patterns of positive and negative religious coping with major life stressors. *Journal for the Scientific Study of Religion, 37,* 710–724.

Pargament, K. I., Trevino, K., Mahoney, A., & Silverman, I. (2007). They killed our lord: The perception of Jews as desecrators of Christianity as a predictor of anti-Semitism. *Journal for the Scientific Study of Religion, 46,* 143–158.

Park, J. I., Hong, J. P., Park, S., & Cho, M. J. (2012). The relationship between religion and mental disorders in a Korean population. *Psychiatry Investigation, 9,* 29–35.

Parker, G. B., & Brotchie, H. L. (2004). From diathesis to dimorphism: the biology of gender differences in depression. *Journal of Nervous and Mental Disease, 192,* 210–216.

Parnas, J., & Handest, P. (2003). Phenomenology of anomalous self-experience in early schizophrenia. *Comprehensive Psychiatry, 44,* 121–134.

Parsons, T., & Bales, R. F. (1955). *Family, Socialization and Interaction Process.* Glencoe: Free Press.

Paton, A. (1948). *Cry the Beloved Country: A Story of Comfort in Desolation.* New York: Charles Scribner's Sons.

Pattison, E. M., Lapins, N. A., & Doerr, H. A. (1973). A study of personality and function. *The Journal of Nervous and Mental Disease, 157,* 397–409.

Paul VI, *Mysterium Fidei,* September 3, 1965.

Paul, C., Fitzjohn, J., Eberhart-Phillips, J., Herbison, P., & Dickson, N. (2000). Sexual abstinence at age 21 in New Zealand: The importance of religion. *Social Science and Medicine, 51,* 1–10.

References **289**

Paunonen, S. V., & Jackson, D. N. (2000). What is beyond the Big Five? Plenty! *Journal of Personality, 68*, 821–835.

Pearce, M. J., Jones, S. M., Schwab-Stone, M. E., & Ruchkin, V. (2003). The protective effects of religiousness and parent involvement on the development of conduct problems among youth exposed to violence. *Child Development, 74*, 1682–1696.

Pearlin, L. I., & Schooler, C. (1978). The structure of coping. *Journal of Health and Social Behavior, 19*, 2–21.

Pearson, P. R., & Francis, L. J. (1989). The dual nature of the Eysenckian lie scales: Are religious adolescents more truthful? *Personality and Individual Differences, 10*, 1041–1048.

Pennycook, G., Cheyne, J. A., Seli, P., Koehler, D. J., & Fugelsang, J. A. (2012). Analytic cognitive style predicts religious and paranormal belief. *Cognition, 123*, 335–346.

Pepinsky, T. B., & Welborne, B. C. (2011). Piety and redistributive preferences in the Muslim world. *Political Research Quarterly, 64*, 491–505.

Pepper, S. C. (1942). *World Hypotheses*. Berkeley: University of California Press.

Peregrine, P. (1996). The Birth of the Gods Revisited: A Partial Replication of Guy Swanson's (1960) Cross-Cultural Study of Religion. *Cross-Cultural Research, 30*, 84–112.

Perrin, R. D. (2000). Religiosity and honesty: Continuing the search for the consequential dimension. *Review of Religious Research, 41*, 534–544.

Persinger, M. A. (1983). Religious and mystical experiences as artifacts of temporal lobe function: A general hypothesis. *Perceptual and Motor Skills, 57*, 1255–1262.

Persinger, M. (1988). Increased geomagnetic activity and the occurrence of bereavement hallucinations: Evidence for melatonin-mediated microseizuring in the temporal lobe? *Neuroscience Letters, 88*, 271–274.

Persinger, M. A. (2001). The neuropsychiatry of paranormal experiences. *Journal of Neuropsychiatry and Clinical Neuroscience, 13*, 515–524.

Persinger, M. A., & Healey, F. (2002). Experimental facilitation of the sensed presence: Possible intercalation between the hemispheres induced by complex magnetic fields. *Journal of Nervous and Mental Disease, 190*, 533–541.

Peters, E., Day, S., McKenna, J., & Orbach, G. (1999). Delusional ideation in religious and psychotic populations. *British Journal of Clinical Psychology, 38*, 83–96.

Petersen, A. M., Tenenbaum, J. N., Havlin, S., Stanley, H. E., & Perc, M. (2012). Languages cool as they expand: Allometric scaling and the decreasing need for new words. *Scientific Reports, 2*, 943–953.

Pew Forum (2010). U.S. religious knowledge survey. September 28, 2010; www.pewforum.org

Pfeiffer, J. T. (2002). African independent churches in Mozambique: Healing the afflictions of inequality. *Medical Anthropology Quarterly, 16*, 176–199.

Piaget, J. (1929). *The Child's Conception of the World*. London: Routledge & Kegan Paul.

Piaget, J. (1932/1965). *The Moral Judgment of the Child*. New York: The Free Press.

Piaget, J. (1962). *Play, Dreams, and Imitation in Childhood*. New York: Norton.

Piaget, J. (1967). *The Language and Thought of the Child*. London: Routledge & Kegan Paul.

Piazza, T., and Glock, C. Y. (1979). Images of God and their social meanings. In R. Wuthnow (Ed.), *The Religious Dimension: New Directions in Quantitative Research*. New York: Academic Press.

Piazza, J., Bering, J. M., & Ingram, G. (2011). "Princess Alice is watching you": Children's belief in an invisible person inhibits cheating. *Journal of Experimental Child Psychology, 109*, 311–320.

Pichon, I., & Saroglou, V. (2009). Religion and helping: Impact of target thinking styles and just world beliefs. *Archive for the Psychology of Religion, 31*, 215–236.

Pichon, I., Boccato, G., & Saroglou, V. (2007). Nonconscious influences of religion on prosociality: A priming study. *European Journal of Social Psychology, 37*, 1032–1045.

Pickel, G. (2009). Secularization as a European fate? Results from the Church and religion in an enlarged Europe project 2006. In G. Pickel & O. Müller (Eds.), *Church and Religion in Contemporary Europe: Results from Empirical and Comparative Research* (pp. 89–122). Opladen: VS-Verlag.

Pierre, R. (1977). Caribbean religion: The Voodoo case. *Sociological Analysis, 38*, 25–36.

Pinker, S. (1997). *How the Mind Works*. New York: Norton.

Pinker, S. (2011). *The Better Angels of Our Nature: Why Violence Has Declined*. New York: Viking.

Piven, J. S. (2003). Buddhism, death, and the feminine. *The Psychoanalytic Review, 90*, 498–536.

Platt, S. R. (2012). *Autumn in the Heavenly Kingdom: China, the West, and the Epic Story of the Taiping Civil War*. New York: Knopf.

Poling, T. H., & Kenney, J. F. (1986). *The Hare Krishna Character Type: A Study of the Sensate Personality*. Lewiston, NY: Edwin Mellen Press.

Pollack, D. (2008). Religious change in Europe: Theoretical considerations and empirical findings. *Social Compass, 55*, 168–186.

Pollack, D., & Pickel, G. (2007). Religious individualization or secularization? Testing hypotheses of religious change – the case of Eastern and Western Germany. *British Journal of Sociology, 58*, 603–632.

Poole, R., & Cook, C.C.H. (2011). Praying with a patient constitutes a breach of professional boundaries in psychiatric practice. *British Journal of Psychiatry, 199*, 94–98.

Pope, L. (1942). *Millhands and Preachers: A Study of Gastonia*. New Haven: Yale University Press.

Popp-Baier, U. (2010). From religion to spirituality—Megatrend in contemporary society or methodological artefact? A contribution to the secularization debate from psychology of religion. *Journal of Religion in Europe, 3*, 34–67.

Poppen, P. J. (1995). Gender and patterns of risk-taking in college students. *Sex Roles, 32*, 545–555.

Popper, M. (2001). *Hypnotic Leadership: Leaders, Followers, and the Loss of Self*. Westport, CT: Praeger.

Porges, S. W. (1998). Love: an emergent property of the mammalian autonomic nervous system. *Psychoneuroendocrinology, 23*, 837–861.

Possamai, A. (2003). Alternative spiritualities and the cultural logic of late capitalism. *Culture and Religion, 4*, 31–45.

Potts, C. A. (2008). *Conspirators, Confederates, and Cronies*. Cincinnati, OH: WordTechs Press.

Powell, A. (2001). *Athens and Sparta: Constructing Greek Political and Social History from 478 BC*. London: Routledge.

Powell, R., & Clarke, S. (2012). Religion as an evolutionary byproduct: A critique of the standard model. *British Journal for the Philosophy of Science, 63*, 457–486.

Pratt, J. B. (1920). *The Religious Consciousness: A Psychological Study*. New York: Macmillan.

Preece, P.F.W. & Baxter, J. H. (2000). Scepticism and gullibility: The superstitious and pseudo-scientific beliefs of secondary school students. *International Journal of Science Education, 22*, 1147–1156.

Presser, S., & Chaves, M. (2007). Is religious service attendance declining? *Journal for the Scientific Study of Religion, 46*, 417–423.

Preston, J. L., & Epley, N. (2009). Science and God: An automatic opposition between ultimate explanations. *Journal of Experimental Social Psychology, 45*, 238–241.

Preston, J. L., & Ritter, R. S. (2013). Different effects of God and religion on prosocial behavior. *Personality and Social Psychology Bulletin, 39,* 1471–1483.

Preston, J., Gray, K., & Wegner, D. M. (2006). The godfather of soul. *Behavioral and Brain Sciences, 29,* 482–483.

Preston, J. L., Ritter, R. S., & Hernandez, J. I. (2010). Principles of religious prosociality: A review and reformulation. *Social and Personality Psychology Compass, 4,* 574–590.

Previc, F. H. (2006). The role of the extrapersonal brain systems in religious activity. *Consciousness and Cognition, 15,* 500–539.

Probst, C. J. (2012). *Demonizing the Jews: Luther and the Protestant Church in Nazi Germany.* Bloomington: Indiana University Press.

Proudfoot, W. (1985). *Religious Experience.* Berkeley and Los Angeles: University of California Press.

Ptacek, J. T., Smith, R. E., & Zanas, J. (1992). Gender, appraisal and coping: A longitudinal analysis. *Journal of Personality, 60,* 747–770.

Puchalski, C., Ferrell, B., Virani, R., Otis-Green, S., Baird, P., Bull, J., Chochinov, H., Handzo, G., Nelson-Becker, H., Prince-Paul, M., Pugliese, K., & Sulmasy, D. (2009). Improving the quality of spiritual care as a dimension of palliative care: the report of the Consensus Conference. *Journal of Palliative Medicine, 12,* 885–904.

Pyszczynski, T. A., Greenberg, J., & Solomon, S. (2003). *In the Wake of 9/11: The Psychology of Terror.* Washington, DC: American Psychological Association.

Pyysiäinen, I. (2004). *Magic, Miracles and Religion: A Scientist's Perspective.* Walnut Creek, CA: Alta Vista.

Pyysiäinen, I. (2009). *Supernatural Agents: Why We Believe in Souls, Gods, and Buddhas.* New York: Oxford University Press.

Quinn, N. (2005). Universals of child rearing. *Anthropological Theory, 5,* 477–516.

Ragan, C. H., Malony, H. N., & Beit-Hallahmi, B. (1980). Psychologists and religion: Professional factors and personal belief. *Review of Religious Research, 21,* 208–217.

Raglan, F.R.S. (1936). *The Hero: A Study in Tradition, Myth, and Drama.* London: Methuen.

Raine, A. (1992). Sex differences in schizotypal personality in a non-clinical population. *Journal of Abnormal Psychology, 101,* 361–364.

Ramachandran, V. S., & Blakeslee, S. (1998). *Phantoms in the Brain: Human Nature and the Architecture of the Mind.* London: Fourth Estate.

Rambo, L. R. (1993). *Understanding Religious Conversion.* New Haven: Yale University Press.

Randi, J. (1989). *The Faith Healers.* Amherst, NY: Prometheus Books.

Randolph-Seng, B., & Nielsen, M. E. (2007). Honesty: One effect of primed religious representations. *International Journal for the Psychology of Religion, 17,* 303–315.

Randolph-Seng, B., & Nielsen, M. E. (2008). Is God really watching you? A response to Shariff and Norenzayan (2007). *International Journal for the Psychology of Religion, 18,* 119–122.

Rank, O. (1914). *The Myth of the Birth of the Hero: A Psychological Interpretation of Mythology.* New York: Nervous and Mental Diseases Publishing Co.

Rasic, D., Robinson, J. A., Bolton, J., Bienvenu, O. J., & Sareen, J. (2011). Longitudinal relationships of religious worship attendance and spirituality with major depression, anxiety disorders, and suicidal ideation and attempts: findings from the Baltimore epidemiologic catchment area study. *Journal of Psychiatric Research, 45,* 848–854.

Raybeck, D., Shoobe, J., & Grauberger, J. (1989). Women, stress, and participation in possession cults: A reexamination of the calcium deficiency hypothesis. *Medical Anthropology Quarterly, 3,* 139–161.

Reader, I. (2012). Secularisation, R.I.P.? Nonsense! The 'Rush Hour Away from the Gods' and the decline of religion in contemporary Japan. *Journal of Religion in Japan, 1,* 7–36.

Reavis, D. J. (1995). *The Ashes of Waco: An Investigation.* New York: Simon & Schuster.

Reed, R. (1997). Democracy and religion are not incompatible. *USA Today,* July 1, pp. 26–28.

Rees, D. G. (1967). *Denominational concepts of God.* Unpublished M.A. thesis, University of Liverpool.

Rees, W. D. (1971). The hallucinations of widowhood. *British Medical Journal, 4,* 37–41.

Regnerus, M. D. (2003). Moral communities and adolescent delinquency: Religious contexts and community social control. *The Sociological Quarterly, 44,* 523–554.

Regnerus, M. D. (2007). *Forbidden Fruit: Sex and Religion in the Lives of American Teenagers.* New York: Oxford University Press.

Regnerus, M. D., & Smith, C. (2005). Selection effects in studies of religious influence. *Review of Religious Research, 47,* 23–50.

Regnerus, M. D., & Uecker, J. E. (2006). Finding faith, losing faith: The prevalence and context of religious transformations during adolescence. *Review of Religious Research, 47,* 217–237.

Regnerus, M. D., Smith, C., & Smith, B. (2004). Social context in the development of adolescent religiosity. *Applied Developmental Science, 8,* 27–38.

Reimer, S., & Park, J. Z. (2001). Tolerant (in)civility? A longitudinal analysis of White conservative Protestants' willingness to grant civil liberties. *Journal for the Scientific Study of Religion, 40,* 735–745.

Reiss, J. L. (1967). *The Social Context of Premarital Sexual Permissiveness.* New York: Holt, Rinehart and Winston.

Reiss, S. (2000). Why people turn to religion: A motivational analysis. *Journal for the Scientific Study of Religion, 39,* 47–52.

Renshon, S. A. (1977). *Handbook of Political Socialization.* New York: Free Press.

Requena, M., & Stanek, M. (2013). Secularization in Poland and Spain after the democratic transition: A cohort analysis. *International Sociology, 28,* 84–101.

Reynolds, V., & Tanner, R. (1995). *The Social Ecology of Religion.* New York: Oxford University Press.

Říčan, P. R. (2004). Spirituality: The story of a concept in the psychology of religion. *Archive for the Psychology of Religion, 26,* 135–156.

Rice, T. W. (2003). Believe it or not: Religious and other paranormal beliefs in the United States. *Journal for the Scientific Study of Religion, 42,* 95–106.

Richards, P. S. (1991). The relation between conservative religious ideology and principled moral reasoning: A review. *Review of Religious Research, 32,* 359–368.

Richardson, J. T., & Dewitt, J. (1992). Christian Science, spiritual healing, the law, and public opinion. *Journal of Church and State, 34,* 549–561.

Richardson, J. T., Stewart, M., & Simmonds, R. B. (1979). *Organized Miracles: A Study of A Contemporary Youth, Communal, Fundamentalist Organization.* New Brunswick, NJ: Transaction Books.

Richert, R. A., & Barrett, J. L. (2005). Do you see what I see? Young children's assumptions about God's perceptual abilities. *International Journal for the Psychology of Religion, 15,* 283–295.

Richert, R. A., & Harris, P. L. (2006). The ghost in my body: Children's developing concept of the soul. *Journal of Cognition and Culture, 6,* 409–427.

Richert, R. A., & Harris, P. L. (2008). Dualism Revisited: Body vs. Mind vs. Soul. *Journal of Cognition and Culture, 8,* 99–115.

Rix, H. (1907). *Tent and the Testament: A Camping Out in Palestine with some Notes on Scripture Sites*. London: William and Norgate.

Rizzuto, A.-M. (1979). *The Birth of the Living God: A Psychoanalytic Study*. Chicago: University of Chicago Press.

Roald, A. S. (2001). *Women in Islam: The Western Experience*. London: Routledge.

Robbins, M., Francis, L. J., Haley, J. M., & Kay, W. K. (2001). The personality characteristics of Methodist ministers: Feminine men and masculine women? *Journal for the Scientific Study of Religion, 40,* 123–128.

Robbins, M., Francis, L. J., McIlroy, D., Clarke, R., & Pritchard, L. (2010). Three religious orientations and five personality factors: An exploratory study among adults in England. *Mental Health, Religion and Culture, 13,* 771–775.

Robbins, T., & Anthony, D. (1972). Getting straight with Meher Baba: A study of mysticism, drug rehabilitation and postadolescent role conflict. *Journal for the Scientific Study of Religion, 11,* 122–140.

Robbins, T., & Palmer, S. (Eds.). (1997). *Millennium, Messiahs, and Mayhem*. London: Routledge.

Robbins, T., Anthony, D., & Richardson, J. T. (1978). Theory and research on today's "New religions." *Sociology of Religion, 39,* 95–122.

Roberts, L., Ahmed, I., Hall, S., & Davison, A. (2009). Intercessory prayer for the alleviation of ill health. *Cochrane Database of Systematic Reviews*, Art. No. CD0-00368.

Roberts, T. A. (1991). Gender and the influence of evaluations of self-assessment in achievement settings. *Psychological Bulletin, 109,* 297–308.

Roccas, S. (2005). Religion and value systems. *Journal of Social Issues, 61,* 747–759.

Roccas, S., & Schwartz, S. H. (1997). Church-state relations and the association of religiosity with values: A study of Catholics in six countries. *Cross-Cultural Research: The Journal of Comparative Social Science, 31,* 356–375.

Roccas, S., Schwartz, S. H., & Amit, A. (2010). Personal value priorities and national identification. *Political Psychology, 31,* 393–419.

Roccas, S., Sagiv, L., Schwartz, S., & Knafo, A. (2002). The Big Five personality factors and personal values. *Personality and Social Psychology Bulletin, 28,* 789–801.

Rochford, E. B., Jr. (1989). Factionalism, group defection, and schism in the Hare Krishna movement. *Journal for the Scientific Study of Religion, 28,* 162–179.

Rochford, E. B., Jr. (2007). *Hare Krishna Transformed*. New York: NYU Press.

Rochford, E. B., Jr., Purvis, S., & Eastman, N. (1989). New religions, mental health, and social control. *Research in the Social Scientific Study of Religion, 1,* 57–82.

Rodarmor, W. (1983). The secret life of Swami Muktananda. *Coevolution Quarterly, 40,* 104–111.

Rodgers, D. V., Gindler, J. S., Atkinson, W. L., & Markowitz, L. E. (1993). High attack rates and case fatality during a measles outbreak in groups with religious exemption to vaccination. *Pediatrics Infectious Disease Journal, 12,* 288–292.

Roe, A. (1952). *The Making of a Scientist*. New York: Dodd, Mead.

Roemer, J. E. (1998). Why the poor do not expropriate the rich: An old argument in new garb. *Journal of Public Economics, 70,* 399–424.

Roemer, M. K. (2010a). Religion and subjective well-being in Japan: Do religious devotion and affiliation affect life satisfaction and happiness? *Review of Religious Research, 51,* 411–427.

Roemer, M. K. (2010b). Religion and psychological distress in Japan. *Social Forces, 89,* 559–583.

Roes, F. L., & Raymond, M. (2003). Belief in Moralizing Gods. *Evolution and Human Behavior, 24,* 126–135.

Roheim, G. (1932). Animism and religion. *Psychoanalytic Quarterly*, *6*, 59–112.

Rohrbaugh, J., & Jessor, R. (1975). Religiosity in youth: A personal control against deviant behavior. *Journal of Personality*, *43*, 136–155.

Rokeach, M. (1960). *The Open and Closed Mind*. New York: Basic Books.

Rokeach, M. (1969). Value systems in religion. *Review of Religious Research*, 1969, *11*, 3–38.

Rokeach, M. (1981). *The Three Christs of Ypsilanti*. New York: Columbia University Press.

Ronen, A. (2012). The oldest burials and their significance. In S. C. Reynolds, & A. Gallagher (Eds.), *African Genesis: Perspectives on Hominin Evolution* (pp. 554–570). Cambridge: Cambridge University Press.

Roof, W. C. (1993). *A Generation of Seekers: The Spiritual Journeys of the Baby Boom Generation*. San Francisco: Harper.

Roof, W. C. (2000). *Spiritual Marketplace: Baby Boomers and the Remaking of American Religion*. Princeton: Princeton University Press.

Rose, L. (1971). *Faith Healing*. Harmondsworth, Middlesex: Penguin.

Rosenbaum, R. (2001). *The Secret Parts of Fortune*. New York: Harper Collins.

Ross, M. W. (1985). Mental health in Hare Krishna devotees. *American Journal of Social Psychiatry*, *5*, 65–67.

Roth, L. M., & Kroll, J. C. (2007). Risky business: Assessing risk-preference explanations for gender differences in religiosity. *American Sociological Review*, *72*, 205–220.

Rothschild, Z. K., Abdollahi, A., & Pyszczynski, T. (2009). Does peace have a prayer? The effect of mortality salience, compassionate values, and religious fundamentalism on hostility toward out-groups. *Journal of Experimental Social Psychology*, *45*, 816–827.

Rounding, K., Lee, A., Jacobson, J. A., & Ji, L. J. (2012). Religion replenishes self-control. *Psychological Science*, *23*, 635–642.

Rowatt, W. C., Franklin, L. M., & Cotton, M. (2005). Patterns and personality correlates of implicit and explicit attitudes toward Christians and Muslims. *Journal for the Scientific Study of Religion*, *44*, 29–43.

Rowatt, W. C., LaBouff, J., Johnson, M., Froese, P., & Tsang, J. (2009). Associations among religiousness, social attitudes, and prejudice in a national random sample of American adults. *Psychology of Religion and Spirituality*, *1*, 14–24.

Roy, O. (2010). *Holy Ignorance: When Religion and Culture Part Ways*. London: Hurst & Co.

Rubin, Z., & Peplau, L. A. (1975). Who believes in a just world? *Journal of Social Issues*, *31*, 65–89.

Rubinstein, G. (1996). Two peoples in one land: A validation study of Altemeyer's right-wing authoritarianism scale in the Palestinian and Jewish societies in Israel. *Journal of Cross-Cultural Psychology*, *27*, 216–230.

Ruffle, B. J., & Sosis, R. (2006). Cooperation and the in-group-out-group bias: A field test on Israeli kibbutz members and city residents. *Journal of Economic Behavior & Organization*, *60*, 147–163.

Ruiter, S., & van Tubergen, F. (2009). Religious attendance in cross-national perspective: A multilevel analysis of 60 countries. *American Journal of Sociology*, *115*, 863–895.

Rule, N. O., Garrett, J. V., & Ambady, N. (2010). On the perception of religious group membership from faces. *PLOS ONE*, *5*(12), e14241.

Runciman, S. (1951). *History of the Crusades: The Kingdom of Acre and the Later Crusades*. Cambridge: Cambridge University Press.

Russell, B. (2008). *Authority and the Individual*. London: Hesperides Press.

Rutchick, A. M. (2010). Deus ex machina: The influence of polling place on voting behavior. *Political Psychology*, *31*, 209–225.

Rutjens, B. T., van der Pligt, J., & van Harreveld, F. (2010). Deus or Darwin: Randomness and belief in theories about the origin of life. *Journal of Experimental Social Psychology, 46,* 1078–1080.

Sabatier, C., Mayer, B., Friedlmeier, M., Lubiewska, K., & Trommsdorff, G. (2011). Religiosity, family orientation, and life satisfaction of adolescents in four countries. *Journal of Cross-Cultural Psychology, 42,* 1375–1393.

Sachdeva, S., Iliev, R., & Medin, D. L. (2009). Sinning saints and saintly sinners: The paradox of moral selfregulation. *Psychological Science, 20,* 523–528.

Sack, D. (2009). *Moral Re-Armament: The Reinventions of an American Religious Movement.* New York: Palgrave Macmillan.

Sacks, O. (1985). *Migraine: Understanding a Common Disorder.* Berkeley: University of California Press.

Sagan, C. (1979). *Broca's Brain: Reflections on the Romance of Science.* New York: Random House.

Sagioglou, C., & Forstmann, M. (2013). Activating Christian religious concepts increases intolerance of ambiguity and judgment certainty. *Journal of Experimental Social Psychology, 49,* 933–939.

Salas-Wright, C. P., Vaughn, M. G., Hodge, D. R., & Perron, B. E. (2012). Religiosity profiles of American youth in relation to substance use, violence, and delinquency. *Journal of Youth and Adolescence, 41,* 1560–1575.

Saler, B., & Ziegler, C. A. (2006). Atheism and the apotheosis of agency. *Temenos: Nordic Journal of Comparative Religion, 42,* 7–41.

Sales, S. M. (1972). Economic threat as a determinant of conversion rates in authoritarian and non-authoritarian churches. *Journal of Personality and Social Psychology, 23,* 420–428.

Sallquist, J., Eisenberg, N., French, D. C., Purwono, U., & Suryanti, T. A. (2010). Indonesian adolescents' spiritual and religious experiences and their longitudinal relations with socioemotional functioning. *Developmental Psychology, 46,* 699–716.

Salzman, L. (1953). The psychology of religious and ideological conversion. *Psychiatry, 16,* 177–187.

Sanada, T. (1979). After prophecy fails: A reappraisal of a Japanese case. *Japanese Journal of Religious Studies, 6,* 217–237.

Sanderson, S. K. (2008). Adaptation, evolution, and religion. *Religion, 38,* 141–156.

Saradjian, A., & Nobus, D. (2003). Cognitive distortions of religious professionals who sexually abuse children. *Journal of Interpersonal Violence, 18,* 905–923.

Sargent, W. (1957). *Battle for the Mind: How Evangelists, Psychiatrists, and Medicine Men Can Change Your Beliefs and Behavior.* Garden City, NY: Doubleday.

Saroglou, V. (2002a). Religion and the five factors of personality: A meta-analytic review. *Personality and Individual Differences, 32,* 15–25.

Saroglou, V. (2002b). Beyond dogmatism: the need for closure as related to religion. *Mental Health, Religion & Culture, 5,* 183–194.

Saroglou, V. (2006). Religion's role in prosocial behavior: Myth or reality? *Psychology of Religion Newsletter, 31,* 1–8.

Saroglou, V. (2010). Religiousness as a cultural adaptation of basic traits: A five-factor model perspective. *Personality and Social Psychology Review, 14,* 108–125.

Saroglou, V. (2011). Believing, bonding, behaving, and belonging: The big four religious dimensions and cultural variation. *Journal of Cross-Cultural Psychology, 42,* 1320–1340.

Saroglou, V., Corneille, O., & Van Cappellen, P. (2009). "Speak, Lord, Your Servant Is Listening": Religious priming activates submissive thoughts and behaviors. *International Journal for the Psychology of Religion, 19,* 143–154.

Saroglou, V., Delpierre, V., & Dernelle, R. (2004). Values and religiosity: A meta-analysis of studies using Schwartz's model. *Personality and Individual Differences, 37,* 721–734.

Saroglou, V., Pichon, I., Trompette, L., Verschueren, M., & Dernelle, R. (2005). Prosocial behavior and religion: New evidence based on projective measures and peer ratings. *Journal for the Scientific Study of Religion, 44,* 323–348.

Sasaki, J. Y., Kim, H. S., & Xu, J. (2011). Religion and well-being: The moderating role of culture and an oxytocin receptor polymorphism. *Journal of Cross-Cultural Psychology, 42,* 1394–1405.

Saver, J. L., & Rabin, J. (1997). The neural substrates of religious experience. *Journal of Neuropsychiatry and Clinical Neurosciences, 9,* 498–510.

Saxe, R., & Kanwisher, N. (2003). People thinking about people: The role of the temporoparietal junction in "theory of mind." *NeuroImage, 19,* 1835–1842.

Scheepers, P., Gijsberts, M., & Hello, E. (2002). Religiosity and prejudice against ethnic minorities in Europe: Cross-national tests on a controversial relationship. *Review of Religious Research, 43,* 242–265.

Scheepers, P., Te Grotenhuis, M., & Van Der Slik, F. (2002). Education, religiosity and moral attitudes: Explaining cross-national effect differences. *Sociology of Religion, 63,* 157–176.

Scheve, K., & Stasavage, D. (2006a). Religion and preferences for social insurance. *Quarterly Journal of Political Science, 1,* 255–286.

Scheve, K., & Stasavage, D. (2006b). The political economy of religion and social insurance in the United States, 1910–1939. *Studies in American Political Development, 20,* 132–159.

Schieman, S. (2010). Socioeconomic status and beliefs about God's influence in everyday life. *Sociology of Religion, 71,* 25–51.

Schimel, J. L. (1973). Esoteric identification processes in adolescence and beyond. *The Journal of the American Academy of Psychoanalysis, 1,* 403–415.

Schjødt, U., & Bulbulia, J. (2011). The need to believe in conflicting propositions. *Religion, Brain & Behavior, 1,* 236–239.

Schjødt, U., Stødkilde-Jørgensen, H., Geertz, A. W., & Roepstorff, A. (2009). Highly religious participants recruit areas of social cognition in personal prayer. *Social Cognitive and Affective Neuroscience, 4,* 199–207.

Schjødt, U., Stødkilde-Jørgensen, H., Geertz, A. W., Lund, T. E., & Roepstorff, A. (2011). The power of charisma—Perceived charisma inhibits the frontal executive network of believers in intercessory prayer. *Social Cognitive and Affective Neuroscience, 6,* 119–127.

Schlesinger, A. M., Jr. (1978). Human rights and the American tradition. *Foreign Affairs, 57,* 503–526.

Schlesinger, K. (1976). Origins of the Passover Seder in ritual sacrifice. *The Psychoanalytic Study of Society, 7,* 369–399.

Schneider, F., Habel, U., Kessler, C., Salloum, J. B., & Posse, S. (2000). Gender differences in regional cerebral activity during sadness. *Human Brain Mapping, 9,* 226–238.

Schredl, M. (2010). Nightmare frequency and nightmare topics in a representative German sample. *European Archives of Psychiatry and Clinical Neuroscience, 260,* 565–570.

Schultz, M. (1991). The blood libel: A motif in the history of childhood. In A. Dundes (Ed.), *The Blood Libel Legend: A Casebook in Anti-Semitic Folklore* (pp. 273–297). Madison: University of Wisconsin Press.

Schwadel, P. (2013). Changes in Americans' views of prayer and reading the Bible in public schools: Time periods, birth cohorts, and religious traditions. *Sociological Forum, 28,* 261–282.

Schwartz, G. (1970). *Sect Ideologies and Social Status.* Chicago: University of Chicago Press.

Schwartz, L. J. (1991). Religious matching for adoption: Unraveling the interests behind the "Best interests" standard. *Family Law Quarterly, 25,* 171–192.

Schwartz, S. H. (1992). Universals in the content and structure of values: Theoretical advances and empirical tests in 20 countries. *Advances in Experimental Social Psychology, 25,* 1–65.

Schwartz, S. H., & Huismans, S. (1995). Value priorities and religiosity in four Western religions. *Social Psychology Quarterly, 58,* 88–107.

Scott, J. (1998). Changing attitudes to sexual morality: A cross-national comparison. *Sociology, 32,* 815–845.

Sears, D. O., & Funk, C. L. (1999). Evidence of the long-term persistence of adults' political predispositions. *Journal of Politics, 61,* 1–28.

Secret, M. (2012). In reversal, Espada jurors indicate a verdict may be near. *The New York Times,* May 11, p. A28.

Sedikides, C., & Gebauer, J. E. (2010). Religiosity as self-enhancement: A meta-analysis of the relation between socially desirable responding and religiosity. *Personality and Social Psychology Review, 14,* 17–36.

Segal, R. A. (1989). *Religion and the Social Sciences.* Ithaca, NY: Scholars Press.

Seggar, J. F., & Blake, R. H. (1970). Post-joining nonparticipation: An exploratory study of convert inactivity. *Review of Religious Research, 11,* 204–209.

Sen, B. (2004). Adolescent propensity for depressed mood and help seeking: Race and gender differences. *The Journal of Mental Health Policy and Economics, 7,* 133–145.

Sered, S. S. (1987). Ritual, morality and gender: The religious lives of oriental Jewish women in Jerusalem. *Israel Social Science Research, 5,* 87–97.

Sered, S. S. (1994). *Priestess, Mother, Sacred Sister: Religions Dominated by Women.* New York: Oxford University Press.

Sethi, S., & Seligman, M.E.P. (1993). Optimism and fundamentalism. *Psychological Science, 4,* 256–259.

Sethi, S., & Seligman, M.E.P. (1994). The hope of fundamentalists. *Psychological Science, 5,* 58.

Shaffir, W. (1995). When prophecy is not validated: Explaining the unexpected in a Messianic campaign. *The Jewish Journal of Sociology, 37,* 119–136.

Shafranskee, E. P. (1996). *Religion and the Clinical Practice of Psychology.* Washington, DC: American Psychological Association.

Shahabi, L., Powell, L. H., Musick, M. A., Pargament, K. I., Thoresen, C. E., Williams, D., Underwood, L., & Ory, M. A. (2002). Correlates of self-perceptions of spirituality in American adults. *Annals of Behavioral Medicine, 24,* 59–68.

Shams, M., & Jackson, P. R. (1993). Religiosity as a predictor of well-being and moderator of the psychological impact of unemployment. *British Journal of Medical Psychology, 66,* 341–352.

Shansky, R. M., Glavis-Bloom, C., McRae, P., Benson, C., Miller, K., Cosand, L., Horvath, T. L., & Arnsten, A.F.T. (2004). Estrogen mediates sex differences in stress-induced prefrontal cortex dysfunction. *Molecular Psychiatry, 9,* 531–538.

Shapiro, R. (2008). *Suckers: How Alternative Medicine Makes Fools of Us All.* New York: Vintage.

Sharf, B. F., Stelljes, L. A. and Gordon, H. S. (2005). 'A little bitty spot and I'm a big man': patients' perspectives on refusing diagnosis of treatment for lung cancer. *Psycho-Oncology, 14,* 636–646.

Shariff, A. F., & Aknin, L. B. (2014). The emotional toll of hell: Cross-national and experimental evidence for the negative well-being effects of hell beliefs. *PLOS ONE, 9*(1), e85251.

Shariff, A. F., & Norenzayan, A. (2007). God is watching you: Priming God concepts increases prosocial behavior in an anonymous economic game. *Psychological Science, 18*, 803–809.

Shariff, A. F., & Rhemtulla, M. (2012). Divergent effects of heaven and hell beliefs on national crime. *PLOS ONE, 7*(6), e39048.

Shariff, A. F., Norenzayan, A., & Henrich, J. (2009). The birth of high gods: How the cultural evolution of supernatural policing influenced the emergence of complex, cooperative societies, paving the way for civilization. In M. Schaller, A. Norenzayan, S. Heine, T. Yamagishi, & T. Kameda (Eds.), *Evolution, Culture and the Human Mind* (pp.117–136). Hillsdale, NJ: Lawrence Erlbaum Associates.

Sharp, S. (2013). When prayers go unanswered. *Journal for the Scientific Study of Religion, 52*, 1–16.

Shaver, P. R., Lenauer, M., & Sadd, S. (1980). Religiousness, conversion, and subjective well-being: The "healthy minded" religion of modern American women. *American Journal of Psychiatry, 137*, 1563–1568.

Sheikh, H., Ginges, J., Coman, A., & Atran, S. (2012). Religion, group threat and sacred values. *Judgment and Decision Making, 7*, 110–118.

Shen, M. J., Yelderman, L. A., Haggard, M. C., & Rowatt, W. C. (2013). Disentangling the belief in God and cognitive rigidity/flexibility components of religiosity to predict racial and value-violating prejudice: A post-critical belief scale analysis. *Personality and Individual Differences, 54*, 389–395.

Shenhav, A., Rand, D. G., & Greene, J. D. (2012). Divine intuition: Cognitive style influences belief in God. *Journal of Experimental Psychology: General, 141*, 423–428.

Sherby, L. S., & Odelberg, W. (2001). *The Who's Who of Nobel Prize Winners 1901–2000*. Phoenix: Oryx Press.

Sherkat, D. E. (2002). Sexuality and religious commitment in the United States: An empirical examination. *Journal for the Scientific Study of Religion, 41*, 313–323.

Sherkat, D. E. (2004). Religious intermarriage in the United States: Trends, patterns, and predictors. *Social Science Research, 33*, 606–625.

Sherkat, D. E. (2008). Beyond belief: Atheism, agnosticism, and theistic certainty in the United States. *Sociological Spectrum, 28*, 438–459.

Sherkat, D. E. (2010). Religion and verbal ability. *Social Science Research, 39*, 2–13.

Sherkat, D. E. (2011). Religion and scientific literacy in the United States. *Social Science Quarterly, 92*, 1–17.

Shils, E. A., & Janowitz, M. (1948). Cohesion and disintegration in the Wehrmacht in World War II. *The Public Opinion Quarterly, 12*, 280–315.

Shimoni, G. (2003). *Community and Conscience: The Jews in Apartheid South Africa.* Waltham, MA: Brandeis University Press.

Shires, P. D. (2007). *Hippies of the Religious Right: From the Countercultures of Jerry Garcia to the Subculture of Jerry Falwell.* Waco, TX: Baylor University Press.

Shmueli, A., & Tamir, D. (2007). Health behavior and religiosity among Israeli Jews. *Israel Medical Association Journal, 9*, 703–707.

Shor, R. (1998). Pediatricians in Israel: Factors which affect the diagnosis and reporting of maltreated children. *Child Abuse and Neglect, 22*, 143–153.

Sibley, C. G., & Bulbulia, J. (2012). Faith after an earthquake: A longitudinal study of religion and perceived health before and after the 2011 Christchurch New Zealand earthquake. *PLOS ONE, 7*(12), e49648.

Siddle, R., Haddock, H., Tarrier, N., & Faragher, E. B. (2002). Religious delusions in patients admitted to hospital with schizophrenia. *Social Psychiatry and Psychiatric Epidemiology, 37*, 130–138.

Silverman, W. (1989). Images of the sacred: An empirical study. *Sociological Analysis, 49*, 440–444.

Simmel, E. (1946). *Anti-Semitism: A Social Disease.* New York: International Universities Press.

Simmonds, R. B. (1977). Conversion or addiction? Consequences of joining a Jesus movement group. *American Behavioral Scientist, 20*, 909–924.

Simmonds, R. B., Richardson, J. T., & Harder, M. W. (1976). A Jesus Movement group: An adjective check list assessment. *Journal for the Scientific Study of Religion, 15*, 323–337.

Simon, R. W. (2002). Revisiting the relationships among gender, marital status, and mental health. *American Journal of Sociology, 107*, 1065–1096.

Simon, R. W., & Lively, K. (2010). Sex, anger and depression. *Social Forces, 88*, 1543–1568.

Simoons, F. J. (1994). *Eat Not This Flesh: Food Avoidances from Prehistory to the Present.* Madison, WI: University of Wisconsin Press.

Simpson, E. (2011). Blame narratives and religious reason in the aftermath of the 2001 Gujarat earthquake. *South Asia: Journal of South Asian Studies, 34*, 421–438.

Simpson, J. (1981). Rationalized motifs in urban legends. *Folklore, 92*, 203–207.

Simpson, W. F. (1989). Comparative longevity in a college cohort of Christian Scientists. *JAMA: The Journal of the American Medical Association, 262*, 1657–1658.

Singelenberg, R. (1989). "It separated the wheat from the chaff": The 1975 prophecy and its impact among Dutch Jehovah's Witnesses. *Sociological Analysis, 50*, 23–40.

Singelenberg, R. (1999). Comments on Rodney Stark's "The rise and fall of Christian science." *Journal of Contemporary Religion, 14*, 127–132.

Singer, P. (1981). *The Expanding Circle: Ethics and Sociobiology.* New York: Farrar, Straus and Giroux.

Singh, S., & Edzard, E. (2008). *Trick or Treatment? Alternative Medicine on Trial.* New York: Norton.

Singleton, A. (2012). Beyond heaven? Young people and the afterlife. *Journal of Contemporary Religion, 27*, 453–468.

Sinha, J. W., Cnaan, R. A., & Gelles, R. J. (2007). Adolescent risk behaviors and religion: Findings from a national study. *Journal of Adolescence, 30*, 231–249.

Sinha, S. (1966). Religion in an affluent society. *Current Anthropology, 7*, 189–195.

Sipe, A.W.R. (1990). *A Secret World: Sexuality and the Search for Celibacy.* New York: Brunner/Mazel.

Slater, E., & Beard, A. W. (1963). The schizophrenia-like psychosis of epilepsy. *British Journal of Psychiatry, 109*, 95–150.

Slezkine, Y. (2004). *The Jewish Century.* Princeton: Princeton University Press.

Sloan, R. P. (2006). *Blind Faith: The Unholy Alliance of Religion and Medicine.* New York: St. Martin's Press.

Sloan, R. P. (2007). Attendance at religious services, health, and the lessons of trinity. *Psychosomatic Medicine, 69*, 493–494.

Sloan, R. P., & Bagiella, E. (2002). Claims about religious involvement and health outcomes. *Annals of Behavioral Medicine, 24*, 14–21.

Sloan, R. P., & Ramakrishnan, R. (2006). Science, medicine, and intercessory prayer. *Perspectives in Biology and Medicine, 49*, 504–514.

Sloan, R. P., Bagiella, E., & Powell, T. (1999). Religion, spirituality, and medicine. *Lancet, 353*, 664–667.

300 References

Sloan, R. P., Bagiella, E., VandeCreek, L., Hover, M., Casalone, C., Hirsch, T. J., Hasan, Y., Kreger, R., & Poulos, P. (2000). Should physicians prescribe religious activities? *New England Journal of Medicine, 342*, 1913–1916.

Smelser, N. J. (1962). *Theory of Collective Behaviour*. London: Routledge & Kegan Paul.

Smidt, C. (2005). Religion and American attitudes toward Islam and an invasion of Iraq. *Sociology of Religion, 66*, 243–261.

Smilde, D., and May, M. (2010). The emerging strong program in the sociology of religion. *SSRC Working Papers*. Available at: http://blogs.ssrc.org/tif/wp-content/uploads/2010/02/Emerging-Strong-Program-TIF.pdf

Smith, B. L., & Horne, S. G. (2008). What's faith got to do with it? The role of spirituality and religion in lesbian and bisexual women's sexual satisfaction. *Women and Therapy, 31*, 73–87.

Smith, C. (2003). Theorizing religious effects among American adolescents. *Journal for the Scientific Study of Religion, 42*, 17–30.

Smith, C. (Ed.) (2003). *The Secular Revolution: Power, Interests, and Conflict in the Secularization of American Public Life*. Berkeley: University of California Press.

Smith, C., & Faris, R. (2005). Socioeconomic inequality in the American religious system: An update and assessment. *Journal for the Scientific Study of Religion, 44*, 95–104.

Smith, C., & Snell, P. (2009). *Souls in Transition: The Religious and Spiritual Lives of Emerging Adults*. New York: Oxford University Press.

Smith, J. Z. (1982). *Imagining Religion: From Babylon to Jonestown*. Chicago: University of Chicago Press.

Smith, P. (1913). Luther's early development in the light of psycho-analysis. *The American Journal of Psychology, 24*, 360–377.

Smith, P. (1987). *The Babi and Baha'i Religions: From Messianic Shi'ism to a World Religion*. Cambridge: Cambridge University Press.

Smith, P. C., Range, L. M., & Ulmer, A. (1992). Belief in afterlife as a buffer in suicidal and other bereavement. *Omega: Journal of Death & Dying, 24*, 217–225.

Smith, T. B., McCullough, M. E., & Poll, J. (2003). Religiousness and depression: Evidence for a main effect and the moderating influence of stressful life events. *Psychological Bulletin, 129*, 614–636.

Snoep, L. (2008). Religiousness and happiness in three nations: a research note. *Journal of Happiness Studies, 9*, 207–211.

Snow, C. P. (1965). *The Two Cultures and the Scientific Revolution*. Cambridge: Cambridge University Press.

Snyder, C. R., Sigmon, D. R., & Feldman, D. B. (2002). Hope for the sacred and vice versa: Positive goal-directed thinking and religion. *Psychological Inquiry, 13*, 234–238.

Sober, E., & Wilson, D. S. (1999). *Unto Others: The Evolution and Psychology of Unselfish Behavior*. Cambridge, MA: Harvard University Press.

Solomon, S., Pyszczynski, T., & Greenberg, J. (2010). A terror management analysis of the psychological functions of religion. *Personality and Social Psychology Review, 14*, 84–94.

Solt, F., Habel, P., & Grant, J. T. (2011). Economic inequality, relative power, and religiosity. *Social Science Quarterly, 92*, 447–465.

Sommerville, C. J. (2002). Stark's Age of Faith argument and the secularization of things: A commentary. *Sociology of Religion, 63*, 361–372.

Sørensen, T., Danbolt, L. J., Lien, L., Koenig, H. G., & Holmen, J. (2011). The relationship between religious attendance and blood pressure: The Hunt Study, Norway. *International Journal of Psychiatry in Medicine, 42*, 13–28.

Sorrentino, R. M., & Hardy, J. E. (1974). Religiousness and derogation of an innocent victim. *Journal of Personality, 42*, 372–382.

Sosis, R. (2000). Religion and intragroup cooperation: Preliminary results of a comparative analysis of utopian communities. *Cross-Cultural Research, 34*, 77–88.

Sosis, R., & Bressler, E. (2003). Cooperation and commune longevity: A test of the costly signaling theory of religion. *Cross-Cultural Research, 37*, 211–239.

Sosis, R., & Bulbulia, J. (2011). The behavioral ecology of religion: the benefits and costs of one evolutionary approach, *Religion, 41*, 341–362.

Sosis, R., and Ruffle, B. J. (2003). Religious ritual and cooperation: Testing for a relationship on Israeli religious and secular kibbutzim. *Current Anthropology, 44*, 714–722.

Sosis, R., & Ruffle, B. (2004). Ideology, religion, and the evolution of cooperation: Field tests on Israeli kibbutzim. *Research in Economic Anthropology, 23*, 89–117.

Spanos, N. P., & Hewitt, E. C. (1979). Glossolalia: A test of the "trance" and psychopathology hypotheses. *Journal of Abnormal Psychology, 88*, 427–434.

Spanos, N. P., Cross, W. P., Lepage, M., & Coristine, M. (1986). Glossolalia as learned behavior: An experimental demonstration. *Journal of Abnormal Psychology, 95,* 21–23.

Spence, J. T., & Helmreich, R. L. (1978). *Masculinity and Femininity: Their Psychological Dimensions, Correlates, and Antecedents.* Austin: University of Texas Press.

Sperber, D. (1997). Intuitive and reflective beliefs. *Mind and Language, 12*, 67–83.

Spero, M. H. (1982). Psychotherapeutic procedure with religious cult devotees. *Journal of Nervous and Mental Disease, 170*, 332–344.

Spero, M. H., & Mester, R. (1988). Countertransference envy towards the religious patient. *American Journal of Psychoanalysis, 48*, 43–55.

Spiro, M. E. (1966). Religion: Problems of definition and explanation. In M. Banton (Ed.), *Anthropological Approaches to the Study of Religion* (pp. 85–126). London: Tavistock.

Spiro, M. E., & D'Andrade, R. G. (1960). A cross-cultural study of some supernatural beliefs. *American Anthropologist, 60*, 456–466.

Squarcini, F. (2000). In search of identity within the Hare Krishna Movement: Memory, oblivion and thought style. *Social Compass, 47*, 253–271.

Stacey, W., & Shupe, A. (1982). Correlates of support for the electronic church. *Journal for the Scientific Study of Religion, 21*, 291–303.

Stanovich, K. E., & West, R. F. (2000). Individual differences in reasoning: Implications for the rationality debate. *Behavioral and Brain Sciences, 23*, 645–665.

Staples, C., & Mauss, A. (1987). Conversion or commitment? A reassessment of the Snow and Machalek approach to the study of conversion. *Journal for the Scientific Study of Religion, 26*, 133–147.

Starbuck, E. D. (1899). *The Psychology of Religion.* New York: Scribner.

Stark, R. (1963). On the incompatibility of religion and science: A survey of American graduate students. *Journal for the Scientific Study of Religion, 3*, 3–20.

Stark, R. (1964). Class, radicalism, and religious involvement. *American Sociological Review, 29*, 698–706.

Stark, R. (1996). Religion as context: Hellfire and delinquency one more time. *Sociology of Religion, 57*, 163–173.

Stark, R. (1998). The rise and fall of Christian Science. *Journal of Contemporary Religion, 13*, 189–214.

Stark, R. (2000). Religious effects: In praise of "idealistic humbug." *Review of Religious Research, 41*, 289–310.

Stark, R. (2002a). Gods, rituals, and the moral order. *Journal for the Scientific Study of Religion, 40*, 619–636.

Stark, R. (2002b). Physiology and faith: Addressing the "universal" gender difference in religious commitment. *Journal for the Scientific Study of Religion, 41*, 495–507.

302 References

Stark, R., & Bainbridge, W. S. (1985). *The Future of Religion: Secularization, Revival and Cult Formation.* Berkeley: University of California Press.

Stark, R., & Bainbridge, W. S. (1987). *A Theory of Religion.* New York: Peter Lang.

Stark, R., Foster, B. D., Glock, C. Y., & Quinley, H. E. (1971). *Wayward Shepherds: Prejudice and the Protestant Clergy.* New York: Harper & Row.

Stark, R., Iannaccone, L. R., & Finke, R. (1996). Religion, science, and rationality. *The American Economic Review, 86,* 433–437.

Starks, B., & Robinson, R. V. (2007). Moral cosmology, religion, and adult values for children. *Journal for the Scientific Study of Religion, 46,* 17–35.

Stavrova, O., Fetchenhauer, D., & Schlösser, T. (2013). Why are religious people happy? The effect of the social norm of religiosity across countries. *Social Science Research, 42,* 90–105.

Stefanek, M., McDonald, P. G., & Hess, S. A. (2005). Religion, spirituality and cancer: Current status and methodological challenges. *Psycho-Oncology, 14,* 450–463.

Steffensen-Bruce, I. A. (*1998*). *Marble Palaces, Temples of Art: Art Museums, Architecture, and American Culture, 1890–1930.* Lewisburg, PA: Bucknell University Press.

Steger, M. F., & Frazier, P. (2005). Meaning in life: One link in the chain from religiousness to well-being. *Journal of Counseling Psychology, 52,* 574–582.

Steigmann-Gall, R. (2003). *The Holy Reich: Nazi Conceptions of Christianity, 1919–1945.* New York: Cambridge University Press.

Steinberg, L. (2008). A social neuroscience perspective on adolescent risk-taking. *Developmental Review, 28,* 78–106.

Steinberg, T. (2000). *Acts of God: The Unnatural History of Natural Disaster in America.* New York: Oxford University Press.

Stephens, N. M., Fryberg, S. A., Markus, H. R., & Hamedani, M. G. (2013). Who explains Hurricane Katrina and the Chilean earthquake as an act of God? The experience of extreme hardship predicts religious meaning-making. *Journal of Cross Cultural Psychology, 44,* 607–619.

Stern, R. M., Rasinski, K. A., & Curlin, F. A. (2011). Jewish physicians' beliefs and practices regarding religion/spirituality in the clinical encounter. *Journal of Religion and Health, 50,* 806–817.

Stewart, P. J., & Strathern, A. (2004). *Witchcraft, Sorcery, Rumors, and Gossip.* Cambridge: Cambridge University Press.

Stiffos-Hanssen, H. (1999). Religion and spirituality: What a European ear hears. *The International Journal for the Psychology of Religion, 9,* 25–33.

Stødkilde-Jørgensen, H., Geertz, A. W., & Roepstorff, A. (2008). Rewarding prayers. *Neuroscience Letters, 443,* 165–168.

Stone, L. (1978). Death and its history. *New York Review of Books,* October 12, 1978.

Stone, L. (1991). *Road to Divorce: England 1530–1987.* New York: Oxford University Press.

Stone, M. H. (1992). Religious behavior in the Psychiatric Institute 500. In M. Finn, & J. Gartner (Eds.), *Object Relations Theory and Religion: Clinical Applications* (pp. 141–153). Westport, CT: Praeger.

Stout-Miller, R., Miller, L. S., & Langenbrunner, M. R. (1997). Religiosity and child sexual abuse: A risk factor assessment. *Journal of Child Sexual Abuse, 6,* 15–34.

Straus, M. (1994). *Beating the Devil Out of Them: Corporal Punishment in American Families.* San Francisco: Jossey-Bass.

Strawbridge, W. J., Cohen, R. D., Shema, S. J., & Kaplan, G. A. (1997). Frequent attendance at religious services and mortality over 28 years. *American Journal of Public Health, 87,* 957–961.

Strawbridge, W. J., Shema, S. J., Cohen, R. D., & Kaplan, G. A. (2001). Religious attendance increases survival by improving and maintaining good health behaviors, mental health, and social relationships. *Annals of Behavioral Medicine, 23,* 68–74.

Strayer, J. (1940). The laicization of French and English society in the thirteenth century. In J. F. Benton, and T. N. Bisson (Eds.), *Medieval Statecraft and the Perspectives of History* (pp. 251–265). Princeton: Princeton University Press.

Streib, H., & Hood, R. W., Jr. (2011). "Spirituality" as privatized experience-oriented religion: Empirical and conceptual perspectives. *Journal of Implicit Religion, 14,* 433–453.

Streib, H., Hood, R. W., Jr., Keller, B., Csöff, R.-M., & Silver, C. F. (2010). *Deconversion: Qualitative and Quantitative Results from Cross-Cultural Research in Germany and the United States of America.* Gottingen: Vandenhoeck & Ruprecht.

Streiker, L. D. (1991). *New Age Comes to Main Street: A Non-Hysterical Survey of the New Age Movement.* Nashville: Abingdon Press.

Strenski, I. (1998). Religion, power and final Foucault. *Journal of the American Academy of Religion, 66,* 345–365.

Stromberg, P. G. (1993). *Language and Self-Transformation: A Study of the Christian Conversion Narrative.* Cambridge: Cambridge University Press.

Stroope, S. (2012). Social networks and religion: The role of congregational social embeddedness in religious belief and practice. *Sociology of Religion, 73,* 273–298.

Strozier, C. (1994). *Apocalypse: On the Psychology of Fundamentalism in America.* Boston: Beacon Press.

Strunk, O., Jr. (1957). The present status of the psychology of religion. *Journal of Religion and the Bible, 25,* 287–292.

Sullins, D. P. (2006). Gender and religion: Deconstructing universality, constructing complexity. *American Journal of Sociology, 112,* 838–880.

Sullivan, A. R. (2010). Mortality differentials and religion in the United States: Religious affiliation and attendance. *Journal for the Scientific Study of Religion, 49,* 740–753.

Sullivan, H. S. (1964). *The Fusion of Psychiatry and Social Science.* New York: Norton.

Svensson, I. (2007). Fighting with faith: Religion and conflict resolution in civil wars. *Journal of Conflict Resolution, 51,* 930–949.

Swanson, G. E. (1960). *The Birth of the Gods.* Ann Arbor: University of Michigan Press.

Tabor, J., & Gallagher, J. (1995). *Why Waco? Cults and The Battle for Religious Freedom in America.* Berkeley: University of California Press.

Tajfel, H. (1978). *Differentiation Between Social Groups: Studies in the Social Psychology of Intergroup Relations.* Oxford, UK: Academic Press.

Tajfel, H. (1981). *Human Groups and Social Categories: Studies in Social Psychology.* Cambridge: Cambridge University Press.

Tajfel, H., & Turner, J. C. (1986). The social identity theory of ingroup behavior. In S. Worchel, & W. G. Austin (Eds.), *Psychology of Intergroup Relations* (pp. 7–24). Chicago: Nelson Hall.

Takriti, R. A., Barrett, M., & Buchanan-Barrow, E. (2006). Children's understanding of religion: Interviews with Arab-Muslim, Asian-Muslim, Christian and Hindu children aged 5–11 years. *Mental Health, Religion & Culture, 9,* 29–42.

Takyi, B. K. (2003). Religion and women's health in Ghana: Insights into HIV/AIDS preventive and protective behavior. *Social Science & Medicine, 56,* 1221–1235.

Talwar, V., Harris, P. L., & Schleifer, M. (Eds.). (2011). *Children's Understanding of Death.* New York: Cambridge University Press.

Tamminen, K. (1994). Religious experiences in childhood and adolescence: A viewpoint of religious development between the ages of 7 and 20. *International Journal for the Psychology of Religion, 4,* 61–85.

304 References

Tamres, L., Janicki, D., & Helgeson, V. S. (2002). Sex differences in coping behavior: A meta-analytic review. *Personality and Social Psychology Review, 6*, 2–30.

Tan, J.H.W. (2006). Religion and social preferences: An experimental study. *Economic Letters, 90*, 60–67.

Tan, J.H.W., & Vogel, C. (2008). Religion and trust: An experimental study. *Journal of Economic Psychology, 29*, 832–848.

Tannen, D. (1990). *You Just Don't Understand: Women and Men in Conversation.* New York, NY: Ballantine.

Tannen, D. (1994). *Gender and Discourse.* New York: Oxford University Press.

Tavory, I., & Wincheser, D. (2012). Experiential careers: The routinization and de-routinization of religious life. *Theory and Society, 41*, 351–373.

Taylor, A., & MacDonald, D. A. (1999). Religion and the five factor model of personality: An exploratory investigation using a Canadian university sample. *Personality and Individual Differences, 27*, 1243–1259.

Taylor, S. E., Klein, L. C., Lewis, B. P., Gruenewald, T. L., Gurung, R.A.R., & Updegraff, J. A. (2000). Female responses to stress: Tend and befriend, not fight or flight. *Psychological Review, 107*, 411–429.

Te Grotenhuis, M., & Scheepers, P. (2001). Churches in Dutch: Causes of religious disaffiliation in the Netherlands, 1937–1995. *Journal for the Scientific Study of Religion, 40*, 591–606

Teinonen, T., Vahlberg, T., Isoaho, R., & Kivelä, S.-L. (2005). Religious attendance and 12-year survival in older persons. *Ageing, 34*, 406–409.

Tek, C., & Ulug, B. (2001). Religiosity and religious obsessions in obsessive-compulsive disorder. *Psychiatry Research, 104*, 99–108.

Tepper, L., Rogers, S. A., Coleman, E. M., & Malony, H. N. (2001). The prevalence of religious coping among persons with persistent mental illness. *Psychiatric Services, 52*, 660–665.

Terhune, C. (1997). Current international and domestic issues affecting children: Cultural and religious defenses to child abuse and neglect. *Journal of the American Academy of Matrimonial Lawyers, 152*, 156–192.

Terman, L. M., & Oden, M. (1959). *The Gifted Group at Mid-Life: Thirty-Five Years' Follow-Up of the Superior Child.* Stanford, CA: Stanford University Press.

Thomas, D. (1954). *Under Milk Wood: A Play for Voices.* New York: New Directions.

Thompson, A. D. (1974). Open-mindedness and indiscriminate antireligious orientation. *Journal for the Scientific Study of Religion, 13*, 471–477.

Thompson, E. H. (1991). Beneath the status characteristic: Gender variations in religiousness. *Journal for the Scientific Study of Religion, 30*, 381–394.

Thompson, E. H. Jr., & Remmes, K. R. (2002). Does masculinity thwart being religious? An examination of older men's religiousness. *Journal for the Scientific Study of Religion, 41*, 521–532.

Thornton, R. (1981). Demographic antecedents of a revitalization movement: Population change, population size, and the 1890 Ghost Dance. *American Sociological Review, 46*, 88–96.

Thornton, R. (1986). *We Shall Live Again. The 1870 and 1890 Ghost Dance Movements as Demographic Revitalization.* Cambridge: Cambridge University Press.

Thouless, R. H. (1923). *An Introduction to the Psychology of Religion.* Cambridge: Cambridge University Press.

Tiliouine, H., & Belgoumidi, A. (2009). An exploratory study of religiosity, meaning in life and subjective wellbeing in Muslim students from Algeria. *Applied Research in Quality of Life, 4*, 109–127.

Titarenko, L. (2008). On the shifting nature of religion during the ongoing post-communist transformation in Russia, Belarus and Ukraine. *Social Compass, 55*, 237–254.

Tolin, D. F., Abramowitz, J. S., Kozak, M. J., & Foa, E. B. (2001). Fixity of belief, perceptual aberration, and magical ideation in obsessive-compulsive disorder. *Anxiety Disorders, 15*, 501–510.

Tolstoy, L. (1966). *War and Peace*. New York: Norton.

Tomasson, R. F. (1968). Religion is irrelevant in Sweden. *Trans-action, 6*, 46–53.

Traphagan, J. W. (2004). *The Practice of Concern: Ritual, Well-being, and Aging in Rural Japan*. Durham, NC: Carolina Academic Press.

Tremlin, T. (2006). *Minds and Gods: The Cognitive Foundations of Religion*. Oxford: Oxford University Press.

Triandis, H. C. (1973). Subjective culture and economic development. *International Journal of Psychology, 8*, 163–180.

Trimble, D. E. (1997). The religious orientation scale: review and meta-analysis of social desirability effects. *Educational and Psychological Measurement, 57*, 970–986.

Trimble, M., & Freeman, A. (2006). An investigation of religiosity and the Gastaut–Geschwind syndrome in patients with temporal lobe epilepsy. *Epilepsy & Behavior, 9*, 407–414.

Trivers, R. (1971). The evolution of reciprocal altruism. *Quarterly Review of Biology, 46*, 35–37.

Truett, K. R., Eaves, L. J., Meyer, J. M., & Heath, A. C., *et al.* (1992). Religion and education as mediators of attitudes: a multivariate analysis. *Behavior Genetics, 22*, 43–62.

Tsai, J. L., Miao, F., & Seppala, E. (2007). Good feelings in Christianity and Buddhism: Religious differences in ideal affect. *Personality and Social Psychology Bulletin, 33*, 409–421.

Tschannen, O. (1991). The secularization paradigm: A systematization. *Journal for the Scientific Study of Religion, 30*, 395–415.

Tumminia, D. (1998). How prophecy never fails: Interpretive reason in a flying-saucer group. *Sociology of Religion, 59*, 157–170.

Turiel, E. (1983). *The Development of Social Knowledge: Morality and Convention*. New York: Cambridge University Press.

Turiel, E., & Neff, K. (2000). Religion, culture, and beliefs about reality in moral reasoning. In K. S. Rosengren, C. N. Johnson, & P. L. Harris (Eds.), *Imagining the Impossible: Magical, Scientific, and Religious Thinking in Children* (pp. 269–304). New York: Cambridge University Press.

Turina, I. (2011). Consecrated virgins in Italy: A case study in the renovation of Catholic religious life. *Journal of Contemporary Religion, 26*, 43–55.

Turner, H. A. (1994). Gender and social support: Taking the bad with the good? *Sex Roles, 30*, 521–541.

Twain, M. (1884/1965). *The Adventures of Huckleberry Finn*. New York: Harper & Row.

Tylor, E. B. (1871). *Primitive Culture: Researches into the Development of Mythology, Philosophy, Religion, Art, and Custom*. London: John Murray.

Uecker, J. E., Regnerus, M. D., & Vaaler, M. L. (2007). Losing my religion: The social sources of religious decline in early adulthood. *Social Forces, 85*, 1667–1692.

Ullman, C. (1982). Cognitive and emotional antecedents of religious conversion. *Journal of Personality and Social Psychology, 43*, 183–192.

Underhill, R. (1975). Economic and political antecedents of monotheism: A cross-cultural study. *American Journal of Sociology, 80*, 841–861.

Underwood, L. G. (2006). Ordinary spiritual experience: Qualitative research, interpretive guidelines, and population distribution for the Daily Spiritual Experience Scale. *Archive for the Psychology of Religion, 28*, 181–218.

United Nations (2000/1948). *Universal Declaration of Human Rights*. General Assembly. Resolution 217 A (III); www.unhchr.ch/udhr/lang/eng.htm

United States Department of State (2011). *International Religious Freedom Report for 2011*. Washington, DC: Bureau of Democracy, Human Rights and Labor.

Unnever, J. D., Bartkowski, J. P., & Cullen, F. T. (2010). God imagery and opposition to abortion and capital punishment: A partial test of religious support for the consistent life ethic. *Sociology of Religion, 71*, 307–322.

Urgesi, C., Aglioti, S. M., Skrap, M., & Fabbro, F. (2010). The spiritual brain: Selective cortical lesions modulate human self-transcendence. *Neuron, 65*, 309–319.

Uttley, R. M. (1993). *The Lance and the Shield: The Life and Times of Sitting Bull*. New York: Henry Holt.

Vail III, K. E., Arndt, J., & Abdollahi, A. (2012). Exploring the existential function of religious and supernatural agent beliefs among Christians, Muslims, atheists and agnostics. *Personality and Social Psychology Bulletin, 38*, 1288–1300.

Vail III, K. E., Rothschild, Z. K., Weise, D. R., Solomon, S., Pyszczynski, T., & Greenberg, J. (2010). A terror management analysis of the psychological functions of religion. *Personality and Social Psychology Review, 14*, 84–94.

Vaitl, D., Birbaumer, N., Gruzelier, J., Jamieson, G. A., Kotchoubey, B., Kubler, A., Lehmann, D., Miltner, W.H.R., Ott, U., Putz, P., Sammer, G., Strauch, I., Strehl, U., Wackermann, J., & Weiss, T. (2005). Psychobiology of altered states of consciousness. *Psychological Bulletin, 131*, 98–127.

Van Beest, I., & Williams, K. D. (2011). "Why hast Thou forsaken me?" The effect of thinking about being ostracized by God on well-being and prosocial behavior. *Social Psychological and Personality Science, 2*, 379–386.

Van Cappellen, P., Corneille, O., Cols, S., & Saroglou, V. (2011). Beyond mere compliance to authoritative figures: Religious priming increases conformity to informational influence among submissive people. *International Journal for the Psychology of Religion, 21*, 97–105.

Van den Bos, K., Van Ameijde, J., & Van Gorp, H. (2006). On the psychology of religion: The role of personal uncertainty in religious worldview defense. *Basic and Applied Social Psychology, 28*, 333–341.

Van Der Lans, J. (1987). The value of Sundén's role-theory demonstrated and tested with respect to religious experiences in meditation. *Journal for the Scientific Study of Religion, 26*, 401–412.

van Fossen, A. B. (1988). How do movements survive failures of prophecy? In L. Kreisberg, B. Misztal, and J. Mucha (Eds.), *Research in Social Movements, Conflict, and Change* (pp. 193–212). Greenwich, CT: JAI Press.

van Lommel, P., van Wees, R., Meyers, V., & Elfferich, I. (2001). Near-death experience in survivors of cardiac arrest: A prospective study in the Netherlands. *The Lancet, 358*, 2039–2045.

Van Pachterbeke, M., Freyer, C., & Saroglou, V. (2011). When authoritarianism meets religion: Sacrificing others in the name of abstract deontology. *European Journal of Social Psychology, 41*, 898–903.

Varese, F., & Yaish, M. (2000). The importance of being asked: The rescue of Jews in Nazi Europe. *Rationality and Society, 12*, 307–334.

Vaughan, T. R., Smith, D. H., & Sjoberg, G. (1963). The religious orientations of American natural scientists. *Social Forces, 44*, 519–526.

Veevers, J. E., & Cousineau, D. F. (1980). The heathen Canadians: Demographic correlates of non-belief. *Pacific Sociological Review, 23*, 199–216.

References **307**

Vermeer, P., Janssen, J., & De Hart, J. (2011). Religious socialization and church attendance in the Netherlands between 1983 and 2007: A panel study. *Social Compass, 58*, 373–392.

Verweij, J., Ester, E., & Nauta, R. (1997). Secularization as an economic and cultural phenomenon: A cross-national analysis. *Journal for the Scientific Study of Religion, 36*, 309–324.

Vess, M., Arndt, J., Cox, C. R., Routledge, C., & Goldenberg, J. L. (2009). Exploring the existential function of religion: The effect of religious fundamentalism and mortality salience on faith-based medical refusals. *Journal of Personality and Social Psychology, 97*, 334–350.

Victoria, B. (2006). *Zen at War.* Lanham, MD: Rowman and Littefield.

Vijayakumar, L. (2004). Altruistic suicide in India. *Archives of Suicide Research, 8*, 73–80.

Vilchinsky, N., & Kravetz, S. (2005). How are religious belief and behavior good for you? An investigation of mediators relating religion to mental health in a sample of Israeli Jewish students. *Journal for the Scientific Study of Religion, 44*, 459–471.

Viña, J., Borrás, C., Gambini, J., Sastre, J., & Pallardó, F. V. (2005). Why females live longer than males? Importance of the upregulation of longevity-associated genes by oestrogenic compounds. *FEBS Letters, 579*, 2541–2545.

Vitell, S. J. (2009). The role of religiosity in business and consumer ethics: A review of the literature. *Journal of Business Ethics, 90*, Supplement 2, 155–167.

Voas, D. (2009). The rise and fall of fuzzy fidelity in Europe. *European Sociological Review, 25*, 155–168.

Vogt, D. S., & Colvin, C. R. (2003). Interpersonal orientation and the accuracy of personality judgments. *Journal of Personality, 71*, 267–295.

von Hentig, H. (1948). *The Criminal and His Victim.* New Haven, CT: Yale University Press.

Vorontsova, L., & Filatov, S. (1994). Religiosity and political consciousness in postSoviet Russia. *Religion, State and Society, 22*, 397–402.

Vyse, S. (1997). *Believing In Magic: The Psychology of Superstition.* New York: Oxford University Press.

Waillet, N., & Roskam, I. (2012). Developmental and social determinants of religious social categorization. *The Journal of Genetic Psychology, 173*, 208–220.

Wallace, A.F.C. (1956). Revitalization movements. *American Anthropologist, 58*, 264–281.

Wallace, A.F.C. (1961). Mental illness, biology and culture. In Hsu, F.L.K. (Ed.), *Psychological Anthropology* (pp. 283–287). Homewood, IL: Dorsey Press.

Wallace, A.F.C. (1966). *Religion: An Anthropological View.* New York: Random House.

Wallace, A.F.C. (1970). *The Death and Rebirth of the Seneca.* New York: Knopf.

Wallace, R. A. (1975). A model of change of religious affiliation. *Journal for the Scientific Study of Religion, 14*, 345–355.

Waller, N. G., Kojetin, B. A., Bouchard, T. J., Jr., Lykken, D. T., & Tellegen, A. (1990). Genetic and environmental influences on religious interests, attitudes, and values: A study of twins reared apart and together. *Psychological Science, 1*, 138–142.

Walter, T. (2012).Why different countries manage death differently: a comparative analysis of modern urban societies. *The British Journal of Sociology, 63*, 123–145.

Warburg, M. (2001). Seeking the seekers in the sociology of religion. *Social Compass, 48*, 91–101.

Warneken, F., & Tomasello, M. (2006). Altruistic helping in human infants and young chimpanzees. *Science, 311*, 1301–1303.

Warneken, F., & Tomasello, M. (2007). Helping and cooperation at 14 months of age. *Infancy, 11*, 271–294.

308 References

Warnod, J. (1975). *Le Bateau Lavoir*. Paris: Presses de la Connaissance.

Watson, P. J., Morris, R. J., Hood, R. W., Jr., Miller, L., & Waddell, M. G. (1999). Religion and the experiential system: Relationships of constructive thinking with religious orientation. *International Journal for the Psychology of Religion, 9*, 195–207.

Waxman, S. G., & Geschwind, N. (1975). The interictal behavior syndrome of temporal lobe epilepsy. *Archives of General Psychiatry, 32*, 1580–1586.

Weaver, G. R., & Agle, B. R. (2002). Religiosity as an influence on ethical behavior in organizations: A symbolic interactionist perspective. *Academy of Management Review, 27*, 77–97.

Weber, M. (1951). *The Religion of China*. New York: Free Press.

Webster, D., & Kruglanski, A. (1994). Individual differences in need for cognitive closure. *Journal of Personality and Social Psychology, 67*, 1049–1062.

Weeks, M., Weeks, K. P., & Daniel, M. R. (2008). The implicit relationship between religious and paranormal constructs. *Journal for the Scientific Study of Religion, 47*, 599–611.

Wegner, D. M. (2005). Who is the controller of controlled processes? In R. Hassin, J. S. Uleman, & J. A. Bargh (Eds.), *The New Unconscious* (pp. 19–36). New York: Oxford University Press.

Weinberger-Thomas, C. (1999). *Ashes of Immortality: Widow-Burning in India*. Chicago: University of Chicago Press.

Weisberg, Y. J., DeYoung, C. G., & Hirsh, J. B. (2011). Gender differences in personality across the ten aspects of the Big Five. *Frontiers in Psychology, 2*, 1–11.

Weisenbach, S. L., Rapport, L. J., Briceno, E. M., Haase, B. D., Vederman, A. C., Bieliauskas, L. A., Welsh, R. C., Starkman, M. N., McInnis, M. G., Zubieta, J. K., & Langenecker, S. A. (2014). Reduced emotion processing efficiency in healthy males relative to females. *Social Cognitive and Affective Neuroscience, 9*, 316–325.

Weiser, N. (1974). The effects of prophetic disconfirmation on the committed. *Review of Religious Research, 16*, 19–30.

Weiss, A. S., & Mendoza, R. H. (1990). Effects of acculturation into the Hare Krishna movement on mental health and personality. *Journal for the Scientific Study of Religion, 29*, 173–184.

Weiss, B. L. (1988). *Many Lives, Many Masters*. New York: Simon & Schuster.

Wellman, J. K., Jr., & Tokuno, K. (2004). Is religious violence inevitable? *Journal for the Scientific Study of Religion, 43*, 291–296.

Wells, L. A. (1983). Hallucinations associated with pathologic grief reaction. *Journal of Psychiatric Treatment and Evaluation, 5*, 259–261.

White, A. D. (1896/1993). *A History of the Warfare of Science with Theology in Christendom*. Buffalo, NY: Prometheus Books.

White, S., McAllister, I., & Kryshtanovskaya, O. (1994). Religion and politics in postcommunist Russia. *Religion, State and Society, 22*, 73–88.

Whitlock, F. A., & Hynes, J. V. (1978). Religious stigmatization: an historical and psychophysiological enquiry. *Psychological Medicine, 8*, 185–202.

Widman, D. R., Corcoran, K. E., & Nagy, R. E. (2009). Belonging to the same religion enhances the opinion of others' kindness and morality. *Journal of Social, Evolutionary, and Cultural Psychology, 3*, 281–289.

Wiech, K., Farias, M., Kahane, G., Shackel, N., Tiede, W., & Tracey, I. (2008). An fMRI study measuring analgesia enhanced by religion as a belief system. *Pain, 139*, 467–476.

Wilford, J. (2010). Sacred archipelagos: Geographies of secularization. *Progress in Human Geography, 34*, 328–348.

Wilkinson, P. J., & Coleman, P. G. (2010). Strong beliefs and coping in old age: A case-based comparison of atheism and religious faith. *Aging & Society, 30*, 337–361.

References 309

Willard, A. K., & Norenzayan, A. (2013). Cognitive biases explain religious belief, paranormal belief, and belief in life's purpose. *Cognition, 129,* 379–391.

Williams, R. J., & Watts, F. N. (2014). Attributions in a spiritual healing context: An archival analysis of a 1920s healing movement. *Journal for the Scientific Study of Religion, 53,* 90–108.

Williamson, S., & Carnes, M. (2013). Partisanship, Christianity, and women in the legislature: Determinants of parental leave policy in U.S. states. *Social Science Quarterly, 94,* 1084–1101.

Willoughby, M., Cadigan, J., Burchinal, M., Skinner, D., & the Family Life Investigative Group (2008). An evaluation of the psychometric properties and criterion validity of the religious social support scale. *Journal for the Scientific Study of Religion, 47,* 147–159.

Wills, T. A., Yaeger, A. M., & Sandy, J. M. (2003). Buffering effects of religiosity for adolescent substance use. *Psychology of Addictive Behaviors, 17,* 24–31.

Wilson, B. R. (1967). *Patterns of Sectarianism.* London: Heinemann.

Wilson, B. R. (1976). *Contemporary Transformations of Religion.* New York: Oxford University Press.

Wilson, D. S. (2002). *Darwin's Cathedral: Evolution, Religion, and the Nature of Society.* Chicago: University of Chicago Press.

Wilson, E. O. (2012). *The Social Conquest of the Earth.* New York: Norton.

Wilson, G. E. (1956). Christian Science and longevity. *Journal of Forensic Sciences, 1,* 43–60.

Wilson, J., & Sherkat, D. E. (1994). Returning to the fold. *Journal for the Scientific Study of Religion, 33,* 148–161.

Wilson, W. P. (1972). Mental health benefits of religious salvation. *Diseases of the Nervous System, 33,* 382–386.

Wilson, W. P., Larson, D. B., & Meier, P. D. (1983). Religious life of schizophrenics. *Southern Medical Journal, 78,* 1096–1100.

Winerip, M. (2012). The vanishing of the nuns. *The New York Times,* December 2, p. C4.

WIN-Gallup International, *Global Index of Religion and Atheism* (2012), 2; available at http://redcresearch.ie/wp-content/uploads/2012/08/RED-C-press-release-Religion-and-Atheism-25-7-12.pdf

Winnicott, D. W. (1971). *Playing and Reality.* New York: Basic Books.

Wise, L. A., Zierler, S., Krieger, N., & Harlow, B. L. (2001). Adult onset of major depressive disorder in relation to early life violent victimisation: a case-control study. *Lancet, 358,* 881–887.

Wisneski, D. C., Lytle, B. L., & Skitka, L. J. (2009). Gut reactions: Moral conviction, religiosity, and trust in authority. *Psychological Science, 20,* 1059–1063.

Witkin, H., Goodenough, D., & Oltman, P. (1979). Psychological differentiation: Current status. *Journal of Personality and Social Psychology, 37,* 1127–1145.

Witten, M. G. (1993). *All Is Forgiven: The Secular Message in American Protestantism.* Princeton: Princeton University Press.

Witter, R. A., Stock, W. A., Okun, M. A., & Haring, M. J. (1985). Religion and subjective well-being in adulthood: a quantitative synthesis. *Review of Religious Research, 26,* 332–342.

Witztum, E., Greenberg, D., & Dasberg, H. (1990). Mental illness and religious change. *British Journal of Medical Psychology, 63,* 33–41.

Witztum, E., Greenberg, D., & Buchbinder, J. T. (1990). "A very narrow bridge": Diagnosis and management of mental illness among Bratslav hasidim. *Psychotherapy: Theory, Research, Practice, Training, 27,* 124–131.

310 References

Wohlrab-Sahr, M. (2009). The stable third: non-religiosity in Germany. In S. Bertelsmann (Ed.), *What the World Believes: Analysis and Commentary on the Religion Monitor 2008* (pp.149–166). Gütersloh: Verlag Bertelsmann Stiftung.

Wojtkowiak, J., & Venbrux, E. (2009). From soul to postself: Home memorials in the Netherlands. *Mortality, 14,* 147–158.

Wolf, J. G. (Ed.) (1989). *Gay Priests.* New York: HarperCollins.

Wolpert, L. (2000). *The Unnatural Nature of Science.* Cambridge, MA: Harvard University Press.

Wondimu, H., Beit-Hallahmi, B., & Abbink, J. (2001). *Ethnic Identity, Stereotypes, and Psychological Modernity in Ethiopian Young Adults: Identifying the Potential For Change.* Amsterdam: KIT Publishers.

Wood, J. (1999). *The Broken Estate: Essays on Literature and Belief.* New York: Random House.

Wood, M. (2009). The nonformative elements of religious life: Questioning the "sociology of spirituality" paradigm. *Social Compass, 56,* 237–248.

Woodhead, L. (2008). Gendering secularization theory. *Social Compass, 55,* 187–193.

Woodhead, L. (2009). 'Because I'm worth it': Religion and women's changing lives in the West. In K. Aune, S. Sharma, & G. Vincett (Eds.), *Women and Religion in the West: Challenging Secularisation* (pp. 145–167). Aldershot, UK: Ashgate.

Wooley, S. (2005). Children of Jehovah's Witnesses and adolescent Jehovah's Witnesses: What are their rights? *Archives of Disease in Childhood, 90,* 715–719.

Woolley, J. D. (2000). The development of beliefs about direct mental-physical causality in imagination, magic, and religion. In K. S. Rosengren, C. N. Johnson, & P. L. Harris (Eds.), *Imagining the Impossible: Magical, Scientific, and Religious Thinking in Children* (pp. 99–129). Cambridge, UK: Cambridge University Press.

Wootton, R. J., & Allen, D. F. (1983). Dramatic religious conversion and schizophrenic decompensation. *Journal of Religion and Health, 22,* 212–220.

Worsley, P. (1957). *The Trumpet Shall Sound: A Study of Cargo Cults in Melanesia.* London: MacGibbon and Kee.

Wortis, J. (1954). *Fragments of an Analysis With Freud.* New York: Simon and Schuster.

Wrangham, R. W., & Peterson, D. (1996). *Demonic Males: Apes and the Origins of Human Violence.* Boston: Houghton Mifflin.

Wright, D. (1971). *The Psychology of Moral Behaviour.* Harmondsworth: Penguin.

Wright, D., & Cox, E. (1967). A study of the relationship between moral judgment and religious belief in a sample of British adolescents. *Journal of Social Psychology, 72,* 135–144.

Wright, S. A. (1986). Dyadic intimacy and social control in three cult movements. *Sociological Analysis, 47,* 137–150.

Wright, S. A. (1987). *Leaving Cults: The Dynamics of Defection.* Washington, DC: Society for the Scientific Study of Religion.

Wright, S. A. (Ed.) (1995). *Armageddon in Waco: Critical Perspectives on the Branch Davidian Conflict.* Chicago: University of Chicago Press.

Wright, S. A., & Piper, E. S. (1986). Families and cults: Familial factors related to youth leaving or remaining in deviant religious groups. *Journal of Marriage and the Family, 48,* 15–25.

Wulff, D. M. (1997). *Psychology of Religion: Classic and Contemporary.* New York: J. Wiley & Sons.

Wulff, D. M. (1999). Psychologists define religion: Patterns and prospects of a century-long quest. In J. G. Platvoet, & A. L. Molendijk (Eds.), *The Pragmatics of Defining Religion: Contexts, Concepts, and Contests* (pp. 207–224). Leiden: Brill.

Wulff, D. M. (2003). A field in crisis: is it time for the psychology of religion to start over? In P.H.M.P. Roelofsma, J.M.T. Corveleyn, & J. W. van Saane (Eds.), *One Hundred Years of Psychology and Religion: Issues and Trends in a Century-Long Quest* (pp. 11–32). Amsterdam: VU University Press.

Wulff, D. M. (2007). Empirical research on religion: Perspectives from the psychology of religion. In H.-G. Heimbrock, & C. Scholtz (Eds.), *Religion: Immediate Experience and the Mediacy of Research; Interdisciplinary Studies in Objectives, Concepts and Methodology of Empirical Research in Religion* (pp. 259–273). Göttingen: Vandenhoeck & Ruprecht.

Wunn, I. (2003). The evolution of religions. *Numen, 50,* 387–415.

Wuthnow, R. (1976). Astrology and marginality. *Journal for the Scientific Study of Religion, 15,* 157–168.

Wuthnow, R. (1978). *Experimentation in American Religion: The New Mysticisms and Their Implications for the Churches.* California: University of California Press.

Wuthnow, R. (1985). Science and the sacred. In P. E. Hammond (Ed.), *The Sacred in a Secular Age* (pp. 187–203). Berkeley: University of California Press.

Wuthnow, R. (2000). How religious groups promote forgiving: A national study. *Journal for the Scientific Study of Religion, 39,* 125–139.

Yarom, N. (1992). *Body, Blood and Sexuality: A Psychoanalytic Study of St. Francis' Stigmata and Their Historical Context.* New York: Peter Lang.

Yeager, D. M., Glei, D. A., Au, M., Lin, H., Sloan, R. P., & Weinstein. M. (2006). Religious involvement and health outcomes among older persons in Taiwan. *Social Science and Medicine, 63,* 2228–2241.

Yonker, J. E., Schnabelrauch, C. A., & DeHaan, L. G. (2012). The relationship between spirituality and religiosity on psychological outcomes in adolescents and emerging adults: A meta-analytic review. *Journal of Adolescence, 35,* 299–314.

Ysseldyk, Y., Matheson, K., & Hymie, A. (2010). Religiosity as identity: Toward an understanding of religion from a social identity perspective. *Personality and Social Psychology Review, 14,* 60–71.

Zaki, J., & Mitchell, J. (2013). Intuitive prosociality. *Current Directions in Psychological Science, 22,* 466–470.

Zaretsky, I. I., & Leone, M. P. (Eds.). (1974). *Religious Movements in Contemporary America.* Princeton: Princeton University Press.

Zarifian, E. (1988). *Les Jardiniers de la Folie.* Paris: Odile Jacob.

Zavalloni, M. (1975). Social identity and the recording of reality: Its relevance for cross-cultural psychology. *International Journal of Psychology, 10,* 197–217.

Zeidner, M. and Beit-Hallahmi, B. (1988). Sex, ethnic, and social class differences in parareligious beliefs among Israeli adolescents. *Journal of Social Psychology, 128,* 333–343.

Zelan, J. (1968). Religious apostasy, higher education and occupational choice. *Sociology of Education, 41,* 370–379.

Zerubavel, E. (1982). Easter and Passover: On calendars and group identity. *American Sociological Review, 42,* 284–289.

Zimdars-Swartz, S. L. (1991). *Encountering Mary.* Princeton: Princeton University Press.

Zinnbauer, J. B., & Pargament, K. I. (1998). Spiritual conversion: A study of religious change among college students. *Journal for the Scientific Study of Religion, 37,* 161–180.

Zinnbauer, B. J., Pargament, K. I., Cole, B., Rye, M. S., Butter, E. M., Belavich, T. G., Hipp, K. M., Scott, A. B., & Kadar, J. L. (1997). Religion and spirituality: Unfuzzying the fuzzy. *Journal for the Scientific Study of Religion, 36,* 549–564.

Zivkovic, T. M. (2014). Consuming the lama: Transformations of Tibetan Buddhist bodies. *Body & Society, 20,* 111–132.

312 References

Zizek, S. (2006). Defenders of the faith. *The New York Times*, March 12, p. A 23.

Zuckerman, M. (1994). *Behavioral Expressions and Biosocial Bases of Sensation Seeking*. New York: Cambridge University Press.

Zuckerman, M., Silberman, J., & Hall, J. A. (2013). The relation between intelligence and religiosity: A meta-analysis and some proposed explanations. *Personality and Social Psychology Review*, 17, 1–30.

Zuckerman, P. (2007). Atheism: Contemporary rates and patterns. In M. Martin (Ed.), *The Cambridge Companion to Atheism*. New York: Cambridge University Press.

Zuckerman, P. (2008). *Society Without God: What the Least Religious Nations Can Tell Us About Contentment*. New York: New York University Press.

Zuckerman, P. (2009). Atheism, secularity, and well-being: How the findings in social science counter negative stereotypes and assumptions. *Sociology Compass*, 3(6), 949–971.

Zusne, L., & Jones, W. H. (1982). *Anomalistic Psychology*. Hillsdale, NJ: Lawrence Erlbaum Associates.

Zygmunt, J. F. (1970). Prophetic failure and chiliastic identity: The case of Jehovah's Witnesses. *American Journal of Sociology, 75*, 926–948.

Zygmunt, J. (1972). When prophecies fail: A theoretical perspective on comparative evidence. *American Behavioural Scientist, 16*, 245–268.

INDEX

academics 1, 73-80, 125, 218
adolescence 99, 100, 106, 107, 110-111, 150, 153, 161-162, 163, 165, 166
adoption 49
African-Americans 62, 96, 143, 146, 153, 219
afterlife 54, 65, 66, 74, 92, 114, 117, 134, 179, 214, 224, 227, 230, 234
aggregate measures 123-125
AIDS epidemic 36
altruism 33, 34, 109, 130, 133-134, 147, 187
altruism, parochial 136- 137
ambiguity intolerance 85
analytic cognitive style 25, 71-72, 73, 81
animal sacrifice 13
ancestors 3, 5, 8, 10-11, 46, 64, 138, 204, 224
animism 26-27, 31, 32, 44, 188, 218, 228
Anthropomorphism 7, 9, 24, 26-28, 31, 32, 44, 97, 183, 188, 232
anti-Semitism 14, 145, 147, 157
apartheid 131, 132, 141, 160
apocalyptic dreams 63, 131, 174, 176, 180
apostasy 73, 153, 154, 159-161, 166
Aristotle 140
art and religion 37, 189
astrology 9, 27, 34, 84, 94, 96, 225-228, 231

attachment theory 81-84, 163-164, 198, 200, 228
authoritarianism 67, 81, 84, 86, 88, 145, 146, 163
automatic believing 25

Baptists 60, 147, 154
Beecher, H.W. 140
Beethoven's Ninth Symphony 37
Berg, D.B., 16
Big Five dimensions 85-86
Black Moslems 152
Blood Libel 14
brain 15, 24, 26, 28, 29-30, 31, 32, 38-39, 56, 66, 67-71, 99, 101, 103-105, 110, 114, 116
brain cancer 12
Branch Davidians 176-179

cannibalism, 13-14
Cargo Cults 63-64
celebrated converts 153
Christian Science 63, 126, 219
Cicero 128
civil liberties 143-145
clergy 13, 107, 115, 125, 134, 141, 147, 152, 197, 199, 213, 217, 223, 232
Cognitive shortcuts vii, 31-32, 44
colonialism 131
consecrated virgins 13

314 Index

consequences of religiosity 6, 17, 57, 109-150
consequential dimension 22
consistent life ethic 145
conversion 21, 44, 47, 56, 60, 67, 69, 71, 84, 130, 151-168, 190-192, 199,
Conversion narratives, sex differences in 103
convert-dependent groups 168-181
corruption 10, 139, 155
"creative illness"152
crime 14, 35, 62, 99, 112, 130, 132, 168, 231
cultural specificity 88, 148

Dalit 108, 154
Darwin, C. 7, 129
Deity images 144-145, 197
deprivation 57-64, 95-96, 108, 160, 176, 210, 220
"DNA Catholic"40
divorce 111-112, 163, 199, 222
dogmatism 85, 145
Dostoyevsky, F.M. 128
dualism 27, 29, 31, 38, 97, 220
Durkheim, E. 9, 201-202

Edison, T.A. 220
Eisenhower, D.D. 203
eminence effect 76-78
endogamy 223
Engel v. Vitale 218
Enlightenment 131, 137, 148, 186, 203-206, 213, 216, 224
estrogen 101
European Values Survey 143
Existential insecurity 61, 66, 210, 232
experiential dimension 21
experimentation, psychological 2, 17, 33, 64, 65, 66, 68, 85, 86, 110, 123, 134-136, 146, 148, 171, 198
explaining misfortune 9, 10, 35-36, 204, 209, 218
extraversion 85
Eucharist 13-14

"faith healing"47, 59, 68, 123, 126, 219
Father Divine 16, 162
Five Precepts 127

food taboos 233
Francis (Saint) 172, 242
Frazer, J.G., 4, 15, 36, 217
free will 29-30
Freud, S. 24, 52, 80-81, 83, 120, 144, 160, 167, 170, 182-200, 234
Freud's conversion case 190-192
funerals 10, 14, 36, 224, 234

Generosity 133-136, 138, 229
genetic influences on religiosity 66-67, 119-120, 149
genital mutilation 13, 46, 125, 197, 233
Ghost Dance 59, 63-64
glossalalia 67, 68
grave goods 15

happiness 6, 11, 113, 116, 117, 120, 124, 148-149, 155, 157, 159, 202, 204, 230
health 115-127
Hegel, W.G.H. 129
helping 130, 134-136
Hitler, A. 132
Holocaust 118, 147
homosexuality 107, 111, 143, 156-157, 199
honesty 139
Hume, D. 27, 28

identity 17, 21, 34, 38, 40-55, 56-57, 64, 66, 75, 80, 100, 105, 107, 113, 143, 144, 147-148, 151, 153-161, 165-166, 168-171, 187, 191, 197, 203, 207, 208, 212, 224-225, 228, 233-234
"identity crisis"161
"identity functions"50
ideological dimension 18
immortality 15-17, 36, 55, 76-77, 185, 187, 219, 224,
individualism 98, 159, 202, 206, 208-211, 222-224, 228-229, 234
intellectual dimension 19
intellectualism 73-75, 78-81
intelligence and religiosity 72-73
intuitive mode 25
in vitro fertilization (IVF) 221, 223
ISKCON ("Hare Krishna") 63, 164, 165, 174, 199

Jacob, M. 156-158, 167
James, W., 4, 16, 24, 129, 130, 151, 152, 155-156, 162, 168, 219
Jesus Christ 13, 16, 63, 190
Jesus Movement 181
Jude the Obscure 223
Just World 141-142

Kant, E. 205
"Keech, M." (Dorothy Martin) 172, 176
Khmer Rouge 168
Kidney Heist 35
Kristol, I. 130
Kubler-Ross, E. 16
Kureishi, H. 50
Kurelu 10, 38

Leuba, J.L. 74, 76, 78, 141
Locke, J. 128
love object hypothesis 197-198

Malinowski, B. 234
marriage 13, 95-96, 112, 148, 154, 155, 163, 174, 178, 194, 222, 223, 225
Marx, K. 24, 58, 186, 201, 203, 210
McCullers, C., 15
Mencken, H.L. 140
mental health 113-115
mentalizing 28, 35, 71
miracles 11-12
Militia Company 37
Moorish Science Temple of America 219
Mormons 16, 63, 117, 176
Mrs. Dalloway 152
Mythology 2, 5, 6, 9, 12-14, 193-197

nationalism and religion 54-55, 144
Natural disasters 209
Nazis 131, 132, 157, 168
near-death experiences (NDE) 71
neuroticism 85, 101
"New Age" 5, 9, 84, 94, 225-231
New Guinea 10, 38
new religious movement (NRMs) 169-171, 202, 208
Nighthawks 37
Nobel laureates 77-79
Noble Lie 130, 140

obsessive-compulsive disorder (OCD) 69, 200
Oedipal motifs 182, 193-199
Opposition to vaccinations 127
Osel Tendzin 175
Osho Meditation 174
Oxford Movement 162, 181

pantheons 7, 89-90, 95, 183, 197-198, 213
para-religious beliefs 7, 9, 94, 97, 226
parental influence 40, 44-46, 48, 51, 61
Parliament of the World's Religions 1893 215
Peoples Temple 176, 180
personality traits and religiosity 80-87
philosophers , religiosity in 75
Piaget, J. 26, 133, 161, 183
piercing 13
Pius IX 140
Plato 140
political attitudes 140-145
possession 5, 8, 59, 67, 68, 199-200
possession in women 93, 95-96
prayer 3, 5, 6, 11-12, 28, 46, 52, 66, 84, 92- 94, 101, 106, 110, 113-116, 184, 215
prayer as curative 122-123, 126
prayer groups 136, 168
prejudice 21, 54, 81, 145-148, 187
privatization of religion 202, 208, 214, 224, 228, 230-231, 234
pre-literate cultures 10
Prison conversions 168
pro-sociality and religion 33-34, 84, 119, 123, 127-130, 132-134, 136, 138
"primitive" 9, 10
projection, parental 183, 197-198
psychoanalysis 35, 37, 81, 163, 182-200
Psychological femininity 94, 106-108, 120
PTSD 101

Reed, R. 124
reflective mode 25
reincarnation 8, 16-17, 19, 29, 94, 96, 179, 226
religion as adaptive 32-37
religion as art 14-15
religion, definition 3-5
Religion and art 37

316 Index

religious experiences 21, 28, 43, 56, 67-71, 93, 102, 154, 166, 168, 169
revitalization movements 63, 159
ritualistic dimension 20
Rousseau, J.-J. 129

sacrifice 6, 10, 12-14, 90, 116, 130, 133, 151, 156, 192, 194
Santa Claus 9
scapegoat 13, 14, 59, 192
schizophrenia 69, 70, 102, 113-114, 165-166, 217
schizotypy 69, 77, 102
self-actualization 81, 206, 211, 234
self-control 33, 109-110, 231
Self-enhancement and religiosity 86-87
sect and church 59
sectarianism 59-60, 72, 74, 80
secularization 33, 39, 42, 47, 53, 57, 61, 75, 91, 92, 116, 128, 148, 154, 159, 170, 201-232, 234
secularization among Jews 75-76
secularization, formal explanations 209
seekers 42, 101, 155, 159- 160, 163, 164, 171, 230, 231
Seventh Day Adventists 63, 117, 177
"sex change"159, 220
sex differences in personality 98
sex differences in religiosity 89-108
sexual behavior 111-112
sexual orientation and religiosity 107
Sitting Bull, 13
Smith, J. Jr., 70
social categorization 51-52
social learning 40-55, 56, 67, 68, 105, 154, 183, 234
socialization 44-49, 53, 61, 105, 110, 132, 149, 150, 192, 209
social support 100, 106, 116, 118-119,
social trust 62, 145
Society for Psychical Research 219
Solar Temple 179-180
Sontag, S. 158
Spencer, H. 129
Spirituality 228-231
Spiritualization 173

Strunk, O. Jr. 235-236
Subjective well-being (SWB) 62, 66, 81, 113, 119, 124, 126, 149-150, 209
Succession crises 174-176
suggestibility 98, 108, 126
suicide 115
Swedenborg, E. 70
'switching' 42, 154, 155

Teleological thinking 26, 27, 30, 31, 38, 97, 121, 218, 232
temporal-lobe epilepsy (TLE) 69
Terman, L.M. 73, 91
Terror Management Theory (TMT) 65-66, 147
theophagy 14
Theory of Mind (TOM) 27, 28, 44
The Future of an Illusion 187, 188
The Uncanny 187
Tolstoy, L.N. 117
Treaty of Lisbon 212
Tylor, E.B. 4

Under Milk Wood 37
Unification Church (Moonies) 164, 170, 181
Universal Declaration of Human Rights 203

values and religiosity 87-88
virgin birth 225
Virgin Mary 5, 184, 195, 196-199, 225
Voltaire 129-130

Washington, G. 128
Welfare state 61, 142
When Prophecy Fails 172
Winnicott, D.W. 37, 189
Witchcraft 5, 9-10, 36, 64, 192
Witch killing 59
World Happiness Report 124
World Value Survey 92, 143, 149

Xenophanes 24

Zen Buddhism 132, 160, 226

CPSIA information can be obtained at www.ICGtesting.com
Printed in the USA
BVOW06s2328031016

463745BV00017B/15/P